Programming F# 3.0

Chris Smith

O'REILLY®

Beijing · Cambridge · Farnham · Köln · Sebastopol · Tokyo

Programming F# 3.0

by Chris Smith

Copyright © 2013 Chris Smith. All rights reserved.

Printed in the United States of America.

Published by O'Reilly Media, Inc., 1005 Gravenstein Highway North, Sebastopol, CA 95472.

O'Reilly books may be purchased for educational, business, or sales promotional use. Online editions are also available for most titles (*http://my.safaribooksonline.com*). For more information, contact our corporate/institutional sales department: 800-998-9938 or *corporate@oreilly.com*.

Editor: Rachel Roumeliotis
Production Editor: Holly Bauer
Copyeditor: Jasmine Kwityn

Proofreader: Absolute Service, Inc.
Indexer: Lucie Haskins
Cover Designer: Karen Montgomery
Interior Designer: David Futato
Illustrator: Rebecca Demarest

October 2009:   First Edition
October 2012:   Second Edition

Revision History for the Second Edition:

2012-10-08   First release

See *http://oreilly.com/catalog/errata.csp?isbn=9781449320294* for release details.

Nutshell Handbook, the Nutshell Handbook logo, and the O'Reilly logo are registered trademarks of O'Reilly Media, Inc. *Programming F# 3.0*, the image of a bullfinch, and related trade dress are trademarks of O'Reilly Media, Inc.

Many of the designations used by manufacturers and sellers to distinguish their products are claimed as trademarks. Where those designations appear in this book, and O'Reilly Media, Inc., was aware of a trademark claim, the designations have been printed in caps or initial caps.

While every precaution has been taken in the preparation of this book, the publisher and authors assume no responsibility for errors or omissions, or for damages resulting from the use of the information contained herein.

ISBN: 978-1-449-32029-4

[LSI]

Table of Contents

Part III. Extending the F# Language

Preface

Have you ever been in a hurry and pounded in a nail using something other than a hammer? Or perhaps settled an argument concerning distances with "the length of my arm is about 20 inches, and that's about two arm lengths..."? You might not be willing to fall for such obviously flawed shortcuts, but as your humble author, I will admit that I have.

There is elegance to using the right tool for the job. And, just like a hammer or a tape measure, programming languages are tools like any other. Throughout this book, you will discover that although F# isn't the best tool for every situation, it is the perfect tool for some situations.

This book is about showing you how to use the F# programming language as a general purpose tool, with an emphasis on the specific domains where it can lead to dramatic boosts in productivity.

Along the way, you will pick up a knack for functional programming, a semi-mysterious collection of concepts that can help you rethink your programs regardless of the host programming language.

Introducing F#

So what actually is F#? In a nutshell, F# is a *multiparadigm* programming language built on .NET, meaning that it supports several different *styles* of programming natively. I'll spare you the history of the language and instead just go over the big bullets:

- F# supports imperative programming. In F#, you can modify the contents of memory, read and write files, send data over the network, and so on.

- F# supports object-oriented programming. In F#, you can abstract code into classes and objects, enabling you to simplify your code.

- F# supports functional programming, which is a style of programming that emphasizes *what* a program should do, not explicitly *how* the program should work.

- F# is statically typed. Being statically typed means that type information is known at compile time, leading to type-safe code. F# won't allow you to put a square peg into a round hole.

- F# is a .NET language. It runs on the *Common Language Infrastructure* (CLI) and so it gets things like garbage collection (memory management) and powerful class libraries for free. F# also natively supports all .NET concepts (e.g., delegates, enumerations, structures, P/Invoke, etc.).

Even without all the jargon, it is clear that F# is a powerful language. But don't worry, we'll cover it all step by step.

Who This Book Is For

This book isn't intended to be an introductory text on programming, and assumes familiarity with basic concepts like looping, functions, and recursion. However, no previous experience with functional programming or .NET is required.

If you come from a C# or VB.NET background, then you should feel right at home. Although F# approaches programming from a different viewpoint, you can apply all of your existing .NET know-how to programming in F#.

If you come from an OCaml or Haskell background, then the syntax of F# should look very familiar. F# has most of the features of those languages, and adds many more to integrate well with .NET.

What You Need to Get Going

F# is "in the box" of Visual Studio 11. This includes the F# compiler and project system, and contains all the features (e.g., syntax highlighting and IntelliSense) that you would expect. Outside of Visual Studio and on non-Microsoft platforms, you can still write and deploy F# applications using the open source Mono platform (*http://www.mono-project.com/*).

If you are running F# on Windows, then Chapter 1 will show you how to get set up using Visual Studio. Otherwise, Appendix A will walk you through getting F# set up on non-Microsoft platforms.

Also, it is important to note that all of the examples printed in this book (as well as many more) may be found on GitHub. The best way to learn any new skill is to just start using it, so I highly recommended that you take a moment to fork and explore the repository for this book's source code (*http://github.com/aChrisSmith/Programming-FS-Examples/*).

How the Book Is Organized

This book is divided into three parts. Part I focuses on multiparadigm programming in F#. Early chapters are devoted to programming in a specific F# paradigm, whereas later ones will help flesh out your understanding of language capabilities. By the end of Part I you will be fluent in the F# language and its idioms.

Part II will introduces a few lingering concepts but primarily focuses on applying F# in specialized areas. By the end of Part II you will know how to utilize F# as a scripting language, for parallel programming, and for creating domain specific languages.

Part III should be considered optional for most F# developers, and focuses on advanced language features that allow you to modify and extend the F# language.

Part I

Chapter 1, Introduction to F#
> Presents the F# language and the Visual Studio 11 integrated development environment (IDE). Even if you are familiar with Visual Studio, I recommend you read this chapter, as F# has some unique characteristics when it comes to building and running projects.

Chapter 2, Fundamentals
> Introduces the core types and concepts that will be the foundation for all other chapters.

Chapter 3, Functional Programming
> Introduces functional programming and how to write F# code using this style.

Chapter 4, Imperative Programming
> Describes how to mutate values and change program state in an imperative manner.

Chapter 5, Object-Oriented Programming
> Covers object-oriented programming from creating simple types to inheritance and polymorphism.

Chapter 6, .NET Programming
> Goes over some style independent concepts exposed by the .NET Framework and CLI.

Part II

Chapter 7, Applied Functional Programming

Covers more advanced topics in functional programming, such as tail recursion and functional design patterns.

Chapter 8, Applied Object-Oriented Programming

Describes how to develop and take advantage of a rich type system. Special attention is paid on how to leverage the functional aspects of F# to make object-oriented code better.

Chapter 9, Asynchronous and Parallel Programming

Takes a look at how to use F# to take advantage of multiple cores on a processor and the facilities in the F# and .NET libraries for parallel programming.

Chapter 10, Scripting

Examines F# as a scripting language and how to make the most of F# script files.

Chapter 11, Data Processing

Focuses exclusively on using F# in real-world scenarios for doing distributed computations, interacting with web services, and working in information-rich environments.

Part III

Chapter 12, Reflection

Provides a look at the .NET reflection library and how to use it to create declarative programs.

Chapter 13, Computation Expressions

Introduces an advanced F# language feature that will enable you to eliminate redundant code and add new capabilities to the core F# language.

Chapter 14, Quotations

Introduces F# quotation expressions and explains how they can be used to do metaprogramming, as well as to execute F# code on other computational platforms.

Chapter 15, Type Providers

Explains the F# compiler's special machinery for integrating typed data across multiple domains. (Don't fret, that sentence will make sense when you start the chapter.)

Part IV

This book also features a couple of appendixes to flesh out any extra concepts you might be interested in.

Appendix A

Does a quick sweep through the existing technologies available on the .NET platform and describes how to use them from F#.

Appendix B

Covers how to write F# to interoperate with existing libraries as well as unmanaged code using P/Invoke and COM-interop.

Conventions Used in This Book

The following font conventions are used in this book:

Italic

Used for new concepts as they are defined.

`Constant width`

Used for code examples and F# keywords.

`Constant width bold`

Used for emphasis within program code.

Pay special attention to note styles within this text.

Notes like this are used to add more detail for the curious reader.

Warnings are indicated in this style are to help you avoid common mistakes.

Using Code Examples

This book is here to help you get your job done. In general, you may use the code in this book in your programs and documentation. You do not need to contact us for permission unless you're reproducing a significant portion of the code. For example, writing a program that uses several chunks of code from this book does not require permission. Selling or distributing a CD-ROM of examples from O'Reilly books does require permission. Answering a question by citing this book and quoting example code does not require permission. Incorporating a significant amount of example code from this book into your product's documentation does require permission.

We appreciate, but do not require, attribution. An attribution usually includes the title, author, publisher, and ISBN. For example: "*Programming F# 3.0*, Second Edition, by Chris Smith. Copyright 2012 Chris Smith, 978-1-449-32029-4."

If you think that your use of code examples falls outside fair use or the permission given above, feel free to contact us at *permissions@oreilly.com*.

Safari® Books Online

 Safari Books Online (*www.safaribooksonline.com*) is an on-demand digital library that delivers expert content in both book and video form from the world's leading authors in technology and business.

Technology professionals, software developers, web designers, and business and creative professionals use Safari Books Online as their primary resource for research, problem solving, learning, and certification training.

Safari Books Online offers a range of product mixes and pricing programs for organizations, government agencies, and individuals. Subscribers have access to thousands of books, training videos, and prepublication manuscripts in one fully searchable database from publishers like O'Reilly Media, Prentice Hall Professional, Addison-Wesley Professional, Microsoft Press, Sams, Que, Peachpit Press, Focal Press, Cisco Press, John Wiley & Sons, Syngress, Morgan Kaufmann, IBM Redbooks, Packt, Adobe Press, FT Press, Apress, Manning, New Riders, McGraw-Hill, Jones & Bartlett, Course Technology, and dozens more. For more information about Safari Books Online, please visit us online.

I'd Like to Hear from You

Although I've tested and verified the information in this book, you may find some aspects of the F# language have changed since the time of writing (or perhaps even a bug in the example!). Please let me know of any errors you find, as well as your suggestions for future editions, at: *http://oreil.ly/Programming_F_Sharp_3*.

In addition, you can use analog-mail by writing to:

O'Reilly Media, Inc.
1005 Gravenstein Highway North
Sebastopol, CA 95472
800-998-9938 (in the United States or Canada)
707-829-0515 (international or local)
707-829-0104 (fax)

You can also send messages electronically. To be put on the mailing list or request a catalog, send email to *info@oreilly.com*.

To comment on the book, send email to *bookquestions@oreilly.com*.

For information about this book and others, as well as additional technical articles and discussion on F#, see the O'Reilly website at *http://www.oreilly.com.*

or the O'Reilly .NET DevCenter at *http://www.oreillynet.com/dotnet.*

or the Microsoft Developer Network portal for F# at *http://www.msdn.com/fsharp.*

Acknowledgments

In addition to the F# team at Microsoft for putting out a solid product, I'd like to thank a few people who had a hand in this second edition: Matt Douglass-Riley; Rachel Roumeliotis; my two puppy warriors, Steve and GOB; and, of course, my wife, Kate.

Multiparadigm Programming

Introduction to F#

F# is a powerful language that spans multiple paradigms of development. This chapter provides a brief introduction to the heart of F#—the F# compiler, tools, and its place in Visual Studio 11.

In this chapter, you will create a couple of simple F# applications, and then I'll point out key Visual Studio features for F# development. I won't cover much of Visual Studio here, so I encourage you to explore the IDE on your own.

If you are already familiar with Visual Studio, you should still skim through this chapter. Creating and debugging F# projects works just like C# or VB.NET; however, F# has a unique characteristic when it comes to multiple-file projects. In addition, F# has a feature called *F# Interactive* that will dramatically increase your productivity. Not to be missed!

Getting to Know F#

As with all programming books, it is customary to write a Hello, World application, and I don't want to deviate from tradition. Open up Notepad or your favorite text editor and create a new file named *HelloWorld.fs* with the following text:

```
// HelloWorld.fs

printfn "Hello, World",
```

Success! You've just written your first F# program. To compile this application, use the F# compiler, `fsc.exe`, located in the *Program Files (x86)\Microsoft SDKs\F#\3.0\Frame work\v4.0* folder. (Don't worry, you won't have to remember that.)

The following snippet shows calling the F# compiler on the command line to build and run your application:

```
C:\Programming F# Source\Ch01>fsc HelloWorld.fs
Microsoft (R) F# 3.0 Compiler build 11.0.50522.1
```

```
Copyright (c) Microsoft Corporation. All Rights Reserved.

C:\Programming F# Source\Ch01>HelloWorld.exe
Hello, World!
```

Visual Studio 11

Tools are the lifeblood of any programming language, and F# is no different. Although you can successfully write F# code in your favorite text editor and invoke the compiler from the command line, you'll likely be more productive using tools. Like C# and VB.NET, F# is a first-class citizen in Visual Studio, with all the features that you might expect, including debugger support, IntelliSense, project templates, and so on.

 Alternatively, you can try F# out in your browser (*http://www.tryf sharp.org/*).

Let's revisit our Hello, World application, but this time using Visual Studio.

To create your first F# project, open up the Visual Studio IDE and select File→New Project from the menu bar to open the New Project dialog, which is shown in Figure 1-1. Select Visual F# in the left pane, select F# Application in the right pane, and then click OK.

Figure 1-1. Select F# Application to start your first F# project

After you click OK in the New Project dialog, you'll see an empty code editor—a blank canvas ready for you to create your F# masterpiece. Next, type the following code into the F# editor:

```
printfn "Hello, World"
```

Now press Ctrl-F5 to run your application. When your application starts, a console window will appear and display the entirely unsurprising result shown in Figure 1-2.

Figure 1-2. Hello World in F#

Your Second F# Program

It may be startling to see a program work without an explicit Main method. You will see why this is admissible in Chapter 2, but for now, let's create a more meaningful Hello, World–type program to get a feel for basic F# syntax.

The code in Example 1-1 will create a program that accepts two command-line parameters and prints them to the console. In addition, it displays the current time.

Example 1-1. Mega Hello World

```
// Mega Hello World
//
// Take two command-line parameters and then print
// them along with the current time to the console.

open System

[<EntryPoint>]
let main (args : string[]) =

    if args.Length <> 2 then
```

```
        failwith "Error: Expected arguments <greeting> and <thing>"

    let greeting, thing = args.[0], args.[1]
    let timeOfDay = DateTime.Now.ToString("hh:mm tt")

    printfn "%s, %s at %s" greeting thing timeOfDay

    // Program exit code
    0
```

Hopefully you are curious about what is going on. Let's look at this program line by line to see how it works.

Values

Example 1-1 introduces three values named `greeting`, `thing`, and `timeOfDay`:

```
let greeting, thing = args.[0], args.[1]
let timeOfDay = DateTime.Now.ToString("hh:mm tt")
```

The key thing here is that the `let` keyword binds a *name* to a *value*. It is worth pointing out that unlike most other programming languages, values in F# are *immutable* by default, meaning they cannot be changed once initialized. We will cover why values are immutable in Chapter 3, but for now it is sufficient to say it has to do with "functional programming."

F# is also case sensitive, so any two values with names that only differ by case are considered different:

```
let number = 1
let Number = 2
let NUMBER = 3
```

A value's name can be any combination of letters, numbers, underscores (_), and apostrophes ('). However, the name must begin with a letter or an underscore.

 You can enclose the value's name with a pair of tick marks, in which case the name can contain any character except for tabs and new lines. This allows you to refer to values and functions exposed from other .NET languages that may conflict with F# keywords:

```
let ``this.Isn't %A% good value Name$!@#`` = 5
```

Whitespace Matters

Other languages (e.g., C#) use semicolons and curly braces to indicate when statements and blocks of code are complete. However, programmers typically indent their code to make it more readable anyway, so these extra symbols often just add syntactic clutter.

In F#, whitespace—spaces and newlines—is significant. The F# compiler allows you to use whitespace to delimit code blocks. For example, anything indented more than the if keyword is considered to be in the body of the if statement. Because tab characters can indicate an unknown number of space characters, they are prohibited in F# code.

 You can configure the Visual Studio editor to automatically convert tab characters into spaces by changing the relevant setting under Tools→Options→Text Editor→F#.

Reviewing Example 1-1, notice that the body of the main method was indented by four spaces, and the body of the if statement was indented by another four spaces:

```
let main (args : string[]) =

    if args.Length <> 2 then
        failwith "Error: Expected arguments <greeting> and <thing>"

    let greeting, thing = args.[0], args.[1]
    let timeOfDay = DateTime.Now.ToString("hh:mm tt")

    printfn "%s, %s at %s" greeting thing timeOfDay

    // Program exit code
    0
```

If the body of the if statement, the failwith "..." expression, was dedented four spaces and therefore lined up with the if keyword, the F# compiler would produce a warning. This is because the compiler wouldn't be able to determine whether the failwith was meant for the body of the if statement or the main function:

```
[<EntryPoint>]
let main (args : string[]) =

    if args.Length <> 2 then
    failwith "Error: Expected arguments <greeting> and <thing>"
```

```
Warning FS0058: Possible incorrect indentation: this token is offside of
context started at position (25:5). Try indenting this token further or
using standard formatting conventions.
```

The general rule is that anything belonging to a method or statement must be indented farther than the keyword that began the method or statement. So in Example 1-1, everything in the main method was indented past the first let and everything in the if statement was indented past the if keyword. As you see and write more F# code, you will quickly find that omitting semicolons and curly braces makes the code easier to write and much easier to read.

.NET Interop

Example 1-1 also demonstrates how F# can interoperate with existing .NET libraries:

```
open System

// ...

let timeOfDay = DateTime.Now.ToString("hh:mm tt")
```

This example shows the `DateTime.Now` property from the `System` namespace in the `mscorlib.dll` assembly in use.

The .NET Framework contains a broad array of libraries for everything from graphics to databases to web services. F# can take advantage of any .NET library natively by calling directly into it. Conversely, any code written in F# can be consumed by other .NET languages. This also means that F# applications can run on any platform that supports .NET. So the F# programs you write can run on phones, tablets, PCs, and so on.

 For more information on .NET libraries, see Appendix A for a quick tour of what's available. For more information about F# interoperating with other .NET languages, refer to Appendix B.

Comments

F# allows you to comment your code. To declare a single-line comment, use two slashes (//); everything after them until the end of the line will be ignored by the compiler:

```
// Program exit code
```

For larger comments, you can use (* and *). Everything between the two tokens will be ignored:

```
(*
Comment
spanning
multiple
lines
*)
```

For F# applications written in Visual Studio, there is a third type of comment—an *XML documentation comment*. If a comment starting with three slashes, ///, is placed above an identifier, Visual Studio will display the comment's text when you hover the mouse over the identifier.

Figure 1-3 shows applying an XML documentation comment and its associated tooltip.

```
/// Compute the greatest common divisor of
/// two numbers.
let rec gcd x y =
    if y = 0 then
        x
    else
        gcd y (x % y)


let test1 = gcd 1024 12
```

val gcd : x:int -> y:int -> int

Full name: Program.gcd

Compute the greatest common divisor of two numbers.

Figure 1-3. XML documentation comments

F# Interactive

So far you have written some F# code and executed it, and the rest of the book will have many more examples. Although you *could* leave a wake of new projects to test out code, Visual Studio comes with a tool called *F# Interactive* or FSI. The FSI window will not only make it much easier to work through the examples in this book, but it will also help you write applications.

F# Interactive is a tool known as a *REPL*, which stands for read, evaluate, print, loop. It accepts F# code, compiles and executes it, then prints the results. This allows you to quickly and easily experiment with F# without needing to create new projects or build a full application to test the results of a code snippet.

Most Visual Studio configurations launch the F# Interactive window with the Ctrl-Alt-F keyboard combination. Once the FSI window is available, it accepts F# code until you terminate the input with ;; and a newline. The code entered is compiled and executed as shown in Figure 1-4.

The FSI window prints any new values introduced as well as their types. Figure 1-4 shows val x : int = 42, declaring that a value x of type int was created with value 42. If the FSI window evaluates an expression that was not assigned to a value, it will instead assign it to the name it.

```
        let greeting, thing = args.[0], args.[1]
        let timeOfDay = DateTime.Now.ToString("hh:mm tt")

        printfn "%s, %s at %s" greeting thing timeOfDay
```

```
100 %   ▾ <                                                                    >

F# Interactive                                                          ▾ � ⏸ ✕

Microsoft (R) F# 3.0 Interactive build 11.0.50522.1
Copyright (c) Microsoft Corporation. All Rights Reserved.

For help type #help;;

> let x = 42;;

val x : int = 42

> x + 8;;
val it : int = 50
>

  <

    F# Interactive │ Output

Ready
```

Figure 1-4. The F# Interactive window

As the F# compiler processes FSI input, it will display the name, type, and value of identifiers. For example, in Figure 1-4 the value x was introduced with type int and value 42.

 If you are running F# without Visual Studio, you can find the console version of F# Interactive in the same directory you found fsc.exe with the name fsi.exe.

Try running these other snippets in FSI. Remember that every code snippet is terminated with a ;;:

```
> 2 + 2;;
val it : int = 4
> // Introduce two values
let x = 1
let y = 2.3;;

val x : int = 1
val y : float = 2.3

> float x + y;;
val it : float = 3.3
> let cube x = x * x * x;;
```

```
val cube : int -> int

> cube 4;;
val it : int = 64
```

FSI can dramatically simplify testing and debugging your applications because you can send F# code from your current project to the FSI window by highlighting it and pressing *Alt-Enter*.

After selecting all the code in Example 1-1 within the code editor and pressing *Alt-Enter*, you will see the following in the FSI window:

```
>

val main : string [] -> int
```

This allows you to write code in the Visual Studio editor—which offers syntax highlighting and IntelliSense—but test your code using the FSI window. You can check the main method's implementation by calling it from FSI:

```
> main [| "Hello"; "World" |];;
Hello, World at 10:52 AM
val it : int = 0
```

 The majority of the examples in this book are taken directly from FSI sessions. I encourage you to use FSI to follow along and experiment with the F# language's syntax.

You can find a copy of the source code for all examples in the book on GitHub (*https://github.com/aChrisSmith/Programming-FS-Examples/*).

Managing F# Source Files

When you are starting out with F# programming, most of the programs you write will live only in FSI or perhaps in a single code file. Your F# projects, however, will quickly grow and be broken up across multiple files and eventually multiple projects.

The F# language has some unique characteristics when it comes to managing projects with multiple source files. In F#, the order in which code files are compiled is significant.

You can only call into functions and classes defined earlier in the code file or in a separate code file compiled before the file where the function or class is used. If you rearrange the order of the source files, your program may no longer build!

 The reason for this significance in compilation order is *type inference*, a topic covered in Chapter 2.

F# source files are compiled from top to bottom in the order they are displayed in Visual Studio's *Solution Explorer*. Whenever you add a new code file it is added at the bottom of the list, but if you want to rearrange the source files, you can right click a code file and select "Move Up" or "Move Down," as seen in Figure 1-5. The keyboard shortcut for reordering project files is *Alt-Up* and *Alt-Down*.

Figure 1-5. Reordering files within an F# project

 A feature sorely missing from Visual Studio is the ability to organize an F# project's source code files into subfolders. Although not exposed by the Visual Studio UI, you can edit the project file directly to achieve this. Many of the in-depth examples of this book utilize this technique

Now that you are armed with the logistical know-how for creating, compiling, and testing F# applications, the rest of this book will focuses exclusively on the syntax and semantics of the F# programming language.

In just a few chapters, you'll master the syntax of the F# language and be able to apply it across several programming paradigms. Good luck and have fun!

Fundamentals

In Chapter 1, you wrote your first F# program. I broke it down to give you a feel for what you were doing, but much of the code is still a mystery. In this chapter, I provide the necessary foundation for you to understand that code fully, but more importantly, I present several more examples that you can use to grasp the basics of F# before you move on to the more complex features.

The first section of this chapter covers primitive types, like `int` and `string`, which are the building blocks for all F# programs. I then cover functions so you can manipulate data.

The fourth section details foundational types such as `list`, `option`, and `unit`. Mastering these types enables you to expand into the object-oriented and functional styles of F# code covered in later chapters.

By the end of this chapter, you will be able to write simple F# programs for processing data. In future chapters, you learn how to add power and expressiveness to your code, but for now, let's master the basics.

Primitive Types

A *type* is a concept or abstraction, and is primarily about enforcing safety. Types represent a proof of sorts if a conversion will work. Some types are straightforward (representing an integer), whereas others are far more abstract (like a function). F# is statically typed, meaning that type checking is done at compile time. For example, if a function accepts an integer as a parameter, you will get a compiler error if you try to pass in a string.

Like C# and VB.NET, F# supports the full cast and crew of *primitive .NET types*, which are standard across most programming languages. They are built into the F# language and separate from *user-defined types* that you define yourself.

To create a value, simply use a *let binding* via the `let` keyword. For example, the following code defines a new value x in an FSI session. You can do much more with `let` bindings, but we'll save that for Chapter 3:

```
> let x = 1;;

val x : int = 1
```

Numeric Primitives

Numeric primitives come in two varieties: integers and floating-point numbers. Integer types vary by size, so that some types take up less memory and can represent a smaller range of numbers. Integers can also be signed or unsigned based on whether or not they can represent negative values. Floating-point types vary in size too; in exchange for taking up more memory, they provide more precision for the values they hold.

To define new numeric values, use a `let` binding followed by an integer or floating-point literal with an optional suffix. The suffix determines the type of integer or floating-point number (a full list of available primitive numeric types and their suffixes is provided in Table 2-1):

```
> let answerToEverything = 42UL;;

val answerToEverything : uint64 = 42UL

> let pi = 3.1415926M;;

val pi : decimal = 3.1415926M

> let avogadro = 6.022e23;;

val avogadro : float = 6.022e23
```

Table 2-1. Numerical primitives in F#

Type	Suffix	.NET Type	Range
byte	uy	System.Byte	0 to 255
sbyte	y	System.SByte	−128 to 127
int16	s	System.Int16	−32,768 to 32,767
uint16	us	System.UInt16	0 to 65,535
int, int32		System.Int32	-2^{31} to $2^{31}-1$
uint32	u	System.UInt32	0 to $2^{32}-1$
int64	L	System.Int64	-2^{63} to $2^{63}-1$
uint64	UL	System.UInt64	0 to $2^{64}-1$
float		System.Double	A double-precision floating point based on the IEEE 64 standard. Represents values with approximately 15 significant digits.

Type	Suffix	.NET Type	Range
float32	f	System.Single	A single-precision floating point based on the IEEE 32 standard. Represents values with approximately 7 significant digits.
decimal	M	System.Decimal	A fixed-precision floating-point type with precisely 28 digits of precision.

F# will also allow you to specify values in hexadecimal (base 16), octal (base 8), or binary (base 2) using a prefix 0x, 0o, or 0b:

```
> let hex = 0xFCAF;;

val hex : int = 64687

> let oct = 0o7771L;;

val oct : int64 = 4089L

> let bin = 0b00101010y;;

val bin : sbyte = 42y

> (hex, oct, bin);;
val it : int * int64 * sbyte = (64687, 4089L, 42)
```

If you are familiar with the IEEE 32 and IEEE 64 standards, you can also specify floating-point numbers using hex, octal, or binary. F# will convert the binary value to the floating-point number it represents. When using a different base to represent floating-point numbers, use the LF suffix for float types and lf for float32 types:

```
> 0x401E000000000000LF;;
val it : float = 7.5

> 0x00000000lf;;
val it : float32 = 0.0f
```

Arithmetic

You can use standard arithmetic operators on numeric primitives. Table 2-2 lists all supported operators. Like most programming languages, integer division rounds down, discarding the remainder.

Table 2-2. Arithmetic operators

Operator	Description	Example	Result
+	Addition	1 + 2	3
−	Subtraction	1 − 2	−1
*	Multiplication	2 * 3	6
/	Division	8L / 3L	2L
**	Power[a]	2.0 ** 8.0	256.0

Operator	Description	Example	Result
%	Modulus	7 % 3	1

[a] Power, the ** operator, only works for float and float32 types. To raise the power of an integer value, you must either convert it to a floating-point number first or use the pown function.

By default, arithmetic operators do not check for overflow, so if you exceed the range allowed by an integer value by addition, it will overflow to be negative (similarly, subtraction will result in a positive number if the number is too small to be stored in the integer type):

```
> 32767s + 1s;;
val it : int16 = -32768s

> -32768s + -1s;;
val it : int16 = 32767s
```

 If integer overflow is a cause for concern, you should consider using a larger type or using checked arithmetic, discussed in Chapter 7.

F# features all the standard mathematical functions you would expect, with a full listing in Table 2-3.

Table 2-3. Common mathematical functions

Routine	Description	Example	Result
abs	Absolute value of a number	abs -1.0	1.0
ceil	Round up to the nearest integer	ceil 9.1	10.0
exp	Raise a value to a power of e	exp 1.0	2.718
floor	Round down to the nearest integer	floor 9.9	9.0
sign	Sign of the value	sign -5	-1
log	Natural logarithm	log 2.71828	1.0
log10	Logarithm in base 10	log10 1000.0	3.0
sqrt	Square root	sqrt 4.0	2.0
cos	Cosine	cos 0.0	1.0
sin	Sine	sin 0.0	0.0
tan	Tangent	tan 1.0	1.557
pown	Compute the power of an integer	pown 2L 10	1024L

Conversion Routines

One of the tenets of the F# language is that there are no implicit conversions. This means that the compiler will not automatically convert primitive data types for you behind the scenes, such as converting an int16 to an int64. This eliminates subtle bugs by removing surprise conversions. Instead, to convert primitive values, you must use an explicit conversion function listed in Table 2-4. All of the standard conversion functions accept all other primitive types—including strings and chars.

Table 2-4. Numeric primitive conversion routines

Routine	Description	Example	Result
sbyte	Converts data to an sybte	sbyte -5	-5y
byte	Converts data to a byte	byte "42"	42uy
int16	Converts data to an int16	int16 'a'	97s
uint16	Converts data to a unit16	uint16 5	5us
int32, int	Converts data to an int	int 2.5	2
uint32	Converts data to a uint32	uint32 0xFF	255
int64	Converts data to an int64	int64 -8	-8l
uint64	Converts data to a unit64	uint64 "0xFF"	255UL
float	Converts data to a float	float 3.1415M	3.1415
float32	Converts data to a float32	float32 8y	8.0f
decimal	Converts data to a decimal	decimal 1.23	1.23M

 Although these conversion routines accept strings, they parse strings using the underlying System.Convert family of methods, meaning that they throw System.FormatException exceptions for invalid inputs.

BigInteger

If you are dealing with data larger than 2^{64}, F# has the bigint type for representing arbitrarily large integers. (bigint type is simply an alias for the System.Numerics.Big Integer type.)

bigint is integrated into the F# language, and uses the I suffix for literals. Example 2-1 defines data storage sizes as bigints.

Example 2-1. The BigInt type for representing large integers

```
> open System.Numerics

// Data storage units
let megabyte = 1024I     * 1024I
let gigabyte = megabyte * 1024I
```

```
let terabyte  = gigabyte * 1024I
let petabyte  = terabyte * 1024I
let exabyte   = petabyte * 1024I
let zettabyte = exabyte  * 1024I;;

val megabyte : BigInteger = 1048576
val gigabyte : BigInteger = 1073741824
val terabyte : BigInteger = 1099511627776
val petabyte : BigInteger = 1125899906842624
val exabyte : BigInteger = 1152921504606846976
val zettabyte : BigInteger = 1180591620717411303424
```

 Although bigint is heavily optimized for performance, it is much slower than using the primitive integer data types.

Bitwise Operations

Primitive integer types support bitwise operators for manipulating values at a binary level. Bitwise operators are typically used when reading and writing binary data from files. See Table 2-5.

Table 2-5. Bitwise operators

Operator	Description	Example	Result
&&&	And	0b1111 &&& 0b0011	0b0011
|||	Or	0xFF00 ||| 0x00FF	0xFFFF
^^^	Exclusive Or	0b0011 ^^^ 0b0101	0b0110
<<<	Left Shift	0b0001 <<< 3	0b1000
>>>	Right Shift	0b1000 >>> 3	0b0001

Characters

The .NET platform is based on Unicode, so most text is represented using 2-byte UTF-16 characters. To define a character value, you can put any Unicode character in single quotes. Characters can also be specified using a Unicode hexadecimal character code.

The following snippet defines a list of vowel characters and prints the result of defining a character using a hexadecimal value:

```
> let vowels = ['a'; 'e'; 'i'; 'o'; 'u'];;

val vowels : char list = ['a'; 'e'; 'i'; 'o'; 'u']

> printfn "Hex u0061 = '%c'" '\u0061';;
Hex u0061 = 'a'
val it : unit = ()
```

To represent special control characters, you need to use an escape sequence, listed in Table 2-6. An escape sequence is a backslash followed by a special character.

Table 2-6. Character escape sequences

Character	Meaning
\'	Single quote
\"	Double quote
\\	Backslash
\b	Backspace
\n	Newline
\r	Carriage return
\t	Horizontal tab

If you want to get the numeric representation of a .NET character's Unicode value, you can pass it to any of the conversion routines listed in Table 2-4. Alternatively, you can get the byte representation of a character literal by adding a B suffix:

```
> // Convert value of 'C' to an integer
int 'C';;
val it : int = 67
> // Convert value of 'C' to a byte
'C'B;;
val it : byte = 67uy
```

Strings

String literals are defined by enclosing a series of characters, which can span multiple lines, in double quotes. To access a character from within a string, use the indexer syntax, .[ ], and pass in a zero-based character index:

```
> let password = "abracadabra";;

val password : string = "abracadabra"

> let multiline = "This string
takes up
multiple lines";;

val multiline : string = "This string
takes up
multiple lines"

> multiline.[0];;
val it : char = 'T'
> multiline.[1];;
val it : char = 'h'
```

```
> multiline.[2];;
val it : char = 'i'
> multiline.[3];;
val it : char = 's'
```

Alternatively, F# supports triple quotes, which allow you to put quotation mark characters in strings without the need for escaping them individually. For example:

```
let xmlFragment = """<Ship Name="Prometheus"></foo>"""
```

If you want to specify a long string, you can break it up across multiple lines using a single backslash \. If the last character on a line in a string literal is a backslash, the string will continue on the next line after removing all leading whitespace characters:

```
> let longString = "abc-\
                      def-\
          ghi";;

val longString : string = "abc-def-ghi"
```

You can use the escape sequence characters (such as \t or \\) within a string if you want, but this makes defining file paths and registry keys problematic. You can define a verbatim string using the @ symbol, which takes the verbatim text between the quotation marks and does not encode any escape sequence characters:

```
> let normalString = "Normal.\n.\n.\t.\t.String";;

val normalString : string = "Normal.
.
.        .        .String

> let verbatimString = @"Verbatim.\n.\n.\t.\t.String";;

val verbatimString : string = "Verbatim.\n.\n.\t.\t.String"
```

Similar to adding the B suffix to a character to return its byte representation, adding B to the end of a string will return the string's characters in the form of a byte array (arrays are covered in Chapter 4):

```
> let hello = "Hello"B;;

val hello : byte [] = [|72uy; 101uy; 108uy; 108uy; 111uy|]
```

Boolean Values

For dealing with values that can only be true or false, F# has the bool type (System .Boolean) as well as standard Boolean operators listed in Table 2-7.

Table 2-7. Boolean operators

Operator	Description	Example	Result
&&	And	true && false	false
||	Or	true || false	true
not	Not	not false	true

Example 2-2 builds truth tables for Boolean functions and prints them. It defines a function called `printTruthTable` that takes a function named f as a parameter. That function is called for each cell in the truth table and its result is printed. Later, the operators && and || are passed to the `printTruthTable` function.

Example 2-2. Printing truth tables

```
> // Print the truth table for the given function
let printTruthTable f =
    printfn "        |true   | false |"
    printfn "        +-------+-------+"
    printfn " true   | %5b | %5b |" (f true  true) (f true  false)
    printfn " false  | %5b | %5b |" (f false true) (f false false)
    printfn "        +-------+-------+"
    printfn ""
    ();;

val printTruthTable : (bool -> bool -> bool) -> unit

> printTruthTable (&&);;
        |true   | false |
        +-------+-------+
 true   |  true | false |
 false  | false | false |
        +-------+-------+

val it : unit = ()
> printTruthTable (||);;
        |true   | false |
        +-------+-------+
 true   |  true |  true |
 false  |  true | false |
        +-------+-------+

val it : unit = ()
```

F# uses short circuit evaluation when evaluating Boolean expressions, meaning that if the result can be determined after evaluating the first of the two expressions, then the second value won't be evaluated. For example:

```
true || f()
```

will evaluate to true, without executing function f. Likewise:

```
false && g()
```

will evaluate to false, without executing function g.

Comparison and Equality

You can compare numeric values using standard greater than, less than, and equality operators listed in Table 2-8. All comparison and equality operators evaluate to a Boolean value; the compare function returns −1, 0, or 1 depending on whether the first parameter is less than, equal to, or greater than the second.

Table 2-8. Comparison operators

Operator	Description	Example	Result
<	Less than	1 < 2	True
<=	Less than or equal to	4.0 <= 4.0	True
>	Greater than	1.4e3 > 1.0e2	True
>=	Greater than or equal to	0I >= 2I	False
=	Equal to	"abc" = "abc"	True
<>	Not equal to	'a' <> 'b'	True
Compare	Compare two values	compare 31 31	0

Equality in .NET is a complex topic. There is *value equality* and *referential equality*. For value types, comparison means that the values are identical, such as 1 = 1. For reference types, however, equality is determined by overriding the System.Object method Equals. For more information, refer to the section "Object Equality" (page 137) in Chapter 5.

Functions

Now that we have all of F#'s primitive types under our control, let's define functions in order to manipulate them.

You define functions the same way you define values, except everything after the name of the function serves as the function's parameters. The following defines a function called `square` that takes an integer, x, and returns its square:

```
> let square x = x * x;;

val square : int -> int

> square 4;;
val it : int = 16
```

F# has no `return` keyword. So when you define a function, the last expression to be evaluated in the function is what the function returns.

Let's try another function to add 1 to the function's input:

```
> let addOne x = x + 1;;

val addOne : int -> int
```

The output from FSI shows the function has type `int -> int`, which is read as "a function taking an integer and returning an integer." The signature gets a bit more complicated when you add multiple parameters:

```
> let add x y = x + y;;

val add : int -> int -> int
```

Technically speaking, the type `int -> int -> int` is read as "a function taking an integer which returns a function which takes an integer and returns an integer." Don't worry about this "functions returning functions" jazz just yet. The only thing you need to know for now is that in order to call a function, simply provide its parameters separated by spaces:

```
> add 1 2;;

Val it : int = 3
```

Type Inference

Because F# is statically typed, calling the `add` method you just created with a floating-point value will result in a compiler error:

```
> add 1.0 2.0;;

  add 1.0 2.0;;
  ----.^^^^

stdin(3,5): error FS0001: This expression was expected to have type
        int
but here has type
        float.
```

You might then be wondering: Why does the compiler think that this function only takes integers? The + operator also works on floats too!

The reason is due to *type inference*. The F# compiler doesn't require you to explicitly state the types of all the parameters to a function. The compiler infers their types based on usage.

 Be careful not to confuse type inference with *dynamic typing*. Although F# allows you to omit types when writing code, that doesn't mean that type checking is not enforced at compile time.

Because the + operator works for many different types, such as `byte`, `int`, and `deci mal`, the compiler simply defaults to `int` if there is no additional information.

The following FSI session declares a function that will multiply two values. Just like when + was used, the function is inferred to work on integers because no usage information is provided:

```
> // No additional information to infer usage
let mult x y = x * y;;

val mult : int -> int -> int
```

Now if we have an FSI snippet that not only defines the `mult` function but also calls it passing in floats, then the function's signature will be inferred to be of type `float -> float -> float`:

```
> // Type inference in action
let mult x y = x * y
let result = mult 4.0 5.5;;

val mult : float -> float -> float
val result : float = 22.0
```

However, you can provide a *type annotation*, or hint, to the F# compiler about what the types are. To add a type annotation, simply replace a function parameter with the following form:

`(ident : type)`

Where *type* is the type you wish to force the parameter to be. To constrain the first parameter of our `add` function to be a `float`, simply redefine the function as:

```
> let add (x : float) y =  x + y;;

val add : float -> float -> float
```

Notice that because you added the type annotation for value x, the type of the function changed to `float -> float -> float`. This is because the only overload for + that takes a `float` as its first parameter is `float -> float -> float`, so the F# compiler now infers the type of y to be `float` as well.

Type inference dramatically reduces code clutter by having the compiler figure out what types to use. However, the occasional type annotation is required and can sometimes improve code readability.

Generic Functions

You can write functions that work for any type of a parameter—for example, an identity function that simply returns its input:

```
> let ident x = x;;

val ident : 'a -> 'a

> ident "a string";;
val it : string = "a string"
> ident 1234L;;
val it : int64 = 1234L
```

Because the type inference system did not require a fixed type for value x in the `ident` function, it was left *generic*. If a parameter is generic, it means that the parameter can be of any type, such as an integer, string, or float.

The type of a generic parameter can have the name of any valid identifier prefixed with an apostrophe, but are typically letters of the alphabet starting with "a." The following code redefines the `ident` function using a type annotation that forces x to be generic:

```
> let ident2 (x : 'a) = x;;

val ident2 : 'a -> 'a
```

Writing generic code is important for maximizing code reuse. We will continue to dive into type inference and generic functions as the book progresses, so don't sweat the details just yet. Just note that whenever you see `'a`, it can be an `int`, `float`, `string`, a user-defined type, and so on.

Scope

Each value declared in F# has a specific scope, which is the range of locations where the value can be used. (More formally, this is called a *declaration space*.) By default, values have *module scope*, meaning that they can be used anywhere after their declaration. However, values defined within a function are scoped only to that function. So a function can use any value defined previously on the "outside" of the function, but the outside cannot refer to values defined inside of a function.

In the following example, a value named moduleValue is defined with module scope and used inside of a function, whereas another value named functionValue is defined within a function and raises an error when used outside of its scope:

```
> // Scope
let moduleValue = 10
let functionA x =
    x + moduleValue;;

val moduleValue : int = 10
val functionA : int -> int

> // Error case
let functionB x =
    let functionValue = 20
    x + functionValue

// 'functionValue' not in scope
functionValue;;

    functionValue;;
    ^^^^^^^^^^^^^
error FS0039: The value or constructor 'functionValue' is not defined.
```

The scoping of values may not seem like that important of a detail, but one reason you should be aware of it is because F# allows nested functions. You can declare new function values within the body of a function. Nested functions have access to any value declared in a higher scope, such as the parent function or module, as well as any new values declared within the nested function.

The following code shows nested functions in action. Notice how function g is able to use its parent function f 's parameter fParam:

```
> // Nested functions
let moduleValue = 1

let f fParam =
    let g gParam = fParam + gParam + moduleValue

    let a = g 1
    let b = g 2
    a + b;;

val moduleValue : int = 1
val f : int -> int
```

It may seem like defining functions within functions can only lead to confusion, but the ability to limit the scope of functions is very useful. It helps prevent pollution of the surrounding module by allowing you to keep small, specific functions local to just where they are needed. This will become more apparent once we start programming in the functional style in Chapter 3.

Once you do start using nested functions, it might become tedious to keep all the values in scope straight. What if you want to declare a value named x, but that value is already used in a higher scope? In F#, having two values with the same name doesn't lead to a compiler error; rather, it simply leads to *shadowing*. When this happens, both values exist in memory, except there is no way to access the previously declared value. Instead, the last one declared "wins."

The following code defines a function that takes a parameter x, and then defines several new values each named x as well:

```
> open System.Numerics
// Convert bytes to gigabytes
let bytesToGB x =
    let x = x / 1024I //  B to KB
    let x = x / 1024I // KB to MB
    let x = x / 1024I // MB to GB
    x;;

val bytesToGB : BigInteger -> BigInteger

> let hardDriveSize = bytesToGB 268435456000I;;
val hardDriveSize : BigInteger = 250
```

After each `let` binding in the previous example, the value named x is shadowed and replaced with a new one. This may look like the value of x is changing, but actually it is just creating a new value of x and giving it the same name. The following shows an example of how the code gets compiled:

```
let bytesToGB x =
    let x_2 = x   / 1024I //  B to KB
    let x_3 = x_2 / 1024I // KB to MB
    let x_4 = x_3 / 1024I // MB to GB
    x_4
```

This technique of intentionally shadowing values is useful for giving the illusion of updating values without relying on mutation. If you want to actually update the value of x, you need to resort to mutability, which is covered in Chapter 4.

Control Flow

Within a function, you can branch control flow using the `if` keyword. The condition expression must be of type `bool` and if it evaluates to `true`, then the given code is executed, which in the following snippet prints a message to the console:

```
> // If statements
let printGreeting shouldGreet greeting =
    if shouldGreet then
        printfn "%s" greeting;;

val printGreeting : bool -> string -> unit
```

```
> printGreeting true "Hello!";;
Hello!
val it : unit = ()
> printGreeting false "Hello again!";;
val it : unit = ()
```

More complex code branching can be done using if *expressions*.

if expressions work just like you would expect: if the condition expression evaluates to true, then the first block of code executes; otherwise, the second block of code executes. However, something that makes F# much different from other languages is that if expressions return a value.

For example, in the following example, the value result is bound to the result of the if expression. So if x % 2 = 0, then result's value will be "Yes it is"; otherwise, result's value will be "No it is not":

```
> // If expressions
let isEven x =
    let result =
        if x % 2 = 0 then
            "Yes it is"
        else
            "No it is not"
    result;;

val isEven : int -> string

> isEven 5;;
val it : string = "No it is not"
```

You can nest if expressions to model more complicated branching, but this quickly becomes difficult to maintain:

```
let isWeekend day =
    if day = "Sunday" then
        true
    else
        if day = "Saturday" then
            true
        else
            false
```

F# has some syntactic sugar to help you combat deeply nested if expressions with the elif keyword. With it, you can chain together multiple if expressions without the need for nesting:

```
let isWeekday day =
    if   day = "Monday"  then true
    elif day = "Tuesday" then true
```

```
    elif day = "Wednesday" then true
    elif day = "Thursday"  then true
    elif day = "Friday"    then true
    else false
```

Because the result of the if expression is a value, every clause of an if expression must return the same type:

```
> // ERROR: Different types for if expression clauses
let x =
    if 1 > 2 then
        42
    else
        "a string";;

    else            "a string";;
    -----------------^^^^^^^^^^^

stdin(118,19): error FS0001: This expression was expected to have type
        int
but here has type
        string.
stopped due to error
```

But what if you only have a single if and no corresponding else? In that case, the clause must return unit, which is a special type in F# that means essentially no value. (Alternatively, you can think of unit as a manifestation of void from other programming languages.) We cover unit in more detail shortly.

Core Types

Previously we covered the primitive types available on the .NET platform, but those alone are insufficient for creating meaningful F# programs. The F# library includes several core types that will allow you to organize, manipulate, and process data. Table 2-9 lists a set of foundational types you will use throughout your F# applications.

In fact, these foundational types enable programming in the functional style, as we will see in Chapter 3.

Table 2-9. Core types in F#

Signature	Name	Description	Example
unit	Unit	The unit value	()
int, float	Concrete type	A concrete type	42, 3.14
'a, 'b	Generic type	A generic (free) type	
'a -> 'b	Function type	A function returning a value	fun x -> x + 1
'a * 'b	Tuple type	An ordered grouping of values	("eggs", "ham")
'a list	List type	A list of values	[1; 2; 3], [1 .. 3]

Signature	Name	Description	Example
'a option	Option type	An optional value	Some(3), None

Unit

The unit type is a value signifying nothing of consequence and is represented in code via ( ):

```
> let x = ();;

val x : unit

> ();;
val it : unit = ()
```

if expressions without a matching else must return unit because if they did return a value, what would happen if else-clause was executed instead? Also, in F# every function must return a value, so if the function doesn't conceptually return anything—like printf—then it should return a unit value.

The ignore function can swallow a function's return value if you want to return unit. It is typically used when calling a function for its side effect and you want to ignore its return value:

```
> let square x = x * x;;

val square : int -> int

> ignore (square 4);;
val it : unit = ()
```

Tuple

A tuple (pronounced as either "two-pull" or "tuh-pull") is an ordered collection of data and an easy way to group common pieces of data together. For example, tuples can be used to track the intermediate results of a computation.

 F# tuples use the underlying System.Tuple<_> type, although in practice you will never use the Tuple<_> class directly.

To create an instance of a tuple, separate a group of values with commas, and optionally place them within parentheses. A tuple type is described by a list of the tuple's element's types, separated by asterisks. In the following example, dinner is an instance of a tuple while string * string is the tuple's type:

```
> let dinner = ("green eggs", "ham");;

val dinner : string * string = ("green eggs", "ham")
```

Tuples can contain any number of values of any type. In fact, you can even have a tuple that contains other tuples!

The following code snippet defines two tuples. The first, named `zeros`, defines a tuple of various manifestations of zero. The second, `nested`, defines a nested tuple. The tuple has three elements, the second and third of which are themselves tuples:

```
> let zeros = (0, 0L, 0I, 0.0);;

val zeros : int * int64 * BigInteger * float = (0, 0L, 0I, 0.0)

> let nested = (1, (2.0, 3M), (4L, "5", '6'));;

val nested : int * (float * decimal) * (int64 * string * char) = ...
```

To extract values from two-element tuples, you can use the `fst` and `snd` functions. `fst` returns the first element of the tuple and `snd` returns the second:

```
> let nameTuple = ("John", "Smith");;

val nameTuple : string * string = ("John", "Smith")

> fst nameTuple;;
val it : string = "John"
> snd nameTuple;;
val it : string = "Smith"
```

Alternately, you can extract values from tuples by simply using a `let` binding. If you have `let` followed by multiple identifiers separated by commas, then those names capture the tuple's values.

The following example creates a tuple value named `snacks`. Later the tuple's values are extracted into new identifiers named x, y, and z:

```
> let snacks = ("Soda", "Cookies", "Candy");;

val snacks : string * string * string = ("Soda", "Cookies", "Candy")

> let x, y, z = snacks;;

val z : string = "Candy"
val y : string = "Cookies"
val x : string = "Soda"

> y, z;;
val it : string * string = ("Cookies", "Candy")
```

You will get a compile error if you try to extract too many or too few values from a tuple:

```
> let x, y = snacks;;

  let x, y = snacks;;
  ----------^^^^^^

stdin(8,12): error FS0001: Type mismatch. Expecting a
        string * string
but given a
        string * string * string.
The tuples have differing lengths of 2 and 3.
```

It is possible to pass tuples as parameters to functions, like any value. Likewise, a function can return a tuple. In the following example, the function tupledAdd takes two parameters, x and y, in tupled form. Notice the difference in type signature between the add and the tupledAdd functions:

```
> let add x y = x + y;;

val add : int -> int -> int

> let tupledAdd(x, y) = x + y;;

val tupledAdd : int * int -> int

> add 3 7;;
val it : int = 10

> tupledAdd(3, 7);;
val it : int = 10
```

Functions taking a single tuple as a parameter have a much different meaning when it comes to the functional style of programming; see the section "Partial function application" (page 55) in Chapter 3.

Lists

Whereas tuples group values into a single entity, lists allow you to link data together to form a chain. Doing so allows you to process list elements in bulk using aggregate operators, discussed shortly.

The simplest way to define a list is as a semicolon-delimited collection of values enclosed in brackets, although later you will learn to declare lists using the more powerful list comprehension syntax. The empty list, which contains no items, is represented by [ ]:

```
> // Declaring lists
let vowels = ['a'; 'e'; 'i'; 'o'; 'u']
let emptyList = [];;

val vowels : char list = ['a'; 'e'; 'i'; 'o'; 'u']
val emptyList : 'a list = []
```

In our example, the empty list had type `'a list` because the empty list could be of any type. With more information based on usage, the type inference system would be able to pin it down to a more specific type.

Unlike list types in other languages, F# lists are quite restrictive in how you access and manipulate them. In fact, for a list, there are only two operations you can perform. (To see how this limitation can be used to your advantage, refer to Chapter 7.)

The first primitive list operation is *cons*, represented by the cons operator, ` :: `. This joins an element to the front or *head* of a list. The following example attaches the value `'y'` to the head of the vowels list:

```
> // Using the cons operator
let sometimes = 'y' :: vowels;;

val sometimes : char list = ['y'; 'a'; 'e'; 'i'; 'o'; 'u']
```

The second primitive list operation, known as append, uses the @ operator. Append joins two lists together. The following example joins the list odds and the list evens together, resulting in a new list:

```
> // Using the append operator
let odds  = [1; 3; 5; 7; 9]
let evens = [2; 4; 6; 8; 10]

val odds : int list = [1; 3; 5; 7; 9]
val evens : int list = [2; 4; 6; 8; 10]

> odds @ evens;;
val it : int list = [1; 3; 5; 7; 9; 2; 4; 6; 8; 10]
```

List ranges

Declaring list elements as a semicolon-delimited list quickly becomes tedious, especially for large lists. To declare a list of ordered numeric values, you can use the list range syntax.

The first expression specifies the lower bound of the range and the second specifies the upper bound. The result then is a list of values from the lower bound to the upper bound, each incremented by one:

```
> let x = [1 .. 10];;

val x : int list = [1; 2; 3; 4; 5; 6; 7; 8; 9; 10]
```

If an optional step value is provided, then the result is a list of values in the range between two numbers separated by the stepping value. Note that the stepping value can be negative:

```
> // List ranges
let tens = [0 .. 10 .. 50]
```

```
let countDown = [5L .. -1L .. 0L];;

val tens : int list = [0; 10; 20; 30; 40; 50]
val countDown : int64 list = [5L; 4L; 3L; 2L; 1L; 0L]
```

List comprehensions

The most expressive method for creating lists is to use *list comprehensions*, a rich syntax
that allows you to generate lists inline with F# code. At the simplest level, a list comprehension is some code surrounded by rectangular brackets, [ ]. The body of the list
comprehension will be executed until it terminates, and the list will be made up of
elements returned via the yield keyword (note that the list is fully generated in memory
when created; if you find yourself creating lists with thousands of elements, consider
using a seq<_>, discussed in Chapter 3, instead):

```
> // Simple list comprehensions
let numbersNear x =
    [
        yield x - 1
        yield x
        yield x + 1
    ];;

val numbersNear : int -> int list

> numbersNear 3;;
val it : int list = [2; 3; 4]
```

Most any F# code can exist inside of list comprehensions, including things like function
declarations and for loops. The following code snippet shows a list comprehension that
defines a function negate and returns the numbers 1 through 10, negating the even
ones:

```
> // More complex list comprehensions
let x =
    [ let negate x = -x
      for i in 1 .. 10 do
          if i % 2 = 0 then
              yield negate i
          else
              yield i ];;

val x : int list = [1; -2; 3; -4; 5; -6; 7; -8; 9; -10]
```

When using for loops within list comprehensions, you can simplify the code by using
-> instead of do yield. The following two code snippets are identical:

```
// Generate the first ten multiples of a number
let multiplesOf x = [ for i in 1 .. 10 do yield x * i ]

// Simplified list comprehension
let multiplesOf2 x = [ for i in 1 .. 10 -> x * i ]
```

Using list comprehension syntax will enable you to quickly and concisely generate lists of data, which can then be processed in your code. Example 2-3 shows how you can use list comprehensions to generate all prime numbers smaller than a given integer.

The example works by looping through all numbers between 1 and the given `max` value. Then it uses a list comprehension to generate all the factors of that number. It checks if the generated list of factors has only two elements, then it yields the value because it is prime. There certainly are more efficient ways to compute primes, but this demonstrates just how expressive list comprehensions can be.

Example 2-3. Using list comprehensions to compute primes

```
> // List comprehension for prime numbers
let primesUnder max =
    [
        for n in 1 .. max do
            let factorsOfN =
                [
                    for i in 1 .. n do
                        if n % i = 0 then
                            yield i
                ]

            // n is prime if its only factors are 1 and n
            if List.length factorsOfN = 2 then
                yield n
    ];;

val primesUnder : int -> int list

> primesUnder 50;;
val it : int list = [2; 3; 5; 7; 11; 13; 17; 19; 23; 29; 31; 37; 41; 43; 47]
```

List module functions

The F# Library's `List` module contains many methods to help you process lists. The built-in methods listed in Table 2-10 are the primary ways you will interact with lists in F#.

Table 2-10. Common List module functions

Function and type	Description
`List.length` `'a list -> int`	Returns the length of a list.
`List.head` `'a list -> 'a`	Returns the first element in a list.
`List.tail` `'a list -> 'a list`	Returns the given list without the first element.

Function and type	Description
List.exists ('a -> bool) -> 'a list -> bool	Returns whether or not an element in the list satisfies the search function.
List.rev 'a list -> 'a list	Reverses the elements in a list.
List.tryfind ('a -> bool) -> 'a list -> 'a option	Returns Some(x) where x is the first element for which the given function returns true. Otherwise returns None. (Some and None are covered shortly.)
List.zip 'a list -> 'b list -> ('a * 'b) list	Given two lists with the same length, returns a joined list of tuples.
List.filter ('a -> bool) -> 'a list -> 'a list	Returns a list with only the elements for which the given function returned true.
List.partition ('a -> bool) -> 'a list -> ('a list * 'a list)	Given a predicate function and a list, returns two new lists; the first where the function returned true, the second where the function returned false.

Initially, it may not be clear how to use some of the List module functions, but you'll soon be able to identify what a function does by simply looking at its type signature.

The following example demonstrates the List.partition function, partitioning a list of numbers from 1 to 15 into two new lists: one comprised of multiples of five and the other list made up of everything else. The tricky part to note is that List.partition returns a tuple, and in the example values multOf5 and nonMultOf5 are elements of that tuple being bound at the same time:

```
> // Using List.partition
let isMultipleOf5 x = (x % 5 = 0)

let multOf5, nonMultOf5 =
    List.partition isMultipleOf5 [1 .. 15];;

val isMultipleOf5 : int -> bool
val nonMultOf5 : int list = [1; 2; 3; 4; 6; 7; 8; 9; 11; 12; 13; 14]
val multOf5 : int list = [5; 10; 15]
```

What is List anyways? All of these functions are defined in the List module in the Microsoft.FSharp.Collections namespace. Because the Microsoft.FSharp.Collections module is imported by default, to access any of these methods you just need to specify the List module and the function name.

Aggregate Operators

Although lists offer a way to chain together pieces of data, there really isn't anything special about them. The true power of lists lies in *aggregate operators*, which are a set of powerful functions that are useful for any collection of values. You'll see this set of methods again during the discussion of sequences (Chapter 3) and arrays (Chapter 4).

List.map

`List.map` is a projection operation that creates a new list based on a provided function. Each element in the new list is the result of applying the function to an element of the original list. It has type:

```
('a -> 'b) -> 'a list -> 'b list
```

Visually you can represent mapping a function *f* to list [x; y; z], as shown in Figure 2-1.

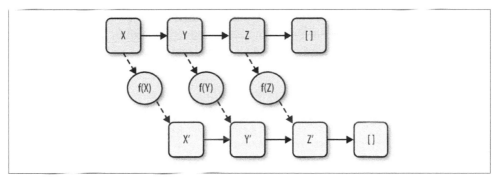

Figure 2-1. Visualizing List.map

Example 2-4 shows the result of mapping a square function to a list of integers.

Example 2-4. Using List.map to square numbers in a list

```
> let square x = x * x;;

val square : int -> int

> List.map square [1 .. 10];;
val it : int list = [1; 4; 9; 16; 25; 36; 49; 64; 81; 100]
```

It may not seem like it right now, but `List.map` is one of the most useful functions in the F# language. It provides an elegant way for you to transform although used repeatedly, can simplify the structure of code you write.

List.fold

Folds represent the most powerful—and, not surprisingly, the most complicated—type of aggregate operator. When you have a list of values and you want to distill it down to a single piece of data, you use a fold.

There are two main types of folds you can use on lists. Let's start with `List.reduce`, which has type:

```
('a -> 'a -> 'a) -> 'a list -> 'a
```

`List.reduce` iterates through each element of a list, building up an *accumulator value*, which is the summary of the processing done on the list so far. Once every list item has been processed, the final accumulator value is returned. The accumulator's initial value in `List.reduce` is the first element of the list.

Example 2-5 demonstrates how to use `List.reduce` to comma-separate a list of strings. The function `insertCommas` takes the accumulator and a value and simply returns a new string that joins the accumulator and the value separated by a comma. When passed to `List.reduce`, the initial value of the accumulator is the first item in the list, so the net result after processing every item in the list is a single string containing all of the list's values separated by commas.

Example 2-5. Comma separating a list of strings using List.reduce

```
> let insertCommas (acc : string) item = acc + ", " + item;;

val insertCommas : string -> string -> string

> List.reduce insertCommas ["Jack"; "Jill"; "Jim"; "Joe"; "Jane"];;
val it : string = "Jack, Jill, Jim, Joe, Jane"
```

The following table shows how the accumulator was built up after processing each list element:

Accumulator	List element
"Jack" (the first list element)	"Jill" (the second list element)
"Jack, Jill"	"Jim"
"Jack, Jill, Jim"	"Joe"
"Jack, Jill, Jim, Joe"	"Jane"

Although the `reduce` fold is helpful, it forces the type of the accumulator to have the same type as the list. But what if you want something more powerful (e.g., reducing a list of items in a shopping cart to a cash value)?

If you want to use a custom accumulator type, you can use `List.fold`. The `fold` function takes three parameters. First, a function that when provided an accumulator and list element returns a new accumulator. Second, an initial accumulator value. The final parameter is the list to fold over. The return value of the `fold` is the final state of the accumulator. Officially the type is:

```
('acc -> 'b -> 'acc) -> 'acc -> 'b list -> 'acc
```

To provide a simple example, consider folding a list of integers into their sum:

```
> let addAccToListItem acc i = acc + i;;

val addAccToListItem : int -> int -> int

> List.fold addAccToListItem 0 [1; 2; 3];;
val it : int = 6
```

But again, the accumulator for `fold` does not need to be the same as the list's elements. Example 2-6 folds the characters of a `string` into a tuple counting the occurrences of each vowel (the number of As, Es, Is, etc.).

The folding function is applied to each letter in the list. If the letter is a vowel, we return an updated accumulator value; otherwise we just return the existing accumulator.

Example 2-6. Counting vowels using List.fold

```
> // Count the number of vowels in a string
let countVowels (str : string) =
    let charList = List.ofSeq str

    let accFunc (As, Es, Is, Os, Us) letter =
        if   letter = 'a' then (As + 1, Es, Is, Os, Us)
        elif letter = 'e' then (As, Es + 1, Is, Os, Us)
        elif letter = 'i' then (As, Es, Is + 1, Os, Us)
        elif letter = 'o' then (As, Es, Is, Os + 1, Us)
        elif letter = 'u' then (As, Es, Is, Os, Us + 1)
        else                  (As, Es, Is, Os, Us)

    List.fold accFunc (0, 0, 0, 0, 0) charList;;

val countVowels : string -> int * int * int * int * int

> countVowels "The quick brown fox jumps over the lazy dog";;
val it : int * int * int * int * int = (1, 3, 1, 4, 2)
```

Folding right-to-left

`List.reduce` and `List.fold` process the list in a left-to-right order. There are alternative functions `List.reduceBack` and `List.foldBack` for processing lists in right-to-left order. Depending on what you are trying to do, processing a list in reverse order can have a substantial impact on performance. For a more in-depth look at the performance implications of list processing, refer to Chapter 7.

List.iter

The final aggregate operator, `List.iter`, iterates through each element of the list and calls a function that you pass as a parameter. It has type:

```
('a -> unit) -> 'a list -> unit
```

Because `List.iter` returns `unit`, it is predominately used for evaluating the *side effect* of the given method. The term side effect simply means that executing the function has some side effect other than its return value; for example, `printfn` has the side effect of printing to the console in addition to returning `unit`.

Example 2-7 uses `List.iter` to iterate through each number in a list and print it to the console.

Example 2-7. Using List.iter to print numbers in a list

```
> // Using List.iter
let printNumber x = printfn "Printing %d" x
List.iter printNumber [1 .. 5];;

Printing 1
Printing 2
Printing 3
Printing 4
Printing 5

val printNumber : int -> unit
```

Option

If you want to represent a value that may or may not exist, the best way to do so is to use the `option` type. The `option` type has only two possible values: `Some('a)` and `None`.

Consider the problem of parsing a `string` as an `int`. If the string is properly formatted, the function should return the integer value, but what if the string is improperly formatted? This is a prime situation where you would use an `option` type.

A common idiom in other languages is to use null to mean the absence of a value. However, null is also used to indicate an uninitialized value. This duality can lead to confusion and bugs. If you use the option type, there is no question what the value represents.

option can be thought of as similar to the System.Nullable type, covered in Chapter 4.

Example 2-8 defines a function isInteger that tries to parse an integer using the Int32.TryParse function. If the parsing is successful, the function will return Some(result); otherwise it will return None. This enables consumers of the function to know that for some inputs the result may not be defined, hence returning None.

Example 2-8. The option type storing if a string parses as an integer

```
> // Using option to return a value (or not)
open System

let isInteger str =
    let successful, result = Int32.TryParse(str)
    if successful
    then Some(result)
    else None;;

val isInteger : string -> int option

> isInteger "This is not an int";;
val it : int option = None
> isInteger "400";;
val it : int option = Some 400
```

To retrieve the value of an option, you can use Option.get. (If Option.get is called on None, an exception will be thrown.) The following snippet defines a function containsNegativeNumbers, which returns Some(_) for all negative numbers in a list. Then, the list's negative numbers are retrieved using Option.get:

```
> // Using Option.get
let isLessThanZero x = (x < 0)

let containsNegativeNumbers intList =
    let filteredList = List.filter isLessThanZero intList
    if List.length filteredList > 0
    then Some(filteredList)
    else None;;

val isLessThanZero : int -> bool
val containsNegativeNumbers : int list -> int list option

> let negativeNumbers = containsNegativeNumbers [6; 20; -8; 45; -5];;
```

```
val negativeNumbers : int list option = Some [-8; -5]

> Option.get negativeNumbers;;
val it : int list = [-8; -5]
```

The Option module contains other helpful functions listed in Table 2-11.

Table 2-11. Common Option module methods

Function and type	Description
Option.isSome 'a option -> bool	Returns true if the option is Some; otherwise false
Option.isNone 'a option -> bool	Returns false if the option is Some; otherwise true

Printf

Writing data to the console is the simplest way to perform I/O and is done using the printf family of functions. printf comes in three main flavors: printf, printfn, and sprintf.

printf takes the input and writes it to the screen, whereas printfn writes it to the screen and adds a line continuation:

```
> // printf and printfn
printf "Hello, "
printfn "World";;

Hello, World
```

 The existing .NET System.Console class can be used for writing text to the screen, but printf is better suited for the functional style because its arguments are strongly typed and therefore contribute to type inference. System.Console.Read should still be used for input, however.

Printing text to the console isn't especially exciting, but printf adds a lot of power in that it has formatting and checking built in. By providing a *format specifier*, listed in Table 2-12, you can drop in data as well:

```
> // Format specifiers
let mountain = "K2"
let height   = 8611
let units    = 'm';;

val mountain : string = "K2"
val height : int = 8611
val units : char = 'm'
```

```
> printfn "%s is %d%c high" mountain height units;;
K2 is 28251m high
val it : unit = ()
```

Best of all, by using F#'s type inference system, the compiler will give you an error if the data doesn't match the given format specifier:

```
> printfn "An integer = %d" 1.23;;

  printfn "An integer = %d" 1.23;;
  -------------------------^^^^^

stdin(2,27): error FS0001: The type 'float' is not compatible with any of the
types byte,int16,int32,int64,sbyte,uint16,uint32,uint64,nativeint,unativeint,
arising from the use of a printf-style format string.
stopped due to error
```

In addition, because the F# compiler knows what type to expect given a list of format specifiers, the type inference system can pin down the types of those values. For example, in the following snippet, the types of the function's parameters are inferred based on usage:

```
> // Type inference from printf
let inferParams x y z =
    printfn "x = %f, y = %s, z = %b" x y z;;

val inferParams : float -> string -> bool -> unit
```

Table 2-12. Printf format specifiers

Specifier	Description	Example	Result
%d, %i	Print any integer	printf "%d" 5	5
%x, %o	Print any integer in Hex or Octal format	printfn "%x" 255	ff
%s	Print any string	printf "%s" "ABC"	ABC
%f	Print any floating-point number	printf "%f" 1.1M	1.100000
%c	Print any character	printf "%c" '\097'	a
%b	Print any Boolean	printf "%b" false	false
%O	Prints any object	printfn "%O" (1,2)	(1, 2)
%A	Print anything	printf "%A" (1, [])	(1, [])

 The %O format specifier boxes the object and calls the Object.To
String virtual method. The %A printf format specifier works the same
way, except that it checks for any special printing instructions from a
[<StructuredFormatDisplay>] attribute before calling Object.To
String. The bottom line is that you should almost always prefer %A
over %O.

`sprintf` is used when you want the result of the printing as a string:

```
> let location = "World";;

val location : string = "World"

> sprintf "Hello, %s" location;;
val it : string = "Hello, World"
```

Organizing F# Code

By now you probably want to take the F# code we have been writing in the FSI window and convert it into *actual* programs. But in reality, every code snippet you have seen so far has been a full program (although, admittedly, not the type of programs you imagined).

Don't worry though. You will see a more real-world view of F# in Chapter 11. For now, we need to focus on the organizational building blocks of any F# application: *modules* and *namespaces*.

Modules

All the code we have written so far has been in a module. By default, F# puts all your code into an *anonymous module* with the same name as the code file with the first letter capitalized. So, if you have a value named `value1`, and your code is in *file1.fs*, you can refer to it by using the fully qualified path: `File1.value1`.

Creating modules

You can explicitly name your code's module by using the `module` keyword at the top of a source file. After that point, every value, function, or type defined will belong to that module:

```
module Alpha

// To refer to this value outside the module
// use: Alpha.x
let x = 1
```

Nested modules

Files can contain nested modules as well. To declare a nested module, use the `module` keyword followed by the name of your module and an equals sign (`=`). Nested modules must be indented to be disambiguated from the "top-level" module:

```
module Utilities

module ConversionUtils =

    // Utilities.ConversionUtils.intToString
    let intToString (x : int) = x.ToString()

    module ConvertBase =
        // Utilities.ConversionUtils.ConvertBase.convertToHex
        let convertToHex x = sprintf "%x" x

        // Utilities.ConversionUtils.ConvertBase.convertToOct
        let convertToOct x = sprintf "%o" x

module DataTypes =

    // Utilities.DataTypes.Point
    type Point = Point of float * float * float
```

Namespaces

The alternative to modules is namespaces. Namespaces are a unit of organizing code just like modules except that namespaces cannot contain values, only type declarations. Also, namespaces cannot be nested in the same way as modules. Instead, you can simply add multiple namespaces to the same file.

Example 2-9 defines several types inside of two namespaces.

Example 2-9. Namespaces

```
namespace PlayingCards

// PlayingCards.Suit
type Suit =
  | Spade
  | Club
  | Diamond
  | Heart

// PlayingCards.PlayingCard
type PlayingCard =
  | Ace    of Suit
  | King   of Suit
  | Queen of Suit
  | Jack   of Suit
  | ValueCard of int * Suit

namespace PlayingCards.Poker

// PlayingCards.Poker.PokerPlayer
type PokerPlayer = { Name : string; Money : int; Position : int  }
```

It may seem strange to have both namespaces and modules in F#. Modules are optimized for rapid prototyping and quickly exploring a solution, like you have seen so far. Namespaces, on the other hand, are geared toward larger-scale projects using an object-oriented approach. The subtle difference in when to use a module over a namespace will become clearer as you see more F# source code. When you are starting out, just put everything in a module and don't worry about namespaces.

Program Startup

Namespaces and modules are ways to organize the code found within F# source files. But where does the execution of code actually start?

In F#, the program starts executing at the top of the last code file, which needs to be a module. Consider this simple F# program consisting of a single code file:

```
// Program.fs
let numbers = [1 .. 10]
let square x = x * x

let squaredNumbers = List.map square numbers

printfn "SquaredNumbers = %A" squaredNumbers

open System

printfn "(press any key to continue)"
Console.ReadKey(true)
```

Now open that project in Visual Studio, and then add a new, empty F# code file. When you press F5 to run your program, nothing will happen. This is because the newest file added to the project—which is blank—was added "last" and thus is what ran when the program started up (again, because *Program.fs* comes before *File1.fs* in Solution Explorer).

This feature is convenient for rapid prototyping and saves you a few keystrokes, but in larger projects it is better to explicitly define the entry point.

For more formal program startup semantics, you can use the [<EntryPoint>] attribute to define a main method. To qualify, your main method must satisfy the following requirements:

- Be the last function defined in the last compiled file in your project. This ensures there is no confusion on where the F# program starts.
- Take a single parameter of type string array, which are the arguments to your program. (Arrays are covered in Chapter 4.)
- Return an integer, which is your program's exit code.

To make the main method explicit then, you could rewrite the previous application as:

```
// Program.fs
open System

[<EntryPoint>]
let main (args : string[]) =
    let numbers = [1 .. 10]
    let square x = x * x

    let squaredNumbers = List.map square numbers

    printfn "SquaredNumbers = %A" squaredNumbers

    printfn "(press any key to continue)"
    Console.ReadKey(true) |> ignore

    // Return 0
    0
```

Now you have all the tools you need to write simple F# programs. In the next chapter, you will learn to program using the functional style, enabling you to write more powerful F# applications and advance on your journey toward becoming a level 9 F# ninja master.

Functional Programming

With the basics out of the way, you can begin to examine F# from the approach of a particular style. This chapter is devoted to F#'s main paradigm: functional programming. In a nutshell, functional programming is about being more declarative in your code. In imperative programming (which we cover in Chapter 4), you spend your time listing out the specific steps to perform a task. In functional programming, you specify *what* is to be done, but not *how*. Even though functional programming is no silver bullet, the result is that programs are much clearer, and some problems—like concurrency and parallel programming—are made much easier.

Functional programming isn't going to replace imperative or object-oriented programming on its own; rather, it just provides a different approach to use so that in certain applications you can be much more productive.

For a language to be considered "functional," it typically needs to support a few key features:

- Immutable data
- Ability to compose functions
- Functions can be treated as data
- Lazy evaluation
- Pattern matching

We go into each of these raw, functional concepts and what they offer throughout the chapter. By the end, you will be able to write purely functional code, and leverage the elegance and simplicity of declarative programming. A deeper look at functional concepts, such as tail recursion and closures, comes later in Chapter 7.

Understanding Functions

The heart of functional programming is thinking about code in terms of mathematical functions. Consider two functions f and g:

```
f(x) = x^2 + x
g(x) = x + 1
```

It follows that:

```
f(2) = (2)^2 + (2)
g(2) = (2) + 1
```

And if you compose the two functions, or put them together, you get:

```
f g (2) = f(g(2))
        = (g(2))^2 + (g(2))
        = (2+1)^2 + (2+1)
        = 12
```

You don't have to be a mathematician to program in F#, but many of the foundations of functional programming are rooted in mathematics. For example, in the previous snippets, there was no explicit return type specified. Does f(x) take an integer or a float? This mathematical notation isn't concerned with data types or return values. The equivalent F# code is:

```
let f x = x ** 2.0 + x
let g x = x + 1.0
```

The fact that the F# code resembles the mathematical notation isn't a coincidence. Functional programming in essence is thinking about computations in an abstract way—again, what is to be computed but not how it gets computed.

You can even think of entire programs as functions with their inputs being mouse and keyboard states and the output being the process exit code. When you begin to view programming in this way, some of the complexity associated with normal programming models goes away.

First, if you think about your program as a series of functions, then you don't need to spend all your time in the details explaining the step-by-step of how to complete a task. Functions simply take their input and produce an output. Second, algorithms are expressed in terms of functions and not classes or objects, so it is easier to translate these concepts using functional programming.

You will see examples of how functional programming can simplify complex code throughout the chapter, but first you need to start thinking in terms of functions. To do so, you need to abandon some of the mind-set built up from existing imperative languages. In the next sections, we introduce the notion of immutability, functions as values, and function composition to demonstrate how to begin to program in the functional style.

Immutability

You may have noticed that I have suspiciously not used the word *variable* before, and instead referred to everything as a *value*. The reason for this is that the names of things you declare are *immutable* by default in functional programming, meaning they cannot be changed.

If a function somehow changes the state of the program—such as writing to a file or mutating a global variable in memory—that is known as a *side effect*. For example, calling the printfn function returns unit, but has the side effect of printing text to the screen. Similarly, if a function updates the value of something in memory, that too is a side effect—something extra the function does in addition to returning a value.

Side effects aren't all that bad, but unintended side effects are the root of many bugs. Even the most well-intentioned programmers can make mistakes if they aren't aware of the side effects of a function. Immutable values help you write safer code because you can't screw up what you can't change.

If you are used to an imperative programming language, then not being able to have variables may seem like a burden. But immutability offers some significant benefits.

Consider the two functions in Example 3-1. Both functions simply sum the squares of a list of numbers with one using the imperative style of mutating data and the other using the functional style. The imperative style makes use of a *mutable* variable, meaning that the value of total changes during the execution of imperativeSum.

Example 3-1. Summing a list of squares using imperative and functional styles

```
let square x = x * x

let imperativeSum numbers =
    let mutable total = 0
    for i in numbers do
        let x = square i
        total <- total + x
    total

let functionalSum numbers =
    numbers
    |> Seq.map square
    |> Seq.sum
```

The first thing you might notice is that the second, functional example is shorter. It starts with the list of numbers, squares each one, and then sums them all up. Although the F# syntax may be unfamiliar, the code is more declarative and maps directly to what you want to have happen.

The imperative version, although easier to walk through in your head, requires you to read through the code to understand what is going on.

You might be thinking that even if it is a little more verbose, the imperative example is better than the functional one because it is more familiar. Please resist this urge, at least for now, because there are some subtle advantages to learning to approach problems in the functional style.

For example, if you wanted to run the imperative version in parallel, then you would have to rewrite the code entirely. Because you were so detailed in how you specified the program to be run, you would need to restate how the program should work in parallel. The functional version, however, wasn't prescriptive on how to do things, so you can easily replace the `map` and `sum` functions with implementations that work in parallel. You will see just how easy F# makes parallel programming in Chapter 11.

 Functional programming languages are referred to as *pure* if they do not allow side effects. F# in this regard is considered impure, as it will allow you to change the values of variables when programming in the imperative style.

Function Values

In most other programming languages, functions and data are regarded as two very different things. However, in a functional programming language, functions are treated just like any other piece of data. For example, functions can be passed as parameters to other functions. In addition, functions can create and return new functions! Functions that take or return other functions as their inputs or outputs are known as *higher-order functions*, and are key for idiomatic functional programming.

This capability enables you to abstract and reuse algorithms in your code. You saw an example of this in Chapter 2 with `List.iter`, `List.map`, and `List.fold`.

Example 3-2 defines a function, `negate`, which negates a single integer. When that function is passed as a parameter to `List.map`, the function is then applied to a whole list, negating every element.

Example 3-2. Example of higher-order functions

```
> let negate x = -x;;

val negate : int -> int

> List.map negate [1 .. 10];;
val it : int list = [-1; -2; -3; -4; -5; -6; -7; -8; -9; -10]
```

Using function values is very convenient, but the result is that you end up writing many simple functions that don't have a lot of value on their own. For example, our `negate` function in Example 3-2 will probably never be used anywhere else in the program except when negating a list.

Rather than naming all the little functions you pass as parameters, you can use an *anonymous function*, also known as a *lambda expression*, to create a function inline.

To create a lambda expression, simply use the `fun` keyword followed by the function's parameters and an arrow, `->`.

The following snippet creates a lambda expression and passes the value 5 as a parameter. When the function is executed, the parameter x is incremented by 3 and the result is 8:

```
> (fun x -> x + 3) 5;;
val it : int = 8
```

We can rewrite our negate list example using a lambda that takes a single parameter i:

```
> List.map (fun i -> -i) [1 .. 10];;
val it : int list = [-1; -2; -3; -4; -5; -6; -7; -8; -9; -10]
```

 Be careful to keep lambdas simple. As they grow larger, they become more difficult to debug. This is especially true if you find yourself copying and pasting lambdas around in your code.

Partial function application

Another example of higher-order functions in practice is *partial function application*. Partial function application is the ability to specify some subset of the parameters of a function, and produce a new function where those parameters are fixed. For example, `f(x, y, z)` can be partially applied with x and y to just be `f'(z)`.

Let's look at a practical example that appends text to a file using the .NET libraries:

```
> // Append text to a file
open System.IO

let appendFile (fileName : string) (text : string) =
    use file = new StreamWriter(fileName, true)
    file.WriteLine(text)
    file.Close();;

val appendFile : string -> string -> unit

> appendFile @"D:\Log.txt" "Processing Event X...";;
val it : unit = ()
```

The `appendFile` function seems simple enough, but what if you wanted to repeatedly write to the same log file? You would have to keep around the path to your log file and always pass it in as the first parameter. It would be nice, however, to create a new version of `appendFile` where the first parameter is fixed to our verbatim string `@"D:\Log.txt"`.

You can achieve this by partially applying the first parameter of `appendFile`, which produces a new function that only takes one parameter, the message to be logged:

```
> // Create a new function, with a partially applied call to appendFile.
let appendLogFile = appendFile @"D:\Log.txt";;

val appendLogFile : (string -> unit)

> // Appends text to to 'D:\Log.txt'
appendLogFile "Processing Event Y...";;

val it : unit = ()
```

Partial function application is why function types have arrows between their arguments. The appendFile function had type:

```
string -> string -> unit
```

So after the first string parameter was passed in, the result was a function that took a string and returned unit, or string -> unit.

To understand what is going on behind the scenes, let me introduce *currying*. The ability to transform a function taking *n* arguments into a chain of *n* functions, each taking one argument, is called currying. The F# compiler "curries" functions to enable partial function application.

There is a huge difference between string * string -> int and string -> string -> int. Both are function types that take two string parameters and return an integer. However, one only accepts its argument in tuple form (string * string). This means that all parameters must be specified at the same time. The other function has had its arguments curried (string -> string -> unit), and so applying a single parameter results in a new function value.

Currying and partial function application may not look particularly powerful, but it can dramatically improve the elegance of your code. Consider the printf function that takes a format string as a parameter followed by the values to fill in that format string. If you just supply the first parameter of "%d", the result is a partially applied function that accepts an integer and prints it to the screen.

The following example shows how you can pass a partially applied version of printf to avoid the need for a lambda expression:

```
> // Non partially applied
List.iter (fun i -> printfn "%d" i) [1 .. 3];;
1
2
3
val it : unit = ()
> // Using printfn applying the "%d" parameter, which returns a new
// function with type int -> unit opposed to string -> int -> unit.
List.iter (printfn "%d") [1 .. 3];;
```

```
1
2
3
val it : unit = ()
```

You will see how to take full advantage of partial function application later in this chapter when we get to function composition and the pipe-forward operator.

 Although partially applied functions can make code simpler, they can also make code harder to debug. Be careful not to abuse currying; otherwise you run the risk of making your programs more complex than they need to be.

Functions returning functions

With functional programming treating functions like data, it is possible for functions to return other functions as values. This can cause some interesting situations when you consider the lifetime of local values.

Example 3-3 defines a function generatePowerOfFunc, which returns a function that raises a given number to a power. Two functions are created, powerOfTwo and powerOf Three, which raise two or three to a given power.

Example 3-3. Functions returning functions

```
> // Functions returning functions
let generatePowerOfFunc baseValue =
  (fun exponent -> baseValue ** exponent);;

val generatePowerOfFunc : float -> float -> float

> let powerOfTwo = generatePowerOfFunc 2.0;;

val powerOfTwo : (float -> float)

> powerOfTwo 8.0;;
val it : float = 256.0
> let powerOfThree = generatePowerOfFunc 3.0;;

val powerOfThree : (float -> float)

> powerOfThree 2.0;;
val it : float = 9.0
```

If you look closer at our generatePowerOfFunc function, you'll notice that its parameter baseValue is used in the two lambdas it returned. But when you call values powerOf Two and powerOfThree later, where does baseValue come from if it isn't a parameter to the function? When generatePowerOfFunc was initially called with the value 2.0 as a parameter, you might be wondering where was that 2.0 was stored.

There is a bit of magic going on here known as a *closure*. Don't concern yourself with this concept or how it works for now. Just know that if a value is in scope, it can be used and perhaps returned by a function. In Chapter 7, we cover closures in depth and see the sorts of things you can do by abusing this magic performed by the F# compiler.

Recursive Functions

A function that calls itself is *recursive*, and these can be very useful when programming in the functional style, as you will see shortly.

To define a recursive function, you simply need to add the rec keyword. The following snippet defines a function for calculating the factorial of a number (the factorial of a number is the product of all positive integers up to and including the number; for example, the factorial of 4 is 4 * 3 * 2 * 1):

```
> // Define a recursive function
let rec factorial x =
    if x <= 1 then
        1
    else
        x * factorial (x - 1);;

val factorial : int -> int

> factorial 5;;
val it : int = 120
```

 The rec keyword may stand out as an artifact because other languages don't require you to explicitly call out recursive functions. The actual purpose of the rec keyword is to inform the type inference system to allow the function to be used as part of the type inference process. rec allows you to call the function before the type inference system has determined the function's type.

By using recursion combined with higher-order functions, you can easily simulate the sort of looping constructs found in imperative languages, only without the need for mutating values. The following example creates functional versions of common *for* and *while* loops. Notice that in the example of the *for* loop, an updated counter is simply passed as a parameter to the recursive call:

```
> // Functional for loop
let rec forLoop body times =
    if times <= 0 then
        ()
    else
        body()
        forLoop body (times - 1)
```

```
// Functional while loop
let rec whileLoop predicate body =
    if predicate() then
        body()
        whileLoop predicate body
    else
        ();;

val forLoop : (unit -> unit) -> int -> unit
val whileLoop : (unit -> bool) -> (unit -> unit) -> unit

> forLoop (fun () -> printfn "Looping...") 3;;
Looping...
Looping...
Looping...
val it : unit = ()
> // A typical work week...
open System

whileLoop
    (fun () -> DateTime.Now.DayOfWeek <> DayOfWeek.Saturday)
    (fun () -> printfn "I wish it were the weekend...");;
I wish it were the weekend...
I wish it were the weekend...
I wish it were the weekend...
    * * * This goes on for several days * * *
val it : unit = ()
```

In fact, in most functional programming languages, recursion is the *only* way to set up looping constructs. (Remember, if you can't mutate variables, you can't increment a loop counter.) F# programs that adhere to the strict functional style prefer the use of recursive functions instead of loops. However, you should always keep your code as clear and simple as possible.

Mutual recursion

Two functions that call each other are known as *mutually recursive*, and present a unique challenge to the F# type inference system. In order to determine the type of the first function, you need to know the type of the second function, and vice versa.

In Example 3-4, the mutually recursive functions fail to compile, because when processing the isOdd function, the isEven function has not been declared yet.

Example 3-4. Mutually recursive functions

```
> // Error: Can't define isOdd without isEven and vice versa.
let isOdd x =
    if x = 0 then    false
    elif x = 1 then true
    else isEven(x - 1)
```

```
let isEven x =
    if x = 0 then    true
    elif x = 1 then false
    else isOdd(x - 1);;

    else isEven(x - 1)
--------^^^^^^
```

In order to define mutually recursive functions, you must join them together with the
and keyword, which tells the F# compiler to perform type inference for both functions
at the same time:

```
> // Mutually recursive functions using "rec" and "and".
let rec isOdd x =
    if x = 0 then    false
    elif x = 1 then true
    else isEven(x - 1)
and isEven x =
    if x = 0 then    true
    elif x = 1 then false
    else isOdd(x - 1);;

val isOdd : int -> bool
val isEven : int -> bool

> isOdd 314;;
val it : bool = false
> isEven 314;;
val it : bool = true
```

Symbolic Operators

Think how difficult programming would be if you couldn't write 1 + 2 and instead had
to write add 1 2 every time. Fortunately, F# not only has built-in symbolic operators
for things like addition and subtraction, but also allows you to define your own symbolic
operators. This allows you to write code in a cleaner and more elegant way.

 Don't think of symbolic functions as a form of operator overloading,
but rather as functions whose names are made out of symbols.

A symbolic operator can be made up of any sequence of !%&*+-./<=>@^|? symbols. The
following code defines a new function ! that computes the factorial of a number:

```
> // Factorial
let rec (!) x =
    if x <= 1 then 1
    else x * !(x - 1);;

val ( ! ) : int -> int

> !5;;
val it : int = 120
```

By default, symbolic functions use *infix* notation when they have more than one parameter. This means that the first parameter comes before the symbol, which is how you most commonly apply symbolic functions. The following example defines a function, ===, which compares a string with a regular expression:

```
> // Define (===) to compare strings based on regular expressions
open System.Text.RegularExpressions;;

let (===) str (regex : string) =
    Regex.Match(str, regex).Success;;

val ( === ) : string -> string -> bool

> "The quick brown fox" === "The (.*) fox";;
val it : bool = true
```

In addition to allowing you to name functions that map more closely to mathematics, symbolic operators can be passed around to higher-order functions if you simply put parentheses around the symbol. For example, if you wanted to sum or multiply the elements of a list, you can write:

```
> // Sum a list using the (+) symbolic function
List.fold (+) 0 [1 .. 10];;
val it : int = 55
> // Multiply all elements using the (*) symbolic function
List.fold (*) 1 [1 .. 10];;
val it : int = 3628800
> let minus = (-);;

val minus : (int -> int -> int)

> List.fold minus 10 [3; 3; 3];;
val it : int = 1
```

Function Composition

Once you get a strong grasp on functions, you can begin to look at combining them to form larger, more powerful functions. This is known as *function composition* and is another tenet of functional programming.

Before we go over how to combine functions, let's look at the problem it solves. Here is an example of what not to do: put everything into one massive function. Consider this code for getting the size of a given folder on disk. I've added type annotations to help clarify return values:

```
open System
open System.IO

let sizeOfFolder folder =

    // Get all files under the path
    let filesInFolder : string [] =
        Directory.GetFiles(
            folder, "*.*",
            SearchOption.AllDirectories)

    // Map those files to their corresponding FileInfo object
    let fileInfos : FileInfo [] =
        Array.map
            (fun (file : string) -> new FileInfo(file))
            filesInFolder

    // Map those fileInfo objects to the file's size
    let fileSizes : int64 [] =
        Array.map
            (fun (info : FileInfo) -> info.Length)
            fileInfos

    // Total the file sizes
    let totalSize = Array.sum fileSizes

    // Return the total size of the files
    totalSize
```

There are three main problems with this code:

- The type inference system cannot determine the correct types automatically, so we must provide a type annotation to the parameters in each lambda expression.

  This is because type inference processes code from left-to-right and top-to-bottom, so it sees the lambda passed to Array.map before it sees the type of the array elements passed. (Therefore, the type of the lambda's parameter is unknown.)

- The result of each computation is just fed as a parameter into the next step of the computation, so the function is littered with unnecessary let statements.

- It's kind of ugly. It takes more time to decipher what is going on than it should.

Function composition is about taking code like this and breaking it down into smaller functions, then composing those into a final result.

The previous example kept feeding the computation of one function into the next. Mathematically, if we want the result of f(x) passed into g(x), we write: g(f(x)). We could have avoided all those let bindings by nesting all the intermediate results, but that is extremely unreadable, as you can see here:

```
let uglySizeOfFolder folder =
    Array.sum
        (Array.map
            (fun (info : FileInfo) -> info.Length)
            (Array.map
                (fun file -> new FileInfo(file))
                (Directory.GetFiles(
                    folder, "*.*",
                    SearchOption.AllDirectories))))
```

Pipe-forward operator

Fortunately, F# solves this problem of passing an intermediate result onto the next function concisely with the pipe-forward operator, |>. It is defined as:

```
let (|>) x f = f x
```

The pipe-forward operator allows you to rearrange the parameters of a function so that you present the last parameter of the function first. Whereas the last parameter to List.iter is the list to iterate through, by using the pipe-forward operator you can now "pipe" the list into List.iter so you specify which list to iterate through first:

```
> [1 .. 3] |> List.iter (printfn "%d");;
1
2
3
val it : unit = ()
```

Technically speaking, the pipe-forward operator and its sister function, the pipe-backward operator, are not actually composing functions. Rather, they just deal in function application.

The benefit of the pipe-forward operator is that you can continually reapply it to chain functions together. So, the result of one function is then piped into the next. We can then rewrite our sizeOfFolder function as the following (note that Directory.Get Files takes its parameters as a tuple and therefore cannot be partially applied; all of its parameters must be specified at the same time):

```
let sizeOfFolderPiped folder =

    let getFiles path =
        Directory.GetFiles(path, "*.*", SearchOption.AllDirectories)

    let totalSize =
```

```
    folder
    |> getFiles
    |> Array.map (fun file -> new FileInfo(file))
    |> Array.map (fun info -> info.Length)
    |> Array.sum

  totalSize
```

The simplicity achieved by using the pipe-forward operator is an example of how useful function currying is. The pipe-forward operator takes a value and a function that only takes one parameter; however, the functions that we used, such as Array.map, clearly take two (a function to map and the array itself). The reason this works is that we partially apply the first argument, resulting in a function that takes only one parameter and therefore can easily be used with the pipe-forward operator.

 Although the pipe-forward operator can greatly simplify code by removing unnecessary declarations for immediate results, this makes debugging piped sequences more difficult because you cannot inspect the value of any intermediate results.

An added benefit of the pipe-forward operator is that it can help the type inference process. You cannot access any properties or methods of a value if the compiler doesn't know what its type is. Therefore, you must use a type annotation to specifically pin down types:

```
> // ERROR: Compiler doesn't know s has a Length property
List.iter
    (fun s -> printfn "s has length %d" s.Length)
    ["Pipe"; "Forward"];;

    (fun s -> printfn "s has length %d" s.Length)
  ----------------------------------------^^^^^^^^

stdin(89,41): error FS0072: Lookup on object of indeterminate type based on
information prior to this program point. A type annotation may be needed prior
to this program point to constrain the type of the object. This may allow the
lookup to be resolved
stopped due to error
```

Because the pipe-forward operator allows the compiler to "see" the last parameter of a function earlier, the type inference system can determine the correct types of a function sooner, reducing the need for type annotations.

In the following snippet, because the pipe-forward operator is used, the parameter of the lambda passed to List.iter is known to be of type string, and therefore does not need a type annotation:

```
> // Using the pipe-forward operator to aid type inference.
["Pipe"; "Forward"] |> List.iter (fun s -> printfn "s has length %d" s.Length);;
s has length 4
s has length 7
val it : unit = ()
```

Forward composition operator

The forward composition operator, >>, joins two functions together with the function on the left being called first:

```
let (>>) f g x = g(f x)
```

When using the pipe-forward operator in functions, you need a placeholder variable to "kick off" the pipelining. In our last example, the function took a `folder` parameter that we directly passed into the first piped function:

```
let sizeOfFolderPiped2 folder =

    let getFiles folder =
        Directory.GetFiles(folder, "*.*", SearchOption.AllDirectories)

    folder
    |> getFiles
    |> Array.map (fun file -> new FileInfo(file))
    |> Array.map (fun info -> info.Length)
    |> Array.sum
```

When using the function composition operator, however, no parameter is needed. We simply compose all of those functions together, resulting in a new function that takes a parameter and computes the result:

```
> // Function Composition

open System.IO

let sizeOfFolderComposed (*No Parameters!*) =

    let getFiles folder =
        Directory.GetFiles(folder, "*.*", SearchOption.AllDirectories)

    // The result of this expression is a function that takes
    // one parameter, which will be passed to getFiles and piped
    // through the following functions.
    getFiles
    >> Array.map (fun file -> new FileInfo(file))
    >> Array.map (fun info -> info.Length)
    >> Array.sum;;

val sizeOfFolderComposed : (string -> int64)
```

```
> sizeOfFolderComposed
    (Environment.GetFolderPath(Environment.SpecialFolder.MyPictures));;
val it : int64 = 904680821L
```

Here is another example of function composition. The following snippet calculates the number of digits in the square of an integer:

```
> // Basic Function Composition
let square x = x * x
let toString (x : int) = x.ToString()
let strLen (x : string) = x.Length
let lenOfSquare = square >> toString >> strLen;;

val square : int -> int
val toString : int -> string
val strLen : string -> int
val lenOfSquare : (int -> int)

> square 128;;
val it : int = 16384
> lenOfSquare 128;;
val it : int = 5
```

Pipe-backward operator

At first glance, the pipe-backward operator, <|, accepts a function on the left and applies it to a value on the right. This seems unnecessary because all it does is separate a function and its last parameter, which you can do without the need of some special operator:

```
let (<|) f x = f x
```

Here's an example of the pipe-backward operator in action:

```
> List.iter (printfn "%d") [1 .. 3];;
1
2
3
val it : unit = ()

> List.iter (printfn "%d") <| [1 .. 3];;
1
2
3
val it : unit = ()
```

You might be surprised, but the pipe-backward operator actually does serve an important purpose: it allows you to change precedence. I've avoided mentioning operator precedence so far, but it is the order in which functions are applied. Functions' arguments are evaluated left-to-right, meaning if you want to call a function and pass the result to another function, you have two choices: add parentheses around the expression or use the pipe-backward operator:

```
> printfn "The result of sprintf is %s" (sprintf "(%d, %d)" 1 2);;
The result of sprintf is (1, 2)
val it : unit = ()

> printfn "The result of sprintf is %s" <| sprintf "(%d, %d)" 1 2;;
The result of sprintf is (1, 2)
val it : unit = ()
```

The pipe-backward operator isn't as common as the pipe-forward or function composition operators, but it serves a solid role in cleaning up F# code.

Backward composition operator

Just like the pipe-backward operator, the composable equivalent is the backward composition operator, <<. The backward composition operator takes two functions and applies the right function first and then the left. It is useful when you want to express ideas in reverse order. It is defined as:

```
let (<<) f g x = f(g x)
```

The following code shows how to take the square of the negation of a number. Using the backward composition operator allows the program text to read exactly like how the function operates:

```
> // Backward Composition
let square x = x * x
let negate x = -x;;

val square : int -> int
val negate : int -> int

> // Using (>>) negates the square
(square >> negate) 10;;
val it : int = -100
> (* But what we really want is the square of the negation
so we need to use (<<) *)
(square << negate) 10;;
val it : int = 100
```

Another example of the backward composition operator is to use it to filter out empty lists in a list of lists. Again, the backward composition operator is used to change the way the code reads to the programmer:

```
> // Filtering lists
[ [1]; []; [4;5;6]; [3;4]; []; []; []; [9] ]
|> List.filter(not << List.isEmpty);;

val it : int list list = [[1]; [4; 5; 6]; [3; 4]; [9]]
```

The |>, <|, >>, and << operators serve as a way to clean up F# code. Idiomatic F# uses these operators where appropriate to make code easier to read and more concise. Avoid these operators if adding them would only add clutter or confusion.

Pattern Matching

All programs need to sort and sift through data. To do this using functional programming you use pattern matching. Pattern matching is similar to a *switch* statement from other programming languages, but it is much more powerful. A pattern match is a series of rules that will execute if the pattern matches the input. The pattern match expression then returns the result of the rule that was matched; therefore, all rules in a pattern match must return the same type.

To perform pattern matching, you use the `match` and `with` keywords with a series of pattern rules, each followed by an arrow, `->`. The following snippet shows the use of pattern matching against the expression `isOdd x` to mimic the behavior of an `if` expression. The first rule matches the `true` value, and if that rule matches, it will print `"x is odd"` to the console:

```
> // Simple pattern matching
let isOdd x = (x % 2 = 1)

let describeNumber x =
    match isOdd x with
    | true  -> printfn "x is odd"
    | false -> printfn "x is even";;

val isOdd : int -> bool
val describeNumber : int -> unit

> describeNumber 4;;
x is even
val it : unit = ()
```

The simplest sort of pattern matching is against constant values. Example 3-5 constructs a truth table for the Boolean function And by matching both values of a tuple simultaneously.

Example 3-5. Constructing a truth table using pattern matching

```
> // Truth table for AND via pattern matching
let testAnd x y =
    match x, y with
    | true,  true  -> true
    | true,  false -> false
    | false, true  -> false
    | false, false -> false;;
```

```
val testAnd : bool -> bool -> bool

> testAnd true true;;
val it : bool = true
```

Note that type inference works on pattern matches. In Example 3-5, because the first rule matches x with the Boolean value `true` and y with another Boolean value, both x and y are inferred to be Boolean values.

The underscore, _, is a wildcard that matches anything. So you can simplify the previous example by using a wildcard to capture any input but `true`, `true`:

```
let testAnd x y =
    match x, y with
    | true,  true -> true
    | _, _         -> false
```

Pattern-matching rules are checked in the order they are declared. So if you had wildcard matches first, subsequent rules will never be checked. (Fortunately, the F# compiler issues a warning in this case.)

Match Failure

You might be wondering what would happen if we left out one of the possible truth table matches in the original version of `testAnd`. For example:

```
let testAnd x y =
    match x, y with
    | true,  true -> true
    | true,  false -> false
    // | false, true -> false - Oops! false, true case omitted!
    | false, false -> false
```

If no match is found during a pattern matching, an exception of type `Microsoft` `.FSharp.Core.MatchFailureException` is raised. You can avoid this by making sure that all possible cases are covered. Fortunately, the F# compiler will issue a warning when it can determine that pattern match rules are incomplete:

```
> // Incomplete pattern matching. OOPS! Not every letter matched.
let letterIndex l =
    match l with
    | 'a' -> 1
    | 'b' -> 2;;

      match l with
   ----------^

stdin(48,11): warning FS0025: Incomplete pattern matches on this expression.
For example, the value '' '' may indicate a case not covered by the pattern(s).

val letterIndex : char -> int
```

```
> letterIndex 'k';;
Microsoft.FSharp.Core.MatchFailureException: The match cases were incomplete
   at FSI_0040.letterIndex(Char l)
   at <StartupCode$FSI_0041>.$FSI_0041.main@()
stopped due to error
```

Named Patterns

So far we have just matched constant values, but you can also use named patterns to actually extract data and bind it to a new value. Consider the following example. It matches against a specific string, but for anything else it captures a new value, x:

```
> // Named patterns
let greet name =
    match name with
    | "Robert"  -> printfn "Hello, Bob"
    | "William" -> printfn "Hello, Bill"
    | x -> printfn "Hello, %s" x;;

val greet : string -> unit

> greet "Earl";;
Hello, Earl
val it : unit = ()
```

The last match rule doesn't match a constant value; instead, it binds the value being matched to a new value you can then use in the match rule's body. Value captures, like wildcards, match anything, so make sure to put more specific rules first.

Matching Literals

Naming patterns is great, but this also prevents you from using an existing value as part of a pattern match. In the previous example, hardcoding the names as part of the pattern match will make the code more difficult to maintain and potentially lead to bugs.

If you want to match against a well-known value, but don't want to copy and paste the literal value into every match rule, you could make the mistake of using a named pattern. This, however, does not work as you intend and just shadows the existing value.

In the following example, the first pattern-match rule doesn't compare the value name against the value bill; rather, it just introduces a new value named bill. This is why the second pattern-match rule yields a warning, because the previous rule already catches all pattern-match input:

```
> // ERROR: Unintentional value captures
let bill = "Bill Gates"
let greet name =
    match name with
    | bill -> "Hello Bill!"
```

```
    | x     -> sprintf "Hello, %s" x;;

     | x     -> sprintf "Hello, %s" x;;
    ------^^

stdin(56,7): warning FS0026: This rule will never be matched.

val bill : string = "Bill Gates"
val greet : string -> string
```

In order to match against an existing value, you must add the [<Literal>] attribute. Any literal value (a constant) marked with this attribute and beginning with a capital can be used inside of a pattern match:

```
> // Define a literal value
[<Literal>]
let Bill = "Bill Gates";;

val Bill : string = "Bill Gates"

> // Match against literal values
let greet name =
    match name with
    | Bill -> "Hello Bill!"
    | x     -> sprintf "Hello, %s" x;;

val greet : string -> string

> greet "Bill G.";;
val it : string - "Hello, Bill G."
> greet "Bill Gates";;
val it : string = "Hello Bill!"
```

 Attributes are a way to annotate .NET code with metadata. For more information about attributes and .NET metadata, refer to Chapter 12.

Only integers, characters, Booleans, strings, and floating-point numbers can be marked as literals. If you want to match against more complex types like a dictionary or map, you must use a when guard.

when Guards

While pattern matching is a powerful concept, sometimes you need custom logic to determine whether a rule should match. This is what when guards are for. If a pattern is matched, the optional when guard will execute and the rule will fire if and only if the when expression evaluates to true.

The following example implements a simple game where you guess a random number. when guards are used to check if the guess is higher, lower, or equal to the secret number:

```
> // High / Low game
open System

let highLowGame () =

    let rng = new Random()
    let secretNumber = rng.Next() % 100

    let rec highLowGameStep () =

        printfn "Guess the secret number:"
        let guessStr = Console.ReadLine()
        let guess = Int32.Parse(guessStr)

        match guess with
        | _ when guess > secretNumber
            -> printfn "The secret number is lower."
               highLowGameStep()

        | _ when guess = secretNumber
            -> printfn "You've guessed correctly!"
               ()

        | _ when guess < secretNumber
            -> printfn "The secret number is higher."
               highLowGameStep()

    // Begin the game
    highLowGameStep();;

val highLowGame : unit -> unit

> highLowGame();;
Guess the secret number: 50
The secret number is lower.
Guess the secret number: 25
The secret number is higher.
Guess the secret number: 37
You've guessed correctly!
val it : unit = ()
```

Grouping Patterns

As your pattern matches contain more and more rules, you might want to combine patterns together. There are two ways to combine patterns. The first way is to use Or, represented by a vertical pipe (|), which combines patterns together so the rule will fire if any of the grouped patterns match. The second way is to use And, represented by an ampersand (&), which combines patterns together so that the rule will fire only if all of the grouped patterns match:

```
let vowelTest c =
    match c with
    | 'a' | 'e' | 'i' | 'o' | 'u'
        -> true
    | _ -> false

let describeNumbers x y =
    match x, y with
    | 1, _
    | _, 1
        -> "One of the numbers is one."
    | (2, _) & (_, 2)
        -> "Both of the numbers are two"
    | _ -> "Other."
```

The And pattern has little use in normal pattern matching; however, it is invaluable when using active patterns (Chapter 7).

Matching the Structure of Data

Pattern matching can also match against the structure of data.

Tuples

You have already seen how to match against tuples. If the tuple's elements are separated by commas in the pattern match, each element will be matched individually. However, if a tuple input is used in a named pattern, the bound value will have a tuple type.

In the following example, the first rule binds value tuple, which captures both values x and y. Other rules match against tuple elements individually:

```
let testXor x y =
    match x, y with
    | tuple when fst tuple <> snd tuple
        -> true
    | true,  true  -> false
    | false, false -> false
```

Lists

Example 3-6 demonstrates how you can pattern match against the structure of lists. The function listLength matches against lists of fixed size; otherwise, it recursively calls itself with the tail of the list.

Example 3-6. Determining the length of a list

```
let rec listLength l =
    match l with
    | []        -> 0
    | [_]       -> 1
    | [_; _]    -> 2
    | [_; _; _] -> 3
    | hd :: tail -> 1 + listLength tail
```

The first four pattern-match rules match against lists of specific lengths, using wildcards to indicate that list elements are not important. The last line of the pattern match, however, uses the cons operator (::) to match the first element of the list, hd, and the rest of the list, tail. tail could be any list, from an empty list [] on up to a list with a million elements. (However, because of the first four rules in the pattern match, we can infer that tail is at least three elements long.)

Options

Pattern matching also provides a more functional way to use option types:

```
let describeOption o =
    match o with
    | Some(42) -> "The answer was 42, but what was the question?"
    | Some(x)  -> sprintf "The answer was %d" x
    | None     -> "No answer found."
```

Outside of Match Expressions

Pattern matching is an extremely powerful concept, but its secret is that it doesn't have to be used exclusively in a "match with" expression. Pattern matching occurs throughout the F# language.

let bindings

let bindings are actually pattern-match rules. So if you write:

```
let x = f()
...
```

You can think of it as if you had written:

```
match f() with
| x -> ...
```

This is how we use let bindings to extract values from tuples:

```
// This...
let x, y = (100, 200)

// ... is the same as this...
match (100, 200) with
| x, y -> ...
```

This is why F# suspiciously accepts the code:

```
let 1 = 2
```

Try it in an FSI window, and see what happens.

Function parameters

Parameters to functions are pattern matches in disguise too!

```
// Given a tuple of option values, return their sum
let addOptionValues = fun (Some(x), Some(y)) -> x + y
```

Wildcard patterns

Imagine you wanted to write a function but didn't care about one of the parameters, or perhaps want to ignore values from a tuple. In that case, you could use a wildcard pattern:

```
> List.iter (fun _ -> printfn "Step...") [1 .. 3];;
Step...
Step...
Step...
val it : unit = ()

> let _, second, _ = (1, 2, 3);;

val second : int = 2
```

Alternate Lambda Syntax

The final use for pattern matching is simplified lambda syntax. In writing F# code, you will find that it's common to pass the parameter directly into a pattern-match expression, such as:

```
let rec listLength theList =
    match theList with
    | []          -> 0
    | [_]         -> 1
    | [_; _]      -> 2
    | [_; _; _]   -> 3
    | hd :: tail  -> 1 + listLength tail
```

A simpler way to write this is to use the `function` keyword, which acts much like the `fun` keyword for creating lambdas, except that `function` lambdas only accept one parameter that must be placed within a pattern match. The following example rewrites the `listLength` function using the `function` keyword:

```
> // The 'function' keyword
let rec funListLength =
    function
    | []          -> 0
    | [_]         -> 1
```

```
    | [_; _]      -> 2
    | [_; _; _] -> 3
    | hd :: tail -> 1 + funListLength tail;;

val funListLength : 'a list -> int

> funListLength [1 .. 5];;
val it : int = 5
```

Discriminated Unions

A foundational type in functional programming is the *discriminated union*, which is a type that can only be one of a set of possible values. Each possible value of a discriminated union is referred to as a *union case*. With the invariant that discriminated unions can only be one of a set of values, the compiler can do additional checks to make sure your code is correct. In particular, the F# compiler ensures that pattern matches cover all discriminated union cases.

 You've already been taking advantage of discriminated union types. The option type is a discriminated union with two union cases: Some('a) and None.

To define a discriminated union, use the type keyword, followed by the type's name, and then each union case separated by a pipe, |. In a standard deck of cards, a card's suit can be represented with the following discriminated union:

```
> // Discriminated union for a card's suit
type Suit =
    | Heart
    | Diamond
    | Spade
    | Club;;

type Suit =
   | Heart
   | Diamond
   | Spade
   | Club

> let suits = [ Heart; Diamond; Spade; Club ];;

val suits : Suit list = [Heart; Diamond; Spade; Club]
```

You can also optionally associate data with each union case. To continue the playing card example, each card can be associated with a suit, and value cards with an integer and suit pair (the int * Suit syntax may look familiar—it is the type signature of a tuple):

```
// Discriminated union for playing cards
type PlayingCard =
    | Ace     of Suit
    | King  of Suit
    | Queen of Suit
    | Jack  of Suit
    | ValueCard of int * Suit

// Use a list comprehension to generate a deck of cards.
let deckOfCards =
    [
        for suit in [ Spade; Club; Heart; Diamond ] do
            yield Ace(suit)
            yield King(suit)
            yield Queen(suit)
            yield Jack(suit)
            for value in 2 .. 10 do
                yield ValueCard(value, suit)
    ]
```

It is also possible to declare discriminated unions on the same line, with the first pipe (|) optional:

```
type Number = Odd | Even
```

Discriminated unions can also be recursive. If you need to define a set of mutually recursive discriminated unions, just like functions, they need to be linked together with the and keyword.

The following defines a simple format for describing a programming language:

```
// Program statements
type Statement =
    | Print     of string
    | Sequence of Statement * Statement
    | IfStmt    of Expression * Statement * Statement

// Program expressions
and Expression =
    | Integer      of int
    | LessThan     of Expression * Expression
    | GreaterThan of Expression * Expression

(*
    if (3 > 1)
        print "3 is greater than 1"
    else
        print "3 is not"
        print "greater than 1"
*)
let program =
    IfStmt(
        GreaterThan(
```

```
            Integer(3),
            Integer(1)),
    Print("3 is greater than 1"),
    Sequence(
        Print("3 is not"),
        Print("greater than 1")
    )
)
```

Using Discriminated Unions for Tree Structures

Discriminated unions are ideal for representing tree-like data structures, like in the previous code snippet.

Example 3-7 defines a binary tree and a function for traversing it in only 11 lines of code.

Example 3-7. Binary tree using discriminated unions

```
type BinaryTree =
    | Node of int * BinaryTree * BinaryTree
    | Empty

let rec printInOrder tree =
    match tree with
    | Node (data, left, right)
        -> printInOrder left
           printfn "Node %d" data
           printInOrder right
    | Empty
        -> ()

(*
        2
       / \
      1   4
         / \
        3   5
*)
let binTree =
    Node(2,
        Node(1, Empty, Empty),
        Node(4,
            Node(3, Empty, Empty),
            Node(5, Empty, Empty)
        )
    )
```

When evaluated within an FSI session, the previous example prints the following:

```
> printInOrder binTree;;
Node 1
```

```
Node 2
Node 3
Node 4
Node 5
val it : unit = ()
```

Pattern Matching

You can pattern match against discriminated unions by using just the case labels as patterns. If the union label has data associated with it, then you can match its value against a constant, a wildcard, or capture the value just like a normal pattern match.

The following example demonstrates the power of pattern matching and discriminated unions by describing two "hole cards" in a game of poker:

```
// Describe a pair of cards in a game of poker
let describeHoleCards cards =
    match cards with
    | []
    | [_]
        -> failwith "Too few cards."
    | cards when List.length cards > 2
        -> failwith "Too many cards."

    | [ Ace(_);  Ace(_)  ] -> "Pocket Rockets"
    | [ King(_); King(_) ] -> "Cowboys"

    | [ ValueCard(2, _); ValueCard(2, _)]
        -> "Ducks"

    | [ Queen(_); Queen(_) ]
    | [ Jack(_);  Jack(_)  ]
        -> "Pair of face cards"

    | [ ValueCard(x, _); ValueCard(y, _) ] when x = y
        -> "A Pair"

    | [ first; second ]
        -> sprintf "Two cards: %A and %A" first second
```

You can also have recursive discriminated unions in pattern matches. Notice in the following example, the third rule uses a nested pattern to match only Manager values that have exactly two Worker employees:

```
type Employee =
    | Manager of string * Employee list
    | Worker  of string

let rec printOrganization worker =
    match worker with
    | Worker(name) -> printfn "Employee %s" name
```

```
// Manager with a worker list with one element
| Manager(managerName, [ Worker(employeeName) ] )
    -> printfn "Manager %s with Worker %s" managerName employeeName

// Manager with a worker list of two elements
| Manager(managerName, [ Worker(employee1); Worker(employee2) ] )
    -> printfn
            "Manager %s with two workers %s and %s"
            managerName employee1 employee2

// Manager with a list of workers
| Manager(managerName, workers)
    -> printfn "Manager %s with workers..." managerName
        workers |> List.iter printOrganization
```

The previous example would result in the following FSI session:

```
> let company = Manager("Tom", [ Worker("Pam"); Worker("Stuart") ] );;

val company : Employee = Manager ("Tom",[Worker "Pam"; Worker "Stuart"])

> printOrganization company;;
Manager Tom with two workers Pam and Stuart
val it : unit = ()
```

Because the compiler knows every possible data tag associated with a discriminated union at compile time, any incomplete pattern match will issue a warning. For example, if the Ace union case were left out of the pattern match, then F# compiler would know:

```
> // OOPS! Forgot about the Ace union case...
let getCardValue card =
    match card with
    | King(_) | Queen(_) | Jack(_) -> 10
    | ValueCard(x, _)              -> x;;

    match card with
    ----------^^^^

stdin(53,11): warning FS0025: Incomplete pattern matches on this expression.
For example, the value 'Ace (_)' may indicate a case not covered by the
pattern(s).

val getCardValue : PlayingCard -> int
```

 Be careful when using a wildcard to match against a discriminated union. If the union is ever extended later, you will get a warning for each instance where the pattern match is not exhaustive. However, no warning will be issued if you use a wildcard because it will consume all additional cases. Being warned where your code could cause a match failure at runtime goes a long way toward preventing defects.

Methods and Properties

You can add more power to discriminated unions by adding methods and properties. In the following snippet, a property `Value` is added so given any `PlayingCard` object, you can get its value (for more information on adding methods and properties, refer to Chapter 5):

```
type PlayingCard =
    | Ace   of Suit
    | King  of Suit
    | Queen of Suit
    | Jack  of Suit
    | ValueCard of int * Suit

    member this.Value =
        match this with
        | Ace(_) -> 11
        | King(_) | Queen (_)| Jack(_)  -> 10
        | ValueCard(x, _) when x <= 10 && x >= 2
                        -> x
        | ValueCard(_) -> failwith "Card has an invalid value!"

let highCard = Ace(Spade)
let highCardValue = highCard.Value
```

Records

Discriminated unions are great for defining a hierarchy of data, but when trying to get values out of a discriminated union, they have the same problem as tuples. Namely, that there is no meaning associated with each value—rather, data is lumped together in some fixed ordering. For example, consider a single-case discriminated union for describing a person. Are its two string fields referring to the first and then last name, or the last and then first name?

```
type Person =
    | Person of string * string * int

let steve = Person("Steve", "Holt", 17)
let gob = Person("Bluth", "George Oscar", 36)
```

When you want to group your data into a structured format without needing hefty syntax, you can use F# *record* types. Records give you a way to organize values into a type, as well as name those values through *fields*.

To define a record, you simply define a series of name/type pairs enclosed in curly braces. To create an instance of a record, simply provide a value for each record field and type inference will figure out the rest. See Example 3-8.

Example 3-8. Constructing and using records

```
> // Define a record type
type PersonRec = { First : string; Last : string; Age : int};;

type PersonRec =
  {First: string;
   Last: string;
   Age: int;}

> // Construct a record
let steve = { First = "Steve"; Last = "Holt"; Age = 17 };;

val steve : PersonRec = {First = "Steve";
                         Last = "Holt";
                         Age = 17;}

> // Use '.field' to access record fields
printfn "%s is %d years old" steve.First steve.Age;;
Steve is 17 years old
val it : unit = ()
```

 To the seasoned .NET developer, it may look like records are just a simplified version of standard .NET classes. You can easily create properties and methods in F#, so why use a record? Records offer several distinct advantages over traditional object-oriented data structures.

- Type inference can infer a record's type. No need for superfluous type annotations.

- Record fields are immutable by default, whereas class types offer no safety guarantee.

- Records cannot be subclassed, giving a future guarantee of safety.

- Records can be used as part of standard pattern matching; classes cannot without resorting to active patterns or when guards.

- Records (and discriminated unions) get structural comparison and equality semantics for free. Equality and comparison in .NET are covered in Chapter 6.

Cloning Records

Records can easily be cloned using the with keyword:

```
type Car =
    {
        Make  : string
        Model : string
        Year  : int
```

```
        }
    let thisYear's = { Make = "FSharp"; Model = "Luxury Sedan"; Year = 2012 }
    let nextYear's = { thisYear's with Year = 2013 }
```

This is equivalent to writing:

```
    let nextYear's =
        {
            Make  = thisYear's.Make
            Model = thisYear's.Model
            Year  = 2013
        }
```

Pattern Matching

You can pattern match on records, providing value capture and literal matching. Note that not every record field needs to be a part of the pattern match. In the following example, a list of Car is filtered to just those where the Model field is equal to "Coup". Fields Make and Year are not considered:

```
    let allCoups =
        allNewCars
        |> List.filter
            (function
                | { Model = "Coup" } -> true
                | _                  -> false)
```

Type Inference

One distinct advantage of records is how they work with F#'s type inference system. Whereas .NET class types must be annotated in order to be used, record types can be inferred by the fields you access.

In Example 3-9, no type annotation is provided for values pt1 and pt2. Because fields X and Y were accessed and the compiler knows of a record type with an X and Y field, the type of pt1 and pt2 was inferred to be of type Point.

Example 3-9. Type inference for records

```
> type Point = { X : float; Y : float };;

type Point =
  {X: float;
   Y: float;}

> // Distance between two points. (No type annotations required!)
let distance pt1 pt2 =
    let square x = x * x
    sqrt <| square (pt1.X - pt2.X) + square (pt1.Y - pt2.Y);;
```

```
val distance : Point -> Point -> float

> distance {X = 0.0; Y = 0.0} {X = 10.0; Y = 10.0};;
val it : float = 14.14213562
```

When using two records that have identical field names, the type inference system will either issue an error or infer types that were different than what you intended. To combat this, you can either provide type annotations or fully qualify the record fields:

```
type Point   = { X: float; Y: float;}
type Vector3 = { X : float; Y : float; Z : float }

// Provide a type annotation to not infer pt1 and pt2 to be Vector3
// (since Vector3 was defined last with fields X and Y)
let distance (pt1 : Point) (pt2 : Point) =
    let square x = x * x
    sqrt <| square (pt1.X - pt2.X) + square (pt1.Y - pt2.Y)

// Disambiguate a Point from the Vector type by
// fully qualifying record fields.
let origin  = { Point.X = 0.0; Point.Y = 0.0 }
```

This provides all the necessary information for the type inference system to figure out what you mean.

Methods and Properties

Just like discriminated unions, you can add methods and properties to records as well:

```
> // Add a property to a record type Vector =
type Vector =
    { X : float; Y : float; Z : float }
    member this.Length =
        sqrt <| this.X ** 2.0 + this.Y ** 2.0 + this.Z ** 2.0;;

type Vector =
  {X: float;
   Y: float;
   Z: float;}
  with
    member Length : float
  end

> let v = { X = 10.0; Y = 20.0; Z = 30.0 };;

val v : Vector = {X = 10.0;
                  Y = 20.0;
                  Z = 30.0;}

> v.Length;;
val it : float = 37.41657387
```

Lazy Evaluation

The code we have written so far has been evaluated *eagerly*, meaning it was executed as soon as we sent it to FSI. The same is true if you compiled and ran your F# program. However, there are situations when you only want to evaluate code on demand—for example, you want to perform computationally expensive operations only if necessary. This is known as *lazy evaluation*.

Using lazy evaluation can lead to a dramatic reduction in memory footprint because you are only creating values in memory as you need them.

F# supports lazy evaluation in two ways—through the Lazy type and sequences (the seq<'a> type).

Lazy Types

A Lazy type is a thunk or placeholder for some computation. Once created, you can pass around the lazy value as if it has been evaluated. But it will only be evaluated once, and only when forced.

Example 3-10 creates two values, x and y, both of which have the side effect of printing to the console. Because they are initialized lazily, they are not evaluated when declared. Only when the value of y is desired is y's evaluation forced, which in turn forces the evaluation of x.

To construct a lazy value, you can use the lazy keyword or Lazy<_>.Create.

Example 3-10. Using lazy evaluation

```
> // Define two lazy values
let x = Lazy<int>.Create(fun () -> printfn "Evaluating x..."; 10)
let y = lazy (printfn "Evaluating y..."; x.Value + x.Value);;

val x : System.Lazy<int> = Value is not created.
val y : Lazy<int> = Value is not created.

> // Directly requesting y's value will force its evaluation
y.Value;;
Evaluating y...
Evaluating x...
val it : int = 20

> // Accessing y's value again will use a cached value (no side effects)
y.Value;;
val it : int = 20
```

Sequences

The most common use of lazy evaluation is through the sequence or **seq** type in F#, which represents an ordered sequence of items, much like a `List`. The following snippet defines a sequence of five elements and iterates through them using the `Seq.iter` function (just like the `List` module, there are a whole slew of available functions to operate on sequences):

```
> let seqOfNumbers = seq { 1 .. 5 };;

val seqOfNumbers : seq<int>

> seqOfNumbers |> Seq.iter (printfn "%d");;
1
2
3
4
5
val it : unit = ()
```

 seq is just an alias for the .NET interface `System.Collections.Gener ic.IEnumerable<'a>`.

So why have two types when you can just use a `list`? The answer has to do with the impact that the `seq<_>` and `list` types have on memory.

The contents of lists are stored entirely in memory, whereas sequence elements are generated dynamically in a so-called "pull" fashion. You can define an infinite sequence quite easily, but an infinite list would run out of memory. Also, with lists, you must know the value of each element ahead of time, whereas sequence elements may take program events into account.

Example 3-11 defines a sequence of all positive 32-bit integers represented as strings. It then tries to create an equivalent list, but fails due to memory.

Example 3-11. A sequence of all integers

```
> // Sequence of all positive integers
let allPositiveIntsSeq =
    seq { for i in 1 .. System.Int32.MaxValue do
                yield i };;

val allPositivesIntsSeq : seq<int>

> allPositiveIntsSeq;;
val it : seq<int> = seq [1; 2; 3; 4; ...]
```

```
> // List of all positive integers - ERROR: Can't fit in memory!
let allPositiveIntsList = [ for i in 1 .. System.Int32.MaxValue -> i ];;
System.OutOfMemoryException: Exception of type 'System.OutOfMemoryException'
was thrown.
```

Sequence Expressions

We can use the same list comprehension syntax to define sequences (technically referred to as *sequence expressions*). You begin a sequence by writing seq followed by curly braces:

```
> let alphabet = seq { for c in 'A' .. 'Z' -> c };;

val alphabet : seq<char>

> Seq.take 4 alphabet;;
val it : seq<char> = seq ['A'; 'B'; 'C'; 'D']
```

Sequences are evaluated lazily, so every time an element is yielded, the code executing inside the sequence is still running. Let's try the previous example again, but this time adding a side effect every time an element is returned. Instead of returning a letter of the alphabet, it will print that letter to the console as well:

```
> // Sequence with a side effect
let noisyAlphabet =
    seq {
        for c in 'A' .. 'Z' do
            printfn "Yielding %c..." c
            yield c
    };;

val noisyAlphabet : seq<char>

> let fifthLetter = Seq.nth 4 noisyAlphabet;;
Yielding A...
Yielding B...
Yielding C...
Yielding D...
Yielding E...

val fifthLetter : char = 'E'
```

An interesting aspect of sequence expressions is that they can be recursive. By using the yield! (pronounced "yield bang") keyword, you can return a subsequence, the result of which is merged into the main sequence in order.

Example 3-12 shows how to leverage yield! within a sequence expression. The function allFilesUnder returns a seq<string>, which recursively gets all files under a given folder. Directory.GetFiles returns an array of strings containing all the files in the basePath folder. Because array is compatible with seq, the yield! returns all of those files.

Example 3-12. Sequence for listing all files under a folder

```
open System.IO

let rec allFilesUnder basePath =
    seq {
        // Yield all files in the base folder
        yield! Directory.GetFiles(basePath)

        // Yield all files in its sub folders
        for subdir in Directory.GetDirectories(basePath) do
            yield! allFilesUnder subdir
    }
```

Seq Module Functions

The Seq module contains many helpful functions for using sequence types.

Seq.take

Returns the first *n* items from a sequence:

```
> // Sequence of random numbers
open System
let randomSequence =
    seq {
        let rng = new Random()
        while true do
            yield rng.Next()
    };;

val randomSequence : seq<int>

> randomSequence |> Seq.take 3;;
val it : seq<int> = seq [2101281294; 1297716638; 1114462900]
```

Seq.unfold

Seq.unfold generates a sequence using the provided function. It has type ('a -> ('b * 'a) option) -> 'a -> seq<'b>.

The supplied function takes an input value, and its result is an option type with a tuple of the next value in the sequence combined with the input to the next iteration of Seq.unfold. The function returns None to indicate the end of the sequence. Example 3-13 generates all Fibonacci numbers under 100 (the nth Fibonacci number is the sum of the two previous items in the sequence; or 1, 1, 2, 3, 5, 8, etc.). The example also uses the Seq.toList function, which converts a sequence to a list.

Example 3-13. Using Seq.unfold

```
> // Generate the next element of the Fibonacci sequence given the previous
// two elements. To be used with Seq.unfold.
let nextFibUnder100 (a, b) =
    if a + b > 100 then
        None
    else
        let nextValue = a + b
        Some(nextValue, (nextValue, a));;

val nextFibUnder100 : int * int -> (int * (int * int)) option

> let fibsUnder100 = Seq.unfold nextFibUnder100 (0, 1);;

val fibsUnder100 : seq<int>

> Seq.toList fibsUnder100;;
val it : int list = [1; 1; 2; 3; 5; 8; 13; 21; 34; 55; 89]
```

Other useful Seq module functions can be found in Table 3-1.

Table 3-1. Common Seq module functions

Function and Type	Description
Seq.length seq<'a> -> int	Returns the length of the sequence.
Seq.exists ('a -> bool) -> seq<'a> -> bool	Returns whether or not an element in the sequence satisfies the search function.
Seq.tryFind ('a -> bool) -> seq<'a> -> 'a option	Returns Some(x) for the first element x in which the given function returns true. Otherwise returns None.
Seq.filter ('a -> bool) -> seq<'a> -> seq<'a>	Filters out all sequence elements for which the provided function does not evaluate to true.
Seq.concat (seq< #seq<'a> > -> seq<'a>	Flattens a series of sequences so that all of their elements are returned in a single seq.

Aggregate Operators

The Seq module also contains the same aggregate operators available in the List module.

Seq.iter

Iterates through each item in the sequence:

```
> // Print odd numbers under 10
let oddsUnderN n = seq { for i in 1 .. 2 .. n -> i }
Seq.iter (printfn "%d") (oddsUnderN 10);;
1
3
5
7
9

val oddsUnderN : int -> seq<int>
```

Seq.map

Produces a new sequence by mapping a function onto an existing sequence. The map operation is not performed, however, until the values are requested from the output sequence. The mapping is done only on demand:

```
> // Sequence of words (Arrays are compatible with sequences)
let words = "The quick brown fox jumped over the lazy dog".Split( [| ' ' |]);;

val words : string [] =
  [|"The"; "quick"; "brown"; "fox"; "jumped"; "over"; "the"; "lazy"; "dog"|]

> // Map strings to string, length tuples
words |> Seq.map (fun word -> word, word.Length);;
val it : seq<string * int> =
  seq [("The", 3); ("quick", 5); ("brown", 5); ("fox", 3); ...]
```

Seq.fold

Reduces the sequence to a single value. Because there is only one way to iterate through sequences, there is no equivalent to `List.foldBack`:

```
> Seq.fold (+) 0 <| seq { 1 .. 100 };;
val it : int = 5050
```

Queries

Sequences combined with the pipe-forward operator provide all the power you need for transforming data, and will make up the backbone of your F# applications. However, there are times when querying sequences of data can become cumbersome, even in terse F# code.

Consider the following snippet, which shows a pipeline over a sequence of customers:

```
// Return the zip codes of all known customers in a given state.
let customerZipCodesByState stateName =
    allCustomers
    |> Seq.filter (fun customer -> customer.State = stateName)
    |> Seq.map (fun customer -> customer.ZipCode)
    |> Seq.distinct
```

The previous example is declarative and functional; it also shows off the expressiveness of sequences when used with pipelines. But compare it to the following:

```
let customerZipCodesByState2 stateName =
    query {
        for customer in allCustomers do
        where (customer.State = stateName)
        select customer.ZipCode
        distinct
    }
```

Although the first version is slightly shorter, the second is undeniably clearer. The reason is that rather than using generic data transformation operators like `Seq.filter` and `Seq.map`, the second example uses a (potentially) more familiar SQL-like syntax.

The second example is using a feature of the F# language called *query expressions*.

Querying data is a common part of any program—be it gathering specific nodes from an XML document, gathering results from a SQL database, or even something as simple as filtering a sequence of customers.

F# query expressions provide a way to describe the nature of a "query" in a declarative manner, rather than relying on the step-by-step details of a sequence pipeline. Doing so not only can make code cleaner, this abstraction also enables new capabilities such as automatically converting program code into a SQL query (as opposed to querying all data rows from the database and then sorting through it on the client).

The scope of F# query expressions and its underlying technologies could easily fit within another book, so for now we just focus on queries over in-memory sequences. Later, in Chapter 15, we look at feeding more sophisticated data sources into F#'s query expression machinery.

Advanced readers will notice that F#'s query expressions are just wrappers on top of the .NET `IQueryable<T>` interface, the same thing that powers C# and VB.NET's LINQ feature. As such, the same powers and limitations apply.

For a more in-depth look at the implementation details of query expressions, refer to Chapter 13.

Query Expressions

Query expressions can be thought of as syntactic sugar on top of sequence expressions. In exchange for slightly less expressiveness, they offer more power. In general, you should prefer query expressions over sequence expressions if you are returning raw data (and don't need to rely on map operations to transform the data source).

To create a query expression, use the same format as a sequence expression, except use query instead of seq. Within the body of a query expression, new operators are available to you, such as where, join, groupJoin, and so on:

```
> open System.Diagnostics

let activeProcCount =
    query {
        for activeProc in Process.GetProcesses() do
        count }


let memoryHog =
    query {
        for activeProcess in Process.GetProcesses() do
        sortByDescending activeProcess.WorkingSet64
        head
    };;
val activeProcCount : int = 66
val memoryHog : System.Diagnostics.Process =
  System.Diagnostics.Process (devenv)

> printfn
    "'%s' has a working set of:\n%d bytes"
    memoryHog.MainWindowTitle memoryHog.WorkingSet64;;
'QueryExpressions.fsx - Microsoft Visual Studio' has a working set of:
254578688 bytes
val it : unit = ()
```

Query Operators

The types of operators allowed inside of query expressions are quite similar to the existing methods we have already seen in the Seq module. For example, ending a query expression with count will return the number of selected items, similar to the Seq.length method.

Selection operators

Selection from a query expression is different than element selection in a sequence expression though. You don't control each individual item returned (like you did with the yield keyword). Instead, query expressions can only have one return point, and the type of the query result depends on the operator used.

The most common is simply `select`, which is an analog to `Seq.map`, returning each element of the query except those filtered, skipped, and otherwise ignored:

```
> // Returns all processes displaying a UI.
let windowedProcesses =
    query {
        for activeProcess in Process.GetProcesses() do
        where (activeProcess.MainWindowHandle <> nativeint 0)
        select activeProcess }

let printProcessList procSeq =
    Seq.iter (printfn "%A") procSeq;;

val windowedProcesses : seq<Process>
val printProcessList : seq<'a> -> unit

> printProcessList windowedProcesses;;
System.Diagnostics.Process (chrome)
System.Diagnostics.Process (devenv)
System.Diagnostics.Process (explorer)
System.Diagnostics.Process (WINWORD)
System.Diagnostics.Process (notepad)
val it : unit = ()
```

But many times you don't want a sequence of values, but rather you just want to know something *about* that sequence of values. Fortunately, the result of a query expression can be specialized.

The `contains` operator allows you to check if the resulting query contains at least one element satisfying a predicate (e.g., `Seq.exists`):

```
> let isChromeRunning =
    query {
        for windowedProc in windowedProcesses do
        select windowedProc.ProcessName
        contains "chrome" };;

val isChromeRunning : bool = true
```

The count operator returns the number of items returned (e.g., `Seq.length`):

```
> let numOfServiceProcesses =
    query {
        for activeProcess in Process.GetProcesses() do
        where (activeProcess.MainWindowHandle = nativeint 0)
        select activeProcess
        count };;

val numOfServiceProcesses : int = 59
```

The `distinct` operator dedupes returned elements based on their hash code (e.g., `Seq.distinct`):

```
> // Using the distinct operator
let oneHundredNumbersUnderFifty =
    let rng = new System.Random()
    seq {
        for i = 1 to 100 do
            yield rng.Next() % 50 }

let distinctNumbers =
    query {
        for randomNumber in oneHundredNumbersUnderFifty do
        select randomNumber
        distinct };;

val oneHundredNumbersUnderFifty : seq<int>
val distinctNumbers : seq<int>

> oneHundredNumbersUnderFifty;;
val it : seq<int> = seq [36; 7; 25; 9; ...]
> printfn "%d distinct numbers found." <| Seq.length distinctNumbers;;
43 distinct numbers found.
val it : unit = ()
```

Beyond contains, count, and distinct, there are other selection operations you can
use in place of select. Consider the following example, which selects a value based on
the maxBy operator, which returns the highest value given a selection projection:

```
> // The number of threads used by the process with the most threads.
let highestThreadCount =
    query {
        for proc in Process.GetProcesses() do
        maxBy proc.Threads.Count };;

val highestThreadCount : int = 134
```

Table 3-2 lists common selection operators.

Table 3-2. Common selection operators over a Seq<'a>

Operator	Result Type	Description
Head	'a	Returns the first element.
Last	'a	Returns the last element.
exactlyOne	'a	Returns the first element. If the resulting elements are zero or more than one, an exception is thrown.
exists	bool	Returns whether or not an element exists in the queried elements which satisfy a predicate.
find	'a	Returns the first queried element that satisfies a predicate. If no element is found, an exception is thrown.
all	bool	Returns whether or not all queried elements satisfy a predicate.

Sorting operators

Sorting is a common operation and can be part of the query expression by using the sortBy and sortByDescending operators. In fact, you can further refine the sort order by using the thenBy and thenByDescending operators.

In the example, notice the let binding introduces a new value. Introducing local values can be useful for identifying custom sorting criteria:

```
// Active processes sorted by whether or not they have a UI, then by name.
let sortedProcs =
    query {
        for proc in Process.GetProcesses() do
        let isWindowed = proc.MainWindowHandle <> nativeint 0
        sortBy isWindowed
        thenBy proc.ProcessName
        select proc }
```

 There are many more query operators not covered here—groupJoin, leftOuterJoin, takeWhile, and thenByNullableDescending to name a few. See the MSDN documentation online for a complete set.

You now know the main aspects of writing functional code (although it is perfectly OK if the advantages of function composition and lazy evaluation aren't immediately obvious). The majority of the examples in this book are written in the functional style, and over time you will begin to see how to formulate solutions in the functional style.

Finishing this chapter was your first step into exploring a new world. Welcome.

Imperative Programming

Until now, most of the programs we've written have been *pure*, meaning that they never changed state. Whenever a function does something other than just return a value, it is known as a *side effect*. Although pure functions have some interesting features (e.g., composability), the fact of the matter is that programs aren't interesting unless they do something: save data to disk, print values to the screen, issue network traffic, and so on. These side effects are where things actually get done.

This chapter covers how to change program state and alter control flow, which is known as *imperative programming*. This style of programming is considered to be more error prone than functional programming because it opens up the opportunity for getting things wrong. The more detailed the instructions given to the computer to branch, or write certain values into memory, the more likely the programmer will make a mistake. When you programmed in the functional style, all of your data was immutable, so you couldn't assign a wrong value by accident. However, if used judiciously, imperative programming can be a great boon for F# development.

Some potential benefits for imperative programming are:

- Improved performance
- Ease of maintenance through code clarity
- Interoperability with existing code

Imperative programming is a style in which the program performs tasks by altering data in memory. This typically leads to patterns where programs are written as a series of statements or commands. Example 4-1 shows a hypothetical program for using a killer robot to take over the Earth. The functions don't return values, but do impact some part of the system, such as updating an internal data structure.

Example 4-1. Taking over the Earth with imperative programming

```
let robot = new GiantKillerRobot()

robot.Initialize()

robot.EyeLaserIntensity <- Intensity.Kill
robot.Target <- [| Animals; Humans; Superheroes |]

// Sequence for taking over the Earth
let earth = Planets.Earth
while robot.Active && earth.ContainsLife do
    if robot.CurrentTarget.IsAlive then
        robot.FireEyeLaserAt(robot.CurrentTarget)
    else
        robot.AquireNextTarget()
```

Although the code snippet makes taking over the Earth look fairly easy, you don't see all the hard work going on behind the scenes. The Initialize function may require powering up a nuclear reactor; and if Initialize is called twice in a row, the reactor might explode. If Initialize were written in a purely function style, its output would only depend on the function's input. Instead, what happens during the function call to Initialize depends on the current state of memory.

Although this chapter won't teach you how to program planet-conquering robots, it does detail how to write F# programs that can change the environment they run in. You will learn how to declare *variables*, the values of which you can change during the course of your program. You'll learn how to use mutable collection types, which offer an easier to use alternative to F#'s list type. Finally, you will learn about control flow and exceptions, allowing you to alter the order in which code executes.

Understanding Memory in .NET

Before you can start making changes to memory, you first need to understand how memory works in .NET. Values in .NET applications are stored in one of two locations: on the *stack* or in the *heap*. (Experienced programmers may already be familiar with these concepts.) The stack is a fixed amount of memory for each process where *local variables* are stored. Local variables are temporary values used only for the duration of the function, like a loop counter. The stack is relatively limited in space, whereas the heap (also called RAM) may contain several gigabytes of data. .NET uses both the stack and the heap to take advantage of the cheap memory allocations on the stack when possible, and storing data on the heap when more memory is required.

The area in memory where a value is stored affects how you can use it.

Value Types Versus Reference Types

Values stored on the stack are known as *value types*, and values stored on the heap are known as *reference types*.

Values types have a fixed size of bytes on the stack. int and float are both examples of value types, because their size is constant. Reference types, on the other hand, only store a *pointer* on the stack, which is the address of some blob of memory on the heap. So while the pointer has a fixed size—typically four or eight bytes—the blob of memory it points to can be much, much larger. list and string are both examples of reference types.

This is visualized in Figure 4-1. The integer 5 exists on the stack, and has no counterpart on the heap. A string, however, exists on the stack as a memory address, pointing to some sequence of characters on the heap.

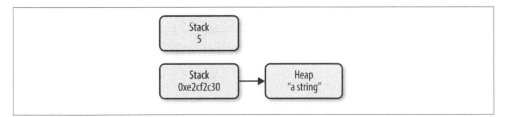

Figure 4-1. Value types versus reference types

Default Values

So far, each value you have declared in F# has been initialized as soon as it has been created, because in the functional style of programming values cannot be changed once declared. In imperative programming, however, there is no need to fully initialize values because you can update them later. This means there is a notion of a *default value* for both value and reference types. That is, the value something has before it has been initialized.

To get the default value of a type, you can use the *type function* Unchecked.default of<'a>. This will return the default value for the type specified.

A type function is a special type of function that takes no arguments other than a generic type parameter. There are several helpful type functions that you will explore in forthcoming chapters:

- `Unchecked.defaultof<'a>` gets the default value for `'a`.
- `typeof<'a>` returns the `System.Type` object describing `'a`.
- `sizeof<'a>` returns the underlying stack size of `'a`.

For value types, their default value is simply a zero-bit pattern. Because the size of a value type is known once it is created, its size in bytes is allocated on the stack, with each byte being given the value `0b00000000`. The default value for reference types is a little more complicated.

Before reference types are initialized, they first point to a special address called `null`. This is used to indicate an uninitialized reference type. In F#, you can use the `null` keyword to check if a reference type is equal to `null`. The following code defines a function to check if its input is `null` or not, and then calls it with an initialized and an uninitialized string value:

```
> let isNull = function null -> true | _ -> false;;

val isNull : obj -> bool

> isNull "a string";;
val it : bool = false
> isNull (null : string);;
val it : bool = true
```

However, reference types defined in F# do not have `null` as a proper value, meaning that they cannot be assigned to be `null`:

```
> type Thing = Plant | Animal | Mineral;;

type Thing =
  | Plant
  | Animal
  | Mineral

> // ERROR: Thing cannot be null
let testThing thing =
    match thing with
    | Plant   -> "Plant"
    | Animal  -> "Animal"
    | Mineral -> "Mineral"
    | null    -> "(null)";;

    | null -> "(null)";;
```

```
------^^^^^
```

```
stdin(9,7): error FS0043: The type 'Thing' does not have 'null' as a proper
value.
```

This seems like a strange restriction, but it eliminates the need for excessive null checking. (If you call a method on an uninitialized reference type, your program will throw
a NullReferenceException, so defensively checking all function parameters for null
in other .NET languages is typical.) If you do need to represent an uninitialized state in
F#, consider using the Option type instead of a reference type with value null, where
the value None represents an uninitialized state and Some('a) represents an initialized
state.

 You can attribute some F# types to accept null as a proper value to ease
interoperation with other .NET languages (see Appendix B for more
information).

Also, that appendix covers the System.Nullable<T> type, which is used
in other .NET languages as a primitive form of F#'s option type.

Reference Type Aliasing

It is possible that two reference types point to the same memory address on the heap.
This is known as *aliasing*. When this happens, modifying one value will silently modify
the other because they both point to the same memory address. This situation can lead
to bugs if you aren't careful.

Example 4-2 creates one instance of an array (covered shortly), but has two values that
point to the same instance. Modifying value x also modifies y and vice versa.

Example 4-2. Aliasing reference types

```
> // Value x points to an array, while y points
// to the same memory address that x does
let x = [| 0 |]
let y = x;;

val x : int [] = [|0|]
val y : int [] = [|0|]

> // If you modify the value of x...
x.[0] <- 3;;
val it : unit = ()
> // ... x will change...
x;;
```

```
val it : int [] = [|3|]
> // ... but so will y...
y;;
val it : int [] = [|3|]
```

Changing Values

Now that you understand the basics of where and how data is stored in .NET, you can look at how to change that data. *Mutable variables* are those that you can change, and can be declared using the `mutable` keyword. To change the contents of a mutable value, use the left arrow operator, `<-`:

```
> let mutable message = "World";;

val mutable message : string = "World"

> printfn "Hello, %s" message;;
Hello, World
val it : unit = ()

> message <- "Universe";;
val it : unit = ()
> printfn "Hello, %s" message;;
Hello, Universe
val it : unit = ()
```

There are several limitations on mutable values, all stemming from security-related CLR restrictions. This prevents you from writing some code using mutable values. Example 4-3 tries to define an inner-function `incrementX`, which captures a mutable value x in its closure (meaning it can access x, even though it wasn't passed in as a parameter). This leads to an error from the F# compiler, because mutable values can only be used in the same function they are defined in.

Example 4-3. Errors using mutable values in closures

```
> // ERROR: Cannot use mutable values except in the function they are defined
let invalidUseOfMutable() =
    let mutable x = 0

    let incrementX() = x <- x + 1
    incrementX()

    x;;

    let incrementX() = x <- x + 1
----------------------^^^^^^^^^^
```

```
stdin(16,24): error FS0407: The mutable variable 'x' is used in an invalid way.
Mutable variables may not be captured by closures. Consider eliminating this use
 of mutation or using a heap-allocated mutable reference cell via 'ref' and '!'.
```

The two restrictions related to mutable values are as follows:

- Mutable values cannot be returned from functions (a copy is made instead)
- Mutable values cannot be captured in inner-functions (closures)

If you ever run into one of these issues, the simple work around is to store the mutable data on the heap using a `ref` cell.

Reference Cells

The `ref` type, sometimes referred to as a `ref` *cell*, allows you to store mutable data on the heap, enabling you to bypass limitations with mutable values that are stored on the stack. To retrieve the value of a `ref` cell, use the ! symbolic operator, and to set the value, use the := operator.

`ref` is not only the name of a type, but also the name of a function that produces `ref` values, which has the signature:

```
val ref: 'a -> 'a ref
```

The `ref` function takes a value and returns a copy of it wrapped in a `ref` cell. Example 4-4 shows passing a list of planets to the `ref` function and then later altering the contents of the returned `ref` cell.

Example 4-4. Using ref cells to mutate data

```
let planets =
    ref [
        "Mercury";  "Venus";     "Earth";
        "Mars";     "Jupiter";   "Saturn";
        "Uranus";   "Neptune";   "Pluto"
    ]

// Oops! Sorry Pluto...

// Filter all planets not equal to "Pluto"
// Get the value of the planets ref cell using (!),
// then assign the new value using (:=)
planets := !planets |> List.filter (fun p -> p <> "Pluto")
```

C# programmers should take care when using ref types and Boolean values. !x is simply the value of x, not the Boolean not function applied to x:

```
> let x = ref true;;

val x : bool ref

> !x;;

val it : bool = true
```

The F# library has two functions, decr and incr, to simplify incrementing and decrementing int ref types:

```
> let x = ref 0;;

val x : int ref = {contents = 0;}

> incr x;;
val it : unit = ()
> x;;
val it : int ref = {contents = 1;}
> decr x;;
val it : unit = ()
> x;;
val it : int ref = {contents = 0;}
```

Mutable Records

Mutability can be applied to more than just single values; record fields can be marked as mutable as well. This allows you to use records with the imperative style. To make a record field mutable, simply prefix the field name with the mutable keyword.

The following example creates a record with a mutable field Miles, which can be modified as if it were a mutable variable. Now you can update record fields without being forced to clone the entire record:

```
> // Mutable record types
open System

type MutableCar = { Make : string; Model : string; mutable Miles : int }

let driveForASeason car =
    let rng = new Random()
    car.Miles <- car.Miles + rng.Next() % 10000;;

type MutableCar =
  {Make: string;
   Model: string;
   mutable Miles: int;}
val driveForASeason : MutableCar -> unit
```

```
> // Mutate record fields
let kitt = { Make = "Pontiac"; Model = "Trans Am"; Miles = 0 }

driveForASeason kitt
driveForASeason kitt
driveForASeason kitt
driveForASeason kitt;;

val kitt : MutableCar = {Make = "Pontiac";
                         Model = "Trans Am";
                         Miles = 4660;}
```

As Uncle Ben once said, "With great power comes great responsibility." And the ability to mutate values is no different. Fortunately, in F#, it is difficult to get into too much trouble with incorrect mutations because of the type system's ability to enforce correctness.

Units of Measure

There are several universal truths in this world: the acceleration of gravity is 9.8 meters per second squared, water will boil at over 100 degrees Celsius (at one atmosphere of pressure), and any programmer, no matter how talented or careful, will have bugs related to units of measure.

If you are ever writing code that deals with real-world units, you will invariably get it wrong. For example, you might pass in seconds when the function takes minutes, or mistake acceleration for velocity. The result of these sorts of bugs in software has ranged from minor annoyances to loss of life.

The problem is that if you represent a value with just a floating-point number, you have no additional information about what that number means. If I give you a float with value 9.8, you have no idea if it is in miles, meters per second, hours, or even megabytes.

A powerful language feature for combating these dimensional analysis issues is *units of measure*. Units of measure allow you to pass along unit information with a floating-point value—float, float32, decimal—or signed integer types in order to prevent an entire class of software defects. Consider Example 4-5, which describes a temperature. Notice how the parameter temp is encoded to only take fahrenheit values. We will cover exactly what float<_> means later in this section.

Example 4-5. Converting Fahrenheit to Celsius with units of measure

```
[<Measure>]
type fahrenheit

let printTemperature (temp : float<fahrenheit>) =

    if   temp < 32.0<_>  then
```

```
    printfn "Below Freezing!"
elif temp < 65.0<_>  then
    printfn "Cold"
elif temp < 75.0<_>  then
    printfn "Just right!"
elif temp < 100.0<_> then
    printfn "Hot!"
else
    printfn "Scorching!"
```

Because the function only accepts fahrenheit values, it will fail to work with any floating-point values encoded with a different unit of measure. Calling the function with an invalid unit of measure will result in a compile-time error (and prevent potentially disastrous results at runtime):

```
> let seattle = 59.0<fahrenheit>;;

val seattle : float<fahrenheit> = 59.0

> printTemperature seattle;;
Cold
val it : unit = ()
> // ERROR: Different units
[<Measure>]
type celsius

let cambridge = 18.0<celsius>;;

[<Measure>]
type celsius
val cambridge : float<celsius> = 18.0

> printTemperature cambridge;;

  printTemperature cambridge;;
  ----------------^^^^^^^^^

stdin(18,18): error FS0001: Type mismatch. Expecting a
    float<fahrenheit>
but given a
    float<celsius>.
The unit of measure 'fahrenheit' does not match the unit of measure 'celsius'
```

Units of measure also can be compounded by multiplication or division. So if you divide a meter unit of measure by another such as second, the result will be encoded as float<meter/second>:

```
> // Define a measure for meters
[<Measure>]
type m;;

[<Measure>]
```

```
type m

> // Multiplication, goes to meters squared
1.0<m> * 1.0<m>;;

val it : float<m ^ 2> = 1.0
> // Division, drops unit entirely
1.0<m> / 1.0<m>;;

val it : float = 1.0
> // Repeated division, results in 1 / meters
1.0<m> / 1.0<m> / 1.0<m>;;

val it : float</m> = 1.0
```

Defining Units of Measure

To define a unit of measure, simply add the [<Measure>] attribute on top of a type declaration. A unit of measure type can only contain static methods and properties, and typically they are defined as *opaque types*, meaning they have no methods or properties at all. Unit of measure types can also be abbreviated to be relative to other units of measure. In Example 4-6, a new unit of measure, s, for seconds, is defined as well as a relative unit of measure Hz, for hertz, which stands for cycles per second. Because the units are relative to one another, two values with the same semantic meaning are considered equal.

Example 4-6. Defining new units of measure

```
> // Define seconds and hertz
[<Measure>]
type s

[<Measure>]
type Hz = s ^ -1;;

[<Measure>]
type s
[<Measure>]
type Hz =/s

> // If Hz was not convertible to s, this
// would result in a compile error.
3.0<s ^ -1> = 3.0<Hz>;;
val it : bool = true
```

Sometimes it can be quite useful to add functions for conversions between units of measures to the measure type itself. The following snippet defines units of measure for Fahrenheit and Celsius like before, except with the addition of static methods to do conversion between the two. Note the use of the and keyword—it is required so that the type far can reference type cel as part of its declaration:

```
> // Adding methods to units of measure
[<Measure>]
type far =
    static member ConvertToCel(x : float<far>) =
        (5.0<cel> / 9.0<far>) * (x - 32.0<far>)

and [<Measure>] cel =
    static member ConvertToFar(x : float<cel>) =
        (9.0<far> / 5.0<cel> * x) + 32.0<far>;;

[<Measure>]
type far =
  class
    static member ConvertToCel : x:float<far> -> float<cel>
  end
[<Measure>]
and cel =
  class
    static member ConvertToFar : x:float<cel> -> float<far>
  end

> far.ConvertToCel(100.0<far>);;
val it : float<cel> = 37.77777778
```

Although defining units of measure is an easy task, all of the common elements of the *international system of units* have been defined in the F# library. They are separated into two namespaces in case you wish to refer to units by their abbreviated form or by name:

```
// UnitSymbols contains the abbreviated versions of SI units.
open Microsoft.FSharp.Data.UnitSystems.SI.UnitSymbols

// In candela, the SI unit of luminous intensity.
let flaslightIntensity = 80.0<cd>

// The UnitNames contains the full-names of SI units.
open Microsoft.FSharp.Data.UnitSystems.SI.UnitNames

// This might be worth a few dollars, euros, yen, etc.
let world'sLargestGoldNugget = 280.0<kilogram>
```

Converting Between Units of Measure

Not every function takes a measured value as a parameter. To convert between a measured parameter and the base type, simply pass the value to the appropriate conversion function. Example 4-7 shows how to drop units of measure when calling the sin and cos trigonometric functions, because they do not accept values marked with a unit of measure.

Example 4-7. Converting units of measure

```
> // Radians
[<Measure>]
type rads;;

[<Measure>]
type rads

> let halfPI = System.Math.PI * 0.5<rads>;;

val halfPI : float<rads>

> // ERROR: Pass a float<_> to a function accepting a float
sin halfPI;;

  sin halfPI;;
  ----^^^^^^^

stdin(7,5): error FS0001: The type 'float<rads>' does not match type 'float'.
> // Drop the units from value halfPi, to convert float<_> to float
sin (float halfPI);;
val it : float = 1.0
```

Generic Units of Measure

Relying on custom conversion can be a pain, especially if you want to create a generic function. Fortunately, you can allow the F# type system to infer a unit of measure type. If you leave the unit of measure type off and use float<_> instead, the F# type inference system will define the value as having a generic unit of measure:

```
> let squareMeter (x : float<m>) = x * x;;

val squareMeter : float<m> -> float<m ^ 2>

> let genericSquare (x : float<_>) = x * x;;

val genericSquare : float<'u> -> float<'u ^ 2>

> genericSquare 1.0<m/s>;;
val it : float<m ^ 2/s ^ 2> = 1.0
> genericSquare 9.0;;
val it : float = 81.0
```

If you want to create a type that is generic with regard to a unit of measure, add the [<Measure>] attribute to a generic type parameter. That generic type parameter will allow you to refer to the unit of measure, but it cannot be anything else. In fact, the compiled form of the type will not expose the generic type parameter at all.

Example 4-8 shows defining a point type that preserves a unit of measure.

Example 4-8. Creating a type that is generic with respect to a unit of measure

```
// Represents a point respecting the unit of measure
type Point< [<Measure>] 'u >(x : float<'u>, y : float<'u>) =

    member this.X = x
    member this.Y = y

    member this.UnitlessX = float x
    member this.UnitlessY = float y

    member this.Length =
        let sqr x = x * x
        sqrt <| sqr this.X + sqr this.Y

    override this.ToString() =
        sprintf
            "{%f, %f}"
            this.UnitlessX
            this.UnitlessY
```

When executed in an FSI session, Example 4-8 looks like the following. Notice how the unit of measure is persisted through the Length property—taking the square root of the sum of two squares:

```
> let p = new Point<m>(10.0<m>, 10.0<m>);;

val p : Point<m>

> p.Length;;
val it : float<m> = 14.14213562
```

 Units of measure are a feature specific to the F# language and not to the Common Language Runtime. As a result, custom types you create in F# will not have their units of measure types exposed across assembly boundaries. So types that are float<'a> will only be exported as float when referenced from C#.

Units of measure are not only suited for real-world values. They can also be helpful when dealing with abstract units as well, such as clicks, pixels, game tiles, and so on.

Arrays

Until now, when you've needed to join multiple pieces of data together, you've used lists. Lists are extremely efficient at adding and removing elements from the beginning of a list, but they aren't ideal for every situation. For example, random access of list elements is very slow. In addition, if you needed to change the last element of a list, you would need to clone the entire list. (The performance characteristics of lists are covered more in-depth in Chapter 7.)

When you know ahead of time how many items you will need in your collection and would like to be able to update any given item, arrays are the ideal type to use.

Arrays in .NET are a contiguous block of memory containing zero or more elements, each of which can be modified individually. (This is unlike lists, which are immutable.)

Arrays can be constructed using *array comprehensions*, which are identical to list comprehensions (discussed in Chapter 2), or manually via a list of values separated by semicolons and enclosed between [| |]:

```
> // Using the array comprehension syntax
let perfectSquares = [| for i in 1 .. 7 -> i * i |];;

val perfectSquares : int [] = [|1; 4; 9; 16; 25; 36; 49|]

> // Manually declared
let perfectSquares2 = [| 1; 4; 9; 16; 25; 36; 49; 64; 81 |];;

val perfectSquares2 : int []
```

Indexing an Array

To retrieve an element from the array, you can use an indexer, . [ ], which is a zero-based index into the array:

```
> // Indexing an array
printfn
    "The first three perfect squares are %d, %d, and %d"
    perfectSquares.[0]
    perfectSquares.[1]
    perfectSquares.[2];;
The first three perfect squares are 1, 4, and 9
val it : unit = ()
```

Example 4-9 uses array indexers to change individual characters of a character array to implement a primitive form of encryption known as ROT13, which works by simply taking each letter and rotating it 13 places forward in the alphabet. The example achieves this by converting each letter to an integer, adding 13, and then converting it back to a character.

Example 4-9. ROT13 encryption in F#

```
open System

// Encrypt a letter using ROT13
let rot13Encrypt (letter : char) =
```

```
// Move the letter forward 13 places in the alphabet (looping around)
// Otherwise ignore.
if Char.IsLetter(letter) then
    let newLetter =
        (int letter)
        |> (fun letterIdx -> letterIdx - (int 'A'))
        |> (fun letterIdx -> (letterIdx + 13) % 26)
        |> (fun letterIdx -> letterIdx + (int 'A'))
        |> char
    newLetter
else
    letter

// Loop through each array element, encrypting each letter
let encryptText (text  : char[]) =

    for idx = 0 to text.Length - 1 do
        let letter = text.[idx]
        text.[idx] <- rot13Encrypt letter

let text =
    Array.ofSeq "THE QUICK BROWN FOX JUMPED OVER THE LAZY DOG"

printfn "Original = %s" <| new String(text)
encryptText(text)
printfn "Encrypted = %s" <| new String(text)

// A unique trait of ROT13 is that to decrypt, simply encrypt again
encryptText(text)
printfn "Decrypted = %s" <| new String(text)
```

The output of our simple program is:

```
Original = THE QUICK FOX JUMPED OVER THE LAZY DOG
Encrypted = GUR DHVPX SBK WHZCRQ BIRE GUR YNML QBT
Decrypted = THE QUICK FOX JUMPED OVER THE LAZY DOG
```

Unlike C# and VB.NET, indexers in F# require using the dot notation. You can think of an indexer then as just another method or property:

```
// Incorrect
x[0]
// Correct
x.[0]
```

Attempting to access an element in the array with an index either less than zero or greater than or equal to the number of elements in the array will raise an IndexOutOfRangeEx ception exception (exceptions are covered later in this chapter). Fortunately, arrays have a Length property, which will return the number of items in the array. Because array indexes are zero-based, you need to subtract one from Length to get the index of the last element in the array:

```
> let alphabet = [| 'a' .. 'z' |];;

val alphabet : char []

> // First letter
alphabet.[0];;

val it : char = 'a'
> // Last leter
alphabet.[alphabet.Length - 1];;

val it : char = 'z'
> // Some nonexistent letter
alphabet.[10000];;

System.IndexOutOfRangeException: Index was outside the bounds of the array.
    at <StartupCode$FSI_0012>.$FSI_0012._main()
stopped due to error
```

Array Slices

When you're analyzing data stored in arrays, it is sometimes convenient to just work with a subset of the data. In F#, there is a special syntax for taking a *slice* of an array, where you specify optional lower and upper bounds for the subset of data. The syntax for taking a slice is:

```
array.[lowerBound..upperBound]
```

If no lower bound is specified, 0 is used. If no upper bound is specified, then the length of the array − 1 is used. If neither a lower nor upper bound is specified, by using *, then the entire array is copied.

Example 4-10 shows the various ways for taking a slice of an array, but we will break it down line by line shortly.

Example 4-10. Using array slices

```
open System
let daysOfWeek = Enum.GetNames( typeof<DayOfWeek> )

// Standard array slice, elements 2 through 4
daysOfWeek.[2..4]

// Just specify lower bound, elements 4 to the end
daysOfWeek.[4..]
```

```
// Just specify an upper bound, elements 0 to 2
daysOfWeek.[..2]

// Specify no bounds, get all elements (copies the array)
daysOfWeek.[*]
```

The first way we sliced an array was specifying both an upper and lower bound; this returned all array elements within that range:

```
> // Standard array slice, elements 2 through 4
daysOfWeek.[2..4];;
val it : string [] = [|"Tuesday"; "Wednesday"; "Thursday"|]
```

Next we specified just a lower or just an upper bound. This returns each element from the lower bound to the end of the array, or from the beginning of the array to the upper bound:

```
> // Just specify lower bound, elements 4 to the end
daysOfWeek.[4..];;
val it : string [] = [|"Thursday"; "Friday"; "Saturday"|]

> // Just specify an upper bound, elements 0 to 2
daysOfWeek.[..2];;
val it : string [] = [|"Sunday"; "Monday"; "Tuesday"|]
```

And finally we just copied the entire array using an *. Note that for every slice operation, a new array is returned, so there will never be problems with aliasing:

```
> // Specify no bounds, get all elements (copies the array)
daysOfWeek.[*];;
```

Creating Arrays

Array comprehensions and manually specifying each element aren't the only ways to construct arrays. You can also use the Array.init function, which takes a function used to generate each array element based on its index. To create an uninitialized array, use the Array.zeroCreate function. With that function, each element is initialized to its default value—zero or null.

Example 4-11 shows how to use Array.init and Array.zeroCreate to construct arrays.

Example 4-11. Initializing arrays using Array.init

```
> // Initialize an array of sin-wave elements
let divisions = 4.0
let twoPi = 2.0 * Math.PI;;

val divisions : float = 4.0
val twoPi : float = 6.283185307

> Array.init (int divisions) (fun i -> float i * twoPi / divisions);;
val it : float [] = [|0.0; 1.570796327; 3.141592654; 4.71238898|]
```

```
> // Construct empty arrays
let emptyIntArray    : int [] = Array.zeroCreate 3
let emptyStringArray : string [] = Array.zeroCreate 3;;

val emptyIntArray : int [] = [|0; 0; 0|]
val emptyStringArray : string [] = [|null; null; null|]
```

 The CLR limits arrays to take up no more than 2GB of memory, even on 64-bit machines. If you need to allocate an array to store a massive amount of data, then use a custom data structure instead.

Pattern Matching

Pattern matching against arrays is just as easy as using lists. And just like pattern matching against lists, when matching against arrays, you can capture element values as well as match against the structure of the array. Example 4-12 shows matching an array value against null or an array with 0, 1, or 2 elements.

Example 4-12. Pattern matching against arrays

```
> // Describe an array
let describeArray arr =
    match arr with
    | null       -> "The array is null"
    | [| |]      -> "The array is empty"
    | [| x |]    -> sprintf "The array has one element, %A" x
    | [| x; y |] -> sprintf "The array has two elements, %A and %A" x y
    | a -> sprintf "The array had %d elements, %A" a.Length a;;

val describeArray : 'a [] -> string

> describeArray [| 1 .. 4 |];;
val it : string = "The array had 4 elements, [|1; 2; 3; 4|]"
> describeArray [| ("tuple", 1, 2, 3) |];;
val it : string = "The array has one element, ("tuple", 1, 2, 3)"
```

Array Equality

Arrays in F# are compared using structural equality. Two arrays are considered equal if they have the same rank, length, and elements (rank is the dimensionality of the array, something we cover in the next section):

```
> [| 1 .. 5 |] = [| 1; 2; 3; 4; 5 |];;
val it : bool = true
> [| 1 .. 3 |] = [| |];;
val it : bool = false
```

This is different from the behavior of equality on arrays in C#. In F#, the = operator contains special logic for comparing arrays so the default referential equality is not used. For more information on object equality in .NET, refer to Chapter 5.

Array Module Functions

Just like the List and Seq modules, there is an Array module containing methods like Array.iter, Array.map, and Array.fold. Among these methods in the Array module are a pair used for creating new arrays, detailed in Table 4-1.

Table 4-1. Array construction methods

Function	Description
Array.init int -> (int -> 'a) -> 'a[]	Creates a new array with the given number of elements; each element is initialized by the result of the provided function.
Array.zeroCreate int -> 'a[]	Creates an array with the given length where each entry is the type's default value.

partition

Array.partition divides the given array into two new arrays. The first array contains only elements where the provided function returns true, the second array contains elements where the provided function returns false:

```
> // Simple Boolean function
let isGreaterThanTen x = (x > 10);;

val isGreaterThanTen : int -> bool

> // Partitioning arrays
[| 5; 5; 6; 20; 1; 3; 7; 11 |]
|> Array.partition isGreaterThanTen;;
val it : int [] * int [] = ([|20; 11|], [|5; 5; 6; 1; 3; 7|])
```

tryFind and tryFindIndex

Array.tryFind returns Some of the first element for which the given function returns true. Otherwise, it returns None. Array.tryFindIndex works just like Array.tryFind, except rather than returning the element, it returns its index in the array:

```
> // Simple Boolean function
let rec isPowerOfTwo x =
    if x = 2 then
        true
    elif x % 2 = 1  (* is odd *) then
        false
    else isPowerOfTwo (x / 2);;
```

```
val isPowerOfTwo : int -> bool

> [| 1; 7; 13; 64; 32 |]
|> Array.tryFind isPowerOfTwo;;
val it : int option = Some 64
> [| 1; 7; 13; 64; 32 |]
|> Array.tryFindIndex isPowerOfTwo;;
val it : int option = Some 3
```

 Array.tryFind and Array.tryFindIndex illustrate why the Option type is so powerful. In C#, functions similar to tryFindIndex will return –1 to indicate failure (as opposed to None). However, if trying to implement tryFind, –1 could both indicate a failure to find an array element or finding an element with value –1.

Aggregate operators

The Array module also contains the aggregate operators of the List module. Namely, fold, foldBack, map, and iter. In addition, there are also index-aware versions of these methods. Example 4-13 demonstrates the iteri function, which behaves just like iter except that in addition to the array element, the element's index is provided as well.

Example 4-13. Using the iteri array aggregate function

```
> let vowels = [| 'a'; 'e'; 'i'; 'o'; 'u' |];;

val vowels : char [] = [|'a'; 'e'; 'i'; 'o'; 'u'|]

> Array.iteri (fun idx chr -> printfn "vowel.[%d] = %c" idx chr) vowels
vowel.[0] = a
vowel.[1] = e
vowel.[2] = i
vowel.[3] = o
vowel.[4] = u
val it : unit = ()
```

Multidimensional Arrays

Arrays are helpful for storing data in a linear fashion, but what if you need to represent data as a two-, three-, or higher-dimensional grid? You can create *multidimensional arrays*, which enable you to treat data as a block indexed by several values.

Multidimensional arrays come in two flavors: rectangular and jagged. The difference is illustrated in Figure 4-2. Rectangular arrays are in a solid block whereas jagged arrays are essentially arrays of arrays.

Figure 4-2. Jagged and rectangular arrays

Which type of multidimensional array to use depends on the situation. Using jagged arrays allows you to save memory if each row doesn't need to be the same length; however, rectangular arrays are more efficient for random access because the elements are stored in a contiguous block of memory (and therefore can benefit from your processor's cache).

Rectangular arrays

Rectangular arrays are rectangular blocks of *n* by *m* elements in memory. Rectangular arrays are indicated by rectangular brackets with a comma separating them for each new dimension. Also, just like single-dimensional arrays, there are the `Array2D` and `Array3D` modules for creating and initializing rectangular arrays:

```
> // Creating a 3x3 array
let identityMatrix : float[,] = Array2D.zeroCreate 3 3
identityMatrix.[0,0] <- 1.0
identityMatrix.[1,1] <- 1.0
identityMatrix.[2,2] <- 1.0;;


val identityMatrix : float [,] = [[1.0; 0.0; 0.0]
                                  [0.0; 1.0; 0.0]
                                  [0.0; 0.0; 1.0]]
```

Two-dimensional rectangular arrays can also take slices, using the same syntax but providing a slice for each dimension:

```
> // All rows for columns with index 1 through 2
identityMatrix.[*, 1..2];;
val it : float [,] = [[0.0; 0.0]
                      [1.0; 0.0]
                      [0.0; 1.0]]
```

Jagged arrays

Jagged arrays are simply single-dimensional arrays of single-dimensional arrays. Each row in the main array is a different array, each needing to be initialized separately:

```
> // Create a jagged array
let jaggedArray : int[][]  = Array.zeroCreate 3
jaggedArray.[0] <- Array.init 1 (fun x -> x)
jaggedArray.[1] <- Array.init 2 (fun x -> x)
jaggedArray.[2] <- Array.init 3 (fun x -> x);;


val jaggedArray : int [] [] = [|[|0|]; [|0; 1|]; [|0; 1; 2|]|]
```

Mutable Collection Types

Often you will need to store data, but you won't know how many items you will have ahead of time. For example, you might be loading records from a database. If you used an array, you run the risk of allocating too many elements and wasting memory, or even worse, not enough and crashing instead.

Mutable collection types allow you to dynamically add and remove elements over time. Although mutable collection types can be problematic when doing parallel and asynchronous programming, they are very simple to work with.

List<'T>

The List type in the System.Collections.Generic namespace—not to be confused with the F# list type—is a wrapper on top of an array that allows you to dynamically adjust the size of the array when adding and removing elements. Because List is built on top of standard arrays, retrieving and adding values is typically very fast. But once the internal array is filled up, a new, larger one will need to be created and the List's contents copied over.

Example 4-14 shows basic usage of a List. Again, we're denying poor Pluto the title of planet.

Example 4-14. Using the List type

```
> // Create a List<_> of planets
open System.Collections.Generic
let planets = new List<string>();;

val planets : Collections.Generic.List<string>

> // Add individual planets
planets.Add("Mercury")
planets.Add("Venus")
planets.Add("Earth")
planets.Add("Mars");;
> planets.Count;;
val it : int = 4
> // Add a collection of values at once
planets.AddRange( [| "Jupiter"; "Saturn"; "Uranus"; "Neptune"; "Pluto" |] );;
val it : unit = ()
> planets.Count;;
val it : int = 9
> // Sorry bro
planets.Remove("Pluto");;
val it : bool = true
> planets.Count;;
val it : int = 8
```

Table 4-2 shows common methods on the List type.

Table 4-2. Methods and properties on the List<'T> type

Function and type	Description
Add: 'a -> unit	Adds an element to the end of the list.
Clear: unit -> unit	Removes all elements from the list.
Contains: 'a -> bool	Returns whether or not the item can be found in the list.
Count: int	Property for the number of items in the list.
IndexOf: 'a -> int	Returns a zero-based index of the given item in the list. If it is not present, returns −1.
Insert: int * 'a -> unit	Inserts the given item at the specified index into the list.
Remove: 'a -> bool	Removes the given item if present from the list.
RemoveAt: int -> unit	Removes the item at the specified index.

Dictionary<'K,'V>

The `Dictionary` type in the `System.Collections.Generic` namespace contains key-value pairs. Typically you would use a dictionary when you want to store data and require a friendly way to look it up, rather than an index, such as using a name to look up someone's phone number.

Example 4-15 shows using a dictionary to map element symbols to a custom `Atom` type. Note the use of F#'s units of measure feature to encode an atom's weight in *atomic mass units*.

Example 4-15. Using a dictionary

```
// Atomic Mass Units
[<Measure>]
type amu

type Atom = { Name : string; Weight : float<amu> }

open System.Collections.Generic
let periodicTable = new Dictionary<string, Atom>()

periodicTable.Add( "H", { Name = "Hydrogen";  Weight = 1.0079<amu> })
periodicTable.Add("He", { Name = "Helium";    Weight = 4.0026<amu> })
periodicTable.Add("Li", { Name = "Lithium";   Weight = 6.9410<amu> })
periodicTable.Add("Be", { Name = "Beryllium"; Weight = 9.0122<amu> })
periodicTable.Add( "B", { Name = "Boron ";    Weight = 10.811<amu> })
// ...

// Lookup an element
let printElement name =

    if periodicTable.ContainsKey(name) then
        let atom = periodicTable.[name]
        printfn
            "Atom with symbol with '%s' has weight %A."
            atom.Name atom.Weight
    else
        printfn "Error. No atom with name '%s' found." name

// Alternate syntax to get a value. Return a tuple of 'success * result'
let printElement2 name =

    let (found, atom) = periodicTable.TryGetValue(name)
    if found then
        printfn
            "Atom with symbol with '%s' has weight %A."
            atom.Name atom.Weight
    else
        printfn "Error. No atom with name '%s' found." Name
```

Table 4-3 shows common methods on the `Dictionary<'k,'v>` type.

Table 4-3. Methods and properties on the Dictionary<'k, 'v> type

Function and Type	Description
`Add:` `'k * 'v -> unit`	Adds a new key-value pair to the dictionary.
`Clear:` `unit -> unit`	Removes all items from the dictionary.
`ContainsKey:` `'k -> bool`	Checks if the given key is present in the dictionary.
`ContainsValue:` `'v -> bool`	Checks if the given value is present in the dictionary.
`Count:` `int`	Returns the number of items in the dictionary.
`Remove:` `'k -> unit`	Removes a key-value pair from the dictionary with then given key.

HashSet<'T>

A `HashSet`, also defined in the `System.Collections.Generic` namespace, is an efficient collection for storing an unordered set of items. Let's say you were writing an application to crawl web pages. You would need to keep track of which pages you have visited before so you didn't get stuck in an infinite loop; however, if you stored the page URLs you have already visited in a `List`, it would be very slow to loop through each element to check if a page had already been visited. A `HashSet` stores a collection of unique values based on their *hash code*, so checking if an element exists in the set can be done rather quickly.

Hash codes are better explained in Chapter 5, but for now you can just think of them as a way to uniquely identify an object. They are the reason why looking up elements in a `HashSet` or `Dictionary` is fast.

Example 4-16 shows using a `HashSet` to check if a film has won the Oscar for Best Picture.

Example 4-16. Using the HashSet type

```
open System.Collections.Generic

let bestPicture = new HashSet<string>()
bestPicture.Add("The Artist")
bestPicture.Add("The King's Speech")
bestPicture.Add("The Hurt Locker")
bestPicture.Add("Slumdog Milionaire")
bestPicture.Add("No Country for Old Men")
bestPicture.Add("The Departed")
// ...
```

```
// Check if it was a best picture
if bestPicture.Contains("Manos: The Hands of Fate") then
    printfn "Sweet..."
    // ...
```

Table 4-4 shows common methods on the HashSet<'T> type.

Table 4-4. Methods and properties on the HashSet<'T> type

Function and Type	Description
Add: 'a -> unit	Adds a new item to the HashSet.
Clear: unit -> unit	Removes all items from the HashSet.
Count: int	Returns the number of items in the HashSet.
IntersectWith: seq<'a> -> unit	Modifies the HashSet to contain only elements that are also contained in the given sequence.
IsSubsetOf: seq<'a > -> bool	Returns whether the HashSet is a subset of the sequence; that is, every element in the HashSet is found in the sequence.
IsSupersetOf: seq<'a > -> bool	Returns whether the HashSet is a superset of the sequence; that is, every element in the sequence is contained in the HashSet.
Remove: 'a -> unit	Removes the given item from the HashSet.
UnionWith: seq<'a> -> unit	Modifies the HashSet to contain at least every element in the given sequence.

Looping Constructs

F# has the traditional sorts of looping constructs seen in imperative languages. These allow you to repeat the same function or piece of code a set number of times or until a condition is met.

While Loops

while expressions loop until a Boolean predicate evaluates to false. (For this reason, while loops cannot be used in a purely functional style; otherwise the loop would never terminate because you could never update the predicate.)

Note that the while loop predicate must evaluate to bool and the body of the loop must evaluate to unit. The following code shows how to use a while loop to count up from zero:

```
> // While loop
let mutable i = 0
while i < 5 do
```

```
    i <- i + 1
    printfn "i = %d" i;;
i = 1
i = 2
i = 3
i = 4
i = 5

val mutable i : int = 5
```

The predicate for the `while` loop is checked before the loop starts, so if the initial value of the predicate is `false`, the loop will never execute.

For Loops

When you need to iterate a fixed number of times, you can use a `for` expression, of which there are two flavors in F#: simple and enumerable.

Simple for loops

Simple `for` loops introduce a new integer value and count up to a fixed value. The loop won't iterate if the counter is greater than the maximum value:

```
> // For loop
for i = 1 to 5 do
    printfn "%d" i;;
1
2
3
4
5
val it : unit = ()
```

To count down, use the `downto` keyword. The loop won't iterate if the counter is less than the minimum value:

```
> // Counting down
for i = 5 downto 1 do
    printfn "%d" i;;
5
4
3
2
1
val it : unit = ()
```

Numerical `for` loops are only supported with integers as the counter, so if you need to loop more than `System.Int32.MaxValue` times, you will need to use enumerable `for` loops.

Enumerable for loop

The more common type of for loop is one that iterates through a sequence of values. Enumerable for loops work with any seq type, such as array or list. The following example loops over a list literal:

```
> // Enumerable loop
for i in [1 .. 5] do
    printfn "%d" i;;
1
2
3
4
5
val it : unit = ()
```

What makes enumerable for loops more powerful than a foreach loop in C# is that enumerable for loops can take advantage of pattern matching. The element that follows the for keyword is actually a pattern-match rule, so if it is a new identifier like i, it simply captures the pattern-match value. But more complex pattern-match rules can be used instead.

In Example 4-17, a discriminated union is introduced with two union cases, Cat and Dog. The for loop iterates through a list but only executes when the element in the list is an instance of the Dog union case.

Example 4-17. For loops with pattern matching

```
> // Pet type
type Pet =
    | Cat of string * int // Name, Lives
    | Dog of string       // Name
;;

type Pet =
    | Cat of string * int
    | Dog of string

> let famousPets = [ Dog("Lassie"); Cat("Felix", 9); Dog("Rin Tin Tin") ];;

val famousPets : Pet list = [Dog "Lassie"; Cat ("Felix",9); Dog "Rin Tin Tin"]

> // Print famous dogs. (Prints warning due to incomplete match.)
for Dog(name) in famousPets do
    printfn "%s was a famous dog." name;;
Lassie was a famous dog.
Rin Tin Tin was a famous dog.
val it : unit = ()
```

There are no break or continue keywords in F#. If you want to exit prematurely in the middle of a for loop, you will need to create a mutable value and convert the for loop to a while loop.

Exceptions

Every programmer knows things don't always happen as planned. I've been careful in examples so far to avoid showing you code where things fail. But dealing with the unexpected is a crucial aspect of any program and, fortunately, the .NET platform supports a powerful mechanism for handling the unexpected.

An *exception* is a failure in a .NET program that causes an abnormal branch in control flow. If an exception occurs, the function immediately exits, as well as its calling function, and its calling function, and so on until the exception is *caught* by an *exception handler*. If the exception is never caught, then the program terminates.

The simplest way to report an error in an F# program is to use the failwith function. This function takes a string as a parameter and, when called, throws an instance of System.Exception. An alternate version exists called failwithf that takes a format string similar to printf and sprintf:

```
> // Using failwithf
let divide x y =
    if y = 0 then failwithf "Cannot divide %d by zero!" x
    x / y;;

val divide : int -> int -> int

> divide 10 0;;
System.Exception: Cannot divide 10 by zero!
   at FSI_0003.divide(Int32 x, Int32 y)
   at <StartupCode$FSI_0004>.$FSI_0004._main()
stopped due to error
```

In the previous example, FSI indicated an exception was thrown, displaying the two most important properties on an exception type: the exception message and stack trace. Each exception has a Message property, which is a programmer-friendly description of the problem. The Stacktrace property is a string printout of all the functions waiting on a return value before the exception occurred, and is invaluable for tracking down the origin of an exception. Because the stack *unwinds* immediately after an exception is thrown, the exception could be caught far away from the where the exception originated.

Although a descriptive message helps programmers debug the exception, it is a best practice in .NET to use a specific exception type, because using typed exceptions makes it far easier to catch and deal with any problems appropriately. To throw a more specific type of exception, you use the raise function. This takes a custom exception type (any type derived from System.Exception) and throws the exception just like failwith:

```
> // Raising a DivideByZeroException
let divide2 x y =
    if y = 0 then raise <| new System.DivideByZeroException()
    x / y;;

val divide2 : int -> int -> int

> divide2 10 0;;
System.DivideByZeroException: Attempted to divide by zero.
   at FSI_0005.divide2(Int32 x, Int32 y)
   at <StartupCode$FSI_0007>.$FSI_0007._main()
stopped due to error
```

 It is tempting to throw exceptions liberally when your program reaches an unexpected situation; however, throwing exceptions incurs a significant performance hit. Whenever possible, situations that would throw an exception should be obviated.

Handling Exceptions

To handle an exception, you catch it using a try-catch expression. Any exceptions raised while executing code within a try-catch expression will be handled by a with block, which is a pattern match against the exception type.

Because the exception handler to execute is determined by pattern matching, you can combine exception handlers for multiple types using Or. Similarly, you can use a wildcard to catch any exception. If an exception is thrown within a try-catch expression and an appropriate exception handler cannot be found, the exception will continue bubbling up until caught or the program terminates.

try-catch expressions return a value, just like a pattern match or if expression. So naturally the last expression in the try block must have the same type as each rule in the with pattern match.

Example 4-18 shows some code that runs through a minefield of potential problems, with each possible exception handled by an appropriate exception handler. In the example, the :? dynamic type test operator is used to match against the exception type; this operator is covered in more detail in Chapter 5.

Example 4-18. Try–catch expressions

```
open System.IO

[<EntryPoint>]
let main (args : string[]) =

    let exitCode =
        try
            let filePath = args.[0]

            printfn "Trying to gather information about file:"
            printfn "%s" filePath

            // Does the drive exist?
            let matchingDrive =
                Directory.GetLogicalDrives()
                |> Array.tryFind (fun drivePath -> drivePath.[0] = filePath.[0])

            if matchingDrive = None then
                raise <| new DriveNotFoundException(filePath)

            // Does the folder exist?
            let directory = Path.GetPathRoot(filePath)
            if not <| Directory.Exists(directory) then
                raise <| new DirectoryNotFoundException(filePath)

            // Does the file exist?
            if not <| File.Exists(filePath) then
                raise <| new FileNotFoundException(filePath)

            let fileInfo = new FileInfo(filePath)
            printfn "Created  = %s" <| fileInfo.CreationTime.ToString()
            printfn "Access   = %s" <| fileInfo.LastAccessTime.ToString()
            printfn "Size     = %d" fileInfo.Length

            0

        with
        // Combine patterns using Or
        | :? DriveNotFoundException
        | :? DirectoryNotFoundException
            ->  printfn "Unhandled Drive or Directory not found exception"
                1
        // Bind the exception value to value ex
        | :? FileNotFoundException as ex
            ->  printfn "Unhandled FileNotFoundException: %s" ex.Message
                3
        | :? IOException as ex
            ->  printfn "Unhandled IOException: %s" ex.Message
                4
        // Use a wildcard match (ex will be of type System.Exception)
        | _ as ex
```

```
        ->  printfn "Unhandled Exception: %s" ex.Message
            5

    // Return the exit code
    printfn "Exiting with code %d" exitCode
    exitCode
```

Because not catching an exception might prevent unmanaged resources from being freed, such as closing file handles or flushing buffers, there is a second way to catch process exceptions: try-finally expressions. In a try-finally expression, the code in the finally block is executed whether or not an exception is thrown, giving you an opportunity to do required cleanup work.

Example 4-19 demonstrates a try-finally expression in action.

Example 4-19. Try–finally expressions

```
> // Try-finally expressions
let tryFinallyTest() =
    try
        printfn "Before exception..."
        failwith "ERROR!"
        printfn "After exception raised..."
    finally
        printfn "Finally block executing..."

let test() =
    try
        tryFinallyTest()
    with
    | ex -> printfn "Exception caught with message: %s" ex.Message;;

val tryFinallyTest : unit -> unit
val test : unit -> unit

> test();;
Before exception...
Finally block executing...
Exception caught with message: ERROR!
val it : unit = ()
```

Unlike C#, Java, and other languages, there is no try-catch-finally expression in F#. If you need to clean up any resources within an exception handler, you must do it for each exception handler or simply after the try-catch block.

Reraising Exceptions

Sometimes, despite your best efforts to take corrective action for raised exceptions, you just can't fix the problem. In those situations, you can *reraise* the exception, which will allow the original exception to continue bubbling up from within an exception handler.

Example 4-20 demonstrates reraising an exception by using the `reraise` function.

Example 4-20. Reraise exceptions

```
// Retry a function throwing an exception N times before failing.
let tryWithBackoff f times =
    let mutable attempt = 1
    let mutable success = false

    while not success do
        try
            f()
            success <- true
        with ex ->
            attempt <- attempt + 1
            if attempt >= times then
                reraise()
```

Defining Exceptions

The reason for throwing specialized exceptions is for consumers of your code to only catch the exceptions they know how to handle. Other exceptions will then continue to bubble up until an appropriate exception handler is found.

You can define your own custom exceptions by creating types that inherit from `System.Exception`, which you will see in Chapter 5. However, in F#, there is an easier way to define exceptions using a lightweight exception syntax. Declaring exceptions in this way allows you to define them with the same syntax as discriminated unions.

Example 4-21 shows creating several new exception types, some of which are associated with data. The advantage of these lightweight exceptions is that when they are caught, they are easier to extract the relevant data from because you can use the same syntax for pattern matching against discriminated unions. Also, there is no need for a dynamic type test operator, `:?`, which we saw in previous examples.

Example 4-21. Lightweight F# exception syntax

```
open System
open System.Collections.Generic

exception NoMagicWand
exception NoFullMoon of int * int
exception BadMojo of string

let castHex (ingredients : HashSet<string>) =
```

```
try

    let currentWand = Environment.MagicWand

    if currentWand = null then
        raise NoMagicWand

    if not <| ingredients.Contains("Toad Wart") then
        raise <| BadMojo("Need Toad Wart to cast the hex!")

    if not <| isFullMoon(DateTime.Today) then
        raise <| NoFullMoon(DateTime.Today.Month, DateTime.Today.Day)

    // Begin the incantation...
    let mana =
        ingredients
        |> Seq.map (fun i -> i.GetHashCode())
        |> Seq.fold (+) 0

    sprintf "%x" mana
with
| NoMagicWand
    -> "Error: A magic wand is required to hex!"
| NoFullMoon(month, day)
    -> "Error: Hexes can only be cast during a full moon."
| BadMojo(msg)
    -> sprintf "Error: Hex failed due to bad mojo [%s]" msg
```

In Chapter 3, you looked at the functional style of programming, which provided some interesting ways to write code, but doesn't quite stand on its own. The purely functional style doesn't integrate well with the existing .NET framework class libraries and sometimes requires complicated solutions for simple problems.

In this chapter, you learned how to update values, which enables you to write new types of programs. Now you can use efficient collections to store program results, loop as necessary, and should any problems occur, throw exceptions.

Now you can make a choice for how to approach problems, and you can begin to see the value of multiparadigm computing. Some problems can be solved by simply building up a mutable data structure, whereas others can be built up through combining simple functions to transform immutable data. In F#, you have options.

In the next chapter, we look at object-oriented programming. This third paradigm of F# doesn't necessarily add much more computational power, but does provide a way for programmers to organize and abstract code.

Object-Oriented Programming

In this chapter, we cover the most widely used programming paradigm today: object-oriented programming. Mastering object-oriented programming is crucial for taking advantage of the existing frameworks and libraries available on .NET, as well as writing F# code that can be integrated into those libraries.

Programming with Objects

Software systems are the some of the most complex things created by man. Consider your typical .NET program: thousands if not millions of lines of source code, transformed into some intermediate language by compilers, then compiled again to machine code via a JITer, which then executes on a processor. Knowing the details about how each step works is just too much to handle.

Rather than sweating all the details of a program, object-oriented programming enables you to organize batches of code into conceptual objects, so that you can limit your interactions with code to small and well-defined interfaces.

The Benefits of OOP

There are several benefits to object-oriented programming:

Encourages code reuse
> By encapsulating your code into objects, it can be reused, which ultimately saves time and enhances productivity.

Tame complexity
> Rather than dealing with myriad individual functions and global variables, OOP allows you to deal with one item at a time. Any mutable state is scoped to just the object.

Specialization through inheritance

Using polymorphism, you can write code that deals with a base type of object, and still accepts any specialized instances of that type. This is another form of code reuse and is discussed later in this chapter.

Where OOP Breaks Down

Although OOP may work well for modeling some concepts, it isn't a silver bullet. To quote Bernard Baruch:

> *If all you have is a hammer, everything looks like a nail.*

OOP has a tough time encoding algorithms and abstract concepts. In order to represent these concepts, *design patterns* have cropped up to help describe abstractions in terms of objects and their relationships.

Although design patterns are helpful, they are often compensation for OOP's inability to simply express certain concepts. In addition, they can be a burden to the programmer by forcing the creation of boilerplate code in order to define the contract and relationships between objects.

F# not only offers object-oriented constructs, but also a new set of primitives—like discriminated unions and function values. These augment existing object-oriented facilities and remove the need for most boilerplate code found when implementing design patterns. In fact, some design patterns aren't necessary when using a functional language. For example, the *Command Pattern* (from *Design Patterns*, by Gamma et al., Addison-Wesley, 1995) describes an object that can be passed around and executed. You can achieve the same result by using higher order functions, which are baked into the F# language.

Understanding System.Object

.NET offers a rich type system that can check the identity of objects and guarantee type safety at runtime. By keeping track of the type of an object, the .NET runtime can ensure that square pegs aren't put into round holes.

To achieve this notion of object identity, everything from integers to strings to discriminated unions are instances of `System.Object` (abbreviated in F# by `obj`). An instance of `System.Object` isn't useful on its own, because it doesn't have any customizations. However, it is important to know the methods available on `System.Object` because they are available on every object you encounter in .NET.

If you are already familiar with .NET programming, feel free to skip ahead to the "Generated Equality" (page 139) section.

Common Methods

Each instance of `System.Object` comes with several methods that can be overridden or customized. For custom F# types (discriminated unions and records), some of these methods are overridden by the F# compiler automatically.

ToString

`ToString` produces a human-readable string representation of the object. In F#, this is the value that the `printf` format specifier `%A` or `%O` displays to the console. No formal guidelines exist for what this should return, although the result from `ToString` should be adequate to differentiate the object from others, as well as an aid in debugging. The default value is the full name of the class itself.

The following example defines a type `PunctuationMark` and provides an implementation of its `ToString` method. Without overriding `ToString`, the default message would look something like `"FSI_0002+PunctuationMark"`:

```
> // Overriding ToString
type PunctuationMark =
    | Period
    | Comma
    | QuestionMark
    | ExclamationPoint
    override this.ToString() =
        match this with
        | Period -> "Period (.)"
        | Comma    -> "Comma (,)"
        | QuestionMark      -> "QuestionMark (?)"
        | ExclamationPoint  -> "ExclamationPoint (!)";;

type PunctuationMark =
  | Period
  | Comma
  | QuestionMark
  | ExclamationPoint
  with
    override ToString : unit -> string
  end

> let x = Comma;;
```

```
val x : PunctuationMark = Comma

> x.ToString();;
val it : string = "Comma (,)"
```

GetHashCode

GetHashCode returns a hash value for the object. Overriding this function is crucial for the type to be used in collections such as Dictionary, HashSet, and Set. A hash code is a pseudo-unique identifier that describes a particular instance of the type. This makes it much more efficient to check if two objects are identical:

```
> "alpha".GetHashCode();;
val it : int = -1898387216
> "bravo".GetHashCode();;
val it : int = 1946920786
> "bravo".GetHashCode();;
val it : int = 1946920786
```

The default implementation is good enough for most situations, but if you ever override Equals, then you should also override GetHashCode.

 When overriding GetHashCode, you must ensure the following invariants in order for the type to work correctly in collections. Otherwise, the type will behave incorrectly when used with data structures that require a hash code (e.g., Dictionary<K, V>):

- If two objects are equal, then their hash code must be identical. The converse is not true; two different objects may have the same hash code. However, you should take care to avoid these hash collisions whenever possible.

- An object's hash code must remain consistent if no changes have been made to the object. If its internal state has been changed, then the hash code may change accordingly.

Equals

The equals function compares if two objects are equal. Equality in .NET is a complex topic; see the section "Object Equality" (page 137) later in this chapter.

```
> "alpha".Equals(4);;
val it : bool = false
> "alpha".Equals("alpha");;
val it : bool = true
```

If you override Equals, you must also override GetHashCode because if two objects are considered equal, then their hash codes must also match.

GetType

Finally, the GetType method returns an instance of System.Type, which is the type of the actual object. This is important for understanding what something is at runtime, and you will see much more of this when we cover reflection in Chapter 12:

```
> let stringType = "A String".GetType();;

val stringType : System.Type = System.String

> stringType.AssemblyQualifiedName;;
val it : string
= "System.String, mscorlib, Version=4.0.0.0, Culture=neutral,
  PublicKeyToken=b77a5c561934e089"
```

Object Equality

Equality among .NET types is a difficult subject that revolves around the fundamental type or identity of an object. As mentioned in Chapter 4, there are value types and reference types, and each has a different default mechanism for equality.

By default, value types are compared using a bit pattern, so for two objects that exist on the stack, each byte is compared to determine if they are identical. This is sufficient for primitive types:

```
> // Value type equality
let x = 42
let y = 42;;

val x : int = 42
val y : int = 42

> x = y;;
val it : bool = true
```

Reference types, on the other hand, need more complex semantics. In Example 5-1, values x and y are both instances of class ClassType constructed with the same value. However, despite having the same conceptual meaning they are not considered equal.

Example 5-1. Referential equality

```
> // Referential Equality
type ClassType(x : int) =
    member this.Value = x

let x = new ClassType(42)
let y = new ClassType(42);;
```

```
type ClassType =
  class
    new : x:int -> ClassType
    member Value : int
  end
val x : ClassType
val y : ClassType

> x = y;;
val it : bool = false
> x = x;;
val it : bool = true
```

The default meaning of equality for reference types is *referential equality*, which means that the two references point to the same object. In the previous example, x = x evaluated to true because x and x refer to the same memory address. However x = y evaluated to false because x and y refer to different memory addresses. This is not sufficient for many applications.

By overriding Object.Equals for a type, you can customize the meaning of equality. The following example defines ClassType2, which has a more meaningful notion of equality:

```
> // Overriding Equals
type ClassType2(x : int) =
    member this.Value = x
    override this.Equals(o : obj) =
        match o with
        | :? ClassType2 as other -> (other.Value = this.Value)
        | _ -> false
    override this.GetHashCode() = x

let x = new ClassType2(31)
let y = new ClassType2(31)
let z = new ClassType2(10000);;

type ClassType2 =
  class
    new : x:int -> ClassType2
    override Equals : o:obj -> bool
    override GetHashCode : unit -> int
    member Value : int
  end
val x : ClassType2
val y : ClassType2
val z : ClassType2
```

```
> x = y;;
val it : bool = true
> x = z;;
val it : bool = false
```

Generated Equality

Tuples, discriminated unions, and records behave exactly like you would expect; that is, two instances with the same set of values are considered equal, just like value types.

Tuples are considered equal if both tuples have the same number of elements, and each element is equal:

```
> let x = (1, 'a', "str");;

val x : int * char * string = (1, 'a', "str")

> x = x;;
val it : bool = true
> x = (1, 'a', "different str");;
val it : bool = false
> // Nested tuples
(x, x) = (x, (1, 'a', "str"));;
val it : bool = true
```

Records are considered equal if all of their fields have the same value:

```
> // Record equality
type RecType = { Field1 : string; Field2 : float }

let x = { Field1 = "abc"; Field2 = 3.5 }
let y = { Field1 = "abc"; Field2 = 3.5 }
let z = { Field1 = "XXX"; Field2 = 0.0 };;

type RecType =
  {Field1: string;
   Field2: float;}
val x : RecType = {Field1 = "abc";
                   Field2 = 3.5;}
val y : RecType = {Field1 = "abc";
                   Field2 = 3.5;}
val z : RecType = {Field1 = "XXX";
                   Field2 = 0.0;}

> x = y;;
val it : bool = true
> x = z;;val it : bool = false
```

Discriminated unions are considered equal if both values are of the same union case, and the tuples of data associated with the tags are equal:

```
> // Discriminated Union Equality
type DUType =
```

```
    | A of int * char
    | B

let x = A(1, 'k')
let y = A(1, 'k')
let z = B;;

type DUType =
   | A of int * char
   | B
val x : DUType = A (1,'k')
val y : DUType = A (1,'k')
val z : DUType = B

> x = y;;
val it : bool = true
> x = z;;
val it : bool = false
```

In reality, tuples, discriminated unions, and records are all reference types. So by default they should use reference equality, meaning that all the comparisons in the previous examples would evaluate to false. The reason this works is because the F# compiler overrides Equals and GetHashCode for you (providing what is known as *structural equality* semantics).

You can change the default behavior of generated equality should the need arise, either by overriding Equals and GetHashCode yourself, or by adding the ReferenceEquali ty attribute.

Example 5-2 shows creating a discriminated union type that uses referential equality.

Example 5-2. Customizing generated equality

```
> // Referential Equality on Functional Types
[<ReferenceEquality>]
type RefDUType =
    | A of int * char
    | B;;

type RefDUType =
   | A of int * char
   | B

> // Declare two conceputally equal values
let x = A(4, 'A')
let y = A(4, 'A');;

val x : RefDUType = A (4,'A')
val y : RefDUType = A (4,'A')
```

```
> x = y;;
val it : bool = false
> x = x;;
val it : bool = true
```

Understanding Classes

With knowledge of what a basic obj can do, let's look at how we can create class types of our own. Classes on the simplest level are functions glued to data. Data associated with a class are known as *fields*. Functions associated with a class are known as either *properties* or *members*.

We cover each aspect of fields, methods, properties, and related concepts all in due time. But creating a new class isn't going to be useful unless you can initialize it with some initial state. Classes have special methods called *constructors*, whose job is to initialize the class's fields.

A class's constructor is called when it is created by a call to new, and may not be invoked again once the class has been instantiated.

F# features two separate syntaxes for defining class constructors: explicit constructors and implicit constructors. One is in line with F#'s simple yet terse syntax, whereas the other allows for more explicit control over how the class is generated.

Explicit Construction

The explicit class construction syntax is the least pleasant way to construct a class, but provides the greatest degree of control. When you define a class using this syntax, you must explicitly name each class field and initialize each field within a constructor.

Class fields are prefixed with the val keyword and are accessed by using the *self identifier*, discussed later. Example 5-3 defines a new class called Point that has two fields, m_x and m_y. The class has two constructors, one that takes two parameters and another that takes none.

Example 5-3. Explicit class construction syntax

```
type Point =
    val m_x : float
    val m_y : float

    // Constructor 1 - Takes two parameters
    new (x, y) = { m_x = x; m_y = y }

    // Constructor 2 - Takes no parameters
    new () = { m_x = 0.0; m_y = 0.0 }

    member this.Length =
        let sqr x = x * x
```

```
        sqrt <| sqr this.m_x + sqr this.m_y

let p1 = new Point(1.0, 1.0)
let p2 = new Point()
```

 In C#, a default constructor is provided if you don't define any custom constructors. This is not the case in F#. In F#, you can define a class without a constructor, but then there would be no way to instantiate that class!

You can have arbitrary code execute before or after the class's fields are initialized to perform a limited set of setup actions. To perform an action before the class's fields are set, simply write code after the equals sign; to perform actions after the fields are initialized, use the then keyword followed by an expression, which must evaluate to unit.

Example 5-4 adds an explicit constructor to our Point type that takes a string, called text, as a parameter. Then, several new values are introduced as the string is parsed. Next, the class's fields, m_x and m_y, are initialized. Finally, after the fields are initialized, a message is printed to the console.

Example 5-4. Arbitrary execution before explicit constructor

```
open System

type Point2 =
    val m_x : float
    val m_y : float

    // Parse a string, e.g. "1.0, 2.0"
    new (text : string) as this =
        // Do any required pre processing
        if text = null then
            raise <| new ArgumentException("text")

        let parts = text.Split([| ',' |])
        let (successX, x) = Double.TryParse(parts.[0])
        let (successY, y) = Double.TryParse(parts.[1])

        if not successX || not successY then
            raise <| new ArgumentException("text")
        // Initialize class fields
        { m_x = x; m_y = y }
        then
            // Do any post processing
            printfn
                "Initialized to [%f, %f]"
                this.m_x
                this.m_y
```

Implicit Class Construction

Although explicit class construction follows typical object-oriented programming styles, it seems rather unnatural in functional programming. Implicit class construction is a simpler way to define classes and fits more naturally with the F# language.

With an implicit constructor, there are no explicit fields (val-bindings); instead, you can use let-bindings inside of the type's definition. When the class is compiled, the let-bindings will be compiled as class fields or simply optimized away. So although the implicit class construction syntax doesn't allow you to explicitly specify class fields, it does clean up the code for creating classes.

To create a type with an implicit constructor, simply add parentheses and arguments after the type name. The arguments will serve as parameters to the type's *primary constructor*. Any let-bindings or do-bindings in the body of the class will execute during its construction. Additional constructors defined must end up calling the primary constructor, which ensures all let-bindings are initialized.

Example 5-5 shows creating a class using the implicit class construction syntax. The example performs the same task of parsing a 2-D point from a string, except it adds an additional constructor that takes two floating-point values. This will serve as the class's primary constructor.

Example 5-5. Implicit class construction

```
type Point3(x : float, y : float) =

    let length =
        let sqr x = x * x
        sqrt <| sqr x + sqr y
    do printfn "Initialized to [%f, %f]" x y

    member this.X = x
    member this.Y = y
    member this.Length = length

    // Define custom constructors, these must
    // call the 'main' constructor
    new() = new Point3(0.0, 0.0)

    // Define a second constructor.
    new(text : string) =
        if text = null then
            raise <| new ArgumentException("text")

        let parts = text.Split([| ',' |])
        let (successX, x) = Double.TryParse(parts.[0])
        let (successY, y) = Double.TryParse(parts.[1])
```

```
    if not successX || not successY then
        raise <| new ArgumentException("text")
    // Calls the primary constructor
    new Point3(x, y)
```

The primary constructor's parameters, as well as any let-bindings, are accessible anywhere within the class and do not need to be prefixed with the self identifier. In the previous example, the values x and y—parameters of the primary constructor—were available as well as the length value defined in a let-binding.

 Having two syntaxes for creating classes seems redundant. The preferred way to create classes is to use the implicit class construction format, and only rely on the explicit class construction syntax when you need to have explicit control over the class's fields.

Generic Classes

In Chapter 2, we covered generic functions, or functions that accepted input of any type. This concept also extends to classes, enabling you to define a type that can be a collection of other types. For example, the F# list and seq types are generic, because you can have lists and sequences of any type (e.g., a list of strings or a seq of floats).

To add a generic type parameter to a class, use angle brackets after the class name. From then on, refer to the type parameter name if you need to refer to the generic type. For example:

```
    type GenericClass<'a, 'b>() = ...
```

Just like in generic functions, generic type parameters are prefixed with an apostrophe ('). It is the convention in F# to name generic type parameters 'a, 'b, 'c, and so on.

Example 5-6 defines a generic class Arrayify whose primary constructor takes a generic parameter, x, and contains properties that return arrays filled with x of various sizes.

Example 5-6. Defining generic classes

```
> // Define a generic class
type Arrayify<'a>(x : 'a) =
    member this.EmptyArray : 'a[] = [| |]
    member this.ArraySize1 : 'a[] = [| x |]
    member this.ArraySize2 : 'a[] = [| x; x |]
    member this.ArraySize3 : 'a[] = [| x; x; x |];;

type Arrayify<'a> =
  class
    new : x:'a -> Arrayify<'a>
    member ArraySize1 : 'a []
    member ArraySize2 : 'a []
```

```
      member ArraySize3 : 'a []
      member EmptyArray : 'a []
   end

> let arrayifyTuple = new Arrayify<int * int>( (10, 27) );;

val arrayifyTuple : Arrayify<int * int>

> arrayfiyTuple.ArraySize3;;
val it : (int * int) [] = [|(10, 27); (10, 27); (10, 27)|]
```

It is worth noting that the generic type may be omitted by using a wildcard (<_>) and having the parameter's type be inferred by the F# compiler. In the following snippet, based on the value of x passed to Arrayify's constructor, the generic type parameter is inferred to be of type string:

```
> let inferred = new Arrayify<_>( "a string" );;

val inferred : Arrayify<string>
```

Records and discriminated unions can be declared generic as well. The following snippet defines a generic discriminate union type:

```
> // Generic discriminated union
type GenDU<'a> =
    | Tag1 of 'a
    | Tag2 of string * 'a list;;

type GenDU<'a> =
  | Tag1 of 'a
  | Tag2 of string * 'a list

> Tag2("Primary Colors", [ 'R'; 'G'; 'B' ]);;
val it : GenDU<char> = Tag2 ("Primary Colors",['R'; 'G'; 'B'])
```

The following snippet defines a generic record type:

```
> type GenRec<'a, 'b> = { Field1 : 'a; Field2 : 'b };;

type GenRec<'a,'b> =
  {Field1: 'a;
   Field2: 'b;}

> let x = { Field1 = "Blue"; Field2 = 'C' };;

val x : GenRec<string,char> = {Field1 = "Blue";
                               Field2 = 'C';}
```

The Self Identifier

In the previous examples, you may have noticed a curious `this` before each method name. In the examples, `this` was the name of the self identifier, which allows you to refer to the instance of the class inside of any of its methods. It doesn't have to be called `this`; in fact, it could be called any valid identifier.

Example 5-7 shows defining a class with oddly named self identifiers. Note that the identifier used to name the self identifier is only scoped to the method or property.

Example 5-7. Naming the this-pointer

```
open System

type Circle =
    val m_radius : float

    new(r) = { m_radius = r }
    member foo.Radius = foo.m_radius
    member bar.Area = Math.PI * bar.Radius * bar.Radius
```

 Obviously, the name of the self identifier should be consistent for every member of a class.

The examples in this book typically name it `this`, to closer match the C# equivalent. However, in idiomatic F# code, you'll rarely need to refer to the self identifier, so it is common to give it a short name such as `x`, or even a double underscore, `__`. (A single underscore, `_`, is not a valid self identifier name.)

Methods and Properties

Classes are given meaning by their methods and properties. Methods are actions—verbs—that describe what the type can do or have done to it. Properties, on the other hand, are attributes—adjectives—that help describe the type.

Properties

The best way to describe when to use properties is to identify the problems that they solve.

How should a type expose its data? In order to interact with a type, it might seem useful to expose its internal fields so that clients can manipulate them. However, this anti-pattern can lead to some bad situations:

```
// Class for controlling all global proton streams.
// (Not valid F# code)
type StreamManager =
```

```
// Public field exposing rather delicate data...
val public streams : List<Stream>

new() = { streams = new List<Stream>() }

// Verifies that the streams aren't crossed. What would happen if
// they do happen to get in a bad state? From Dr. Spengler:
//
// "Try to imagine all life as you know it stopping  instantaneously
// and every molecule in your body exploding at the speed of light."
member this.CheckStreamsAren'tCrossed() = ...
```

Don't worry if you missed the movie reference in snippet above, but the moral of the story is that—in addition to not crossing the streams—you should avoid exposing data directly to clients. The solution is to create *accessor* methods in front of fields.

The following snippet wraps an internal field of type Widget by a *getter* and *setter* accessor method:

```
type FancyMachine() =
    let mutable m_widget = Widget.FromSerialNumber("tuacm-2004")

    member this.GetWidget() = m_widget
    member this.SetWidget(newWidget) =
        // Clone newWidget so that it may change after this call to
        // SetWidget without modifying m_widget.
        m_widget <- newWidget.Clone()
```

Although the getters and setters make sure the type can be used correctly, the approach makes code a little more cumbersome to read. This is where properties come in.

In short, properties are simply syntactic sugar on top of accessor methods, and come in three different flavors: read-only, write-only, and read/write. A property *getter* is defined with the get keyword and returns the property value, whereas a property *setter*, defined with the set keyword, updates the property value.

The syntax for defining a read-only property is simply a method with no arguments. For more explicit control, you can provide with get and with set methods.

Example 5-8 shows creating a simple read-only property as well as a more complex property with both a getter and a setter. To invoke the setter, use the left arrow operator, <-, as if setting a mutable value.

Example 5-8. Defining class properties

```
> // Define a WaterBottle type with two properties
[<Measure>]
type ml

type WaterBottle() =
    let mutable m_amount = 0.0<ml>
```

```
    // Read-only property
    member this.Empty = (m_amount = 0.0<ml>)

    // Read/write property
    member this.Amount with get ()      = m_amount
                        and  set newAmt = m_amount <- newAmt;;


[<Measure>]
type ml
type WaterBottle =
  class
    new : unit -> WaterBottle
    member Amount : float<ml>
    member Empty : bool
    member Amount : float<ml> with set
  end

> let bottle = new WaterBottle();;

val bottle : WaterBottle

> bottle.Empty;;
val it : bool = true
> bottle.Amount <- 1000.0<ml>;;
val it : unit = ()
> bottle.Empty;;
val it : bool = false
```

Auto-properties

Creating a mutable classfield, and exposing it through a property, is a common practice
and semi-tedious. To simplify this pattern, F# supports *automatically implemented
properties*, which adds *even more* syntactic sugar to accessor methods by hiding the
backing field.

The previous WaterBottle example could be rewritten as the following:

```
    type WaterBottle() =
        member this.Empty = (this.Amount = 0.0<ml>)

        // Auto-property, initialized to 0.0<ml>
        member val Amount = 0.0<ml> with get, set
```

The val ... get, set means that both a getter and setter should be automatically
generated with the backing field initialized to 0.0<ml>.

Auto-properties should be used whenever you don't need any custom logic in the property getter or setter. This approach might seem unnecessary compared to just exposing the field itself, but by requiring clients to access data through a property now, you can later add custom logic in front of the data access without requiring a breaking change. That is, changing the auto-property to a regular one with custom logic.

Setting Properties in the Constructor

Properties simply provide an easy way to access data for a type, but it is worth noting that you can set properties as additional arguments to a class's constructor. This simplifies the code required to construct an object and set it up the way you want.

Example 5-9 shows two ways for constructing an identical Form object, in the System.Windows.Forms namespace. The first way constructs the object and sets properties individually. The second sets the properties as part of the class's constructor. This is just syntactic sugar for setting the properties individually after the constructor has executed.

Example 5-9. Setting properties after the class's constructor

```
open System.Windows.Forms

// Attempt one - The hard way
let f1 = new Form()
f1.Text    <- "Window Title"
f1.TopMost <- true
f1.Width   <- 640
f1.Height  <- 480
f1.ShowDialog()

// Attempt two - The easy way
let f2 = new Form(Text    = "Window Title",
                  TopMost = true,
                  Width   = 640,
                  Height  = 480)
f2.ShowDialog()
```

Methods

To add methods to a class, specify a self identifier followed by the function name after the member keyword. Just like function values, any pattern rules after the function's name are its parameters. And, just like functions, to define a method that takes no parameters, simply have it take unit as a parameter:

```
type Television =

    val mutable m_channel : int
    val mutable m_turnedOn : bool
```

```
new() = { m_channel = 3; m_turnedOn = true }

member this.TurnOn() =
    printfn "Turning on..."
    this.m_turnedOn <- true

member this.TurnOff() =
    printfn "Turning off..."
    this.m_turnedOn <- false

member this.ChangeChannel(newChannel : int) =
    if this.m_turnedOn = false then
        failwith "Cannot change channel, the TV is not on."

    printfn "Changing channel to %d..." newChannel
    this.m_channel <- newChannel

member this.CurrentChannel = this.m_channel
```

Class methods can be partially applied, just like function values. However, this is not recommended, because other .NET languages do not support this. The best practice is to have all parameters wrapped in a single tuple. When referenced from other languages, your F# code won't look like it takes a single parameter of type Tuple, but rather a parameter for each element of the tuple, like you would expect:

```
> // Demonstration of tupled args versus "curried" args.
type Adder() =
    // AddTwoParams can be partially applied. Providing one parameter
    // will return a function object, accepting one more parameter.
    member this.AddTwoParams x y = x + y
    // Normal arguments
    member this.AddTwoTupledParams(x, y) = x + y;;

type Adder =
  class
    new : unit -> Adder
    member AddTwoParams : x:int -> y:int -> int
    member AddTwoTupledParams : x:int * y:int -> int
  end

> let adder = new Adder();;

val adder : Adder

> let add10 = adder.AddTwoParams 10;;

val add10 : (int -> int)

> adder.AddTwoTupledParams(1, 2);;
val it : int = 3
```

A notable difference between class methods and function values is that class methods can be recursive without needing to use the rec keyword.

.NET design guidelines state that methods and properties should be named in Pascal case, meaning every word is capitalized including the first word. DoStuff is a recommending naming instead of doStuff or do_stuff.

For more information on .NET conventions, see *Framework Design Guidelines* by Abrams and Cwalina (Addison-Wesley, 2008).

Static Methods, Properties, and Fields

We've now seen methods and properties, which are functions associated with a particular instance of a type. But what if you want a method that is associated with the type itself and not a particular instance? For example, the Environment class in the System namespace has properties to describe the current computer, like the machine name. The current machine name isn't conceptually associated with a particular instance of System.Environment so it seems strange to require an instance of the type in order to access the MachineName property. (The MachineName property should already exist in memory, and not require allocating a new object.)

To declare a method or property that can be accessed without an instance of the type, you need to mark it as *static*. This means that the method or property cannot access anything referenced from the self identifier, such as class fields, but can be called without having an instance of the type.

To define a static method, simply use the static keyword before a method declaration without declaring a self identifier. Example 5-10 shows creating a static method for class SomeClass. To call a static method, you must fully qualify the type and the method name; otherwise it will lead to a compiler error.

Example 5-10. Static methods

```
> // Declaring a static method
type SomeClass() =
    static member StaticMember() = 5;;

type SomeClass =
  class
    new : unit -> SomeClass
    static member StaticMember : unit -> int
  end

> SomeClass.StaticMember();;
val it : int = 5
> let x = new SomeClass();;
```

```
val x : SomeClass

> x.StaticMember();;

  x.StaticMember();;
  ^^^^^^^^^^^^^^^^^

stdin(39,1): error FS0809: StaticMember is not an instance method
```

Static methods are usually associated with utility classes and are not typical in F# code. When you find the need to write many static methods relating to a type, consider organizing methods into an F# module.

Static fields

Class fields can also be marked as `static`, meaning there is a piece of data associated with a type that is accessible through any instance (rather than having a custom copy of the value for each instance of the class).

Static fields typically serve as global constants. However, mutable static fields can be useful as well. Example 5-11 defines a class `RareType` which whenever its primary constructor executes, the static field is decremented by one. Once the static field `m_num Left` is zero, an exception is raised preventing the class from being instantiated again. Without one shared value between each instance of `RareType`, this wouldn't be possible.

Example 5-11. Creating and using static fields

```
// Static fields
type RareType() =

    // There is only one instance of m_numLeft for all instances of RareType
    static let mutable m_numLeft = 2

    do
        if m_numLeft <= 0 then
            failwith "No more left!"
        m_numLeft <- m_numLeft - 1
        printfn "Initialized a rare type, only %d left!" m_numLeft

    static member NumLeft = m_numLeft
```

The following FSI session shows the type winding down:

```
> let a = new RareType();;

val a : RareType

Initialized a rare type, only 1 left!
> let b = new RareType();;
```

```
val b : RareType

Initialized a rare type, only 0 left!
> let c = new RareType();;

val c : RareType

System.Exception: No more left!
   at FSI_0012.RareType..ctor() in C:\Users\chrsmith\Desktop\Ch05.fsx:line 18
   at <StartupCode$FSI_0015>.$FSI_0015._main()
stopped due to error
> RareType.NumLeft;;
val it : int = 0
```

Method Overloading

Often you'll create a very useful method that you want to customize with different sets of parameters. This saves you the hassle of needing to convert your data into the exact types the method needs. Creating a method that has the same name but accepts a different number or different types of arguments is known as *method overloading*.

For example, the System.Console.WriteLine method has 19 different overloads! This might seem like a lot, but if you want to print an integer, you can use the overload that takes an int:

```
System.Console.WriteLine(42)
```

Otherwise, you would need to convert the int parameter to a string first, which would quickly become annoying:

```
System.Console.WriteLine((42).ToString())
```

In Example 5-12, the method CountBits is overridden to accept arguments of any primitive integer types.

Example 5-12. Method overloading in F#

```
type BitCounter =

    static member CountBits (x : int16) =
        let mutable x' = x
        let mutable numBits = 0
        for i = 0 to 15 do
            numBits <- numBits + int (x' &&& 1s)
            x' <- x' >>> 1
        numBits

    static member CountBits (x : int) =
        let mutable x' = x
        let mutable numBits = 0
        for i = 0 to 31 do
            numBits <- numBits + int (x' &&& 1)
```

```
        x' <- x' >>> 1
    numBits

static member CountBits (x : int64) =
    let mutable x' = x
    let mutable numBits = 0
    for i = 0 to 63 do
        numBits <- numBits + int (x' &&& 1L)
        x' <- x' >>> 1
    numBits
```

Accessibility Modifiers

You can now create classes to encapsulate the complex inner workings of your abstractions. However, if consumers of your classes can access every method, property, or field, they could inadvertently modify some internal state and introduce bugs.

Limiting member visibility is important so that when you share your type across assembly boundaries, consumers can only use the methods and properties you specify.

In F#, you can control the visibility of a type or method by providing an *accessibility modifier*. In Example 5-13, the type Ruby is marked internal, and its primary constructor is private, whereas its other constructors are all public. Attempting to call or access a private value, method, property, or constructor will lead to a compiler error.

Example 5-13. Accessibility modifiers

```
open System

type internal Ruby private(shininess, carats) =

    let mutable m_size = carats
    let mutable m_shininess = shininess

    // Polishing increases shiness but decreases size
    member this.Polish() =
        this.Size    <- this.Size - 0.1
        m_shininess <- m_shininess + 0.1

    // Public getter, private setter
    member public  this.Size with get ()     = m_size
    member private this.Size with set newSize = m_size <- newSize

    member this.Shininess = m_shininess

    public new() =
        let rng = new Random()
        let s = float (rng.Next() % 100) * 0.01
        let c = float (rng.Next() % 16) + 0.1
        new Ruby(s, c)
```

```
public new(carats) =
    let rng = new Random()
    let s = float (rng.Next() % 100) * 0.01
    new Ruby(s, carats)
```

The specific visibility for all three types of accessibility modifiers in F# is described in Table 5-1. The default accessibility for types, members, and functions in F# is `public`. The default accessibility for class fields (`val` and `let` bindings) is `private`.

Table 5-1. Accessibility modifiers

Accessibility Modifier	Visibility
public	`public` visibility means that the method or property is visible from anywhere. This is the default for all types, values, and functions in F#.
private	`private` visibility limits the value to only be available in that class. Outside callers cannot access the value, nor can derived classes. This is the default for class fields.
internal	`internal` visibility is the same as `public`; however, this only extends to the current assembly. `internal` types will not be accessible from another assembly—as if they had originally been declared `private`.

 Unlike C#, there is no *protected* visibility. However, F# will honor protected visibility on types inherited from languages that support protected inheritance.

Accessibility modifiers on module values

Accessibility modifiers can be applied to more than just classes; they work on values defined in modules as well.

Example 5-14 defines a `Logger` module, which has a private mutable value, `m_file sToWriteTo`. This value is only visible from within the module, so it can safely expose methods `AddLogFile` and `LogMessage` without needing to check that `m_filesToWrite To` is `null` (because if `m_filesToWriteTo` were public, a caller could accidentally replace its value).

Example 5-14. Accessibility modifiers in modules

```
open System.IO
open System.Collections.Generic

module Logger =

    let mutable private m_filesToWriteTo = new List<string>()

    let AddLogFile(filePath) = m_filesToWriteTo.Add(filePath)

    let LogMessage(message : string) =
```

```
      for logFile in m_filesToWriteTo do
          use file = new StreamWriter(logFile, true)
          file.WriteLine(message)
          file.Close()
```

F# signature files

Accessibility modifiers are key to limiting scope and encapsulation, but providing the correct accessibility modifiers to every type method and value adds a lot of clutter to your code. The cleanest way to control accessibility across an entire file is to use an *F# signature file*. A signature file, suffixed with the .fsi extension, allows you to specify a signature for an entire code file. Anything in the code file but not in the signature is assumed to have private accessibility. This provides a simple way to bulk annotate your code.

Example 5-15 shows a code file and the corresponding signature file. The signature file defines a class with a constructor and two methods. In the corresponding implementation file, there are additional methods and properties, and even though those methods and properties aren't explicitly marked private, they will be compiled as such. Also, because the signature file specifies that the type is internal, it will be compiled with that accessibility. If no accessibility is specified in the .fsi file, the member will have public accessibility.

An error will be raised if the implementation file has a lower visibility than the signature file.

 .fsi signature files are best used for F# modules intended to be referenced by other projects. They also form a primitive kind of documentation.

Example 5-15. Example .fsi and .fs files

```
// File.fsi
namespace MyProject.Utilities

type internal MyClass =
    new : unit -> MyClass
    member public Property1 : int
    member private Method1 : int * int -> int

// File.fs
namespace MyProject.Utilities

type internal MyClass() =
```

```
member this.Property1 = 10
member this.Property2 with set (x : int) = ()
member this.Method1 (x, y) = x + y
member this.Method2 () = true
```

Inheritance

So far I have covered classes, but not *polymorphism*, which is the magic that makes object-oriented programming so powerful. Consider the following two classes: a delicious BLTSandwich and the standard TurkeyAndSwissSandwich.

```
type BLTSandwich() =
    member this.Ingredients = ["Bacon"; "Lettuce"; "Tomato"]
    member this.Calories = 450
    override this.ToString() = "BLT"

type TurkeySwissSandwich() =
    member this.Ingredients = ["Turkey"; "Swiss"]
    member this.Calories = 330
    override this.ToString() = "Turkey and Swiss"
```

Even though both classes are nearly identical, they are different entities. So in order to write a function that accepts either an instance of BLTSandwich or an instance of TurkeySwissSandwich, you will need to resort to method overloading. Also, we would have to add a new overload method whenever we added a new sandwich type:

```
member this.EatLunch(sandwich : BLTSandwich) = (*...*)

member this.EatLunch(sandwich : TurkeySwissSandwich) = (*...*)

// This will need to be added later...
member this.EatLunch(sandwich : ClubSandwich) = (*...*)
```

The right way to think about this is that both of these tasty snacks are specializations of the same base type—Sandwich—and can customize the general properties and methods of a Sandwich. Each specialization of Sandwich will have a different calorie count and list of ingredients.

Moreover, you can continue to create a *class hierarchy* to specialize even further—perhaps create a BLTWithPicklesSandwich type. This is exactly how inheritance and polymorphism works.

Inheritance is the ability to create a new class that inherits the methods and properties of a *base class*, as well as the ability to add new methods and properties and/or customize existing ones. So in this example, BLTSandwich is a specialization, or *derived class*, of Sandwich, with its own custom implementations of the Calories and Ingredients properties.

Polymorphism is the ability to treat any derived class like an instance of its base class (because you know that the derived class has all of the methods and properties of its base).

The syntax for inheriting from a class is to add the line **inherit** *type* under the type declaration. The syntax is slightly different between explicit and implicit class construction syntax.

When using the implicit class construction syntax, simply add the base class constructor you want to call immediately after the `inherit` declaration in the primary constructor. Be sure to provide any applicable parameters to the base class's constructor:

```
// Base class
type BaseClass =
    val m_field1 : int

    new(x) = { m_field1 = x }
    member this.Field1 = this.m_field1

// Derived class using implicit class construction
type ImplicitDerived(field1, field2) =
    inherit BaseClass(field1)

    let m_field2 : int = field2

    member this.Field2 = m_field2
```

When using explicit class construction, you call the desired base class constructor by putting **inherit** type (constructor arguments) in the field initialization of the class:

```
// Derived class using explicit class construction
type ExplicitDerived =
    inherit BaseClass

    val m_field2 : int

    new(field1, field2) =
        {
            inherit BaseClass(field1)
            m_field2 = field2
        }

    member this.Field2 = this.m_field2
```

Method Overriding

The key to customization in derived classes is a technique called *method overriding*, which allows you to redefine what a method does.

To communicate that a method or property can be overridden in F#, mark it as ab stract. In Example 5-16, type Sandwich has two abstract properties, Ingredients and Calories. To provide a default implementation for these methods, you use the de fault keyword before the member declaration.

To override or customize the implementation of a base class's method in a derived class, use the override keyword before the member declaration. (Just like you have seen for overriding System.Object's ToString method.) From then on, when that method is called, the derived class's version will be used instead of the base class'.

Example 5-16. Method overriding in F#

```
type Sandwich() =
    abstract Ingredients : string list
    default this.Ingredients = []

    abstract Calories : int
    default this.Calories = 0

type BLTSandwich() =
    inherit Sandwich()

    override this.Ingredients = ["Bacon"; "Lettuce"; "Tomato"]
    override this.Calories    = 330

type TurkeySwissSandwich() =
    inherit Sandwich()

    override this.Ingredients = ["Turkey"; "Swiss"]
    override this.Calories = 330
```

To access the base class explicitly, you use the base keyword. Example 5-17 defines a new class, BLTWithPickleSandwich, which accesses its base class to print its new in-gredients and increase its calories.

Example 5-17. Accessing the base class

```
> // BLT with pickles
type BLTWithPickleSandwich() =
    inherit BLTSandwich()

    override this.Ingredients = "Pickles" :: base.Ingredients
    override this.Calories    = 50 + base.Calories;;

type BLTWithPickleSandwich =
  class
    inherit BLTSandwich
    new : unit -> BLTWithPickleSandwich
    override Calories : int
    override Ingredients : string list
  end
```

```
> let lunch = new BLTWithPickleSandwich();;

val lunch : BLTWithPickleSandwich

> lunch.Ingredients;;
val it : string list = ["Pickles"; "Bacon"; "Lettuce"; "Tomato"]
```

Categories of Classes

With the ability to create a class hierarchy, you have the choice of what to do with the classes higher in the tree and the ones at the very bottom.

Nodes at the top may represent *abstract classes*, which are so general that they might not actually exist. In a previous example, we defined a Sandwich class, for which we provided a default implementation for its abstract members. But not every abstract member has a meaningful default implementation.

To continue with our sandwich example, type Sandwich might inherit from Food, which inherits from System.Object. Class Food cannot provide any meaningful defaults for its methods, and thus would need to be declared abstract.

At the bottom of the class hierarchy are things so specific that they cannot further be specialized. Although BLTNoPicklesLightMayo could be the foundation for BLTNoPick lesLightMayoOrganicLettuce, there isn't a need to customize the behavior of System .String.

In .NET, you can annotate these topmost and bottommost classes in a special way to help define how your classes get used.

Abstract classes

Abstract classes are typically the root objects in hierarchies and are not whole on their own. In fact, you cannot instantiate a class marked as abstract, or otherwise you could potentially call a method that hasn't been defined.

To create an abstract class, simply apply the [<AbstractClass>] attribute to the class declaration. Otherwise you will get an error for not providing a default implementation for abstract remembers:

```
> // ERROR: Define a class without providing an implementation to its members
type Foo() =
    member this.Alpha() = true
    abstract member Bravo : unit -> bool;;

  type Foo() =
  -----^^^

stdin(2,6): error FS0365: No implementation was given for 'abstract member
 Foo.Bravo : unit -> bool'
```

```
> // Properly define an abstract class
[<AbstractClass>]
type Bar() =
    member this.Alpha() = true
    abstract member Bravo : unit -> bool;;

type Bar =
  class
    new : unit -> Bar
    abstract member Bravo : unit -> bool
    member Alpha : unit -> bool
  end
```

Sealed classes

If abstract classes are those that you must inherit from, *sealed classes* are those that you cannot inherit from. To seal a class, simply add the [<Sealed>] attribute.

```
> // Define a sealed class
[<Sealed>]
type Foo() =
    member this.Alpha() = true;;

type Foo =
  class
    new : unit -> Foo
    member Alpha : unit -> bool
  end

> // ERROR: Inherit from a sealed class
type Bar() =
    inherit Foo()
    member this.Bravo() = false;;

    inherit Foo()
----.^^^^^^^^^^^^^

stdin(19,5): error FS0191: Cannot inherit a sealed type
```

Sealing a class enables certain compiler optimizations, because the compiler knows that virtual methods cannot be overridden. It also prevents a certain kind of security bug in which a malicious user creates a derived class for an object used for authentication, allowing her to spoof credentials.

Casting

A key advantage of polymorphism is that you can take an instance of a derived class and treat it like its base class. So in our previous examples, every class in the Sandwich hierarchy had a Calories property and an Ingredients property. To take an instance of a type and convert it to another type in the class hierarchy, you can use a *cast* operator.

Casting is a way to convert types between one another. There are two types of casts—*static* and *dynamic*—which are based on the direction you cast (up or down) the inheritance chain.

Static upcast

A static upcast is where an instance of a derived class is cast as one of its base classes, or cast to something higher up the inheritance tree. It is done using the static cast operator, :>. The result is an instance of the targeted class.

Example 5-18 creates a class hierarchy where Pomeranian is a type of Dog, which is a type of Animal. By using a static upcast we can convert an instance of Pomeranian into an instance of Dog or Animal. Anything can be upcast to obj.

Example 5-18. Static upcasts

```
> // Define a class hierarchy
[<AbstractClass>]
type Animal() =
    abstract member Legs : int

[<AbstractClass>]
type Dog() =
    inherit Animal()
    abstract member Description : string
    override this.Legs = 4

type Pomeranian() =
    inherit Dog()
    override this.Description = "Furry";;

... snip ...


> let steve = new Pomeranian()

val steve : Pomeranian

> // Casting Steve as various types
let steveAsDog    = steve :> Dog
let steveAsAnimal = steve :> Animal
let steveAsObject = steve :> obj;;

val steveAsDog : Dog
val steveAsAnimal : Animal
val steveAsObject : obj
```

Dynamic cast

A dynamic cast is when you cast a base type as a derived type, or cast something down the inheritance tree (therefore, this type of cast cannot be checked statically by the compiler). This allows you to cast any peg—circular or not—into a round hole, which could lead to failures at runtime.

The most common use of a dynamic cast is when you have an instance of System.Object and you know that it is actually something else. To perform a dynamic cast, use the dynamic cast operator, :?>. Building off of our previous example, we can cast our steveAsObj value, which is of type obj to a Dog by employing a dynamic cast:

```
> let steveAsObj = steve :> obj;;

val steveAsObj : obj

> let steveAsDog = steveAsObj :?> Dog;;

val steveAsDog : Dog

> steveAsDog.Description;;
val it : string = "Furry"
```

If a type is converted to something it is not, the error will be caught at runtime and result in a System.InvalidCastException exception:

```
> let _ = steveAsObj :?> string;;
System.InvalidCastException: Unable to cast object of type 'Pomeranian' to
 type 'System.String'.
   at <StartupCode$FSI_0022>.$FSI_0022._main()
stopped due to error
```

Pattern matching against types

When you use dynamic casts, if the cast fails, an exception is raised, so you cannot test the type of an object without the unnecessary overhead of exception handling. Fortunately, you can use a dynamic type test as part of a pattern match to simplify type checking using the :? operator.

Example 5-19 shows a function whatIs which takes an object and matches it against several known types. If the type is not known, it calls the GetType method, from System.Object, and prints the name to the console.

It is worth noting that the **as** ident trailing the dynamic type test in the pattern match binds a new value with type equal to the type tested. So in the example, value s has type string and not obj.

Example 5-19. Type tests in a pattern match

```
> // Pattern matching against types
let whatIs (x : obj) =
```

```
  match x with
  | :? string    as s -> printfn "x is a string \"%s\"" s
  | :? int       as i -> printfn "x is an int %d" i
  | :? list<int> as l -> printfn "x is an int list '%A'" l
  | _ -> printfn "x is a '%s'" <| x.GetType().Name;;

val whatIs : obj -> unit

> whatIs [1 .. 5];;
x is an int list '[1; 2; 3; 4; 5]'
val it : unit = ()
> whatIs "Rosebud";;
x is a string "Rosebud"
val it : unit = ()
> whatIs (new System.IO.FileInfo(@"C:\config.sys"));;
x is a 'FileInfo'
val it : unit = ()
```

Although there is plenty more to learn about OOP, and especially object-oriented design, you now can create classes and use inheritance to organize and reuse your code. This enables you to write code in F# to utilize its strengths—data exploration, quantitative computing, etc.—and package the code up to integrate with object-oriented languages like C#.

.NET Programming

The .NET platform is a general-purpose programming platform that can do more than just object-oriented or functional programming. This chapter covers some additional concepts available when using .NET that will offer advantages when you put them to use in your F# code.

In this chapter, you will learn how to use interfaces to build better abstractions, how to create enums and structs that can help performance, and how to use F#'s object expressions for boosting programmer productivity.

The .NET Platform

Let's begin our look at .NET-specific concepts by examining the runtime on which .NET applications execute. This will help you understand how to take full advantage of the platform by seeing the features F# gets for free.

The CLI

The foundation of the .NET platform is the *CLI*, or Common Language Infrastructure. This is a specification for a runtime system that actually runs your F# code. The F# compiler produces a binary file called an *assembly*, which is composed of a high-level assembly language called *MSIL* or Microsoft Intermediate Language.

An implementation of the CLI compiles this MSIL to machine code at runtime to execute the code faster than if it were just interpreted. The compilation happens "just-in-time" as the code is needed, or *JIT*.

Code that is compiled to MSIL and executed through the JITer is referred to as *managed code*—as opposed to *unmanaged code*, which is simply raw machine code (typically from programs written in C or C++).

There are several benefits of running through the CLI/managed code and not compiling your F# directly down to the machine level:

Interoperability between languages
> It would be much more difficult to share code between C#, VB.NET, and F# projects if it weren't for a common language (MSIL).

Ability to work cross-platform
> Because the CLI specification can be implemented anywhere, it is possible to run .NET code on other platforms: on the Web with Microsoft Silverlight, on the X-Box with the XNA and the .NET Compact Framework, or even on Linux through the Mono project.

Machine independence
> The JIT layer takes care of compiling down to machine code, so you don't have to worry about compiling your source code to target a specific architecture like x86 or ARM.

In addition, the .NET runtime offers garbage collection. This frees the programmer from the error-prone process of tracking the allocation and freeing of memory, and (mostly) eliminates an entire class of bugs.

Most of the benefits you don't even need to think about, as things "just work." But the one aspect of .NET programming you should be cognizant about is how the garbage collector works.

Garbage Collection

The garbage collector is an aspect of the .NET runtime that will automatically free any memory that is no longer referenced. As soon as a value is no longer accessible, typically because the execution has left the function scope, the memory the object occupied is marked for deletion and will be freed later by the garbage collector. For example, if a function declares an object named x, as soon as that function exits, there is no longer a way to refer to x and therefore its memory can be safely reclaimed.

As the programmer, you usually don't need to worry about whether or not a section of memory should be freed or not—the garbage collector will take care of that for you.

However, it is still possible to have a memory leak in managed code. If you unintentionally keep a reference to something that you don't need, then the garbage collector won't free it because you could potentially access that memory later.

Having the garbage collector to manage all memory works fine for managed resources, which are the ones created and referenced by the CLI. But things get more complicated when you're dealing with unmanaged resources, which includes pretty much anything existing outside of the CLI environment (e.g., file handles, operating system handles, shared memory, etc.). Those resources must be explicitly managed and freed by the developer.

If, for whatever reason, you need to manually deal with allocating and freeing resources, the recommended pattern to use is the IDisposable interface (interfaces are covered later in this chapter). The IDisposable interface just contains one method, Dispose, which does the freeing of resources. You customize the implementation of Dispose to take care of any cleanup you need, such as closing a file:

```
type IDisposable =
    interface
        abstract member Dispose : unit -> unit
    end
```

But remembering to call Dispose is problematic; in fact, it is just as error prone as manually managing memory in the first place. Fortunately, F# has some syntactic sugar to help you.

If you utilize the use keyword, the F# code will dispose of the item as soon as it is done being used (i.e., as it leaves scope). Syntactically, the use keyword behaves exactly like the let keyword.

The following example defines a new class called MultiFileLogger that implements IDisposable and prints some text to the console window when Dispose is called. Because the value logger is bound with use, as soon as the value leaves scope—such as when the function exits—Dispose will automatically be called:

```
> // Implementing IDisposable
open System
open System.IO
open System.Collections.Generic

type MultiFileLogger() =
    do printfn "Constructing..."
    let m_logs = new List<StreamWriter>()

    member this.AttachLogFile file =
        let newLogFile = new StreamWriter(file, true)
        m_logs.Add(newLogFile)

    member this.LogMessage (msg : string) =
        m_logs |> Seq.iter (fun writer -> writer.WriteLine(msg))

    interface IDisposable with
        member this.Dispose() =
            printfn "Cleaning up..."
            m_logs |> Seq.iter (fun writer -> writer.Close())
            m_logs.Clear();;
```

```
type MultiFileLogger =
  class
    interface IDisposable
    new : unit -> MultiFileLogger
    member AttachLogFile : file:string -> unit
    member LogMessage : msg:string -> unit
  end

> // Write some code using a MultiFileLogger
let task1() =
  use logger = new MultiFileLogger()
  // ...
  printfn "Exiting the function task1.."
  ();;

val task1 : unit -> unit

> task1();;
Constructing...
Exiting the function task1..
Cleaning up...
val it : unit = ()
```

Interfaces

So far in object-oriented programming we have modeled a couple of different relationships. *Is a* relationships can be modeled through inheritance, and *has a* relationships are modeled through aggregation (fields and properties). For example, a BMW *is a* car (inherits from type Car) and *has a* motor (contains a field named m_motor of type Engine).

There is, however, a third type of relationship—the *can do* relationship—which specifies that type X *can do* the operations described by type Y. For example: people, cars, and wine all age. Although there may be no clear relationship between people, cars, or wine, they are all capable of aging.

In .NET programming, the *can do* relationship is modeled via an *interface*, which is a contract that a type can implement to establish that it can perform a certain set of actions. An interface is just a collection of methods and properties. A type can declare that it implements the interface if it provides an implementation for each method or property. Once this contract has been implemented, then the type *can do* whatever the interface describes.

In Example 6-1, several types implement the IConsumable interface. To implement an interface, use the interface keyword followed by the implementation of each interface method or property to fulfill the contract. If a class implements the IConsumable interface, it means that the class has a Tastiness property and an Eat method.

Example 6-1. Interfaces in F#

```
type Tastiness =
    | Delicious
    | SoSo
    | TrySomethingElse

type IConsumable =
    abstract Eat : unit -> unit
    abstract Tastiness : Tastiness

// Protip: Eat one of these a day
type Apple() =
    interface IConsumable with
        member this.Eat() = printfn "Tasty!"
        member this.Tastiness = Delicious

// Not that tasty, but if you are really hungry will do a bind.
type CardboardBox() =
    interface IConsumable with
        member this.Eat() =  printfn "Yuck!"
        member this.Tastiness = TrySomethingElse
```

In C#, it is possible to partially implement an interface, and allow derived classes to provide the rest of the contract. This is not possible in F#. If a type is declared to implement an interface, it must implement each method and property explicitly.

Using Interfaces

Unlike other .NET languages, in F#, the methods and properties of implemented interfaces are not in scope by default. In order to call interface methods, you must cast the type to the corresponding interface. Once you have an instance of the interface, that object can do exactly what the interface specifies:

```
> let apple = new Apple();;

val apple : Apple

> apple.Tastiness;;

  apple.Tastiness;;
  ------^^^^^^^^^

stdin(81,7): error FS0039: The field, constructor or member 'Tastiness' is
 not defined.
> let iconsumable = apple :> IConsumable;;
```

```
val iconsumable : IConsumable

> iconsumable.Tastiness;;
val it : Tastiness = Delicious
```

 Needing to cast F# objects to interfaces before calling interface members is a common source of confusion when interoperating with existing .NET code. This requirement, however, makes it clear whether you are relying on the interface's functionality or the type's.

Defining Interfaces

To create an interface, you simply define a new class type with only abstract methods. The type inference system will infer the type to be an interface. Alternatively, you can use the `interface` keyword, followed by abstract members and properties, followed by the end keyword:

```
> // Define a type inferred to be an interface
type IDoStuff =
    abstract DoThings : unit -> unit;;

// Define an interface explicitly
type IDoStuffToo =
    interface
        abstract member DoThings : unit -> unit
    end;;

type IDoStuff =
  interface
    abstract member DoThings : unit -> unit
  end

type IDoStuffToo =
  interface
    abstract member DoThings : unit -> unit
  end
```

 In .NET code, it is a convention to prefix interfaces with the letter I. This is a relic of Hungarian notation, which was a programming convention to prefix variables with the type of data something contained or the purpose of that value. For example, an integer that contained a column index would be named colX or nX, rather than the ambiguous x.

Because .NET code relies less on tracking machine-level primitives and more about abstractions, the .NET style guidelines dictate that you should not use Hungarian notation with interface definitions being an exception.

Interfaces can inherit from other interfaces, with the derived interface extending the contract of the first.

Example 6-2 defines two interfaces, IDoStuff and IDoMoreStuff, which inherits from IDoStuff. When creating a class that implements the derived interface but not its base, an error is raised.

Example 6-2. Implementing a derived interface

```
> // Inherited interfaces
type IDoStuff =
    abstract DoStuff : unit -> unit

type IDoMoreStuff =
    inherit IDoStuff

    abstract DoMoreStuff : unit -> unit;;

    ... snip ...

> // ERROR: Doesn't implement full interface inheritance heirarchy
type Foo() =
    interface IDoMoreStuff with
        override this.DoMoreStuff() = printfn "Stuff getting done...";;

    interface IDoMoreStuff with
  ----^

stdin(116,5): error FS0191: No implementation was given for 'abstract member
IDoStuff.DoStuff : unit -> unit'. Note that all interface members must be
implemented and listed under an appropriate 'interface' declaration,
e.g. 'interface ... with member ...'
> // Works
type Bar() =
    interface IDoStuff with
        override this.DoStuff() = printfn "Stuff getting done..."

    interface IDoMoreStuff with
        override this.DoMoreStuff() = printfn "More stuff getting done...";;

type Bar =
  class
    interface IDoMoreStuff
    interface IDoStuff
    new : unit -> Bar
  end
```

Object Expressions

Interfaces are useful in .NET, but sometimes you just want an implementation of an interface, without going through the hassle of defining a custom type. For example, in order to sort the elements in a `List<_>`, you must provide a type that implements the `IComparer<'a>` interface. As you require more ways to sort that `List<_>`, you will quickly find your code littered with types that serve no purpose other than to house the single method that defines how to compare two objects.

In F#, you can use an *object expression*, which will create an anonymous class and return an instance of it for you. (The term "anonymous class" just means the compiler will generate the class for you and that you have no way to know its name.) This simplifies the process of creating one-time-use types, much in the same way using a lambda expression simplifies creating one-time-use functions.

The syntax for creating object expressions is a pair of curly braces, { }, beginning with the new keyword followed by the name of an interface, declared like you would normally use them. The result of an object expression is an instance of the anonymous class.

Object Expressions for Interfaces

Example 6-3 shows both using an object expression and an implementation of the `IComparer<'a>` interface, which is used to sort items in a collection. Each object expression defines a different way to sort a list of names. Without the use of object expressions, this would take two separate type definitions, each implementing `IComparer<'a>`. Instead, with the help of object expressions, no new explicit types are required.

Example 6-3. Sorting a list using IComparer<'a>

```
open System.Collections.Generic

type Person =
    { First : string; Last : string }
    override this.ToString() = sprintf "%s, %s" this.Last this.First

let people =
    new List<_>(
        [|
            { First = "Jomo";  Last = "Fisher" }
            { First = "Brian"; Last = "McNamara" }
            { First = "Joe";   Last = "Pamer" }
        |] )

let printPeople ()  =
    Seq.iter (fun person -> printfn "\t %s" (person.ToString())) people

// Now sort by last name

printfn "Initial ordering:"
printPeople()

// Sort people by first name
people.Sort(
```

```
    {
        new IComparer<Person> with
            member this.Compare(l, r) =
                if   l.First > r.First then  1
                elif l.First = r.First then  0
                else                        -1
    } )

printfn "After sorting by first name:"
printPeople()

// Sort people by last name
people.Sort(
    {
        new IComparer<Person> with
            member this.Compare(l, r) =
                if   l.Last > r.Last then  1
                elif l.Last = r.Last then  0
                else                      -1
    } )

printfn "After sorting by last name:"
printPeople()
```

The output in FSI is as follows:

```
Initial ordering:
        Fisher, Jomo
        McNamara, Brian
        Pamer, Joe
After sorting by first name:
        McNamara, Brian
        Pamer, Joe
        Fisher, Jomo
After sorting by last name:
        Fisher, Jomo
        McNamara, Brian
        Pamer, Joe
```

Object Expressions for Derived Classes

In addition to implementing interfaces, you can also use object expressions to create derived classes. However, types declared in object expressions cannot add any new methods or properties. They can only override abstract members of the base type.

Example 6-4 uses an object expression to create a new instance of the abstract class Sandwich, without explicitly declaring a type.

Example 6-4. Object expressions for creating derived classes

```
> // Abstract class
[<AbstractClass>]
type Sandwich() =
    abstract Ingredients : string list
    abstract Calories : int

// Object expression for a derived class
let lunch =
    {
        new Sandwich() with
            member this.Ingredients = ["Peanutbutter"; "Jelly"]
            member this.Calories = 400
    };;

type Sandwich =
  class
    abstract member Calories : int
    abstract member Ingredients : string list
    new : unit -> Sandwich
  end
val lunch : Sandwich

> lunch.Ingredients;;
val it : string list = ["Peanutbutter"; "Jelly"]
```

A situation where object expressions are especially useful is when writing unit tests. In unit tests, you typically want to create a *stub object*, or a class that simulates behavior that is otherwise slow or complicated to isolate, such as stubbing out the database connection so your tests don't hit a real database. Using object expressions, you can easily create anonymous types that can serve as placeholders without the need to define a plethora of custom types.

Extension Methods

There are times when you are working with a type and may not be able to make changes, either because you don't have the source code or because you are programming against an older version. This poses a problem when you want to extend that type in some way.

Extension methods provide a simple extension mechanism without needing to modify a type hierarchy or modify existing types. Extension methods are special types of methods you can use to augment existing types and use as if they were originally members of the type. This prevents you from having to rebuild base libraries or resort to using inheritance in order to add a few methods. Once extension methods have been added, you can use types as if they had the additional methods and properties, even if they weren't originally written for the type.

To declare an extension method, write `type` *ident* `with` followed by the extension methods, where *ident* is the fully qualified class name.

Note that because extension methods are not actually part of the class, they cannot access private or internal data. They are simply methods that can be called as if they were members of a class.

In Example 6-5, `System.Int32` is extended to provide the `ToHexString` method.

Example 6-5. Using an extension method

```
> (1094).ToHexString();;

  (1094).ToHexString();;
  -------^^^^^^^^^^^

stdin(131,8): error FS0039: The field, constructor or member 'ToHexString' is
 not defined.

> // Extend the System.Int32 AKA int type
type System.Int32 with
    member this.ToHexString() = sprintf "0x%x" this;;

  type Int32 with
    member ToHexString : unit -> string

> (1094).ToHexString();;
val it : string = "0x446"
```

Type extensions must be defined within modules, and are only available once the given module has been opened. In other words, people need to opt in to use extension methods by opening the defining module.

 Extension methods created in F# are not proper extension methods, in that they cannot be consumed from C# and VB.NET as extension methods. Rather, extension methods defined in F# code only extend types in other F# assemblies.

Extending Modules

Modules in F# can be extended by simply creating a new module with the same name. As long as the new module's namespace is opened, all new module functions, types, and values will be accessible.

The following snippet creates a new namespace called `FSCollectionExtensions`. Once this namespace is opened, its two modules will be available, adding new functions to the `List` and `Seq` modules:

```
namespace FSCollectionExtensions

open System.Collections.Generic

module List =

    /// Skips the first n elements of the list
    let rec skip n list =
        match n, list with
        | _, []       -> []
        | 0, list     -> list
        | n, hd :: tl -> skip (n - 1) tl

module Seq =

    /// Reverse the elements in the sequence
    let rec rev (s : seq<'a>) =
        let stack = new Stack<'a>()
        s |> Seq.iter stack.Push
        seq {
            while stack.Count > 0 do
                yield stack.Pop()
        }
```

Enumerations

We have covered discriminated unions, which are helpful for defining types of things within a set. However, each discriminated union case is a distinctly different class and is too heavyweight of a construct in some situations. Many times you simply want to define a group of related constant integral values, and in those situations you can use *enumerations*.

An enumeration is a primitive integral type, such as int or sbyte, which also contains a series of named constant values. An enumeration is just a wrapper over that integral type, however, so an instance of an enumerated type can have a value not defined within that enumeration.

Creating Enumerations

To create an enumeration, you use the same syntax for creating discriminated unions, but each data tag must be given a constant value of the same type. Example 6-6 shows creating an enumeration type for chess pieces. Each enumeration field value must be unique. In the example, the field values correspond to the chess piece's material value.

Example 6-6. Declaring an enumeration

```
type ChessPiece =
    | Empty  = 0
    | Pawn   = 1
    | Knight = 3
    | Bishop = 4
    | Rook   = 5
    | Queen  = 8
    | King   = 1000000
```

To use an enumeration value, simply use the fully qualified field name. Example 6-7 initializes an eight-by-eight array to represent locations on a chessboard.

With our `ChessPiece` enum as is, it would be impossible to differentiate between a black piece and a white piece. However, because each `ChessPiece` value is simply an integer, we can get sneaky and treat black pieces as their `ChessPiece` values, and white pieces as the negative. So `-1 * ChessPiece.Bishop` would represent a white bishop. The mechanics of converting enumeration values between their underlying primitives will be covered in the next section.

Example 6-7. Initializing a chessboard enum array

```
/// Create a 2-D array of the ChessPiece enumeration
let createChessBoard() =
    let board = Array2D.init 8 8 (fun _ _ -> ChessPiece.Empty)

    // Place pawns
    for i = 0 to 7 do
        board.[1,i] <- ChessPiece.Pawn
        board.[6,i] <- enum<ChessPiece> (-1 * int ChessPiece.Pawn)

    // Place black pieces in order
    [| ChessPiece.Rook; ChessPiece.Knight; ChessPiece.Bishop; ChessPiece.Queen;
       ChessPiece.King; ChessPiece.Bishop; ChessPiece.Knight; ChessPiece.Rook |]
    |> Array.iteri(fun idx piece -> board.[0,idx] <- piece)

    // Place white pieces in order
    [| ChessPiece.Rook;  ChessPiece.Knight; ChessPiece.Bishop; ChessPiece.King;
       ChessPiece.Queen; ChessPiece.Bishop; ChessPiece.Knight; ChessPiece.Rook |]
    |> Array.iteri(fun idx piece ->
                    board.[7,idx] <- enum<ChessPiece> (-1 * int piece))

    // Return the board
    board
```

Enumerations can be used in pattern matching, but unlike discriminated unions, each enumeration field must be fully qualified through their type name:

```
let isPawn piece =
    match piece with
    | ChessPiece.Pawn
        -> true
    | _ -> false
```

Conversion

To construct an enumeration value, simply use the `enum<_>` function. The function converts its argument to the enum type of its generic type parameter.

The following snippet converts the value 42 to an instance of `ChessPiece`:

```
let invalidPiece = enum<ChessPiece>(42)
```

To get values from an enumeration, simply use the typical primitive value conversion functions, such as `int`:

```
let materialValueOfQueen = int ChessPiece.Queen
```

When to Use an Enum Versus a Discriminated Union

Enumerations and discriminated unions have two significant differences. First, enumerations don't offer a safety guarantee. Whereas a discriminated union can only be one of a known set of possible values, an enumeration is syntactic sugar over a primitive type. So if you are given an enumeration value, there is no implicit guarantee that the value is something meaningful.

For example, if the value −711 were converted to a `ChessPiece` enum, it would make no sense and likely introduce bugs when encountered. When you have obtained an enum value from an external source, be sure to check it with the `Enum.IsDefined` method:

```
> System.Enum.IsDefined(typeof<ChessPiece>, int ChessPiece.Bishop);;
val it : bool = true
> System.Enum.IsDefined(typeof<ChessPiece>, -711);;
val it : bool = false
```

Second, enumerations only hold one piece of data—their value. Discriminated union data tags can each hold a unique tuple of data.

However, enumerations represent a common .NET idiom and offer significant performance benefits over discriminated unions. Whereas enums are simply a few bytes on the stack, discriminated unions are reference types and require separate memory allocations. So populating an array with a large number of enums will be much faster than populating that array with discriminated unions.

A useful benefit to enums is bit flags, shown in Example 6-8. By giving the enum fields powers of two as values, each bit of an underlying enum is treated as a Boolean flag. This way, flags can be combined using bitwise OR (|||) and tested using bitwise AND (&&&). Using this technique, you can store up to 32 flags within an int based enum, or up to 64 flags in an int64 based enum.

Example 6-8. Combining enumeration values for flags

```
open System

// Enumeration of flag values
type FlagsEnum =
    | OptionA = 0b0001
    | OptionB = 0b0010
    | OptionC = 0b0100
    | OptionD = 0b1000

let isFlagSet (enum : FlagsEnum) (flag : FlagsEnum) =
    let flagName = Enum.GetName(typeof<FlagsEnum>, flag)
    if enum &&& flag = flag  then
        printfn "Flag [%s] is set." flagName
    else
        printfn "Flag [%s] is not set." flagName
```

The following FSI session is from Example 6-8:

```
> // Check if given flags are set
let customFlags = FlagsEnum.OptionA ||| FlagsEnum.OptionC

isFlagSet customFlags FlagsEnum.OptionA
isFlagSet customFlags FlagsEnum.OptionB
isFlagSet customFlags FlagsEnum.OptionC
isFlagSet customFlags FlagsEnum.OptionD
;;
Flag [OptionA] is set.
Flag [OptionB] is not set.
Flag [OptionC] is set.
Flag [OptionD] is not set.

val customFlags : FlagsEnum = 5
```

Structs

We have covered classes before and gone through the complexities of overriding Equals to create equality semantics that make sense. However, for simple types, there is a better way. Rather than trying to simulate value type semantics through overriding Equals, why not just create a new value type? *Structs* are similar to classes, the main difference being that they are a value type, and therefore may be put on the stack. Struct instances take up much less memory than that of a class and, if stack allocated, will not need to be garbage collected.

Creating Structs

To create a struct, define a type like you normally would, but add the [<Struct>] attribute. Alternately, you could use the struct and end keywords before and after the struct's body:

```
[<Struct>]
type StructPoint(x : int, y : int) =
    member this.X = x
    member this.Y = y


type StructRect(top : int, bottom : int, left : int, right : int) =
    struct
        member this.Top    = top
        member this.Bottom = bottom
        member this.Left   = left
        member this.Right  = right

        override this.ToString() =
            sprintf "[%d, %d, %d, %d]" top bottom left right
    end
```

Structs have many of the features of classes but may be stored on the stack rather than the heap. Therefore, equality (by default) is determined by simply comparing the values on the stack rather than references:

```
> // Define two different struct values
let x = new StructPoint(6, 20)
let y = new StructPoint(6, 20);;

val x : StructPoint = FSI_0011+StructPoint
val y : StructPoint = FSI_0011+StructPoint

> x = y;;
val it : bool = true
```

One difference between structs and classes, however, is how they are constructed. Whereas classes only have the constructors you provide, structs automatically get a *default constructor*, which assigns the default value to each struct field (which you might recall is zero for value types and null for reference types):

```
> // Struct for describing a book
[<Struct>]
type BookStruct(title : string, pages : int) =
    member this.Title = title
    member this.Pages = pages

    override this.ToString() =
        sprintf "Title: %A, Pages: %d" this.Title this.Pages;;

type BookStruct =
  struct
```

```
      new : title:string * pages:int -> BookStruct
      override ToString : unit -> string
      member Pages : int
      member Title : string
    end

> // Create an instance of the struct using the constructor
let book1 = new BookStruct("Philosopher's Stone", 309);;

val book1 : BookStruct = Title: "Philosopher's Stone", Pages: 309

> // Create an instance using the default constructor
let namelessBook = new BookStruct();;

val namelessBook : BookStruct = Title: <null>, Pages: 0
```

To create a struct in which you can modify its fields, you must explicitly declare each mutable field in a val binding and add the [<DefaultValue>] attribute. In addition, in order to mutate a struct's fields, the instance of that struct must be declared mutable.

The following snippet defines a struct MPoint with two mutable fields. It then creates a mutable instance of that struct, pt, and updates the struct's fields:

```
> // Define a struct with mutable fields
[<Struct>]
type MPoint =
    val mutable X : int

    val mutable Y : int

    override this.ToString() =
        sprintf "{%d, %d}" this.X this.Y;;

type MPoint =
  struct
    val mutable X: int
    val mutable Y: int
    override ToString : unit -> string
  end

> let mutable pt = new MPoint();;

val mutable pt : MPoint = {0, 0}

> // Update the fields
pt.X <- 10
pt.Y <- 7;;
> pt;;
val it : MPoint = {10, 7}
> let nonMutableStruct = new MPoint();;

val nonMutableStruct : MPoint = {0, 0}
```

```
> // ERROR: Update a nonmutable struct's field
nonMutableStruct.X <- 10;;

  nonMutableStruct.X <- 10;;
  ^^^^^^^^^^^^^^^^^

stdin(54,1): error FS0256: A value must be mutable in order to mutate the
  contents of a value type, e.g. 'let mutable x = ...'
```

Restrictions

Structs have several restrictions in place in order to enforce their characteristics:

- Structs cannot be inherited; they are implicitly marked with [<Sealed>].
- Structs cannot override the default constructor. (The default constructor always exists and zeros out all memory.)
- Structs cannot use let bindings as with the implicit constructor syntax from class types.

When to Use a Struct Versus a Record

Because F# offers both structs and records as lightweight containers for data, it can be confusing to know when to use which.

The main benefit of using structs over records is the same benefit of using structs over classes—namely, that they offer different performance characteristics. When you're dealing with a large number of small objects, allocating the space on the stack to create new structs is much faster than allocating many small objects on the heap. Similarly, with structs there is no additional garbage collection step, because the stack is cleared as soon as the function exits.

For the most part, however, the performance gain for struct allocation is negligible. In fact, if used thoughtlessly, structs can have a detrimental impact on performance due to excessive copying when passing structs as parameters. Also, the .NET garbage collector and memory manager are designed for high-performance applications. When you think you have a performance problem, use the Visual Studio code profiler to identify what the bottleneck is first before prematurely converting all of your classes and records to structs.

Programming F#

Applied Functional Programming

Most of the programming you have done so far has been in the functional style. Although this has enabled you to write succinct, powerful programs, you never quite used the functional style to its full potential. Functional programming means more than just treating functions as values. Embracing the functional programming paradigm and having it help shape your thought process will enable you to write programs that would otherwise be prohibitively difficult in an imperative style.

In this chapter, we build on what you learned about functional programming back in Chapter 3, and introduce new language features that help you to be more productive in the functional style. For example, using active patterns allows you to increase the power of your pattern matching and eliminate the need for when guards, and by creating auto-opened modules, you can extend common F# modules.

In addition, we look at some of the more mind-bending aspects of functional programming. You will learn how to use advanced forms of recursion to avoid stack overflows and write more efficient programs using lists. We also take a look at some common design patterns and data structures for functional code.

To begin, let's look at how to take pattern matching from "switch statements on steroids" to an entirely new level.

Active Patterns

Pattern matching adds power to your programming by giving you a way to be much more expressive in code branching than using if expressions alone. It allows you to match against constants, capture values, and match against the structure of data. However, pattern matching has a significant limitation—namely, it only has the ability to match against literal values such as string, or a limited range of class types like arrays and lists.

Ideally, pattern matching could be used to match against higher-level concepts such as elements in a seq<_>. The following is an example of what you would like to write, however, it fails to compile:

```
// Does not compile
let containsVowel (word : string) =
    let letters = word :> seq<char>
    match letters with
    | ContainsAny [ 'a'; 'e'; 'i'; 'o'; 'u' ]
        -> true
    | SometimesContains [ 'y' ]
        -> true
    | _ -> false
```

To check if elements exist in a seq<_>, you need to resort to using when guards, which are ugly at best. The following snippet creates a Set type filled with the letters of a string, and then searches for specific letters in a pattern match rule's when guard:

```
let containsVowel (word : string) =
    let letters = word |> Set.of_seq
    match letters with
    | _ when letters.Contains('a') || letters.Contains('e') ||
             letters.Contains('i') || letters.Contains('o') ||
             letters.Contains('u') || letters.Contains('y')
        -> true
    | _ -> false
```

Fortunately, in F#, there is a feature called *active patterns* that captures all the succinct expressiveness you want with the elegance of pattern matching.

Active patterns are just special functions that can be used inside of pattern-match rules. Using them eliminates the need for when guards as well as adding clarity to the pattern match. This has the extra benefit of making the code look as if it maps more closely to the problem you are solving.

Active patterns take on several forms; each takes an input and converts it into one or more new values:

- Single-case active patterns convert the input into a new value.
- Partial-case active patterns carve out an incomplete piece of the input space (e.g., only matching against strings that contain the letter "e").
- Multicase active patterns partition the input space into one of several values (e.g., partitioning all possible integers into odds, evens, or zero).

Single-Case Active Patterns

The simplest type of active pattern is the single-case active pattern, which converts data from one type to another. This enables you to use the existing pattern-match syntax on classes and values that couldn't otherwise be expressed in a pattern-match rule. We see an example of this shortly.

To define an active pattern, define the function with the name enclosed with *banana clips* or (| |).

Example 7-1 defines an active pattern for converting a file path into its extension. This allows you to pattern-match against the file extension, without needing to resort to using a when guard.

To use the `FileExtension` active pattern, simply use it in place of a pattern-match rule. The result of the active pattern will come immediately after the active pattern's name, and will behave just like any other pattern-match rule. So in the example, the constant value ".jpg" is matched against the result of the active pattern. In the last pattern-match rule, a new value ext is bound to the result of the active pattern.

Example 7-1. Single-case active pattern

```
open System.IO

// Convert a file path into its extension
let (|FileExtension|) filePath = Path.GetExtension(filePath)

let determineFileType (filePath : string) =
    match filePath with

    // Without active patterns
    | filePath when Path.GetExtension(filePath) = ".txt"
        -> printfn "It is a text file."

    // Converting the data using an active pattern
    | FileExtension ".jpg"
    | FileExtension ".png"
    | FileExtension ".gif"
        -> printfn "It is an image file."

    // Binding a new value
    | FileExtension ext
        -> printfn "Unknown file extension [%s]" ext
```

Partial Active Patterns

Single-case active patterns are helpful for cleaning up pattern matches, but there are many situations where there isn't a 1:1 correspondence between input and output. For example, what happens when you write an active pattern for converting strings to integers? Not every string can be converted to an integer:

```
> // Active pattern for converting strings to ints
open System
let (|ToInt|) x = Int32.Parse(x);;

val ( |ToInt| ) : string -> int

> // Check if the input string parses as the number 4
let isFour str =
    match str with
    | ToInt 4 -> true
    | _ -> false;;

val isFour : string -> bool

> isFour " 4 ";;
val it : bool = true
> isFour "Not a valid Integer";;
System.FormatException: Input string was not in a correct format.
    at System.Number.StringToNumber(String str, NumberStyles options,
    NumberBuffer& number, NumberFormatInfo info, Boolean parseDecimal)
    at System.Number.ParseInt32(String s, NumberStyles style, NumberFormatInfo info)
    at FSI_0007.IsFour(String str)
    at <StartupCode$FSI_0009>.$FSI_0009._main()
stopped due to error
```

Partial active patterns allow you to define active patterns that don't always convert the input data. To do this, a partial active pattern returns an option type (which, if you recall, has only two values, Some('a) and None). If the match succeeds, it returns Some; otherwise, it returns None. The option type is removed as part of the pattern match when the result is bound.

Example 7-2 shows how to define a partial active pattern that doesn't throw an exception for malformed input. To define a partial active pattern, simply enclose your active pattern with (|*ident*|_|) instead of the usual (|*ident*|). When used in the pattern match, the rule will only match if the partial active pattern returns Some.

Another way to think about partial active patterns is that they are optional single-case active patterns.

Example 7-2. Partial active patterns in action

```
open System
let (|ToBool|_|) x =
    let success, result = Boolean.TryParse(x)
    if success then Some(result)
    else            None

let (|ToInt|_|) x =
```

```
    let success, result = Int32.TryParse(x)
    if success then Some(result)
    else            None

let (|ToFloat|_|) x =
    let success, result = Double.TryParse(x)
    if success then Some(result)
    else            None

let describeString str =
    match str with
    | ToBool  b -> printfn "%s is a bool with value %b" str b
    | ToInt   i -> printfn "%s is an integer with value %d" str i
    | ToFloat f -> printfn "%s is a float with value %f" str f
    | _         -> printfn "%s is not a bool, int, or float" str
```

An example of describeString is as follows:

```
> describeString " 3.141 ";;
 3.141  is a float with value 3.141000
val it : unit = ()
> describeString "Not a valid integer";;
Not a valid integer is not a bool, int, or float
val it : unit = ()
```

Parameterized Active Patterns

Active patterns can take parameters too. Parameters for an active pattern are provided immediately after the active pattern name, but before the result of the active pattern.

Example 7-3 shows creating parameterized active patterns to check if the given string matches a regular expression. Rather than needing to keep track of the regular expression match and teasing out the individual groups, active patterns allow you to check if the regular expression matches, as well as bind values to each group from within a pattern-match rule.

Example 7-3. Parameterized active patterns for regular expression matching

```
open System
open System.Text.RegularExpressions

// Use a regular expression to capture three groups
let (|RegexMatch3|_|) (pattern : string) (input : string) =
    let result = Regex.Match(input, pattern)

    if result.Success then
        match (List.tail [ for g in result.Groups -> g.Value ]) with
        | fst :: snd :: trd :: []
            -> Some (fst, snd, trd)
        | [] -> failwith <| "Match succeeded, but no groups found.\n" +
                            "Use '(.*)' to capture groups"
        | _  -> failwith "Match succeeded, but did not find exactly three groups."
```

```
        else
            None

let parseTime input =
    match input with
    // Match input of the form "6/20/2008"
    | RegexMatch3 "(\d+)/(\d+)/(\d\d\d\d)" (month, day, year)
    // Match input of the form "2004-12-8"
    | RegexMatch3 "(\d\d\d\d)-(\d+)-(\d+)" (year, month, day)
        -> Some( new DateTime(int year, int month, int day) )
    | _ -> None
```

The result of this active pattern can be seen in the following FSI session:

```
> parseTime "1996-3-15";;
val it : DateTime option
= Some 3/15/1996 12:00:00 AM {Date = ...;
                              Day = 15;
                              DayOfWeek = Friday;
                              DayOfYear = 75;
                              Hour = 0;
                              Kind = Unspecified;
                              Millisecond = 0;
                              Minute = 0;
                              Month = 3;
                              Second = 0;
                              Ticks = 629624448000000000L;
                              TimeOfDay = 00:00:00;
                              Year = 1996;}
> parseTime "invalid";;
val it : DateTime option = None
```

 Active patterns can clean up match statements, but should be treated like .NET properties. They should not be computationally expensive to execute nor cause side effects; otherwise it can be difficult to isolate performance problems or anticipate where exceptions could be thrown.

Multicase Active Patterns

Although single-case and partial active patterns are helpful for converting data, they have the drawback that they can only convert the input data into one other format. But sometimes you want to transform that data into multiple types, typically when you want to partition the input space into multiple categories.

Using a *multicase active pattern*, you can partition the input space into a known set of possible values. To define a multicase active pattern, simply use the banana clips again but include multiple identifiers to identify the categories of output.

For example, consider doing a pattern match against a row in your Customers table in a database. You could write multiple partial active patterns to divide the customer into power user, nonuser, valued customer, and so on. Rather than defining a group of partial active patterns to determine which category the input falls into, a multicase active pattern partitions the input space into exactly one of a group of possible results.

 Another way to think about multicase active patterns is that they simply act as a way of converting the input data into a discriminated union type.

Example 7-4 takes a string and breaks it into a Paragraph, Sentence, Word, or White space categories. These categories, and associated data, can then be used as part of a pattern match.

Example 7-4. Multicase active patterns

```
open System

// This active pattern divides all strings into their various meanings.
let (|Paragraph|Sentence|Word|WhiteSpace|) (input : string) =
        let input = input.Trim()

        if input = "" then
            WhiteSpace
        elif input.IndexOf(".") <> -1 then
            // Paragraph contains a tuple of sentence counts and sentences.
            let sentences = input.Split([|"."|], StringSplitOptions.None)
            Paragraph (sentences.Length, sentences)
        elif input.IndexOf(" ") <> -1 then
            // Sentence contains an array of string words
            Sentence (input.Split([|" "|], StringSplitOptions.None))
        else
            // Word contains a string
            Word (input)

// Count the number of letters of a string by breaking it down
let rec countLetters str =
    match str with
    | WhiteSpace -> 0
    | Word x       -> x.Length
    | Sentence words
        -> words
            |> Array.map countLetters
            |> Array.sum
    | Paragraph (_, sentences)
        -> sentences
            |> Array.map countLetters
            |> Array.sum
```

Using Active Patterns

Active patterns can do more than just spice up the standard sort of pattern matches we have seen so far. You can combine, nest, and use active patterns outside of `match` expressions, just like pattern-match rules.

Active patterns can be used in place of any pattern-matching element, which if you recall means that they can be used as part of `let` bindings or as parameters in lambda expressions too.

The following code snippet applies the active pattern `ToUpper` to the first parameter of function `f`:

```
> let (|ToUpper|) (input : string) = input.ToUpper();;

val ( |ToUpper| ) : string -> string

> let f ( ToUpper x ) = printfn "x = %s" x;;

val f : string -> unit

> f "this is lower case";;
x = THIS IS LOWER CASE
val it : unit = ()
```

Combining active patterns

Active patterns can also be combined much like regular pattern-match rules using Or and And. Example 7-5 shows how to combine multiple active patterns into the same pattern match rule using Or |.

Example 7-5. Combining active patterns with Or

```
// Classify movies by genre.
let (|Action|Drama|Comedy|Documentary|Horror|Romance|) movie =
    // ...

// Checks if a movie won a specific award.
let (|WonAward|_|) awardTitle movie =
    // ...

// Determine if the film would make a good date movie.
let goodDateMovie movie =
    match movie with
    // Matching cases of the multicase active pattern
    | Romance
    | Comedy

    // Using the parameterized active pattern
    | WonAward "Best Picture"
```

```
| WonAward "Best Adaptation"
    -> true

| _ -> false
```

And & allows you to test against multiple active patterns simultaneously. Example 7-6 combines active patterns to determine if an image file is too large to send in an email. The example combines a multicase active pattern that converts a file path into one of several size active pattern tags and a second, partial active pattern that will determine if a file path is an image file.

Example 7-6. Combining active patterns with And

```
open System.IO

let (|KBInSize|MBInSize|GBInSize|) filePath =
    let file = File.Open(filePath, FileMode.Open)
    if   file.Length < 1024L * 1024L then
        KBInSize
    elif file.Length < 1024L * 1024L * 1024L then
        MBInSize
    else
        GBInSize

let (|IsImageFile|_|) filePath =
    match filePath with
    | EndsWithExtension ".jpg"
    | EndsWithExtension ".bmp"
    | EndsWithExtension ".gif"
        -> Some()
    | _ -> None

let ImageTooBigForEmail filePath =
    match filePath with
    | IsImageFile & (MBInSize | GBInSize)
        -> true
    | _ -> false
```

Nesting active patterns

With all the power that active patterns have for converting data within pattern matching, a problem you quickly run into is transforming data multiple times. However, binding the result of an active pattern and immediately pattern matching against the value leads to tedious and error-prone code.

Fortunately, just like pattern matching, you can nest active patterns. You can also use an active pattern in place of the result of an active pattern, which will then apply the result of the first active pattern to the second.

Example 7-7 defines a few simple active patterns for parsing XML elements. One is for converting an XML node into its child elements, another is for converting the value of an XML element's attributes, and so on. By nesting active patterns within a single match statement, you can match against the full structure of an XML document within a single rule of a pattern match. This shows the full extent to which active patterns add power to pattern matching.

Example 7-7. Nesting active patterns within a match expression

```
// This example requires a reference to System.Xml.dll
#r "System.Xml.dll"
open System.Xml

// Match an XML element
let (|Elem|_|) name (inp : XmlNode) =
    if inp.Name = name then Some(inp)
    else                    None

// Get the attributes of an element
let (|Attributes|) (inp : XmlNode) = inp.Attributes

// Match a specific attribute
let (|Attr|) attrName (inp : XmlAttributeCollection) =
    match inp.GetNamedItem(attrName) with
    | null -> failwithf "Attribute %s not found" attrName
    | attr -> attr.Value

// What we are actually parsing
type Part =
    | Widget   of float
    | Sprocket of string * int

let ParseXmlNode element =
    match element with
    // Parse a Widget without nesting active patterns
    | Elem "Widget" xmlElement
        -> match xmlElement with
            | Attributes xmlElementsAttributes
                -> match xmlElementsAttributes with
                    | Attr "Diameter" diameter
                        -> Widget(float diameter)

    // Parse a Sprocket using nested active patterns
    | Elem "Sprocket" (Attributes (Attr "Model" model & Attr "SerialNumber" sn))
        -> Sprocket(model, int sn)

    |_ -> failwith "Unknown element"
```

When executed through FSI, Example 7-7 has the following output:

```
> // Load the XML Document
let xmlDoc =
    let doc = new System.Xml.XmlDocument()
    let xmlText =
```

```
             "<?xml version=\"1.0\" encoding=\"utf-8\"?>
             <Parts>
                 <Widget Diameter='5.0' />
                 <Sprocket Model='A' SerialNumber='147' />
                 <Sprocket Model='B' SerialNumber='302' />
             </Parts>
             "
        doc.LoadXml(xmlText)
        doc;;

    val xmlDoc : XmlDocument

    > // Parse each document node
    xmlDoc.DocumentElement.ChildNodes
    |> Seq.cast<XmlElement>
    |> Seq.map ParseXmlNode;;
    val it : seq<Part> = seq [Widget 5.0; Sprocket ("A",1024); Sprocket ("B",306)]
```

Using active patterns, you can easily add a great deal of flexibility to your pattern matching. The best times to use an active pattern is whenever you find yourself writing a lot of similar when guards or when you would like to be more expressive in pattern matches. For instance, XML doesn't lend itself naturally to pattern matching, but with a few simple active patterns, you can then use it as part of any pattern match.

Using Modules

If you recall from Chapter 2, namespaces are a way to organize types. Modules behave much like namespaces, except that instead of only being able to contain types, modules can contain values as well.

Although modules' ability to contain values makes it easy to write simple applications, they are not well suited for being shared with other programmers and .NET languages. A well-designed class can stand on its own, and is simple and intuitive to use because all of its complex inner workings are hidden. With a module, you are given a loose collection of values, functions, and types, and it can be unclear how they all relate.

Identifying when and how to convert a module into a namespace and class is important for mastering functional programming in F#.

Converting Modules to Classes

Simply put, code defined in modules doesn't scale as well as typical object-oriented hierarchies. Ten modules with dozens of values/types are manageable, but hundreds of modules with thousands of values/types are not. Eliminating the loose values and just relying on classes is one way to help combat complexity.

The code in Example 7-8 creates a simple screen scraper, or a program that downloads the images at a particular URL. You can see how code like this can easily grow out of a long FSI session: typing some code in the FSI window until it works and then copying it to the code editor later. Although the code works in the context of a single code file and an FSI session, it cannot easily be integrated into an existing project.

Example 7-8. Web scraper in a module

```
open System.IO
open System.Net
open System.Text.RegularExpressions

let imagesPath = @"D:\Images\"
let url = @"http://oreilly.com/"

// Download the webpage
let req = WebRequest.Create(url)
let resp = req.GetResponse()
let stream = resp.GetResponseStream()
let reader = new StreamReader(stream)
let html = reader.ReadToEnd()


// Extract all images
let results = Regex.Matches(html, "<img src=\"([^\"]*)\"")
let allMatches =
    [
        for r in results do
            for grpIdx = 1 to r.Groups.Count - 1 do
                yield r.Groups.[grpIdx].Value
    ]

let fullyQualified =
    allMatches
    |> List.filter (fun url -> url.StartsWith("http://"))

// Download the images
let downloadToDisk (url : string) (filePath : string) =
    use client = new System.Net.WebClient()
    client.DownloadFile (url, filePath)

fullyQualified
|> List.map(fun url -> let parts = url.Split( [| '/' |] )
                       url, parts.[parts.Length - 1])
|> List.iter(fun (url, filename) -> downloadToDisk url (imagesPath + filename))
```

The problem with Example 7-8 is that it is an unorganized series of values. Although the code makes perfect sense when executing a series of steps from top to bottom, the next programmer just sees module properties like `results` and `allMatches`, which are meaningless out of context.

The first step to convert this code is to abstract elements into a series of functions, removing the need for any purely local values. By indenting everything four spaces and adding a function declaration up top, the module's contents could be placed inside of a function. Doing this allows us to break up the code into several pieces:

```
let downloadWebpage (url : string) =
    let req = WebRequest.Create(url)
    let resp = req.GetResponse()
    let stream = resp.GetResponseStream()
    let reader = new StreamReader(stream)
    reader.ReadToEnd()

let extractImageLinks html =
    let results = Regex.Matches(html, "<img src=\"([^\"]*)\"")
    [
        for r in results do
            for grpIdx = 1 to r.Groups.Count - 1 do
                yield r.Groups.[grpIdx].Value
    ] |> List.filter (fun url -> url.StartsWith("http://"))

let downloadToDisk (url : string) (filePath : string) =
    use client = new System.Net.WebClient()
    client.DownloadFile (url, filePath)

let scrapeWebsite destPath (imageUrls : string list) =
    imageUrls
    |> List.map(fun url ->
            let parts = url.Split( [| '/' |] )
            url, parts.[parts.Length - 1])
    |> List.iter(fun (url, filename) ->
            downloadToDisk url (Path.Combine(destPath, filename)))
```

This refactoring would enable you to use the web scrapper in the following fashion:

```
downloadWebpage "http://oreilly.com/"
|> extractImageLinks
|> scrapeWebsite @"C:\Images\"
```

But loose functions aren't that useful for the same reasons that loose values aren't useful. Namely, they don't abstract or simplify anything. You still need to figure out how to get the functions to work together. So the next step would be to create classes that could then be used by other programmers. All you need to do is replace the function value with a type declaration, and its parameters are simply parameters to the constructor.

In Example 7-9, all the loose functions are brought into the class, so that they are encapsulated. This leaves only a class with a constructor and a member SaveImagesToDisk.

Example 7-9. Web scraper converted to a class

```
type WebScraper(url) =

    let downloadWebpage (url : string) =
        let req = WebRequest.Create(url)
        let resp = req.GetResponse()
        let stream = resp.GetResponseStream()
        let reader = new StreamReader(stream)
        reader.ReadToEnd()

    let extractImageLinks html =
        let results = Regex.Matches(html, "<img src=\"([^\"]*)\"")
        [
            for r in results do
                for grpIdx = 1 to r.Groups.Count - 1 do
                    yield r.Groups.[grpIdx].Value
        ] |> List.filter (fun url -> url.StartsWith("http://"))

    let downloadToDisk (url : string) (filePath : string) =
        use client = new System.Net.WebClient()
        client.DownloadFile (url, filePath)

    let scrapeWebsite destPath (imageUrls : string list) =
        imageUrls
        |> List.map(fun url ->
                let parts = url.Split( [| '/' |] )
                url, parts.[parts.Length - 1])
        |> List.iter(fun (url, filename) ->
                downloadToDisk url (Path.Combine(destPath, filename)))

    // Add class fields
    let m_html   = downloadWebpage url
    let m_images = extractImageLinks m_html

    // Add class members
    member this.SaveImagesToDisk(destPath) =
        scrapeWebsite destPath m_images
```

Modules serve a valuable purpose in F# code, especially in the development of simple programs. However, mastering the conversion of modules to classes is important for sharing and reusing your F# code with other .NET languages.

Intentional Shadowing

In F#, the notion of a value is simply a name bound to some data. By declaring a new value with the same name you can shadow the previous value with that name:

```
let test() =
    let x = 'a'
    let x = "a string"
    let x = 3
    // The function returns 3
    x
```

In the same vein, opening a module dumps a series of new name/value pairs into the current environment, potentially shadowing existing identifiers. So if you have a value in scope named x, and you open a module that also contains a value named x, after the module is opened, x will refer to the module's value. This will silently shadow the previous value x, leaving no way to access it.

Although this has the potential for introducing subtle bugs, using modules to intentionally shadow values can be beneficial too. This is exactly the approach F# uses for checking for arithmetic overflow.

Consider the case of *checked arithmetic* (i.e., arithmetic that throws an exception if there is an overflow). By default, F#'s mathematical operators do not support this, so when you overflow the bounds of an integer value, it just wraps around:

```
> let maxInt = System.Int32.MaxValue;;

val maxInt : int = 2147483647

> maxInt;;
val it : int = 2147483647
> maxInt + 1;;
val it : int = -2147483648
```

The Microsoft.FSharp.Core.Operators.Checked module defines common arithmetic operators such as +, -, and so on, that check for overflow conditions and throw the OverflowException. By opening the Checked module, you shadow all of the existing arithmetic functions and essentially replace them with new ones. Opening that module effectively redefines all those operators for you:

```
> let maxInt = System.Int32.MaxValue;;

val maxInt : int

> open Checked;;
> maxInt + 1;;
System.OverflowException: Arithmetic operation resulted in an overflow.
   at <StartupCode$FSI_0009>.$FSI_0009._main()
stopped due to error
```

The reason you only need to write open Checked instead of open Microsoft.FSharp.Core.Operators.Checked is because F# automatically opens the Microsoft.FSharp.Core.Operators namespace for you.

This ability to intentionally shadow values can be handy for customizing the behavior of code in a file, but you should be careful about making sure you have the right usage semantics for the modules you write.

Controlling Module Usage

What if a library writer wants to ensure that people are only accessing module values through the module's name? For example, opening the List module would bring a lot of simple functions like map and length into scope, but would be easy to confuse those functions with other common functions like Seq.map or Array.length:

```
open List
open Seq

// Confusion: Is this List.length or Seq.length?
length [1 .. 10];;
```

To prevent a module from being opened in this way, you can simply add [<RequireQua lifiedAccess>] to the module, which bars it from being imported:

```
[<RequireQualifiedAccess>]
module Foo

let Value1 = 1

[<RequireQualifiedAccess>]
module Bar =
    let Value2 = 2
```

When you try to open a module with the [<RequireQualifiedAccess>] attribute, you will get an error. For example, in the F# library, the List module requires qualified access:

```
> open List;;

  open List;;
  ^^^^^^^^^

stdin(10,1): error FS0191: This declaration opens the module
 'Microsoft.FSharp.Collections.List', which is marked as 'RequireQualifiedAccess'.
Adjust your code to use qualified references to the elements of the module instead,
e.g. 'List.map' instead of 'map'. This will ensure that your code is robust as new
constructs are added to libraries
```

However, some modules are especially useful and always having their values and types in scope would be good. In Chapter 6, you learned about extension methods, which allowed you to augment the members of a class. If you define a set of extension methods that are especially useful when used with a given namespace, you can mark the module to be automatically opened as soon as the parent namespace is opened with the [<AutoOpen>] attribute.

A good example of this in the F# libraries is the Linq.NullableOperators module. As soon as the Microsoft.FSharp.Linq namespace is opened, the NullableOperators module is automatically opened, importing custom operators like (?+) and (?>=?).

Example 7-10 defines a namespace that contains an auto-opened module. After opening the parent namespace with open Alpha.Bravo, you can access any values in the module Charlie without needing to fully qualify them, because module Charlie was opened implicitly.

Example 7-10. The AutoOpen attribute

```
namespace Alpha.Bravo

[<AutoOpen>]
module Charlie =
    let X = 1
```

The first half of this chapter showed you how to take advantage of language elements in F# and syntax to enable you to write code in the functional style. The rest of the chapter focuses not on syntax, but theory. Specifically, it shows you how to take full advantage of the unique characteristics of functional programming.

Mastering Lists

Whereas arrays and the List<_> type make up the backbone data structure for imperative programming, immutable lists are the cornerstone of functional programming. This guarantee of immutability helps support function composition and recursion, as well as freeing you from needing to allocate all the memory up front (as you would when using fixed size arrays).

Although lists are pervasive when programming in the functional style, I have not yet covered how to use them efficiently. Lists in F# have unique performance characteristics that you should be aware of or else you run the risk of unexpectedly poor performance.

F# lists are represented as a linked list, visualized in Figure 7-1. Every element of the list has a value as well as a reference to the next element in the list (except of course the last element of the list).

Figure 7-1. Structure of an FSharpList type

List Operations

Perhaps the greatest benefit of the FSharpList type is how simple it is to use. Although the List module offers plenty of functionality for using existing lists, when you build up lists dynamically, there are only two operations to choose from: *cons* and *append*.

Cons

The cons operator, ::, adds an element to the front of an existing list. When the cons operator is used, the result is a new list; the input list is unchanged because all the work is done by simply allocating a new list element and setting its next element to the start of the input list.

This can be seen visually in Figure 7-2. Notice that a new list is returned, and the input list is reused:

```
> let x = [2; 3; 4];;

val x : int list = [2; 3; 4]

> 1 :: x;;
val it : int list = [1; 2; 3; 4]

> x;;
val it : int list = [2; 3; 4]
```

Figure 7-2. Cons operator on lists

Because only one list node is introduced, the cons operation for lists is very fast. Remember, if you were adding an element to a List<_>, and the internal array was already filled, a new array would then need to be allocated, resulting in a very expensive operation. With lists, cons will always be fast.

Append

The append function, @, joins two lists together. Rather than the last element of the first list ending, it instead points to the beginning of the second list (forming a new, longer list). However, because the last element of the first list provided to append needs to be modified, an entire copy of that list is made.

Visually this can be seen in Figure 7-3:

```
> // Append
let x = [2; 3; 4]
let y = [5; 6; 7];;

val x : int list = [2; 3; 4]
val y : int list = [5; 6; 7]

> x @ y;;
val it : int list = [2; 3; 4; 5; 6; 7]
```

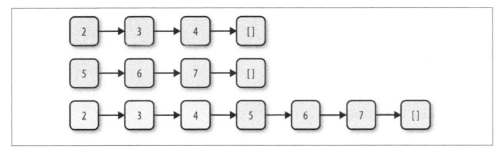

Figure 7-3. Append operator on lists

Looking at Figures 7-2 and 7-3, it is easy to see that cons is a very fast operation because all you do is create a new element and you are done. Append, on the other hand, is potentially more expensive because you need to clone the first list, meaning that for very long lists, append takes a proportionally long time. (Copying the list not only takes twice as much time but also twice as much memory!)

Using Lists

Once you know the performance characteristics of lists, you can then use them effectively. Cons should almost always be preferred over append, except in special circumstances.

Consider Example 7-11. Both functions remove consecutive duplicate elements in a list. The first implementation uses a fold, going from left to right. This makes producing the list costly, because append must be used in each iteration of the fold. (For those familiar with asymptotic time complexity, this is an O(n^2) operation.) Notice that the accumulator for fold is a tuple of the last element and the new list with duplicate items removed.

The second implementation uses foldBack, which means this implementation can build up the list in order by using cons. This is precisely the reason for having two separate fold operations. For this particular problem, foldBack enables the use of cons rather than append, making it a better approach than fold.

Example 7-11. Effective list manipulation

```
(*
Removes consecutive duplicate numbers.
e.g., [1; 1; 2; 2; 3; 4] => [1; 2; 3; 4]
*)

// Slow implementation...
let removeConsecutiveDupes1 lst =

    let foldFunc acc item =
        let lastNumber, dupesRemoved = acc
        match lastNumber with
        | Some(c) when c = item
                    -> Some(c), dupesRemoved
        | Some(c) -> Some(item), dupesRemoved @ [item]
        | None    -> Some(item), [item]

    let (_, dupesRemoved) = List.fold foldFunc (None, []) lst
    dupesRemoved

// Fast implementation...
let removeConsecutiveDupes2 lst =
    let f item acc =
        match acc with
        | []
            -> [item]
        | hd :: tl when hd <> item
            -> item :: acc
        | _ -> acc

    List.foldBack f lst []
```

When using lists, think of append as a "code smell"—it is usually indicative of a suboptimal solution.

Tail Recursion

You can now use lists to process large amounts of data efficiently, but there is trouble looming. Because lists are immutable, the most common way to build them—other than list comprehensions—is with recursion. Consider the following two ways to construct two lists of integers:

```
> // Creating a List<_> of 100,000 integers
open System.Collections.Generic

let createMutableList() =
    let l = new List<int>()
    for i = 0 to 100000 do
        l.Add(i)
    l;;

val createMutableList : unit -> List<int>

> // Creating a list of 100,000 integers
let createImmutableList() =
    let rec createList i max =
        if i - max then
            []
        else
            i :: createList (i + 1) max
    createList 0 100000;;

val createImmutableList : unit -> int list
```

Both solutions look identical, but the createImmutableList function won't work. (In fact, it will crash.) I'll explain the reason why the function is flawed as well as how to fix it by introducing tail recursion.

You may have heard of *tail recursion* before; in fact, you may have even written tail-recursive functions without even knowing it. Tail recursion is a special form of recursion, where the compiler can optimize the recursive call to not consume any additional stack space.

In general, when a function makes a recursive call, the rest of the calling function may still need to execute some code, so the state of what's left to execute is stored on the stack.

However, as recursive functions call themselves deeper and deeper, the limited stack space can be exhausted leading to an unrecoverable type of CLR error: the dreaded StackOverflowException. Because tail recursion doesn't use any additional stack space, it allows you a way to use recursion safely.

Understanding tail recursion is crucial for writing efficient and safe functional code. As you saw in the previous sections, many functional data structures are constructed using recursion to be built up. With this reliance on recursion, stack overflows can become a real threat and limit the size of data a recursive function can process. However, by writing functions in a tail-recursive style, this can be avoided.

Understanding the Stack

Before you can identify and write tail-recursive functions, you need to understand the stack and how it works with regard to recursive functions.

Whenever you call a function, the *instruction pointer*—the address in the program code that identifies the next operation to execute—is pushed onto the stack. Once the called function returns a value, the stack is cleared and the instruction pointer is restored (which resumes the calling function in its previous state).

Consider this simple, recursive function for computing the factorial of a number:

```
let rec factorial x =
    if x <= 1
    then 1     // Base case
    else x * factorial (x - 1)
```

If you set a breakpoint on the base case and call `factorial` with a value of 10, and attach the Visual Studio debugger you will see this call stack in Figure 7-4. Notice that each recursive call creates a new stack frame. Here you can clearly see the recursive function breaking the parameter x down into smaller and smaller values until x is less than or equal to 1 and the base case is executed.

Figure 7-4. Call stack while executing the factorial function

Once the base case executes, it will return the value 1. The stack will be restored to when `factorial` was called with 2 as its parameter, which will return 2 * 1. Then the stack will be restored to when `factorial` was called with 3 as its parameter, returning 3 * 2, and so on.

But remember that the stack is in a fixed block of memory, and generally limited to 1MB. So the `factorial` function will exhaust the stack for sufficiently large values. An easier demonstration of this is in the `infLoop` function in Example 7-12. Notice how `fsi.exe` is launched from the command line and when the `StackOverflow` exception is thrown, the process terminates. That is because you cannot catch the `StackOverflowException`.

Example 7-12. Overflowing the stack with recursion

```
C:\Program Files (x86)\Microsoft SDKs\F#\3.0\Framework\v4.0>Fsi.exe

Microsoft (R) F# 3.0 Interactive build 11.0.50522.1
Copyright (c) Microsoft Corporation. All Rights Reserved.

For help type #help;;

> let rec infLoop() = 1 + infLoop();;

val infLoop : unit -> int

> // Go hunting for a StackOverflowException
- try
-     printfn "%d" <| infLoop()
- with
- | _ -> printfn "Exception caught";;

Process is terminated due to StackOverflowException.

C:\Program Files (x86)\Microsoft SDKs\F#\3.0\Framework\v4.0>
```

Figure 7-5 shows the same `infLoop` program but from within the Visual Studio debugger.

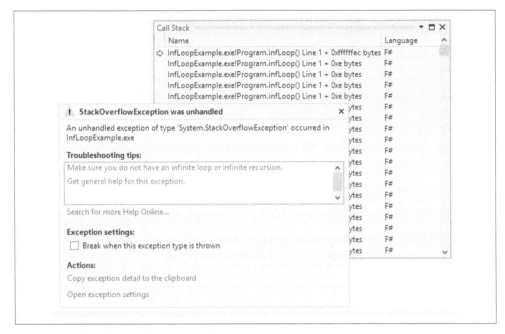

Figure 7-5. The dreaded StackOverflow exception

Introducing Tail Recursion

How can you solve this problem of recursive calls consuming too much stack space? Tail recursion.

If there are no additional instructions to execute, then there is no need to store the instruction pointer on the stack, because the only thing left to do once the recursive call exits is restore the stack to the previous function. So rather than needlessly modifying the stack, *tail calls* (or recursive calls from a tail-recursive function) drop the current stack frame before making the recursive call. And once the recursion eventually succeeds, the function will return to the original instruction pointer location.

The previous implementation of `factorial` was not tail recursive because after the recursive call to `factorial (x-1)` completed, the function needed to multiply that result by x, the original parameter. This is made clearer if you rewrite the function as follows:

```
let rec factorial x =
    if x <= 1
    then
        1
    else
        // Recurse
        let resultOfRecusion = factorial (x - 1)
        // Instruction Pointer needed to be stored
```

```
// so that this instance of the function
// can be resumed at a later time.
let result = x * resultOfRecusion
result
```

Example 7-13 is the tail-recursive version of `factorial`. By passing the data around as an extra parameter, you remove the need to execute code after the recursive function call, so no additional stack space is required. Instead, the result is built up to be returned in the base case rather than being unwound from all the recursive calls.

Example 7-13. Tail-recursive version of factorial

```
let factorial x =
    // Keep track of both x and an accumulator value (acc)
    let rec tailRecursiveFactorial x acc =
        if x <= 1 then
            acc
        else
            tailRecursiveFactorial (x - 1) (acc * x)
    tailRecursiveFactorial x 1
```

When the F# compiler identifies a function as tail recursive, it generates the code differently. For example, the `tailRecursiveFactorial` function would be generated as the following C# code. Notice how the recursion is simply replaced with a `while` loop:

```
// tailRecursiveFactorial function as it would get compiled in C#.
public static int tailRecursiveFactorial (int x, int acc)
{
    while (true)
    {
        if (x <= 1)
        {
            return acc;
        }
        acc *= x;
        x--;
    }
}
```

If you fire up the Visual Studio debugger and set a breakpoint on the base case of the `tailRecursiveFactorial` function, you see that only one stack frame has been used, as shown in Figure 7-6.

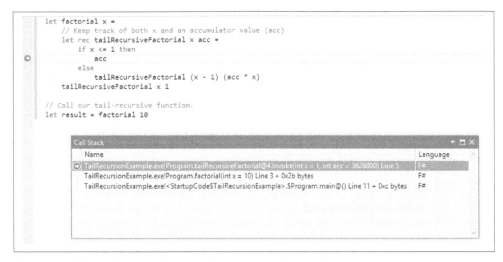

```
let factorial x =
    // Keep track of both x and an accumulator value (acc)
    let rec tailRecursiveFactorial x acc =
        if x <= 1 then
            acc
        else
            tailRecursiveFactorial (x - 1) (acc * x)
    tailRecursiveFactorial x 1

// Call our tail-recursive function.
let result = factorial 10
```

Call Stack			▾ □ ×
Name			Language
⊙ TailRecursionExample.exe!Program.tailRecursiveFactorial@4.Invoke(int x = 1, int acc = 3628800) Line 5			F#
TailRecursionExample.exe!Program.factorial(int x = 10) Line 3 + 0x2b bytes			F#
TailRecursionExample.exe!<StartupCode$TailRecursionExample>.$Program.main@() Line 11 + 0xc bytes			F#

Figure 7-6. The call stack when the function is tail recursive

To sum up, here are the benefits of using tail recursion:

- The function executes slightly faster, because fewer stack pushes and pops are required.
- The function can recurse indefinitely.
- No StackOverflowException is thrown.

And to review, a function is considered tail recursive if and only if there is no work to be performed after a recursive call is executed. We see more examples of this in the next section.

 There is no indication from Visual Studio if a function will be compiled as tail recursive. When you write recursive functions in the functional style, be careful to write them as tail recursive.

Tail-Recursive Patterns

There are two main ways to ensure that a recursive function is tail recursive. The simplest applies to when you are whittling down the input while at the same time building up the answer. The second, and much more mind-bending approach, is used when you need to have two recursive calls and branch code flow.

Accumulator pattern

The simplest way to master tail recursion is to have your code follow certain patterns of usage. The easiest thing to do is to add additional parameters, just like in the previous example of `tailRecursiveFactorial`. This is known as the *accumulator pattern*. Rather than waiting for a recursive call to return, instead you pass an accumulator parameter to the recursive call so that the base case will return the final state of the accumulator.

To illustrate the point, let's write a naïve implementation of `List.map`, which transforms a list based on a provided function:

```
let rec map f list =
    match list with
    | []      -> []
    | hd :: tl -> (f hd) :: (map f tl)
```

However, that code is not tail recursive because on the fourth line; the recursive call to `map` completes and then the cons operation completes. To combat this, you can use the accumulator pattern to simply store the completed result. In Example 7-14, a nested recursive function is defined that takes the mapped list as a parameter and returns it in the base case.

Example 7-14. The accumulator pattern

```
let map f list =
    let rec mapTR f list acc =
        match list with
        | []      -> acc
        | hd :: tl -> mapTR f tl (f hd :: acc)
    mapTR f (List.rev list) []
```

For simple recursive functions, the accumulator pattern is all you need. But what if there is some sort of branching? A function where in order for the function to return, you need to make two recursive calls? (This is called *binary recursion*.) One recursive call at the very least won't be in tail position. Consider Example 7-15, which is an implementation of a binary tree and an `iter` operation that applies a function to each node in the tree.

Example 7-15. Non-tail-recursive iter implementation

```
type BinTree<'a> =
    | Node of 'a * BinTree<'a> * BinTree<'a>
    | Empty

let rec iter f binTree =
    match binTree with
    | Empty -> ()
    | Node(x, l, r) ->
        f x
        iter f l  // NOT in tail position
        iter f r  // In tail position
```

Because there are two recursive calls to make, there simply is no way to use the accumulator pattern. Is all hope lost? Is the dream of entirely tail-recursive code a myth? Fortunately, no. But it will take some functional programming magic to achieve.

Continuations

Imagine rather than passing the current state of the accumulator "so far" as a parameter to the next function call, you instead passed a function value representing the rest of the code to execute. That is, rather than storing "what's left" on the stack, you store it in a function. This is known as the *continuation passing style* or simply using a *continuation*.

Continuations are function values that represent the rest of the code to execute when the current recursive call completes. This allows you to write tail-recursive functions even though there is more work to be done. Conceptually, you are trading stack space (the recursive calls) with heap space (the function values).

Consider Example 7-16, which prints a list of integers in reverse. The printing is done as part of the continuation, which grows larger with each recursive call. In the base case, the continuation is called. The function `printListRevTR` and the built continuation are both tail recursive, so no matter how much input was processed or how large the resulting continuation becomes, it will not overflow the stack.

Example 7-16. Building up a function value

```
> // Print a list in revere using a continuation
let printListRev list =
    let rec printListRevTR list cont =
        match list with
        // For an empy list, execute the continuation
        | [] -> cont()
        // For other lists, add printing the current
        // node as part of the continuation.
        | hd :: tl ->
            printListRevTR tl (fun () -> printf "%d " hd
                                         cont() )

    printListRevTR list (fun () -> printfn "Done!");;

val printListRev : int list -> unit

> printListRev [1 .. 10];;
10 9 8 7 6 5 4 3 2 1 Done!
val it : unit = ()
```

Admittedly, the act of building up a function value is a little mind-bending. But this technique allows you to write functions that otherwise would be impossible to implement in a tail-recursive fashion.

Let's revisit the binary tree `iter` operation. This operation needed to perform two recursive calls, and therefore the function cannot be tail recursive using the accumulator pattern. However, in order to write code that can perform operations on large trees, you need to convert the function to be tail recursive.

There are several ways to do this using continuations, but the simplest is to use a *custom iterator type*. This is a pattern where rather than building up a single continuation to perform all the computation you need in tail-recursive fashion, you *linearrize* what needs to happen through a custom data type.

Example 7-17 defines a custom iterator type `ContinuationStep`, which has two data tags `Finished` and `Step`. `Step` is a tuple of a value and a function to produce the next `ContinuationStep`.

The function `linearize` uses a continuation to convert the binary tree into a `ContinuationStep` object. Each node is converted into a `Step` union tag in addition to breaking the recursive calls to the left and right sub-trees in lambdas. Finally, the `processSteps` function breaks apart the `ContinuationStep` object to actually perform the `iter` operation on the binary tree.

Example 7-17. Building a custom iterator

```
type ContinuationStep<'a> =
    | Finished
    | Step of 'a * (unit -> ContinuationStep<'a>)

let iter f binTree =

    let rec linearize binTree cont =
        match binTree with
        | Empty -> cont()
        | Node(x, l, r) ->
            Step(x, (fun () -> linearize l (fun() -> linearize r cont)))

    let steps = linearize binTree (fun () -> Finished)

    let rec processSteps step =
        match step with
        | Finished -> ()
        | Step(x, getNext)
            ->  f x
                processSteps (getNext())

    processSteps steps
```

Although this example will take some time staring at to make sense, it is one way to break apart recursive functions and write tail-recursive code.

Admittedly, such a complicated solution is likely not the best one. Perhaps using a mutable data structure to store nodes to visit, in the order to visit them, would make more sense. (For example, one could keep a mutable `Stack<_>` of nodes.) But when programming in F#, you have options to find the solution that works best for you.

Programming with Functions

Although tail recursion and modules allow you to get more out of the functional style of programming, there is still more to learn about functions as values. Next we look at function currying and closures. Although they may not be the most important aspect of functional programming, having a good understanding of their capabilities will make it easier for you to write code in the purely functional style.

Partial Function Application

Recall that partial function application is the ability to specify a subset of a function's parameters and return new functions taking fewer parameters. On the surface this seems like a strange feature to add. What does only providing a subset of a function's parameters actually buy you? The most visible benefit of partial function application is the pipe forward operator, which makes data transformation much more elegant:

```
getCustomers()
|> List.filter (fun cust -> datesEqual cust.Birthday DateTime.Today)
|> List.map (fun cust -> cust.EmailAddress)
|> List.filter Option.isSome
|> sendSpam "Happy Birthday... Now buy our product!"
```

Each line of the previous expression is a curried function whose last parameter is provided by the previous line of code. Programming in this style enables you to write code exactly the way you conceptualize it in your head. But partial function application has another way of cleaning up your code as well.

Passing functions as parameters

Higher-order functions (treating functions like values) can potentially eliminate the need for many lambda expressions. Consider the following code, which maps the function f to all the elements of a list:

```
List.map (fun x -> f x) lst
```

Note that the lambda's parameter x is passed as the last parameter to the function f. Whenever you see code like this, you can remove the lambda altogether, because f can be passed as a parameter to the function List.map (this is the way you see most functions passed to List.map):

```
List.map f lst
```

In much the same vein, you can simplify functions even if they accept more than one parameter. In the following example, g takes four parameters, a, b, c, and x. However, because the lambda only takes one parameter, x, you can just pass the partially applied function value as a parameter:

```
List.map (fun x -> g a b c x) lst
```

Again, when the lambda's parameter is the last parameter passed to the function, the code can be simplified again by just currying the function:

```
List.map (g a b c) lst
```

 Although passing functions as parameters can be elegant, it can also obfuscate code. Remember that one day someone else will be debugging your programs, so always take care to ensure that they are readable.

Eliminating Redundant Code

A common objective of refactoring is to eliminate redundancy through reuse, typically through inheritance in object-oriented code. However, you can also eliminate redundant code in the functional style using higher-order functions.

Consider these two functions to aid you in picking what to get for dinner. pickCheap est returns the cheapest entrée from the list, whereas pickHealthiest returns the item with the fewest calories. Remember that reduce behaves just like fold except that the initial value of the accumulator is the first element of the list:

```
[<Measure>]
type usd

type Entree = { Name : string; Price : float<usd>; Calories : int }

// Picks the cheapest item on the menu
let pickCheapest menuItems =
    List.reduce
        (fun acc item -> if item.Price < acc.Price
                         then item
                         else acc)
        menuItems

let pickHealthiest menuItems =
    List.reduce
        (fun acc item -> if item.Calories < acc.Calories
                         then item
                         else acc)
        menuItems
```

Both of these functions are nearly identical and differ only in how they compare the given element. Why not factor that out? If you define the compare function as a parameter, you can swap out implementations much more easily and potentially result in more readable code. Note that the functions pickCheapest2 and pickHealthiest2 rely on their partially applied call to pickItem:

```
let private pickItem cmp menuItems =
    let reduceFunc acc item =
        match cmp acc item with
        | true  -> acc
        | false -> item
    List.reduce reduceFunc menuItems

let pickCheapest2   = pickItem (fun acc item -> item.Price < acc.Price)
let pickHealthiest2 = pickItem (fun acc item -> item.Calories < acc.Calories)
```

Closures

Closure is the term used to describe an inner or nested function that can access values not explicitly passed in as parameters to that function. Like currying, this too may seem like some strange concept that isn't particularly applicable, but you have actually been using closures constantly throughout the book without even knowing it.

A simple example of a closure would be the following function mult, which multiplies every element in a list by a given number. Notice that i is a parameter to the first function, but not a parameter to the lambda expression. So you might be wondering how i can be used inside that lambda if it isn't explicitly passed in as a parameter. That's the beauty of closures. Because value i is in scope, it is *captured* by the closure of the lambda, and therefore accessible. Behind the scenes, the compiler actually links the value i to the lambda so that at runtime the value is accessible, but this is all done for you:

```
> let mult i lst = List.map (fun x -> x * i) lst;;

val mult : int -> int list -> int list

> mult 10 [1; 3; 5; 7];;
val it : int list = [10; 30; 50; 70]
```

In essence, with closures, a function may capture some additional data with it, which enables the function to know about values in the scope where the function was declared. With this we can achieve some interesting results.

Imagine creating an abstract data type, like a class, without any explicit fields to store the type's state. It doesn't sound like it is possible—because in order for the type to have some meaning, it must store its internal data somewhere. But with closures, that isn't the case.

Consider Example 7-18, which defines a record type Set whose two fields are functions; one to add items to the Set, and another to check if an item exists in the set. To create an instance of Set, simply access the static property Empty. Once you have an instance of Set, adding and removing items works entirely by capturing the data in closures. The function makeSet receives a list—which are the items contained in the set. When new items are added to the list, a recursive call to makeSet is returned, capturing the original set's item list and the new item to be added in the closure of the updated Add function.

Example 7-18. Data encapsulation via closures

```
// Data type for a set. Notice the implementation is
// stored in record fields...
type Set =
    {
        // Add an item to the set
        Add    : int -> Set
        // Checks if an element exists in the set
        Exists : int -> bool
    }

    // Returns an empty set
    static member Empty =
        let rec makeSet lst =
            {
                Add    = (fun item -> makeSet (item :: lst))
                Exists = (fun item -> List.exists ((=) item) lst)
            }
        makeSet []
```

You can see the Set type in action in the following FSI session:

```
> // Set in action
let s    = Set.Empty
let s'   = s.Add(1)
let s''  = s'.Add(2)
let s''' = s''.Add(3);;

val s : Set
val s' : Set
val s'' : Set
val s''' : Set

> s.Exists 2;;
val it : bool = false
> s'''.Exists 2;;
val it : bool = true
```

Just like writing super-complicated continuations, there are likely better ways to write types than by storing internal data entirely in closures. However, understanding that functions can contain more than just their parameters opens up new possibilities.

Functional Patterns

Now that we have covered some advanced concepts in the functional style of programming, let's examine some common design patterns they enable. Describing solutions to problems in terms of design patterns makes it easier to explain and reuse such solutions.

Memoization

When you write in the functional style, most of the functions you write will be pure, meaning that for the same input they will always produce the same output. Therefore, if you call the same pure function many times, it can be a waste of resources to recompute known values. Instead, it would be more efficient to store those values in a Dictionary<_,_> type that maps input values to function results.

The process of storing known input/result pairs of a function is known as *memoization*, and can be done automatically by taking advantage of higher-order functions and closures in F#.

Example 7-19 defines a memoize function, which takes a function as a parameter and returns a memoized version of that function as its result. The memoized version stores a dictionary of previous results in its closure, and only calls the provided function when necessary.

Example 7-19. Memoizing pure functions

```
open System.Collections.Generic

let memoize (f : 'a -> 'b) =
    let dict = new Dictionary<'a, 'b>()

    let memoizedFunc (input : 'a) =
        match dict.TryGetValue(input) with
        | true,  x -> x
        | false, _ ->
            // Evaluate and add to lookup table
            let answer = f input
            dict.Add(input, answer)
            answer

    // Return our memoized version of f dict is captured in the closure
    memoizedFunc
```

The following FSI session shows the memoize function in action. The function f simply waits a given number of seconds, and calling the function twice with the same input will cause it to wait twice. Calling the memoized version will simply look up the cached value the second time, so the function doesn't need to be evaluated:

```
> // Some long running function...
let f x =
    // Sleep for x seconds
    System.Threading.Thread.Sleep(x * 1000)
    // Return x
    x;;

val f : int -> int

> // Benchmark
#time;;

--> Timing now on

> f 10;;
Real: 00:00:10.007, CPU: 00:00:00.000, GC gen0: 0, gen1: 0, gen2: 0
val it : int = 10
> f 10;;
Real: 00:00:10.008, CPU: 00:00:00.000, GC gen0: 0, gen1: 0, gen2: 0
val it : int = 10
> let memoizedF = memoize f;;
Real: 00:00:00.004, CPU: 00:00:00.000, GC gen0: 0, gen1: 0, gen2: 0

val memoizedF : (int -> int)

> memoizedF 10;;
Real: 00:00:10.009, CPU: 00:00:00.000, GC gen0: 0, gen1: 0, gen2: 0
val it : int = 10
> memoizedF 10;;
Real: 00:00:00.000, CPU: 00:00:00.000, GC gen0: 0, gen1: 0, gen2: 0
val it : int = 10
```

Memoizing recursive functions

Memoizing recursive functions can be a bit trickier. In Example 7-19, the function
memoize took a function f and returned a new function that checked if the value of f
has already been computed for a given input. However, what if in its evaluation f calls
itself? Unfortunately, it will call the non-memoized version—which eliminates any benefits of memoization. Memoization will only occur for the first input value to the function, it will not check for memoized values for recursive calls.

The correct thing to do is have any recursive calls to the function be through the memoized version. If you think about it, this shouldn't work, because the memoized function
needs to be called before the memoized function is even finished being defined! Fortunately, the F# compiler does the extra work to make it happen, albeit with a warning.

Example 7-20 shows an FSI session illustrating both the correct and incorrect way of
memoizing the fib function. Notice how the function fib in the definition of mem
Fib2 calls memFib2 (the memoized function) instead of recursively calling itself.

Example 7-20. Memoization of recursive functions

```
> // WRONG way to memoize the function - fib doesn't call the
// memoized version recursively.
let wrongMemFib =
    let rec fib x =
        match x with
        | 0 | 1 -> 1
        | 2 -> 2
        | n -> fib (n - 1) + fib (n - 2)

    memoize fib;;

val wrongMemFib : (int -> int)

> // CORRECT way to memoize the function - fib  does call
// the memoized version recursively.
let rec rightMemFib =
    let fib x =
        match x with
        | 0 | 1 -> 1
        | 2 -> 2
        | n -> rightMemFib (n - 1) + rightMemFib (n - 2)

    memoize fib;;

val rightMemFib : (int -> int)

> #time;;

--> Timing now on

> wrongMemFib 45;;
Real: 00:00:21.553, CPU: 00:00:21.528, GC gen0: 0, gen1: 0, gen2: 0
val it : int = 1836311903
> rightMemFib 45;;
Real: 00:00:00.001, CPU: 00:00:00.000, GC gen0: 0, gen1: 0, gen2: 0
val it : int = 1836311903
```

Mutable Function Values

Function values provide a simple way to pass around the implementation of a function. However, a function value can also be mutable, allowing you to easily swap out the *implementation* of a function. Much in the same way a mutable integer allows you to update its value, a mutable function can be updated as well.

Example 7-21 shows how you can change out the implementation of the generateWidg et function on the fly. This allows customization of implementation without resorting to heavyweight solutions like polymorphism and inheritance.

In the example, the `generateWidget` function is initialized to generate Sprockets. However, once the `generateWidget` function is updated, subsequent calls will generate Cogs.

Example 7-21. Using mutable function values

```
> // Code to produce Widgets, the backbone of all .NET applications
type Widget =
    | Sprocket of string * int
    | Cog of string * float

let mutable generateWidget =
    let count = ref 0
    (fun () -> incr count
               Sprocket("Model A1", !count));;

type Widget =
    | Sprocket of string * int
    | Cog of string * float
val mutable generateWidget : (unit -> Widget)

> // Produce a Widget
generateWidget();;
val it : Widget = Sprocket ("Model A1",1)
> // ... and another
generateWidget();;
val it : Widget = Sprocket ("Model A1",2)
> // Now update the function...
generateWidget <-
    let count = ref 0
    (fun () -> incr count
               Cog( (sprintf "Version 0x%x" !count), 0.0));;
val it : unit = ()
> // Produce another Widget   with the updated function
generateWidget();;
val it : Widget = Cog ("Version 0x1",0.0)
> generateWidget();;
val it : Widget = Cog ("Version 0x2",0.0)
```

To be clear, calling a function when you aren't 100% sure what it does can lead to heinous bugs. But being able to change the implementation of a function can be very helpful in certain situations.

Lazy Programming

Lazy programming was brought up briefly in Chapter 3, but it is a style in and of itself. In short, lazy programming means only computing values when needed—as opposed to *eagerly*, which is as soon as they are declared.

Lazy programming can have a few distinct advantages if used correctly.

Reducing memory usage

Earlier we looked at continuations as a way of making operations on a binary tree tail recursive. But even if you didn't need to worry about overflowing the stack, for very large trees, those operations can take a long time to compute. What if you wanted to map a function to every node in a tree with a million elements? Moreover, what if you only needed to access a small subset of the resulting nodes? If you lazily evaluated the map operation, you only compute the values you need.

Example 7-22 defines a binary tree where the nodes are evaluated lazily. So in the implementation of map, the function f is only applied to the child nodes once their evaluation has been forced (by accessing the Value property).

Defining the map operation in this way, the input tree isn't duplicated. Instead, new nodes are only created as they are accessed. So for very large trees that are minimally inspected, using lazy programming can lead to a dramatic savings in memory usage.

Example 7-22. Lazy type

```
type LazyBinTree<'a> =
    | Node of 'a * LazyBinTree<'a> Lazy * LazyBinTree<'a> Lazy
    | Empty

let rec map f tree =
    match tree with
    | Empty -> Empty
    | Node(x, l, r) ->
        Node(
            f x,
            lazy(
                let lfNode = l.Value
                map f lfNode
            ),
            lazy(
                let rtNode = r.Value
                map f rtNode
            )
        )
```

Abstracting data access

Another example of lazy programming is abstracting data access. Example 7-23 loads an entire directory full of comma separated value (CSV) files and returns the data as a single sequence of string arrays. However, the files aren't actually opened and accessed until necessary, so although on the surface the result of processFile looks to be a constant sequence of data, it is in fact opening and closing separate files behind the scenes. With Seq.map and Seq.concat, the file provided to processFile isn't opened until the actual sequence elements are required. Or put another way, the sequences are produced lazily.

Example 7-23. Lazy programming for processing CSV files

```
open System
open System.IO

let processFile (filePath : string) =
    seq {
        use fileReader = new StreamReader(filePath)

        // Skip header row
        fileReader.ReadLine() |> ignore

        while not fileReader.EndOfStream do
            let line = fileReader.ReadLine()
            yield line.Split( [| ',' |] )
    }

let rootPath = @"D:\DataFiles\"
let csvFiles = Directory.GetFiles(rootPath, "*.csv")

let allCsvData =
    csvFiles
    |> Seq.map processFile
    |> Seq.concat
```

Functional Data Structures

In Chapter 4, we looked at a few data structures that had efficient access for data such as the HashSet<T> and Dictionary<K,V> types. However, those types don't lend themselves well to functional programming.

For example, consider passing a dictionary as a parameter to a function. If that function modifies that dictionary in any way, then the calling function's expectations of that dictionary might have been violated.

This leads to the following question: Are there data structures designed specifically for functional use? As it turns out, yes.

Functional Set

In the F# libraries are the Set<_> and Map<_,_> types, which behave much like the HashSet<_> and Dictionary<_,_> except that they are immutable. The Add method, rather than returning unit, returns new instance of the Set<_> or Map<_,_> with the new element included.

Example 7-24 uses the Set<_> type to get the list of unique words from a given web page, which in the example is the text of Mary Shelley's *Frankenstein*.

Notice how the Set<_> type is built up using the Array.fold method. In order to fill a functional collection type, you must use some form of recursion. Also, just as the List and Seq modules provide a series of functions for working with types of the same name, there is a Set module containing methods like Set.add and Set.count.

Example 7-24. Using the Set type

```
> // The functional Set type
open System
open System.IO
open System.Net

let getHtml (url : string) =
    let req = WebRequest.Create(url)
    let rsp = req.GetResponse()

    use stream = rsp.GetResponseStream()
    use reader = new StreamReader(stream)

    reader.ReadToEnd()

let uniqueWords (text : string) =
    let words = text.Split([| ' ' |], StringSplitOptions.RemoveEmptyEntries)

    let uniqueWords =
        Array.fold
            (fun (acc : Set<string>) (word : string) -> Set.add word acc)
            Set.empty
            words

    uniqueWords;;

val getHtml : string -> string
val uniqueWords : string -> Set<string>

> let urlToShelley'sFrankenstein = "http://www.gutenberg.org/files/84/84.txt";;

val urlToShelley'sFrankenstein : string =
  "http://www.gutenberg.org/files/84/84.txt"

> // Produce the Set of unique words
let wordsInBook =
    urlToShelley'sFrankenstein
    |> getHtml |> uniqueWords;;

val wordsInBook : Set<string> = ...

> Set.count wordsInBook;;
val it : int = 16406
```

Functional Map

Example 7-25 uses the Map<_,_> type to associate each word with the number of times it is used in the book. Then, the Map<_,_> is converted to a sequence of key-value tuples, sorted, and the top 20 most frequently occurring words are printed to the screen.

Just like how the Set<_> was built up in the previous example, the Map<_,_> is also produced during a fold operation.

Example 7-25. Using the Map type

```
> // The functional Map type
let wordUsage (text : string) =
    let words = text.Split([| ' ' |], StringSplitOptions.RemoveEmptyEntries)

    let wordFrequency =
        Array.fold
            (fun (acc : Map<string, int>) (word : string) ->
                if Map.containsKey word acc then
                    let timesUsed = acc.[word]
                    Map.add word (timesUsed + 1) acc
                else
                    Map.add word 1 acc)
            Map.empty
            words

    wordFrequency

let printMostFrequentWords (wordFrequency : Map<string, int>) =
    let top20Words =
        wordFrequency
        |> Map.toSeq
        |> Seq.sortBy (fun (word, timesUsed) -> -timesUsed)
        |> Seq.take 20

    printfn "Top Word Usage:"
    top20Words
    |> Seq.iteri(fun idx (word, timesUsed) ->
        printfn "%d\t '%s' was used %d times" idx word timesUsed);;

val wordUsage : string -> Map<string,int>
val printMostFrequentWords : Map<string,int> -> unit

> // Print the most frequent words
urlToShelley'sFrankenstein
|> getHtml |> wordUsage |> printMostFrequentWords
;;
Top Word Usage:
0        'the' was used 3408 times
1        'and' was used 2569 times
2        'of' was used 2405 times
3        'I' was used 2333 times
```

```
4          'to' was used 1900 times
5          'my' was used 1389 times
6          'a' was used 1212 times
7          'in' was used 980 times
8          'that' was used 876 times
9          'was' was used 874 times
10         'with' was used 573 times
11         'had' was used 571 times
12         'but' was used 480 times
13         'me' was used 478 times
14         'which' was used 465 times
15         'as' was used 437 times
16         'not' was used 432 times
17         'his' was used 413 times
18         'by' was used 411 times
19         'you' was used 404 times
val it : unit = ()
```

 For more information on functional data structures and how to implement them, see *Purely Functional Data Structures* by Chris Okasaki
(Cambridge University Press, 1999).

Applied Object-Oriented Programming

This chapter could also be called "being functional in an object-oriented world." By now you've mastered the F# syntax and style, but there is still plenty to be said about using F# in the object-oriented landscape of the .NET platform.

In this chapter, you learn how to create F# types that integrate better with other object-oriented languages like C#. For example, with operator overloading, you can allow your types to be used with symbolic code. Also, events enable your classes to notify consumers to receive notifications when certain actions occur. This not only enables you to be more expressive in your F# code, but also reduces the friction with non-F# developers when sharing your code.

Operators

A symbolic notation for manipulating objects can simplify your code by eliminating methods like Add and Remove, and instead using more intuitive counterparts like + and -. Also, if an object represents a collection of data, being able to index directly into it with the .[ ] or .[*expr* .. *expr*] notation can make it much easier to access the data an object holds.

Operator Overloading

Operator overloading is a term used for adding new meaning to an existing operator, like + or -. Instead of only working on primitive types, you can *overload* those operators to accept custom types you create. Operator overloading in F# can be done by simply adding a static method to a type. After that, you can use the operator as if it natively supported the type. The F# compiler will simply translate the code into a call to your static method.

Be sure to use an operator that makes sense. For example, overloading + for a custom type shouldn't subtract values or remove items from a collection.

When you overload an operator, the operator's name must be in parentheses. For example, (+) overloads the plus operator. To overload a unary operator, simply prefix the operator with a tilde (~).

Example 8-1 overloads the + and – operators to represent operators on a bottle. Note the ~- operator allows for unary negation.

Example 8-1. Operator overloading

```
[<Measure>]
type ml

type Bottle(capacity : float<ml>) =

    new() = new Bottle(0.0<ml>)

    member this.Volume = capacity

    static member (+) ((lhs : Bottle), rhs) =
        new Bottle(lhs.Volume + rhs)

    static member (-) ((lhs : Bottle), rhs) =
        new Bottle(lhs.Volume - rhs)

    static member (~-) (rhs : Bottle) =
        new Bottle(rhs.Volume * -1.0<1>)

    override this.ToString() =
        sprintf "Bottle(%.1fml)" (float capacity)
```

Once the proper operators have been added, then you can intuitively use the class using the standard symbolic operators you would expect (well, a bottle really can't have a negative volume, but you get the idea):

```
> let half = new Bottle(500.0<ml>);;

val half : Bottle = Bottle(500.0ml)

> half + 500.0<ml>;;
val it : Bottle = Bottle(1000.0ml) {Volume = 1000.0;}
> half - 500.0<ml>;;
val it : Bottle = Bottle(0.0ml) {Volume = 0.0;}
> -half;;
val it : Bottle = Bottle(-500.0ml) {Volume = -500.0;}
```

You can also add overloaded operators to discriminated unions and record types the same way they are added to class types:

```
type Person =
    | Boy of string
    | Girl of string
    | Couple of Person * Person
    static member (+) (lhs, rhs) =
        match lhs, rhs with
        | Couple(_), _
        | _, Couple(_)
            -> failwith "Three's a crowd!"
        | _ -> Couple(lhs, rhs)
```

Using the + operator, we can now take two Person objects and convert them into a Couple union case:

```
Boy("Dick") + Girl("Jane");;
val it : Person = Couple (Boy "Dick",Girl "Jane")
```

F# allows you to define arbitrary symbolic operators for types; however, only a subset of these can be used natively with C# and VB.NET. Only the following operators are recognized by those languages:

Binary operators:

```
+, -, *, /, %, &, |, <<, >>
+=, -=, *=, /=, %=
```

Unary operators:

```
~+, ~-, ~!, ~++, ~--
```

Otherwise the method will be exposed as a friendly name describing the symbols used. For example, operator +-+ will be exposed as a static method named op_PlusMinusPlus.

Note that this list does not contain > and <. To define binary comparison operators you must implement IComparable.

Indexers

For types that are a collection of values, an indexer is a natural way to extend the metaphor by enabling developers to index directly into the object. For example, you can get an arbitrary element of an array by using the .[ ] operator.

In F#, you can add an indexer by simply adding a property named Item. This property will be evaluated whenever you call the .[ ] method on the class.

Example 8-2 creates a class Year and adds an indexer to allow you to look up the *n*th day of the year.

Example 8-2. Adding an indexer to a class

```
open System

type Year(year : int) =

    member this.Item (idx : int) =
        if idx < 1 || idx > 365 then
            failwith "Invalid day range"

        let dateStr = sprintf "1-1-%d" year
        DateTime.Parse(dateStr).AddDays(float (idx - 1))
```

The following FSI session shows using the indexer for type `Year`:

```
> // Using a custom indexer
let eightyTwo   = new Year(1982)
let specialDay = eightyTwo.[171];;

val eightyTwo : Year
val specialDay : DateTime = 6/20/1982 12:00:00 AM

> specialDay.Month, specialDay.Day, specialDay.DayOfWeek;;
val it : int * int * DayOfWeek = (6, 20, Sunday)
```

But what if you want to not only read values from an indexer, but write them back as well? Also, what if you wanted the indexer to accept a non-integer parameter? The F# language can accommodate both of those requests.

Example 8-3 defines an indexer for a type that accepts a non-integer parameter. In a different take on the `Year` class example, the indexer takes a month and date tuple.

Example 8-3. Non-integer indexer

```
type Year2(year : int) =

    member this.Item (month : string, day : int) =
        let monthIdx =
            match month.ToUpper() with
            | "JANUARY" -> 1  | "FEBRUARY" -> 2  | "MARCH"     -> 3
            | "APRIL"   -> 4  | "MAY"      -> 5  | "JUNE"      -> 6
            | "JULY"    -> 7  | "AUGUST"   -> 8  | "SEPTEMBER" -> 9
            | "OCTOBER" -> 10 | "NOVEMBER" -> 11 | "DECEMBER"  -> 12
            | _ -> failwithf "Invalid month [%s]" month

        let dateStr = sprintf "1-1-%d" year
        DateTime.Parse(dateStr).AddMonths(monthIdx - 1).AddDays(float (day - 1))
```

Year2 uses a more intuitive indexer that makes the type easier to use:

```
> // Using a non-integer index
let O'seven = new Year2(2007)
let randomDay = O'seven.["April", 7];;
```

```
val O'seven : Year2
val randomDay : DateTime = 4/7/2007 12:00:00 AM

> randomDay.Month, randomDay.Day, randomDay.DayOfWeek;;
val it : int * int * DayOfWeek = (4, 7, Saturday)
```

The read-only indexers you've seen so far aren't ideal for every situation. What if you wanted to provide a read/write indexer to not only access elements but to also update their values? To make a read/write indexer, simply add an explicit getter and setter to the Item property.

Example 8-4 defines a type WordBuilder that allows you to access and update letters of a word at a given index.

Example 8-4. Read/write indexer

```
open System.Collections.Generic

type WordBuilder(startingLetters : string) =
    let m_letters = new List<char>(startingLetters)

    member this.Item
        with get idx   = m_letters.[idx]
        and  set idx c = m_letters.[idx] <- c

    member this.Word = new string (m_letters.ToArray())
```

The syntax for writing a new value using the indexer is the same as when updating a value in an array:

```
> let wb = new WordBuilder("Jurassic Park");;

val wb : WordBuilder

> wb.Word;;
val it : string = "Jurassic Park"
> wb.[10];;
val it : char = 'a'
> wb.[10] <- 'o';;
val it : unit = ()
> wb.Word;;
val it : string = "Jurassic Pork"
```

Adding Slices

Similar to indexers, slices allow you to index into a type that represents a collection of data. The main difference is that where an indexer returns a single element, a slice produces a new collection of data. Slices work by providing syntax support for providing an optional lower bound and an optional upper bound for an indexer.

To add a one-dimensional slice, add a method named `GetSlice` that takes two option types as parameters. Example 8-5 defines a slice for a type called `TextBlock` where the slice returns a range of words in the body of the text.

Example 8-5. Providing a slice to a class

```
type TextBlock(text : string) =
    let words = text.Split([| ' ' |])

    member this.AverageWordLength =
        words |> Array.map float |> Array.average

    member this.GetSlice(lowerBound : int option, upperBound : int option) =
        let words =
            match lowerBound, upperBound with
            // Specify both upper and lower bounds
            | Some(lb), Some(ub) -> words.[lb..ub]
            // Just one bound specified
            | Some(lb), None     -> words.[lb..]
            | None,     Some(ub) -> words.[..ub]
            // No lower or upper bounds
            | None,     None -> words.[*]
        words
```

Using our `TextBlock` class we can see:

```
> // Using a custom slice operator
let text = "The quick brown fox jumped over the lazy dog"
let tb = new TextBlock(text);;

val text : string = "The quick brown fox jumped over the lazy dog"
val tb : TextBlock

> tb.[..5];;
val it : string [] = [|"The"; "quick"; "brown"; "fox"; "jumped"; "over"|]
> tb.[4..7];;
val it : string [] = [|"jumped"; "over"; "the"; "lazy"|]
```

If you need a more refined way to slice your data, you can provide a two-dimension slicer. This allows you to specify two ranges of data. To define a 2-D slice, simply add a method called `GetSlice` again, except that the method should now take four option-type parameters. In order, they are: first-dimension lower bound, first-dimension upper bound, second-dimension lower bound, and second-dimension upper bound.

Example 8-6 defines a class that encapsulates a sequence of data points. The type provides a 2-D slice that returns only those points within the given range.

Example 8-6. Defining a two-dimensional slice

```
open System

type DataPoints(points : seq<float * float>) =
```

```
member this.GetSlice(xlb, xub, ylb, yub) =

    let getValue optType defaultValue =
        match optType with
        | Some(x) -> x
        | None    -> defaultValue

    let minX = getValue xlb Double.MinValue
    let maxX = getValue xub Double.MaxValue

    let minY = getValue ylb Double.MinValue
    let maxY = getValue yub Double.MaxValue

    // Return if a given tuple representing a point is within range
    let inRange (x, y) =
        (minX < x && x < maxX &&
         minY < y && y < maxY)

    Seq.filter inRange points
```

The following FSI session shows the 2-D slice in action. The slice allows you to only get data points that fall within a specific range, allowing you to isolate certain sections for further analysis:

```
> // Define 1,000 random points with value between 0.0 to 1.0
let points =
  seq {
      let rng = new Random()
      for i = 0 to 1000 do
          let x = rng.NextDouble()
          let y = rng.NextDouble()
          yield (x, y)
  };;

val points : seq<float * float>

> points;;
val it : seq<float * float> =
  seq
    [(0.6313018304, 0.8639167859); (0.3367836328, 0.8642307673);
     (0.7682324386, 0.1454097885); (0.6862907925, 0.8801649925); ...]

> let d = new DataPoints(points);;

val d : DataPoints

> // Get all values where the x and y values are greater than 0.5.
d.[0.5.., 0.5..];;

val it : seq<float * float> =
  seq
    [(0.7774719744, 0.8764193784); (0.927527673, 0.6275711235);
```

```
        (0.5618227448, 0.5956258004); (0.9415076491, 0.8703156262); ...]
> // Get all values where the x-value is between 0.90 and 0.99,
// with no restriction on the y-value.
d.[0.90 .. 0.99, *];;

val it : seq<float * float> =
  seq
    [(0.9286256581, 0.08974070246); (0.9780231351, 0.5617941956);
     (0.9649922103, 0.1342076446); (0.9498346559, 0.2927135142); ...]
```

Slices provide an expressive syntax for extracting data from types. However, you cannot add a slice notation for a type higher than two dimensions.

Generic Type Constraints

Adding generic type parameters to a class declaration enables the type to be used in conjunction with any other type. However, what if you want the class to actually *do* something with that generic type? Not just hold a reference to an instance 'a, but do something meaningful with 'a as well. Because 'a could be anything, you are out of luck.

Fortunately, you can add a *generic type constraint*, which will enable you to still have the class be generic but put a restriction on the types it accepts. For example, you can force the generic class to only accept types that implement a specific interface. This allows you to restrict which types can be used as generic type parameters so that you can do more with those generic types.

A generic type constraint is simply a form of type annotation. Whenever you would have written a generic type 'a, you can add type constraints using the when keyword.

Example 8-7 defines a generic class GreaterThanList where the type parameter must also implement the IComparable interface. This allows instances of the generic type to be cast to the IComparable interface, and ultimately enables items to be checked to be sure they are greater than the first element in the list.

Example 8-7. Generic type constraints

```
open System
open System.Collections.Generic

exception NotGreaterThanHead

/// Keep a list of items where each item added to it is
/// greater than the first element of the list.
type GreaterThanList< 'a when 'a :> IComparable<'a> >(minValue : 'a) =

    let m_head = minValue

    let m_list = new List<'a>()
```

```
do m_list.Add(minValue)


member this.Add(newItem : 'a) =
    // Casting to IComparable wouldn't be possible
    // if 'a weren't constrainted
    let ic = newItem :> IComparable<'a>

    if ic.CompareTo(m_head) >= 0 then
        m_list.Add(newItem)
    else
        raise NotGreaterThanHead

member this.Items = m_list :> seq<'a>
```

There are many ways to constrain types in F#. Using multiple type constraints allows you to refine a type parameter; to combine multiple type constraints, simply use the and keyword:

```
/// Given a type x which contains a constructor and implements IFoo,
/// returns an instance of that type cast as IFoo.
let fooFactory<x : 'a when 'a : (new : unit -> 'a) and
                'a :> IFoo>() =

    // Creating new instance of 'a because the type constraint enforces
    // that there be a default constructor.
    let clone = new 'a()

    // Comparing x with a new instance, because we know 'a implements IFoo
    let ifoo = x :> IFoo
    ifoo
```

Most type constraints deal with kind of "type" Value type constraint

The value type constraint enforces that the type argument must be a value type. The syntax for the value type constraint is as follows:

```
'a : struct
```

Reference type constraint

The reference constraint enforces that the type argument must be a reference type. The syntax for the reference constraint is as follows:

```
'a : not struct
```

Enumeration constraint

With the enumeration constraint, the type argument must be an enumeration type whose underlying type must be of the given base type (such as int). The syntax for the enumeration constraint is as follows:

```
'a : enum<basetype>
```

Null constraint

The null constraint requires that the type argument be assignable to `null`. This is true for all objects, except those defined in F# without the [`<AllowNullLiter al>`] attribute:

```
'a : null
```

Unmanaged constraint

The provided type must be unmanaged (either a primitive value type like `int` or `float`, or a non-generic struct with only unmanaged types as fields):

```
'a : unmanaged
```

Delegate constraint

The delegate constraint requires that the type argument must be a delegate type, with the given signature and return type. (Delegates are covered in the next section.) The syntax for defining a delegate constraint is as follows:

```
'a : delegate<tupled-args, return-type>
```

The second set of constraints has to do with the capabilities of the type; these are the most common types of generic constraints.

Type constraint

The subtype constraint enforces that the generic type parameter must match or be a subtype of a given type. (This also applies to implementing interfaces.) This allows you to cast `'a` as a known type. The syntax for a subtype constraint is as follows:

```
'a :> type
```

Constructor constraint

The default constructor constraint enforces that the type parameter must have a default (parameter-less) constructor. This allows you to instantiate new instances of the generic type. The syntax for a default constructor constraint is as follows:

```
'a : (new : unit -> 'a)
```

Equality constraint

The type must support equality. Nearly all .NET types satisfy this constraint by the use of the default referential equality. F# types annotated with the [`<NoEquali ty>`] attribute do not satisfy this constraint.

```
'a : equality
```

Comparison constraint

The type must support comparison by implementing the `System.IComparable` interface. F# records and discriminated unions support the comparison constraint by default unless annotated with the [`<NoComparison>`] attribute.

```
'a : comparison
```

Delegates and Events

So far, the classes and types we have created have been useful, but they needed to be acted upon in order for something to happen. However, it would be beneficial if types could be *proactive* instead of *reactive*. That is, you want types that act upon others, and not the other way around.

Consider Example 8-8, which defines a type `CoffeeCup` that lets interested parties know when the cup is empty. This is helpful in case you wanted to automatically get a refill and avoid missing out on a tasty cup of joe. This is done by keeping track of a list of functions to call when the cup is eventually empty.

Example 8-8. Creating proactive types

```
open System.Collections.Generic

[<Measure>]
type ml

type CoffeeCup(amount : float<ml>) =
    let mutable m_amountLeft = amount
    let mutable m_interestedParties = List<(CoffeeCup -> unit)>()

    member this.Drink(amount) =
        printfn "Drinking %.1f..." (float amount)
        m_amountLeft <- max (m_amountLeft - amount) 0.0<ml>
        if m_amountLeft <= 0.0<ml> then
            this.LetPeopleKnowI'mEmpty()

    member this.Refil(amountAdded) =
        printfn "Coffee Cup refilled with %.1f" (float amountAdded)
        m_amountLeft <- m_amountLeft + amountAdded

    member this.WhenYou'reEmptyCall(func) =
        m_interestedParties.Add(func)

    member private this.LetPeopleKnowI'mEmpty() =
        printfn "Uh ho, I'm empty! Letting people know..."
        for interestedParty in m_interestedParties do
            interestedParty(this)
```

When used in an FSI session, the following transpires after a refreshing cup of coffee has been emptied:

```
> let cup = new CoffeeCup(100.0<ml>);;

val cup : CoffeeCup

> // Be notified when the cup is empty
cup.WhenYou'reEmptyCall(
    (fun cup ->
```

```
        printfn "Thanks for letting me know..."
        cup.Refil(50.0<ml>) ));;
val it : unit = ()

> cup.Drink(75.0<ml>);;

Drinking 75.0...
val it : unit = ()

> cup.Drink(75.0<ml>);;
Drinking 75.0...
Uh ho, I'm empty! Letting people know...
Thanks for letting me know...
Coffee Cup refilled with 50.0
val it : unit = ()
```

Abstractly, we can describe the CoffeeCup class as a pattern enabling *consumers*—people who have an instance of the class—to subscribe to an *event*—when the cup is empty. This turns out to be very useful, and makes up the foundation of most graphical programming environments (so-called *event-driven* programming). For example, windowing systems allow you to provide functions to be called when a button is clicked or when a check box is toggled. However, our custom implementation of keeping a list of function values is clunky at best.

Fortunately, the .NET framework has rich support for this pattern through the use of *delegates* and *events*. A *delegate* is very similar to F#'s function values. An *event* is simply the mechanism for calling the functions provided by all interested parties.

When used together, delegates and events form a contract. The first class *publishes* an event, which enables other classes to *subscribe* to that event. When the class's event is fired, the delegates provided by all subscribers are executed.

Delegates can be thought of as an alternate form of function values. They represent a function pointer to a method and can be passed around as parameters or called directly, just like function values. Delegates, however, offer a couple of advantages over the F# functions you are used to, as we see shortly.

Defining Delegates

To define a delegate, simply use the following syntax. The first type represents the parameters passed to the delegate and the second type is the return type of the delegate when called:

```
type ident = delegate of type1 -> type2
```

Example 8-9 shows how to create a simple delegate and how similar it is to a regular function value. To instantiate a delegate type, you use the new keyword and pass the body of the delegate in as a parameter. To execute a delegate, you must call its Invoke method.

Example 8-9. Defining and using delegates

```
let functionValue x y =
    printfn "x = %d, y = %d" x y
    x + y

// Defining a delegate
type DelegateType = delegate of int * int -> int

// Construct a delegate value
let delegateValue1 =
    new DelegateType(
        fun x y ->
            printfn "x = %d, y = %d" x y
            x + y
    )

// Calling function values and delegates
let functionResult = functionValue 1 2
let delegateResult = delegateValue1.Invoke(1, 2)
```

F# has a bit of magic that eliminates the need for instantiating some delegate types. If a class member takes a delegate as a parameter, rather than passing an instance of that delegate type, you can pass in a lambda expression, provided it has the same signature as the delegate.

The following code snippet defines a delegate `IntDelegate` and a class method `Apply Delegate`. `ApplyDelegate` is called twice, the first using an explicit instance of `Int Delegate`, and again using an implicit instance. The lambda expression provided would create a valid instance of `IntDelegate` and so the F# compiler creates one behind the scenes.

This dramatically cleans up F# code that interacts with .NET components that expect delegates, such as the Parallel Extensions to the .NET Framework, discussed in Chapter 11:

```
type IntDelegate = delegate of int -> unit

type ListHelper =
    /// Invokes a delegate for every element of a list
    static member ApplyDelegate (l : int list, d : IntDelegate) =
        l |> List.iter (fun x -> d.Invoke(x))

// Explicitly constructing the delegate
ListHelper.ApplyDelegate([1 .. 10], new IntDelegate(fun x -> printfn "%d" x))

// Implicitly constructing the delegate
ListHelper.ApplyDelegate([1 .. 10], (fun x -> printfn "%d" x))
```

Combining Delegates

Although delegates are very similar to function values, there are two key differences. First, delegates can be combined. Combining multiple delegates together allows you to execute multiple functions with a single call to Invoke. Delegates are coalesced by calling the Combine and Remove static methods on the System.Delegate type, which is the base class for all delegates.

Example 8-10 shows combining delegates so that a single call to Invoke will execute multiple delegates at once.

Example 8-10. Combining delegates

```
open System.IO

type LogMessage = delegate of string -> unit

let printToConsole =
    LogMessage(fun msg -> printfn "Logging to console: %s..." msg)

let appendToLogFile =
    LogMessage(fun msg -> printfn "Logging to file: %s..." msg
                          use file = new StreamWriter("Log.txt", true)
                          file.WriteLine(msg))

let doBoth = LogMessage.Combine(printToConsole, appendToLogFile)
let typedDoBoth = doBoth :?> LogMessage
```

The following is the output from the FSI session. Invoking the typedDoBoth delegate executes both the printToConsole delegate and the appendToLogFile delegate. F# function values cannot be combined in this way:

```
> typedDoBoth.Invoke("[some important message]");;
Logging to console: [some important message]...
Logging to file: [some important message]...
val it : unit = ()
```

The second main difference between delegate types and function values is that you can invoke a delegate asynchronously, so the delegate's execution will happen on a separate thread and your program will continue as normal. To invoke a delegate asynchronously, call the BeginInvoke and EndInvoke methods.

Unfortunately, delegates created in F# do not have the BeginInvoke and EndInvoke methods, so to create delegates that can be invoked asynchronously you must define them in VB.NET or C#. In Chapter 11, we look at parallel and asynchronously programming in F# and simple ways to work around this.

Events

Now that you understand delegates, let's look at how to take advantage of them to create events. Events are just syntactic sugar for properties on classes that are delegates. So when an event is raised, it is really just invoking the combined delegates associated with the event.

Creating Events

Let's start with a simple example and work backward from that. Unlike C# or VB.NET, there is no event keyword in F#.

Example 8-11 creates a NoisySet type that fires events whenever items are added or removed from the set. Rather than keeping track of event subscribers manually, it uses the Event<'Del, 'Arg> type, which is discussed shortly.

Example 8-11. Events and the Event<_,_> type

```
type SetAction = Added | Removed

type SetOperationEventArgs<'a>(value : 'a, action : SetAction) =
    inherit System.EventArgs()

    member this.Action = action
    member this.Value = value

type SetOperationDelegate<'a> = delegate of obj * SetOperationEventArgs<'a> -> unit

// Contains a set of items that fires events whenever
// items are added.
type NoisySet<'a when 'a : comparison>() =
    let mutable m_set = Set.empty : Set<'a>

    let m_itemAdded =
        new Event<SetOperationDelegate<'a>, SetOperationEventArgs<'a>>()

    let m_itemRemoved =
        new Event<SetOperationDelegate<'a>, SetOperationEventArgs<'a>>()

    member this.Add(x) =
        m_set <- m_set.Add(x)
        // Fire the 'Add' event
        m_itemAdded.Trigger(this, new SetOperationEventArgs<_>(x, Added))

    member this.Remove(x) =
        m_set <- m_set.Remove(x)
        // Fire the 'Remove' event
        m_itemRemoved.Trigger(this, new SetOperationEventArgs<_>(x, Removed))
```

```
// Publish the events so others can subscribe to them
member this.ItemAddedEvent   = m_itemAdded.Publish
member this.ItemRemovedEvent = m_itemRemoved.Publish
```

Delegates for events

The first thing to point out in the example is the delegate used for the event. In .NET, the idiomatic way to declare events is to have the delegate return unit and take two parameters. The first parameter is the source, or object raising the event, the second parameter is the delegate's arguments passed in an object derived from System.Event Args.

In the example, the SetOperationEventArgs type stores all relevant information for the event, such as the value of the item being added or removed. Many events, however, are raised without needing to send any additional information, in which case the Event Args class is not inherited from.

Creating and raising the event

Once the delegate has been defined for the event, the next step is to actually create the event. In F#, this is done by creating a new instance of the Event<_,_> type:

```
let m_itemAdded =
        new Event<SetOperationDelegate<'a>, SetOperationEventArgs<'a>>()
```

We cover the Event<_,_> type shortly, but note that whenever you want to raise the event or add subscribers to the event, you must use that type. Raising the event is done by calling the Trigger method, which takes the parameters to the delegates to be called:

```
// Fire the 'Add' event
m_itemAdded.Trigger(this, new SetOperationEventArgs<_>(x, Added))
```

Subscribing to events

Finally, to subscribe to a class's events, use the AddHandler method on the event property. From then on, whenever the event is raised, the delegate you passed to AddHandler will be called.

If you no longer want your event handler to be called, you can call the RemoveHandler method.

 Be sure to remove an event handler when an object no longer needs to subscribe to an event. Otherwise, the event raiser will still have a reference to the object and therefore will prevent the subscriber from being garbage collected. This is a very common way to introduce memory leaks in .NET applications.

Example 8-12 shows the `NoisySet<_>` type in action.

Example 8-12. Adding and removing event handlers

```
> // Using events
let s = new NoisySet<int>()

let setOperationHandler =
    new SetOperationDelegate<int>(
        fun sender args ->
            printfn "%d was %A" args.Value args.Action
    )

s.ItemAddedEvent.AddHandler(setOperationHandler)
s.ItemRemovedEvent.AddHandler(setOperationHandler);;

val s : NoisySet<int>
val setOperationHandler : SetOperationDelegate<int>

> s.Add(9);;
9 was Added
val it : unit = ()
> s.Remove(9);;
9 was Removed
val it : unit = ()
```

As you can see from Example 8-12, all the work of combining delegates and eventually raising the event was handled by the `Event<'Del, 'Arg>` class. But what is it exactly? And why does it need two generic parameters?

The Event<_,_> Class

The `Event<'Del, 'Arg>` type keeps track of the delegates associated with the event, and makes it easier to fire and publish an event. The type takes two generic parameters. The first is the type of delegate associated with the event, which in the previous example was `SetOperationDelegate`. The second generic parameter is the type of the delegate's argument, which was `SetOperationEventArgs`. (Note that this ignores the delegate's actual first parameter, the sender object.)

If your events don't follow this pattern where the first parameter is the sender object, then you should use the `DelegateEvent<'del>` type instead. It is used the same way, except that its arguments are passed in as an `obj` array.

Example 8-13 defines a clock type with a single event that gets fired every second, notifying subscribers of the current hour, minute, and second. Note that in order to trigger an event with type `DelegateEvent<_>` you must pass in an `obj array` for all of its parameters. As a reminder, the `box` function converts its parameter to type `obj`.

Example 8-13. The DelegateEvent type

```
open System

type ClockUpdateDelegate = delegate of int * int * int -> unit

type Clock() =

    let m_event = new DelegateEvent<ClockUpdateDelegate>()

    member this.Start() =
        printfn "Started..."
        while true do
            // Sleep one second...
            Threading.Thread.Sleep(1000)

            let hour   = DateTime.Now.Hour
            let minute = DateTime.Now.Minute
            let second = DateTime.Now.Second

            m_event.Trigger( [| box hour; box minute; box second |] )

    member this.ClockUpdate = m_event.Publish
```

When finally run, Example 8-13 produces the following output:

```
> // Non-standard event types
let c = new Clock();;

val c : Clock

> // Adding an event handler
c.ClockUpdate.AddHandler(
    new ClockUpdateDelegate(
        fun h m s -> printfn "[%d:%d:%d]" h m s
    )
);;
val it : unit = ()

> c.Start();;
Started...
[14:48:27]
[14:48:28]
[14:48:29]
```

The Observable Module

Using events as a way to make class types proactive and notify others when particular events occur is helpful. However, events in F# don't have to be associated with a particular class, much like functions in F# don't have to be members of a particular class.

The `Observable` module defines a series of functions for creating instances of the `I Observable<_>` interface, which allows you to treat events like first-class citizens much like objects and functions. This way you can use functional programming techniques like composition and data transformation on events.

Example 8-14 defines a `JukeBox` type that raises an event whenever a new song is played. (The specifics of the mysterious `CLIEvent` attribute are covered later.)

Example 8-14. Compositional events

```
[<Measure>]
type minute

[<Measure>]
type bpm = 1/minute

type MusicGenre = Classical | Pop | HipHop | Rock | Latin | Country

type Song = { Title : string; Genre : MusicGenre; BPM : int<bpm> }

type SongChangeArgs(title : string, genre : MusicGenre, bpm : int<bpm>) =
    inherit System.EventArgs()

    member this.Title = title
    member this.Genre = genre
    member this.BeatsPerMinute = bpm

type SongChangeDelegate = delegate of obj * SongChangeArgs -> unit

type JukeBox() =
    let m_songStartedEvent = new Event<SongChangeDelegate, SongChangeArgs>()

    member this.PlaySong(song) =
        m_songStartedEvent.Trigger(
            this,
            new SongChangeArgs(song.Title, song.Genre, song.BPM)
        )

    [<CLIEvent>]
    member this.SongStartedEvent = m_songStartedEvent.Publish
```

Rather than just adding event handlers directly to the `JukeBox` type, we can use the `Observable` module to create new, more specific event handlers. In Example 8-15, the `Observable.filter` and `Observable.partition` methods are used to create two new events, `slowSongEvent` and `fastSongEvent`, which will be raised whenever the Juke Box plays songs that meet a certain criteria.

The advantage is that you can take an existing event and transform it into new events, which can be passed around as values.

Example 8-15. Using the Event module

```
> // Use the Observable module to only subscribe to specific events
let jb = new JukeBox()

let fastSongEvent, slowSongEvent =
    jb.SongStartedEvent
    // Filter event to just dance music
    |> Observable.filter(fun songArgs ->
            match songArgs.Genre with
            | Pop | HipHop | Latin | Country -> true
            | _ -> false)
    // Split the event into 'fast song' and 'slow song'
    |> Observable.partition(fun songChangeArgs ->
            songChangeArgs.BeatsPerMinute >= 120<bpm>);;

val jb : JukeBox
val slowSongEvent : IObservable<SongChangeArgs>
val fastSongEvent : IObservable<SongChangeArgs>

> // Add event handlers to the IObservable event
slowSongEvent.Add(fun args -> printfn
                                "You hear '%s' and start to dance slowly..."
                                args.Title)

fastSongEvent.Add(fun args -> printfn
                                "You hear '%s' and start to dance fast!"
                                args.Title);;
> jb.PlaySong( { Title = "Burnin Love"; Genre = Pop; BPM = 120<bpm> } );;
You hear 'Burnin Love' and start to dance fast!
val it : unit = ()
```

However, `Observable.filter` and `Observable.partition` are not the only useful methods in the module.

Observable.add

`Observable.add` simply subscribes to the event. Typically this method is used at the end of a series of pipe-forward operations and is a cleaner way to subscribe to events than calling `AddHandler` on the event object.

`Observable.add` has the following signature:

```
val add : ('a -> unit) -> IObservable<'a> -> unit
```

Example 8-16 pops up a message box whenever the mouse moves into the bottom half of a form.

Example 8-16. Subscribing to events with Observable.add

```
open System.Windows.Forms

let form = new Form(Text="Keep out of the bottom!", TopMost=true)
```

```
form.MouseMove
|> Observable.filter (fun moveArgs -> moveArgs.Y > form.Height / 2)
|> Observable.add    (fun moveArgs -> MessageBox.Show("Moved into bottom half!")
                                      |> ignore)

form.ShowDialog()
```

Observable.merge

Observable.merge takes two input events and produces a single output event, which will be fired whenever either of its input events is raised.

Observable.merge has the following signature:

```
val merge: IObservable<'a> -> IObservable<'a> -> IObservable<'a>
```

This is useful for when trying to combine and simplify events. For example, in the previous example, if a consumer didn't care about specifically dancing to slow or fast songs, both the song events could be combined into a single justDance event:

```
> // Combine two song events
let justDanceEvent = Observable.merge slowSongEvent fastSongEvent
justDanceEvent.Add(fun args -> printfn "You start dancing, regardless of tempo!");;

val justDanceEvent : System.IObservable<SongChangeArgs>

> // Queue up another song
jb.PlaySong(
    { Title = "Escape (The Pina Colada Song)"; Genre = Pop; BPM = 70<bpm> } );;
You hear 'Escape (The Pina Colada Song)' and start to dance slowly...
You start dancing, regardless of tempo!
val it : unit = ()
```

Observable.map

Sometimes when working with an event value, you want to transform it into some sort of function that is easier to work with. Observable.map allows you to convert an event with a given argument type into another. It has the following signature:

```
val map: ('a -> 'b) -> IObservable<'a> -> IObservable<'b>
```

When using Windows Forms, all mouse click events are given in pixels relative to the top left of the form. So for a given form f, the top left corner is at position (0, 0) and the bottom right corner is at position (f.Width, f.Height). Example 8-17 uses Event.map to create a new Click event that remaps the positions to points relative to the center of the form.

Example 8-17. Transforming event arguments with Event.map

```
> // Create the form
open System.Windows.Forms

let form = new Form(Text="Relative Clicking", TopMost=true)

form.MouseClick.AddHandler(
    new MouseEventHandler(
        fun sender clickArgs ->
            printfn "MouseClickEvent    @ [%d, %d]" clickArgs.X clickArgs.Y
    )
)

// Create a new click event relative to the center of the form
let centeredClickEvent =
    form.MouseClick
    |> Observable.map (fun clickArgs -> clickArgs.X - (form.Width  / 2),
                                        clickArgs.Y - (form.Height / 2))
// Subscribe
centeredClickEvent
|> Observable.add (fun (x, y) -> printfn "CenteredClickEvent @ [%d, %d]" x y);;

val form : Form =  System.Windows.Forms.Form, Text: Relative Clicking
val centeredClickEvent : System.IObservable<int * int>

> // The output is from clicking the dialog twice, first in the
// top left corner and then in the center.
form.ShowDialog();;
MouseClickEvent    @ [4, 8]
CenteredClickEvent @ [-146, -142]
MouseClickEvent    @ [150, 123]
CenteredClickEvent @ [0, -27]
val it : DialogResult = Cancel
```

Using the Observable module enables you to think about events in much the same way as function values. This adds a great deal of expressiveness and enables you to do more with events in F# than you can in other .NET events.

Creating .NET Events

There is just one extra step for creating events in F#. To create an event in F# code, you need to create a property that returns an instance of the IEvent<_, _> interface. However, to create an event that can be used by other .NET languages, you must also add the [<CLIEvent>] attribute. This is just a hint to the F# compiler specifying how to generate the code for the class. To F# consumers of your code, the class will behave identically; however, to other .NET languages, rather than being a property of type IEvent<_,_> there will be a proper .NET event in its place.

Example 8-18 revisits our coffee cup example, but rather than keeping an explicit list of functions to notify when the coffee cup is empty, a proper .NET event is used instead.

Example 8-18. Creating .NET compatible events

```
open System

[<Measure>]
type ml

type EmptyCoffeeCupDelegate = delegate of obj * EventArgs ->  unit

type EventfulCoffeeCup(amount : float<ml>) =
    let mutable m_amountLeft = amount
    let m_emptyCupEvent = new Event<EmptyCoffeeCupDelegate, EventArgs>()

    member this.Drink(amount) =
        printfn "Drinking %.1f..." (float amount)
        m_amountLeft <- max (m_amountLeft - amount) 0.0<ml>
        if m_amountLeft <= 0.0<ml> then
            m_emptyCupEvent.Trigger(this, new EventArgs())

    member this.Refil(amountAdded) =
        printfn "Coffee Cup refilled with %.1f" (float amountAdded)
        m_amountLeft <- m_amountLeft + amountAdded

    [<CLIEvent>]
    member this.EmptyCup = m_emptyCupEvent.Publish
```

Asynchronous and Parallel Programming

"Parallel programming" frightens many developers, as the term has become synonymous with complexity and difficult-to-find bugs. However, with the libraries and language features available to F#, any anxiety over parallel programming is misplaced.

In fact, even if parallel programming were difficult—which I contend it is not—it is still worth studying because without it you simply cannot take advantage of your hardware's potential.

This chapter focuses on how to speed up computation in F# using asynchronous and parallel programming. By the end of this chapter, you will be able to execute code in different contexts (threads), use the F# asynchronous workflows library for mastering asynchronous programming, and also take advantage of the Parallel Extensions to .NET.

Before we begin, let's define some of the domains related to "parallel programming":

Asynchronous programming

> *Asynchronous programming* describes programs and operations that once started are executed in the background and terminate at some "later time." For example, in most email clients, new emails are retrieved asynchronously in the background so the user doesn't have to force checking for new mail.

Parallel programming

> *Parallel programming* is dividing up work between processing resources in order to speed up execution. For example, converting a song into an MP3 can be parallelized—dividing the song into pieces and converting each segment in parallel.

Reactive programming

> *Reactive programming* is writing applications in such a way that they respond to events as they occur in real time. For example, an application that updates the user interface whenever the backing data store has been updated.

Although each of these paradigms can add a great deal of complexity to applications, using them provides some clear benefits:

Ability to take advantage of multiple processors and cores
> Modern computers come with multiple processors, each equipped with multiple cores. These logical units allow multiple computations to happen at the same time, so rather than executing your program sequentially, you can take advantage of these extra processors and cores by splitting up your programs. For example, a computer with two quad-core processors can execute eight operations at once.

Asynchronous I/O
> Historically, I/O operations such as reading and writing to disk have been the bottleneck in high-performance applications. Modern hardware has the ability to do asynchronous I/O, which can greatly improve overall performance.

Application responsiveness
> Perhaps the most compelling reason to introduce asynchronous programming into your applications is to increase responsiveness. For any long-running computation, if you run it asynchronously, then your application is still free to process user input. This enables users to continue working or perhaps even cancel operations in progress. Nobody likes staring at a frozen screen.

Working with Threads

Asynchronous and parallel programming is done by using *threads*, which are different computational units. Once started, the operating system will give each thread on the system a certain amount of time to execute before passing control to another thread.

What separates threads from *processes* is that processes are kept isolated from each other. Threads belong to the process that spawned them and can access the same memory heap as any other thread spawned by that process, so communication between threads is as simple as writing data to shared memory. Processes, on the other hand, cannot easily access each other's memory, and so communication is more difficult.

At any given moment, the operating system determines which threads are executing. The ones that aren't executing are suspended, and simply waiting for their next slice of processor time.

Spawning multiple threads on a single-processor system won't hurt anything—but the processor can only execute one of those threads at a time, so there will be time lost switching between the different threads. The same program on a multiprocessor or multicore machine, on the other hand, would be able to execute several threads concurrently, so it will often go much faster.

The drawback with multiple things going on at once is that it can be difficult to keep track of data being read or written. Is the data that thread *alpha* read out of date because thread *beta* just updated the value? What if thread *alpha* needs to access a file that thread *beta* has locked for writing? When you're dealing with multiple threads, several classes of synchronization issues can occur, which we cover later.

Spawning Threads

To spin up a new thread and have it execute in the background, simply create a new instance of `System.Threading.Thread` and pass in a `ThreadStart` delegate to its constructor. Then, call the `Thread` object's `Start` method.

Example 9-1 spawns a couple of threads that each count to five.

 Remember that in F# if a function takes a delegate as a parameter, you can pass in a lambda expression or function value and the compiler will treat it as if you had created an instance of the delegate type. So in the example, threadBody is passed into the constructor of Thread and converted into new instance of ThreadStart.

Example 9-1. Creating threads

```
// Creating new threads
open System
open System.Threading

// What will execute on each thread
let threadBody() =
    for i in 1 .. 5 do
        // Wait 1/10 of a second
        Thread.Sleep(100)
        printfn "[Thread %d] %d..."
            Thread.CurrentThread.ManagedThreadId
            i

let spawnThread() =
    let thread = new Thread(threadBody)
    thread.Start()

// Spawn a couple of threads at once
spawnThread()
spawnThread()
```

When executed, Example 9-1 will output the following (or something like it, depending on how the OS schedules the threads and/or assign thread IDs):

```
[Thread 5] 1...
[Thread 6] 1...
[Thread 5] 2...
[Thread 6] 2...
[Thread 5] 3...
[Thread 6] 3...
[Thread 5] 4...
[Thread 6] 4...
[Thread 5] 5...
[Thread 6] 5...
```

Spawning multiple threads that count to five is a good start, but imagine that the threadBody function calculated insurance premiums or did gene sequence alignment. Getting multiple threads executing code concurrently is actually just as simple as spinning up a new thread and calling Start.

Other than Start, there are two methods on a Thread object that you should be aware of: Sleep and Abort.

Thread.Sleep

Thread.Sleep is a static method that puts the currently executing thread to sleep for a given number of milliseconds. In Example 9-1, both threads had a 100 millisecond sleep—or 1/10th of a second—in between when they printed to the console.

Typically, Thread.Sleep is used to put in a static delay or simply yield execution of the current thread so the OS can devote processor time to a different thread.

Thread.Abort

The Thread.Abort method kills the thread, attempting to stop its execution by raising a ThreadAbortException execution somewhere in the executing thread (with a few exceptions, wherever the thread's instruction pointer happens to be at the time the thread is aborted). With the .NET memory model, the abrupt termination of the thread likely won't leak any memory, but you should always avoid using Thread.Abort.

Later in this chapter, we look at more advanced libraries built on top of System.Thread to enable friendly notions such as task cancellation to avoid the need for Thread.Abort.

The .NET Thread Pool

Spawning new threads can be costly. For example, each thread has its own stack to keep track of its execution that can be several megabytes in size. For short-lived actions, rather than continually allocating memory for new threads, it is recommended that you use the *.NET thread pool*, which is a collection of threads just waiting around to do your bidding.

You can spawn a task on the .NET thread pool by using the `ThreadPool.QueueUser WorkItem` function, which takes a delegate of type `WaitCallback`. The following example does the same printing numbers to the console, except that it doesn't need to manually allocate and start the threads.

`WaitCallback` takes a parameter of type `obj`, because in one overload of the `QueueUser WorkItem` method you can pass in an `obj` parameter, which will be passed to the callback. If no parameter is specified when calling `QueueUserWorkItem`, the callback's parameter will be `null`:

```
open System.Threading

ThreadPool.QueueUserWorkItem(fun _ -> for i = 1 to 5 do printfn "%d" i)

// Our thread pool task, note that the delegate's
// parameter is of type obj
let printNumbers (max : obj) =
    for i = 1 to (max :?> int) do
        printfn "%d" i

ThreadPool.QueueUserWorkItem(new WaitCallback(printNumbers), box 5)
```

Sharing Data

With multiple threads executing, you will want to share data between them for coordination and storing intermediate results. This can lead to a couple of problems: race conditions and deadlocks.

Race conditions

A *race condition* is when you have two threads trying to read or write the same reference at the same time. If two threads are writing a value, the last one wins, and the first write operation is lost forever. Similarly, if one thread reads a value and the other immediately overwrites that value, then the first thread's data is out of date and potentially invalid.

Example 9-2 simply loops through an array and adds up its elements on two threads. Both threads are constantly updating the `total` reference cell, which leads to a data race.

Example 9-2. Race conditions

```
open System.Threading

let sumArray (arr : int[]) =
    let total = ref 0

    // Add the first half
    let thread1Finished = ref false

    ThreadPool.QueueUserWorkItem(
        fun _ -> for i = 0 to arr.Length / 2 - 1 do
```

```
                    total := arr.[i] + !total
                thread1Finished := true
        ) |> ignore

    // Add the second half
    let thread2Finished = ref false

    ThreadPool.QueueUserWorkItem(
        fun _ -> for i = arr.Length / 2 to arr.Length - 1 do
                    total := arr.[i] + !total
                thread2Finished := true
        ) |> ignore

    // Wait while the two threads finish their work
    while !thread1Finished = false ||
          !thread2Finished = false do

        Thread.Sleep(0)

    !total
```

The results of the sumArray function in an FSI session are quite troubling. Not only does this function fail to work, it returns a different value each time! An array with an million elements with value one should sum to exactly one million; instead, sumArray is returning about half that:

```
> // Array of 1,000,000 ones
let millionOnes = Array.create 1000000 1;;

val millionOnes : int [] =
  [|1; 1; 1; 1; 1; 1; 1; 1; 1; 1; 1; 1; 1; 1; 1; 1; 1; 1; 1; 1; 1; 1; 1; 1; 1;
    1; 1; 1; 1; 1; 1; 1; 1; 1; 1; 1; 1; 1; 1; 1; 1; 1; 1; 1; 1; 1; 1; 1; 1; 1;
    1; 1; 1; 1; 1; 1; 1; 1; 1; 1; 1; 1; 1; 1; 1; 1; 1; 1; 1; 1; 1; 1; 1; 1; 1;
    1; 1; 1; 1; 1; 1; 1; 1; 1; 1; 1; 1; 1; 1; 1; 1; 1; 1; 1; 1; 1; 1; 1; 1; 1;
    ...|]

> sumArray millionOnes;;
val it : int = 547392
> sumArray millionOnes;;
val it : int = 579574
> sumArray millionOnes;;
val it : int = 574109
> sumArray millionOnes;;
val it : int = 573321
> sumArray millionOnes;;
val it : int = 550012
```

The problem arises from the fact that updating total consists of three separate operations: reading the value, incrementing it, and then writing it back. Ideally, updating total would occur as a single, atomic operation.

A solution for data races is to *lock* the shared data to prevent other threads from accessing it while you update its value. For example, there would be no problem with the implementation of sumArray if only one thread could read and update the value of total at a time.

In F#, you can lock a value by using the lock function, which has the following signature. It takes a reference value, which is the value being locked on, and will lock that value until the provided function is finished executing:

```
val lock : ('a -> (unit -> 'b) -> 'b) when 'a : not struct
```

Example 9-3 is the same as Example 9-2 except that this time, all access to the total value is done inside of lock, meaning that all other threads must wait to access it until the provided predicate has finished executing.

Example 9-3. Array summing using lock

```
let lockedSumArray (arr : int[]) =
    let total = ref 0

    // Add the first half
    let thread1Finished = ref false
    ThreadPool.QueueUserWorkItem(
        fun _ -> for i = 0 to arr.Length / 2 - 1 do
                    lock (total) (fun () -> total := arr.[i] + !total)
                thread1Finished := true
    ) |> ignore

    // Add the second half
    let thread2Finished = ref false
    ThreadPool.QueueUserWorkItem(
        fun _ -> for i = arr.Length / 2 to arr.Length - 1 do
                    lock (total) (fun () -> total := arr.[i] + !total)
                thread2Finished := true
    ) |> ignore

    // Wait while the two threads finish their work
    while !thread1Finished = false ||
          !thread2Finished = false do

        Thread.Sleep(0)

    !total
```

Now the function works exactly like we want; the sum of an array with a million ones is exactly one million. However, with the locking there is no longer any performance gain from summing the array elements in parallel, because the counting is actually done one element at a time as the lock is released and immediately acquired, over and over again.

Later in this chapter, you will learn to use concurrent data structures that are built for high performance while still using locking internally to maintain data integrity:

```
> lockedSumArray millionOnes;;
val it : int = 1000000
> lockedSumArray millionOnes;;
val it : int = 1000000
> lockedSumArray millionOnes;;
val it : int = 1000000
> lockedSumArray millionOnes;;
val it : int = 1000000
```

Deadlocks

Locking solves the data race problem; however, it unfortunately introduces more problems down the road. What if you need to acquire a lock while you are locking something else? This has the potential to lead to a *deadlock*.

Deadlocks are when you want to access a resource that is locked by another thread, but that other thread won't let up until you release a resource that you have locked. So both you and the other thread are left waiting for the other to release their lock indefinitely.

Whenever you have a lock on an object, you run the risk of a potential deadlock if another thread needs to access that value.

Example 9-4 shows a simple implementation of a bank account and a function to transfer funds between two bank accounts using locking.

Example 9-4. Deadlocks in F#

```
type BankAccount = { AccountID : int; OwnerName : string; mutable Balance : int }

/// Transfer money between bank accounts
let transferFunds amount fromAcct toAcct =

    printfn "Locking %s's account to deposit funds..." toAcct.OwnerName
    lock fromAcct
        (fun () ->
            printfn "Locking %s's account to withdraw funds..." fromAcct.OwnerName
            lock toAcct
                (fun () ->
                    fromAcct.Balance <- fromAcct.Balance - amount
                    toAcct.Balance   <- toAcct.Balance + amount
                )
        )
```

The previous code snippet looks simple enough, but if there is ever a fund transfer between the same two accounts at the same time, then the code will deadlock.

In the following example, the first call to `transferFunds` will lock John Smith's account, whereas on a separate thread, the second call to `transferFunds` will lock Jane Doe's account. Then, when the `transferFunds` routine goes to lock the other account, both threads will stall indefinitely:

```
let john = { AccountID = 1; OwnerName = "John Smith"; Balance = 1000 }
let jane = { AccountID = 2; OwnerName = "Jane Doe";   Balance = 2000 }

ThreadPool.QueueUserWorkItem(fun _ -> transferFunds 100 john jane)
ThreadPool.QueueUserWorkItem(fun _ -> transferFunds 100 jane john)
```

Deadlocking doesn't mean that sharing data between threads is a no-win situation. You just need to be judicious in your use of locking and be aware of what dependencies threads have. There are many ways to write code with locks that do not lead to deadlocks. For example, in the previous example, if the function `transferFunds` always locked the account with the lower `AccountID` first, then there would be no deadlock.

Asynchronous Programming

Armed with a firm understanding of threads, you can now look at how to begin writing asynchronous programs for .NET.

Asynchronous programming is when you begin an operation on a background thread to execute concurrently, and have it terminate at some later time; either ignoring the new task to complete in the background, or polling it at a later time to check on its return value.

Modern hardware has facilities for parallel reading and writing, so performing asynchronous I/O may improve your application's performance. This is especially true if you are writing data to disk that you will not need later—there is no need to "block" the program, waiting for the operation to complete, when you can begin the write asynchronously and continue execution of your program.

The way asynchronous programs have historically been written on .NET has been using the *asynchronous programming model*, or APM.

The APM is a pattern for dividing asynchronous operations into two methods called `BeginOperation` and `EndOperation`. When `BeginOperation` is called, the operation will begin asynchronously, and when the operation completes, a provided delegate callback is executed. The code within that callback must call `EndOperation`, which will retrieve the result of the asynchronous computation. Coordination, such as polling for when the operation has completed, happens through the use of the `IAsyncResult` interface.

Example 9-5 uses the APM to asynchronously open a file, perform some operation on the file's data, and then asynchronously write the updated data to disk. Doing this asynchronously effectively queues up all the I/O operations so that the disk controller can work as fast as it can. More importantly, the thread isn't blocked while the operation completes.

Don't worry if all the AsyncCallback delegates and IAsyncResult interfaces seem complicated. The APM truly is a pain to work with, and in the next section, you will see a way to avoid using this model explicitly.

Example 9-5. Asynchronous I/O using the AMP

```
open System
open System.IO

let processFileAsync (filePath : string) (processBytes : byte[] -> byte[]) =

    // This is the callback from when the AsyncWrite completes
    let asyncWriteCallback =
        new AsyncCallback(fun (iar : IAsyncResult) ->
            // Get state from the async result
            let writeStream = iar.AsyncState :?> FileStream

            // End the async write operation by calling EndWrite
            let bytesWritten = writeStream.EndWrite(iar)
            writeStream.Close()

            printfn
                "Finished processing file [%s]"
                (Path.GetFileName(writeStream.Name))
        )

    // This is the callback from when the AsyncRead completes
    let asyncReadCallback =
        new AsyncCallback(fun (iar : IAsyncResult) ->
            // Get state from the async result
            let readStream, data = iar.AsyncState :?> (FileStream * byte[])

            // End the async read by calling EndRead
            let bytesRead = readStream.EndRead(iar)
            readStream.Close()

            // Process the result
            printfn
                "Processing file [%s], read [%d] bytes"
                (Path.GetFileName(readStream.Name))
                bytesRead

            let updatedBytes = processBytes data

            let resultFile = new FileStream(readStream.Name + ".result",
```

```
                          FileMode.Create)

            let _ =
                resultFile.BeginWrite(
                    updatedBytes,
                    0, updatedBytes.Length,
                    asyncWriteCallback,
                    resultFile)

            ()
        )

    // Begin the async read, whose callback will begin the async write
    let fileStream = new FileStream(filePath, FileMode.Open, FileAccess.Read,
                                    FileShare.Read, 2048,
                                    FileOptions.Asynchronous)

    let fileLength = int fileStream.Length
    let buffer = Array.zeroCreate fileLength

    // State passed into the async read
    let state = (fileStream, buffer)

    printfn "Processing file [%s]" (Path.GetFileName(filePath))
    let _ = fileStream.BeginRead(buffer, 0, buffer.Length,
                                 asyncReadCallback, state)
    ()
```

To the mortal programmer, the code in Example 9-5 demonstrates just how painful and error prone the APM is. Several problems with this pattern stand out:

- If several asynchronous computations happen back to back, you can no longer follow the flow of the program as it is spread across multiple callbacks.

- Forgetting to call EndOperation can lead to adverse effects from memory leaks to exceptions to program hangs.

- Casting any state information from the IAsyncResult.AsyncState property can lead to type cast exceptions at runtime.

- Once you start looping with asynchronous calls, you encounter a nightmare of spaghetti callbacks.

These aren't the only pitfalls when using the APM. What if you wanted to do proper exception handling across the series of asynchronous operations? You can't wrap all of your callbacks inside of a single try-with expression; rather, you need to have an exception handler inside each callback.

The point of introducing the APM wasn't to scare you away from asynchronous programming, but rather to set the stage for how F# can improve upon this.

Ideally, there would be a way to eliminate the need for explicitly dividing up your code into what happens *before* the asynchronous operation (the code that calls `BeginOpera tion`) and what happens *after* the asynchronous operation (the callback, which calls `EndOperation`).

It would be useful if you could write your code in a synchronous fashion, and just have some helper library do the "thread hopping" and "chopping up your computation and passing it to a callback" for you. Ideally, you could write:

```
printfn "Opening file..."
let_wait_until_async_is_done data = openFileAsync filePath

let result = processFile data filePath

printfn "Writing result to disk..."
do_wait_until_async_is_done writeFileAsync (filePath +  ".result") result

printfn "Finished!"
```

As it turns out, you are in luck! In F# you can do just that.

Asynchronous Workflows

F# asynchronous workflows allow you to perform asynchronous operations without the need for explicit callbacks. This allows you to write code as if it was using synchronous execution but in actuality the code will execute asynchronously, suspending and resuming the computation as asynchronous operations complete.

 F# asynchronous workflows don't introduce any new primitives to the .NET platform; rather, F#'s computation expression syntax makes the existing threading libraries much more palatable.

Example 9-6 repeats the same task of asynchronously reading and writing a file, except rather than using the APM, all of the asynchronous operations are handled by the F# asynchronous workflows library. The result is that the code is dramatically simpler to write and understand.

The magic of how async workflows works is discussed shortly. But for now, just notice that the code is wrapped up in the `async` computation expression builder and the asynchronous operations begin with `let!` and `do!`. Also, note that the result of the `async` builder is passed to the mysterious `Async.Start` method.

Example 9-6. Asynchronous file I/O using F# async workflows

```
open System.IO

let asyncProcessFile (filePath : string) (processBytes : byte[] -> byte[]) =
    async {

        printfn "Processing file [%s]" (Path.GetFileName(filePath))

        use fileStream = new FileStream(filePath, FileMode.Open)
        let bytesToRead = int fileStream.Length

        let! data = fileStream.AsyncRead(bytesToRead)

        printfn
            "Opened [%s], read [%d] bytes"
            (Path.GetFileName(filePath))
            data.Length

        let data' = processBytes data

        use resultFile = new FileStream(filePath + ".results", FileMode.Create)
        do! resultFile.AsyncWrite(data', 0, data'.Length)

        printfn "Finished processing file [%s]" <| Path.GetFileName(filePath)
    } |> Async.Start
```

The Async Library

The secret behind asynchronous workflows is that the code is wrapped in an `async` block and doesn't immediately execute. Rather, the computation that the code performs is returned in the form of an `Async<'T>` object, which you can think of as an asynchronous operation that will *eventually* return an instance of `'T`. Exactly how the `'T` will be extracted from the `Async<'T>` is the business of the `Async` module and the `async` computation expression builder.

Whenever a `let!` or `do!`, or similar action is performed, the `async` computation builder will begin the task asynchronously and then execute the rest of the computation once that task completes.

In the previous example, the function `AsyncRead` returns an `Async<byte[]>`. So if the code were written:

```
let data = fileStream.AsyncRead(bytesToRead)
```

The type of `data` would be `Async<byte[]>`.

However, `let!` (pronounced let-bang) was used instead. This starts the `async` builder's machinery to begin the computation asynchronously, and return the result that was a byte array once that operation completes:

```
let! data : byte[] = fileStream.AsyncRead(bytesToRead)
```

 Refer to Chapter 13 for more information about how let! and do! translate to function calls on a computation expression builder.

Starting async tasks

There are several methods available to start asynchronous workflows. The simplest of which is the Async.Start method. Async.Start takes an Async<unit> as a parameter, and simply begins executing it asynchronously. If you want the async task to return a value, then you need to wait for operation to complete by calling Async.RunSynchro nously.

Example 9-7 defines a function getHtml that takes a URL as a parameter and returns the web page's content. The function returns an instance of type Async<string>.

Notice that a value is returned from the async workflow by using the return! keyword. return is also a valid way to return a value from an async workflow, and will have the workflow return an Async<'T> instead of a 'T.

Example 9-7. Retrieving values from async workflows

```
open System.IO
open System.Net

let getHtml (url : string) =
    async {

        let req = WebRequest.Create(url)
        let! rsp = req.AsyncGetResponse()

        use stream = rsp.GetResponseStream()
        use reader = new StreamReader(stream)

        return reader.ReadToEndAsync().Result
    }

let html =
    getHtml "http://en.wikipedia.org/wiki/F_Sharp_programming_language"
    |> Async.RunSynchronously
```

Async.RunSynchronously isn't especially useful on its own, because it blocks the starting thread waiting for the operation to complete—which is exactly the opposite of asynchronous execution. Usually this method is called immediately after the Async.Paral lel method, which takes a seq< Async<'T> >, and starts all of the sequence's computations in parallel. The results are combined into an instance of Async<'T[]>.

The following code snippet builds off the `getHtml` method, and retrieves a series of web pages in parallel:

```
let webPages : string[] =
    [ "http://www.google.com"; "http://www.bing.com"; "http://www.yahoo.com" ]
    |> List.map getHtml
    |> Async.Parallel
    |> Async.RunSynchronously
```

In addition to simplifying asynchronous code, using F# asynchronous workflows has the added benefit of making it easier to handle exceptions and support cancellation, something that is prohibitively difficult when using the APM.

Exceptions

Earlier when we were chopping up asynchronous tasks with `BeginOperation` and `EndOperation`, what if you wanted to properly handle an exception? Rather than having multiple exception handlers—each within an APM callback—when using asynchronous workflows, you can put the exception handler directly in the `async` block.

Even if the body of the `try` has several asynchronous operations (`let!`s and `do!`s) inside of it, the exception will be caught exactly the way you expect:

```
let asncOperation =
    async {
        try
            // ...
        with
        | :? IOException as ioe ->
            printfn "IOException: %s" ioe.Message
        | :? ArgumentException as ae ->
            printfn "ArgumentException: %s" ae.Message
    }
```

But what happens if an exception from an async workflow isn't caught? Does the exception bubble up and eventually bring down the whole process? Unfortunately, yes.

In asynchronous workflows, unhandled exceptions bring down the whole process because by default they are not caught. To catch unhandled exceptions from async workflows, you can use the `Async.StartWithContinuations` method, discussed later, or use the `Async.Catch` combinator.

The `Async.Catch` method takes an async workflow and wraps it into a success or exception result. It has the following signature:

```
val Catch : Async<'T> -> Async< Choice<'T,exn> >
```

The Choice type means that its value has one of several values; this is what multicase active patterns compile to behind the scenes.

The following example uses the `Async.Catch` combinator to enable catching exceptions and then runs the async workflow. If the task completes successfully, the result is printed to the screen, otherwise the exception's message is printed:

```
asyncTaskX
|> Async.Catch
|> Async.RunSynchronously
|> function
    | Choice1Of2 result     -> printfn "Async operation completed: %A" result
    | Choice2Of2 (ex : exn) -> printfn "Exception thrown: %s" ex.Message
```

Cancellation

When you execute code asynchronously, it is important to have a cancellation mechanism just in case the user notices things going awry or gets impatient. Earlier, when we were working with raw threads, the only way to cancel an operation was to literally kill the thread using `Thread.Abort`, and in doing so introduce numerous problems.

Asynchronous workflows can be cancelled, but unlike `Thread.Abort`, cancelling an async workflow is simply a request. The task does not immediately terminate, but rather the next time a `let!`, `do!`, etc., is executed, the rest of the computation will not be run and a cancellation handler will be executed instead.

The simplest way to hook up cancellation is to use the `Async.TryCancelled` method. Similar to `Async.Catch`, it takes an `Async<'T>` and returns an updated `Async<'T>` that will call a provided function in the event that the workflow is cancelled.

Example 9-8 defines a simple task that counts to ten and cancels it later. Notice how the cancellation is done by calling the `Async.CancelDefaultToken` method.

Example 9-8. Cancelling asynchronous operations

```
open System
open System.Threading

let cancelableTask =
    async {
        printfn "Waiting 10 seconds..."
        for i = 1 to 10 do
            printfn "%d..." i
            do! Async.Sleep(1000)
        printfn "Finished!"
    }

// Callback used when the operation is canceled
```

```
let cancelHandler (ex : OperationCanceledException) =
    printfn "The task has been canceled."

Async.TryCancelled(cancelableTask, cancelHandler)
|> Async.Start

// ...

Async.CancelDefaultToken()
```

Cancellation in F# asynchronous workflows is handled using the same mechanism of the Parallel Extensions to .NET, via the `CancellationToken` type. A `CancellationToken` keeps track of whether or not the operation has been cancelled (or more specifically, had cancellation requested). So whenever a `let!` or `do!` is encountered, the `async` builder checks the workflow's `CancellationToken` to see if the operation should continue or terminate early.

The `Async.CancelDefaultToken` method cancels the last asynchronous workflow that was started. This is ideal most of the time but can cause issues if your application starts multiple asynchronous workflows.

If you want to be able to cancel an arbitrary asynchronous workflow, then you'll want to create and keep track of a `CancellationTokenSource` object. A `CancellationTokenSource` is what signals the cancellation, which in turn updates all of its associated `CancellationTokens`.

The following snippet shows how to start an asynchronous workflow whose cancellation is tracked by a `CancellationTokenSource` object:

```
open System.Threading

let computation = Async.TryCancelled(cancelableTask, cancelHandler)
let cancellationSource = new CancellationTokenSource()

Async.Start(computation, cancellationSource.Token)

// ...

cancellationSource.Cancel()
```

The `Async` module may seem a bit complicated with so many ways to start and customize async workflow tasks. Most likely, you will only use one method for hooking into unhandled exceptions and cancellations, and that is the `Async.StartWithContinua` `tions` method. Essentially, it is `Async.Catch`, `Async.TryCancelled`, and `Async.Start` all rolled into one. It takes four parameters:

- The async workflow to execute
- A function to execute when the operation completes

- A function to call in case an exception is thrown
- A function to call in case the operation gets cancelled

The following snippet shows the `Async.StartWithContinuations` method in action:

```
Async.StartWithContinuations(
    superAwesomeAsyncTask,
    (fun result -> printfn "Task completed with result %A" result),
    (fun exn    -> printfn "Task threw an exception: %s" exn.Message),
    (fun oce    -> printfn "Task was cancelled. Message: %s" oce.Message)
)
```

Async Operations

F# asynchronous workflows show the ease at which you can write asynchronous code, but how do you get an instance of `Async<'T>`? You can build your own async objects, as you will see shortly, but most likely you will use the extension methods defined in the F# library.

The `System.IO.Stream` type is extended with several methods for reading and writing data synchronously. You've already seen examples of `AsyncRead` and `AsyncWrite`.

The `System.Net.WebRequest` class is extended with `AsyncGetResponse` for retrieving web pages asynchronously:

```
open System.IO
open System.Net

open Microsoft.FSharp.Control.WebExtensions

let getHtml (url : string) =
    async {

        let req = WebRequest.Create(url)
        let! rsp = req.AsyncGetResponse()

        use stream = rsp.GetResponseStream()
        use reader = new StreamReader(stream)

        return reader.ReadToEnd()
    }
```

The `Async.Sleep` method does a sleep just like `Thread.Sleep` except that it does not block the async workflow thread. Instead, the thread that begins the sleep will be reused by some other task, and when the sleep completes, another thread will be woken up to finish the execution.

The following code snippet suspends and resumes an async workflow each second to update a progress bar attached to a WinForm:

```
#r "System.Windows.Forms.dll"
#r "System.Drawing.dll"

open System.Threading
open System.Windows.Forms

let form = new Form(TopMost = true)

let pb   = new ProgressBar(Minimum = 0, Maximum = 15, Dock = DockStyle.Fill)
form.Controls.Add(pb)

form.Show()

async {
    for i = 0 to 15 do
        do! Async.Sleep(1000)
        pb.Value <- i
} |> Async.Start
```

Custom Async Primitives

You can build your own async workflow primitives by using the Async.FromBeginEnd
function. As parameters, it takes the Begin*Operation* and End*Operation* methods
from the APM, but wraps them so that they can be used with an async workflow. (The
Async.FromBeginEnd function is overloaded to accept various types of APM
operations.)

Example 9-9 defines two extension methods for getting the files in a directory and
copying a file asynchronously. Both async primitives work by using the Func<_,_> type,
which is a way to create function values, except that it works using delegates. Remember
that any delegate type defined in C# or VB.NET comes with a BeginInvoke and End
Invoke method that can serve as the basis for the APM.

Once the two new async primitives AsyncGetFiles and AsyncCopy have been created,
they are used to copy all the files from one folder to another.

 Be careful when creating your own async primitives. Unless there is a
specific reason for executing an operation asynchronously, such as an
OS hook to improve I/O throughput, you won't see any improvement
as the operation will complete synchronously and then switch to a different thread when the async workflow resumes.

Example 9-9. Creating custom async primitives

```
open System
open System.IO

type System.IO.Directory with
```

```
    /// Retrieve all files under a path asynchronously
    static member AsyncGetFiles(path : string, searchPattern : string) =
        let dele = new Func<string * string, string[]>(Directory.GetFiles)
        Async.FromBeginEnd(
            (path, searchPattern),
            dele.BeginInvoke,
            dele.EndInvoke)

type System.IO.File with
    /// Copy a file asynchronously
    static member AsyncCopy(source : string, dest : string) =
        let dele = new Func<string * string, unit>(File.Copy)
        Async.FromBeginEnd((source, dest), dele.BeginInvoke, dele.EndInvoke)


let asyncBackup path searchPattern destPath =
    async {
        let! files = Directory.AsyncGetFiles(path, searchPattern)

        for file in files do
            let filename = Path.GetFileName(file)
            do! File.AsyncCopy(file, Path.Combine(destPath, filename))
    }
```

Limitations

F# asynchronous workflows are great for enabling I/O parallelism; however, because the library simply is a lightweight wrapper on top of the thread pool, using it won't guarantee that you will maximize performance. When executing code in parallel, there are numerous factors to take into account; for example:

- The number of processor cores
- Processor cache coherency
- The existing CPU workload

Although F# asynchronous workflows make it easy to perform multiple computations at once, there is no throttling of executing threads to ensure an optimal usage. For example, if eight threads are vying for CPU time, but the machine is already under a heavy workload, then a lot of time is wasted context switching between those threads. Ideally, a governor would give some threads more processor time to reduce this context switching.

You should use F# asynchronous workflows for asynchronous programming, but for CPU-level parallelism, consider using the .NET Task Parallel Library.

Parallel Programming

Parallel programming is about dividing a computation up into n parts to hopefully obtain an n-times speed up (although in practice this is rarely achievable).

The simplest way to do parallel programming on .NET is through the *Task Parallel Library* (TPL), which is Microsoft-speak for new primitives to make it easier to write parallel programs. By using the TPL, you should have no need to manually control threads or the thread pool.

Parallel.For

The first thing you can do to parallelize your applications is to just swap out your for loops with the Parallel.For and Parallel.ForEach methods in the System.Thread ing namespace. Like their name implies, these functions can replace for loops and execute loop iterations in parallel.

Example 9-10 uses Parallel.For to multiply two matrices. The code to produce each row of the resulting matrix is in the **rowTask** function, so rows of the resulting matrix will be computed in parallel.

Example 9-10. Using Parallel.For

```
open System
open System.Threading.Tasks

/// Multiply two matricies using the TPL
let matrixMultiply (a : float[,]) (b : float[,]) =

    let aRow, aCol = Array2D.length1 a, Array2D.length2 a
    let bRow, bCol = Array2D.length1 b, Array2D.length2 b
    if aCol <> bRow then failwith "Array dimension mismatch."

    // Allocate space for the resulting matrix, c
    let c = Array2D.create aCol bRow 0.0
    let cRow, cCol = aCol, bRow

    // Compute each row of the resulting matrix
    let rowTask rowIdx =
        for colIdx = 0 to cCol - 1 do
            for x = 0 to aRow - 1 do
                c.[colIdx, rowIdx] <-
                    c.[colIdx, rowIdx] + a.[x, colIdx] * b.[rowIdx, x]
        ()

    let _ = Parallel.For(0, cRow, new Action<int>(rowTask))

    // Return the computed matrix
    c
```

```
// Example usage:
// let x = array2D [| [| 1.0; 0.0 |]; [| 0.0; 1.0 |] |]
// let y = array2D [| [| 1.0; 2.0; |]; [| 7.0; 8.0; |] |]
// let result = matrixMultiply y x
```

Blindly swapping out for loops with `Parallel.For` will introduce bugs if the code executing inside the `for` loop depends on the previous iteration (e.g., if you are using a `for` loop to perform a fold-type operation). In the previous example, the order in which rows were computed didn't matter, so the code could safely be parallelized.

You can start to see the benefits of containing mutation and not sharing global state. In F#, you have to "opt-in" for mutating data, so your code by default is thread safe.

The Array.Parallel Module

Built on top of the TPL, for F# developers, is the `Array.Parallel` module that contains some of the methods found in the `Array` module, such as `map`, `mapi`, and `partition`. The only difference is that these methods complete the operation in parallel.

Example 9-11 shows using the `Array.Parallel` module to open and search through files in parallel. Just like using `Parallel.For`, if the operation on each element of the array is independent, you can safely replace the synchronous operations with the parallel ones.

The code retrieves a list of classified files, decrypts them in parallel, then searches for keywords in parallel, and finally encrypts them again... in parallel.

Example 9-11. Using the Array.Parallel library

```
open System.IO

let getSecretData keyword =

    let secretFiles = Directory.GetFiles(@"D:\TopSecret\", "*.classified")

    Array.Parallel.iter File.Decrypt secretFiles

    let secretData =
        Directory.GetFiles(@"D:\TopSecret\", "*.classified")
        |> Array.Parallel.map (fun filePath -> File.ReadAllText(filePath))
        |> Array.Parallel.choose (fun contents ->
                if contents.Contains(keyword)
                then Some(contents)
                else None)

    Array.Parallel.iter File.Encrypt secretFiles

    secretData
```

Task Parallel Library

In the previous section, we looked at how to execute operations in arrays and for loops in parallel; however, not every problem can decompose so nicely. Most likely, you will see a way to cleanly break up a problem, but the divisions may not be equal. Or perhaps one part of the problem may need to be subdivided again and again in a "divide and conquer" approach.

Fortunately, the TPL allows you divide your operations however you see fit and the library will take care of scheduling and executing those pieces in parallel.

The core structure of TPL parallelism is the Task object. Similar to the Async<'T> type, a Task represents a body of work to be completed later. To see what the Task object offers, let's quickly review how to write parallel programs in F#.

Suppose you have two independent, long-running tasks. The naïve implementation simply runs them in serial:

```
let result1 = longTask1()
let result2 = longTask2()
```

You can improve upon this by using the thread pool as you saw earlier; however, this makes a mess of the code and prevents you from cancelling the operation or handling exceptions properly:

```
let mutable completed = false
let mutable result1 = null

ThreadPool.QueueUserWorkItem(fun _ ->
    result1   <- longTask1()
    completed <- true
) |> ignore

let result2 = longTask2()

// Wait until task1 complete
while not completed do
    Thread.Sleep(0)
```

Here is how you can solve this problem using the TPL:

```
open System.Threading.Tasks

let taskBody = new Func<string>(longTask1)
let task = Task.Factory.StartNew<string>(taskBody)

let result2 = longTask2()
let result1 = task.Result
```

Primitives

New tasks can be created using one of the overloads of the `Task.Factory.StartNew` method. Once created, the task will be scheduled to execute in parallel. However, the machinery of the TPL library will determine just how many tasks to spawn at a time, dependent upon factors such as current available CPU resources, number of processors, and so on.

The point is that you don't need to manage this explicitly—the TPL will do it for you. So whereas spawning numerous operations using F# asynchronous workflows would overwhelm the thread pool and CPU, the TPL properly modulates how many tasks are executing at once to get the best performance possible.

To retrieve a task's return value, all you need to do is access its `Result` property:

```
let x = task.Result
```

Accessing `Result` will do one of two things:

- Return the task's stored result if it the task has already completed.
- Block until the task has completed.

You don't have to track individual tasks either. You can combine multiple tasks with synchronization primitives `Task.WaitAll` and `Task.WaitAny`. These functions take an array of tasks and wait until all the tasks have finished or any of the tasks have finished before continuing on.

Example 9-12 shows spawning several tasks to resize images in a directory, and using the `WaitAll` method to wait for all of the parallel operations to complete.

Example 9-12. Using Task.WaitAll to wait for tasks to complete

```
open System
open System.IO
open System.Drawing
open System.Drawing.Imaging
open System.Drawing.Drawing2D
open System.Threading.Tasks

/// Resize images to a new width, height
let resizeImage (newWidth : int, newHeight : int) (filePath : string) =
    let originalImage = Bitmap.FromFile(filePath)

    let resizedImage = new Bitmap(newWidth, newHeight)
    use g = Graphics.FromImage(resizedImage)
    g.InterpolationMode <- InterpolationMode.HighQualityBicubic
    g.DrawImage(originalImage, 0, 0, newWidth, newHeight)

    let fileName = Path.GetFileNameWithoutExtension(filePath)
    let fileFolder = Path.GetDirectoryName(filePath)
```

```
    resizedImage.Save(
        Path.Combine(fileFolder, fileName + ".Resized.jpg"),        ImageFormat.Jpeg)

// Spawns a new TPL task to resize an image
let spawnTask filePath =
    let taskBody = new Action(fun () -> resizeImage (640, 480) filePath)
    Task.Factory.StartNew(taskBody)

let imageFiles = Directory.GetFiles(@"C:\2012-06-20 iPhone\", "*.jpg")

// Spawning resize tasks
let resizeTasks = imageFiles |> Array.map spawnTask

// Wait for them all to complete
Task.WaitAll(resizeTasks)
```

The WaitAny primitive may seem strange—why spawn several tasks and only wait for one to complete? There are two good reasons to use this primitive.

First, if you have a family of algorithms you can use to solve a problem, each with varying degrees of efficiently based on input, then it can make sense to start them all in parallel and just get the first one that completes. (You might want to cancel all the other tasks once you know their results won't be needed though.)

Second, it can be helpful for creating more responsive applications. For example, if there were a UI attached to Example 9-13, the user might want to see the results of the resized images as they came in—not just after all of the operations have completed.

Cancellation

Another benefit of using the Task class unlike manually controlling threads you spawn is to take advantage of cancellation. Just like F# asynchronous workflows, cancellation is a request and doesn't immediately terminate the task. So if you want tasks to behave well when cancelled, you must explicitly check for it.

As mentioned earlier, the Parallel Extensions to .NET use the same cancellation mechanism as F# asynchronous workflows. Specifically, each task can be associated with a CancellationToken object that keeps track of its cancellation status. A CancellationToken is produced by a CancellationTokenSource object, which actually signals cancellation.

Example 9-13 shows starting up a task that will execute for 10 seconds, unless it is otherwise cancelled. The task is started with a CancellationToken associated the long TaskCTS CancellationTokenSource. Once signaled to be cancelled, a task must either shutdown as best it can or simply throw an OperationCancelledException.

Example 9-13. Cancelling tasks

```
open System
open System.Threading
open System.Threading.Tasks

let longTaskCTS = new CancellationTokenSource()

let longRunningTask() =
    let mutable i = 1
    let mutable loop = true

    while i <= 10 && loop do
        printfn "%d..." i
        i <- i + 1
        Thread.Sleep(1000)

        // Check if the task was cancelled
        if longTaskCTS.IsCancellationRequested then
            printfn "Cancelled; stopping early."
            loop <- false

    printfn "Complete!"

let startLongRunningTask() =
    Task.Factory.StartNew(longRunningTask, longTaskCTS.Token)

let t = startLongRunningTask()

// ...

longTaskCTS.Cancel()
```

Exceptions

Handling exceptions in conjunction with the TPL is a bit more involved. If a task throws an exception, it returns an exception of type `System.AggregateException`. It may seem strange that tasks don't surface the exception you originally threw, but remember that tasks are executing in an entirely different context from where the exception will be caught. What if the task had spawned child tasks—and they too threw exceptions?

The `AggregateException` type combines all exceptions originating from the target task, which you can access later via the `InnerExceptions` collection.

Example 9-14 shows using the TPL for searching through a graph structure, which in the example is a magical cave filled with yeti and treasure. Whenever a fork is encountered, new tasks are spawned to visit the left and right branches.

Example 9-14. Using the TPL to search through a graph

```
open System
open System.Threading.Tasks
```

```
type CaveNode =
    | ManEatingYeti of string
    | BottomlessPit
    | Treasure
    | DeadEnd
    | Fork of CaveNode * CaveNode

let rec findAllTreasure node =
    match node with

    // Finding treasure in magical caves ain't easy...
    | ManEatingYeti(n) -> failwithf "Eaten by a yeti named %s" n
    | BottomlessPit    -> failwith "Fell into a bottomless pit"

    // Leaf nodes
    | DeadEnd  -> 0
    | Treasure -> 1

    // Branches. Send half of your expedition left, the other half goes right...
    // ... hopefully not to only be eaten by a Yeti
    | Fork(left, right) ->
        let goLeft  = Task.Factory.StartNew<int>(fun () -> findAllTreasure left)
        let goRight = Task.Factory.StartNew<int>(fun () -> findAllTreasure right)
        goLeft.Result + goRight.Result
```

The following snippet calls the findAllTreasure function and catches the Aggrega teException. Notice how the decomposeAggregEx function is used to extract all the non-AggregateExceptions:

```
let colossalCave =
    Fork(
        Fork(
            DeadEnd,
            Fork(Treasure, BottomlessPit)
        ),
        Fork(
            ManEatingYeti("Umaro"),
            Fork(
                ManEatingYeti("Choko"),
                Treasure
            )
        )
    )

try
    let treasureFindingTask =
        Task.Factory.StartNew<int>(fun () -> findAllTreasure colossalCave)

    printfn "Found %d treasure!" treasureFindingTask.Result

with
```

```
| :? AggregateException as ae ->

    // Get all inner exceptions from the aggregate exception.
    let rec decomposeAggregEx (ae : AggregateException) =
        seq {
            for innerEx in ae.InnerExceptions do
                match innerEx with
                | :? AggregateException as ae -> yield! decomposeAggregEx ae
                | _ -> yield innerEx
        }

    printfn "AggregateException:"

    // Alternately, you can use ae.Flatten() to put all nested
    // exceptions into a single AggregateException collection.
    decomposeAggregEx ae
    |> Seq.iter (fun ex -> printfn "\tMessage: %s" ex.Message)
```

Concurrent Data Structures

Mastering the Task type is crucial for exploiting the TPL and writing parallel programs without a lot of extra fuss. However, the Task.Result property alone is insufficient to store the results for many parallel applications. Ideally, you will have tasks working in concert to fill out a shared data structure.

However, sharing data structures between tasks can be problematic due to the data races you saw early in the chapter. You could lock the data type every single time you access the value, but acquiring an exclusive lock is an expensive operation, and can dramatically hamper performance if it is never used. (That is, you acquire a lock during a time nobody else accesses the data.) Also, should you acquire a lock for a read operation?

The TPL introduces several new collection types to solve this problem. The System.Col lections.Concurrent namespace contains the standard sort of collection types you would expect, except that they can all be shared freely between threads. Each collection uses locking to ensure data is consistent, but does so in a way to maximize performance. (Or, if possible, simply use a lock-free algorithm.)

Concurrent queue

A common pattern in parallel programming is having a list of work to be done and dividing it among various threads. However, there is an inherent contention for the list of things to do. Fortunately, the ConcurrentQueue data type solves this problem.

The type is a first-in, first-out queue that can safely be used across threads. The main methods on the type are TryDequeue and Enqueue. The *Try-* prefix indicates that the function will return true if the operation completes successfully and false if it doesn't. (In the context of concurrent data structures, this is typically due to a data race.)

Similar to `Dictionary.TryGetValue`, the result of `TryDequeue` will be returned as a tuple, with the first element indicating success or failure of the operation:

```
open System.Collections.Concurrent

let cq = new ConcurrentQueue<int>()
[1 .. 10] |> List.iter cq.Enqueue

let success, firstItem = cq.TryDequeue()
if success then
    printfn "%d was successfully dequeued" firstItem
else
    printfn "Data race, try again later"
```

Concurrent dictionary

The `ConcurrentDictionary` type behaves like a normal dictionary. Example 9-15 uses a `ConcurrentDictionary` to associate words with the number of times they are encountered in a set of files.

In the example, the `AddOrUpdate` method is used. The `ConcurrentDictionary` has different methods for adding new items to the dictionary, and `AddOrUpdate` takes a key, a function to generate a value to add if the key doesn't exist, and a function to update the value if the key is already present in the dictionary. Using this method makes it easier to insert items into the dictionary rather than checking the result of `TryAdd`.

Example 9-15. Using the ConcurrentDictionary

```
open System
open System.IO
open System.Collections.Concurrent

// Queue of files to process
let filesToProcess =
    Directory.GetFiles(@"D:\Book\", "*.txt")
    |> (fun files -> new ConcurrentQueue<_>(files))

// Dictionary to store the occurrences of particular words
let wordUsage = new ConcurrentDictionary<string, int>()

let processFile filePath =
    let text = File.ReadAllText(filePath)
    let words =
        text.Split([| ' '; '\r'; '\n' |], StringSplitOptions.RemoveEmptyEntries)
        |> Array.map (fun word -> word.Trim())

    // Add the word to our lookup table. Inserts value '1', or if the key
    // is already present updates it to be 'count + 1'.
    Array.Parallel.iter(fun word ->
        wordUsage.AddOrUpdate(word, (fun _ -> 1), (fun _ count -> count + 1))
        |> ignore
    ) words
```

```
// Begins updating the wordUsage dictionary
let fillDictionary() =
    let mutable continueWorking = true

    while continueWorking do

        let dequeueSuccessful, filePath = filesToProcess.TryDequeue()

        if not dequeueSuccessful then
            // If the queue is empty, then we are done working
            if filesToProcess.IsEmpty then
                continueWorking <- false
            // ... otherwise, two tasks tried to dequeue
            // at the same time. Try again.
            else
                continueWorking <- true

        // Process the file
        processFile filePath

// Start three tasks to count word usage
fillDictionary()
fillDictionary()
fillDictionary()
```

Concurrent bag

The ConcurrentBag class behaves much like the HashSet<_> type we covered in Chapter 4, except that it allows duplicate items to be added. This isn't a world-shattering loss, because once the bag has been filled, you can filter out duplicates on your own.

A ConcurrentBag is ideal for aggregating results found from several tasks you have spawned.

Example 9-16 spawns several tasks to compute a list of prime numbers up to a maximum value in parallel using a ConcurrentBag. If a HashSet<_> type were used instead, some of the values added to the collection would be "dropped," because of the race conditions when trying to update the HashSet's internal data structures. (Or even worse, the data itself could get corrupted.)

The function computePrimes returns the ConcurrentBag cast as a seq<int> and then passed to a HashSet<_>. (ConcurrentBag, like most collection types, implements the IEnumerable<_> interface and therefore can be cast as a seq<_>.)

Example 9-16. Using the ConcurrentBag class to store parallel results

```
open System
open System.Threading.Tasks
open System.Collections.Concurrent
open System.Collections.Generic
```

```
/// Check if a number is prime
let isPrime x =
    let rec primeCheck count =
        // If the counter has reached x, then we know x is prime
        if count = x       then true
        // If x is divisible by the counter, we know x isn't prime
        elif x % count = 0 then false
        else primeCheck (count + 1)
    // Special case 1 as prime
    if x = 1
    then true
    else primeCheck 2

let computePrimes tasksToSpawn maxValue =
    let range = maxValue / tasksToSpawn
    let primes = new ConcurrentBag<int>()

    // Spawn several tasks at once, adding any primes they find
    // to the ConcurrentBag
    let tasks =
        [|
        for i in 0 .. tasksToSpawn - 1 do
            yield Task.Factory.StartNew(
                Action(fun () ->
                    for x = i * range to (i + 1) * range - 1 do
                        if isPrime x then primes.Add(x)
                )
            )
        |]
    Task.WaitAll(tasks)

    new HashSet<_>(primes :> seq<int>)
```

Now you can write asynchronous and parallel programs in F# by taking advantage of
the great libraries available. You can also see why an emphasis on functional programming is beneficial when doing parallel programming: composing pure, immutable
functions makes it easy to decompose tasks to execute independently, without worrying
about introducing bugs.

 Remember that adding parallelism to an application doesn't always
make it perform better. Whenever doing any architectural changes for
performance, be sure to benchmark your application early and often.

Scripting

In previous chapters, you saw how F# can be effective across multiple programming paradigms. But F# is not only well suited for different *styles* of programming, it can also be effective for writing different *types* of programs as well. F# is not only useful for client applications, but can also be effective as a scripting language too.

Scripting is general term used to describe programs that don't have a UI and are focused on solving a particular task. In most scripting languages, the script consists entirely of code—as opposed to an executable program—that is then interpreted by a runtime engine.

Programming in this mode typically sacrifices execution speed for the convenience of being able to easily modify and deploy the program. Rather than creating a complex solution designed to work everywhere, you can simply move a script from machine to machine and modify it as necessary.

Although F# may be best suited for client application programming, using it in a scripting context has one major advantage: you already know it. Rather than learning a separate language for your scripts, employing F# for your scripting needs lets you reuse your existing code and knowledge about F# programming. Also, F# code is never interpreted—it is always compiled first. So F# can be comparatively faster than pure scripting languages.

If you have a simple problem and don't need a complicated interface, consider scripting the solution. In this chapter, you learn about some constructs available to script files as well as see some recipes for creating useful F# scripts that you can put to good use right away.

F# Script Files

When F# is installed on a system, it registers *.fsx* files as *F# Script* files. These are F# source files specifically designed to be easy to execute. Double clicking on an F# script file will bring up Visual Studio to edit the script. Right clicking on the file in Windows Explorer enables you to execute it directly by selecting the *Run with F# Interactive* context menu item, seen in Figure 10-1.

Figure 10-1. Windows shell integration for F# script files

Executing an F# script file simply sends the contents of the file to console version of F# Interactive, `fsi.exe` (located in the *C:\Program Files (x86)\Microsoft SDKs\F#\3.0 \Framework\v4.0* directory.)

F# script files behave just as if you had opened the code file within Visual Studio and sent it all directly to FSI. The code will then be compiled and executed, performing whatever actions are in the script. In F# script files, you have full usage of the F# language and a few additional features to help make writing scripts easier.

Directives

The most noticeable difference between normal F# source files and F# Script files is the usage of compiler directives. These are special hints and commands to the F# compiler.

General Directives

The following directives are available in any F# source program but are mostly applicable to F# scripts.

__SOURCE_DIRECTORY__

The Source Directory directive, available with __SOURCE_DIRECTORY__, returns the current directory of the executing code. This is especially helpful in scripts for determining where the script file is located. Any instance of __SOURCE_DIRECTORY__ will be replaced with a constant string as soon as the file is compiled:

```
C:\Program Files (x86)\Microsoft F#\v4.0>cd C:\Program Files (x86)\Microsoft SDK
s\F#\3.0\Framework\v4.0

C:\Program Files (x86)\Microsoft SDKs\F#\3.0\Framework\v4.0>fsi

Microsoft (R) F# 3.0 Interactive build 4.0.30319.16909
Copyright (c) Microsoft Corporation. All Rights Reserved.

For help type #help;;

> __SOURCE_DIRECTORY__;;
val it : string =
  "C:\Program Files (x86)\Microsoft SDKs\F#\3.0\Framework\v4.0"
> #q;;
```

__SOURCE_FILE__

The __SOURCE_FILE__ directive returns the current filename. When you combine this directive with __SOURCE_DIRECTORY__, you can determine the actual script being executed.

Example 10-1 runs a script that prints the __SOURCE_FILE__ to the console. Like __SOURCE_DIRECTORY__, __SOURCE_FILE__ will be replaced with a string as soon as the file is compiled.

Example 10-1. Using __SOURCE_FILE__ and __SOURCE_DIRECTORY__

```
C:\Programming FS\Ch10>type AwesomestScriptEver.fsx
printfn "__SOURCE_DIRECTORY__ = %s" __SOURCE_DIRECTORY__
printfn "__SOURCE_FILE__      = %s" __SOURCE_FILE__

C:\Programming FS\Ch10>fsi AwesomestScriptEver.fsx
__SOURCE_DIRECTORY__ = C:\Programming FS\Ch10
__SOURCE_FILE__      = AwesomestScriptEver.fsx
```

F# Script-Specific Directives

The following directives are not available in regular F# source files. Rather, they are specifically designed to be used in F# script files to provide an experience as if they were single-file projects within Visual Studio. These directives are also available from within an FSI session in Visual Studio.

#r

The #r directive references an assembly. This allows your F# script file to reference types defined in a separate .NET assembly, perhaps written in another language, such as C#. The string passed to the #r directive can be as simple as the assembly's shortened file name or the full assembly name containing the name, version, culture, and so on.

Note that the #r directive only works in *.fsx* files. For regular F# source files (with the .fs extension), use your IDE's add reference dialog.

Example 10-2 shows how to load the Windows Forms libraries to display a list of files located in the *My Pictures* folder on a data grid.

Example 10-2. Loading assembly references in scripts

```
#r "System.Windows.Forms.dll"
#r "System.Drawing.dll"

open System
open System.IO
open System.Collections.Generic
open System.Drawing
open System.Windows.Forms

// val images : seq<string * System.Drawing.Image>
let images =
    let myPictures =
        Environment.GetFolderPath(Environment.SpecialFolder.MyPictures)

    Directory.GetFiles(myPictures, "*.JPG")
    |> Seq.map (fun filePath ->
            Path.GetFileName(filePath),
            Bitmap.FromFile(filePath))

// Create the data grid and put on a form
let dg = new DataGridView(Dock = DockStyle.Fill)
dg.DataSource <- new List<_>(images)

let f = new Form()
f.Controls.Add(dg)

f.ShowDialog()
```

The order for reference resolution is:

1. The Include Path (discussed next)
2. The same directory as the script
3. The .NET Global Assembly Cache

#I

The #I directive adds a new directory to the search path for references. If you want to keep your scripts and the assemblies they depend upon in separate folders, you can use the #I directive to add a new folder to the search path, so that those assemblies can be found when using #r.

The following example adds several directories to F#'s search path so that when it comes time to actually load a reference with #r, the desired assembly can be found:

```
// Reference whatever version of "SuperAwesomeLib" is installed...
#I @"C:\PW Software\SuperAwesomeLib\1.0.0"
#I @"C:\PW Software\SuperAwesomeLib\1.0.1"
#I @"C:\PW Software\SuperAwesomeLib\1.1.0"
#I @"C:\PW Software\SuperAwesomeLib\1.2.0"

#r "SuperAwesomeLib.dll"
#r "SuperAwesomeLib.Client.dll"

// ...
```

#load

The #load directive opens up another F# file with a relative path and executes it. This is for when you want scripts to be broken up across multiple files, or if you want to reuse some existing F# code. Loading a code file will work as if you had opened the file and sent its entire contents directly into the FSI session. Example 10-3 shows loading a code file for displaying charts and plots while the actual script file does the computation.

Example 10-3. Loading a code file into an F# script

```
#load "Plotting.fs"

open System

let data =
    seq {
        let rng = new Random()
        for i in 1 .. 10000 do
            yield (rng.NextDouble(), rng.NextDouble())
```

```
    }
// Function plot is defined in 'Plotting.fs'
plot "Random plot" data
```

 Use #load sparingly in F# scripts. They make scripts more difficult to maintain and deploy. If your script needs multiple code files to work, consider creating an actual project.

F# Script Recipes

This section highlights some simple utilities that can help make your F# scripts more effective—such as taking advantage of console coloring or automating data input to Microsoft Excel.

Colorful Output

Scripts don't primarily invest in a UI, rather they are often designed not to need any user input. However, taking advantage of a color console can dramatically improve the readability of your script's output. Example 10-4 defines a `cprintfn` function that behaves just like `printfn`, taking a string filled with format specifiers and additional arguments, except that it also takes a color parameter.

Example 10-4. Producing colorful output

```
/// Colorful printing for helpful diagnostics
let cprintfn c fmt =
    Printf.kprintf
        (fun s ->
            let orig = System.Console.ForegroundColor
            System.Console.ForegroundColor <- c;
            System.Console.WriteLine(s)
            System.Console.ForegroundColor <- orig)
        fmt
```

The `cprintfn` function takes advantage of the `Printf.kprintf` function in the F# library, which does all the conversion of the format string, such as `"%d %f %s"`, and the additional arguments, and calls the provided function once they have been combined into the final result. The `cprintfn` function then simply updates the console color before doing the actual printing.

The following code prints text to the console in various colors. The last section of the code uses a little functional programming magic to print a string where each letter is in a different color—see if you can figure out how it works (hint: a `string` type can be treated as if it were a `seq<char>`):

```
open System

cprintfn ConsoleColor.Blue   "Hello, World! in blue!"
cprintfn ConsoleColor.Red    "... and in red!"
cprintfn ConsoleColor.Green "... and in green!"

let rotatingColors =
    let possibleColors = Enum.GetValues(typeof<ConsoleColor>)
    let getColor idx : ConsoleColor = enum (idx % possibleColors.Length)
    Seq.initInfinite getColor

"Experience the rainbow of possibility!"
|> Seq.zip rotatingColors
|> Seq.iter (fun (color, letter) -> cprintfn color "%c" letter)
```

Producing Sound

Similar to using the console's ability to color output as a way of improving your scripts, you can also take advantage of the console's ability to beep. To have your script make sounds, you can use the `System.Console.Beep` method, which takes a frequency and duration as parameters. Although potentially very annoying, having an audible cue for when a script is complete or when a special event has occurred can be helpful.

The following code defines two functions, `victory` and `defeat`, which play sounds to indicate success or failure. `victory` beeps ascending tones to convey the sheer joy of success, while `defeat` beeps a series of increasingly depressing low tones.

```
open System

/// Victory!
let victory() =
    for frequency in [100 .. 50 .. 2000] do
        Console.Beep(frequency, 25)

/// Defeat :(
let defeat() =
    for frequency in [2000 .. -50 .. 37] do
        Console.Beep(frequency, 25)
```

Walking a Directory Structure

You'll often want a script to process all the files under a certain directory. An easy and effective way to process every file is to use the sequence expression defined in Example 10-5. Remember that in a sequence expression, `yield!` merges a sequence of elements into the master sequence, similar to the `Seq.concat` function.

Example 10-5. Getting all sub files under a directory

```
open System.IO

let rec filesUnder basePath =
    seq {
        yield! Directory.GetFiles(basePath)
        for subDir in Directory.GetDirectories(basePath) do
            yield! filesUnder subDir
    }
```

This following script can be applied to walk a directory tree and identify specific files, which can then be processed by your script. Notice that using the __SOURCE_DIRECTO RY__ directive allows you to scan each file under the directory where the script resides. The following code uses the filesUnder function to copy all JPEG files under the script's directory into a new folder:

```
open System.IO

let rec filesUnder basePath =
    seq {
        yield! Directory.GetFiles(basePath)
        for subDir in Directory.GetDirectories(basePath) do
            yield! filesUnder subDir
    }

let NewImageFolder = @"D:\NewImagesFolder\"

__SOURCE_DIRECTORY__
|> filesUnder
|> Seq.filter(fun filePath -> filePath.ToUpper().EndsWith("JPG"))
|> Seq.iter(fun filePath -> let fileName = Path.GetFileName(filePath)
                            let destPath = Path.Combine(NewImageFolder, fileName)
                            File.Copy(filePath, destPath))
```

Starting Processes Easily

Another common task for scripts is to launch a separate tool. The functionality for spawning new processes is built into the .NET base class libraries. The simplest way to do this is to use the Process.Start method, and simply wait for it to complete:

```
open System.Diagnostics
Process.Start("notepad.exe", "file.txt").WaitForExit()
```

For more sophisticated scripts, you will probably need to check the result of the process, either the process exit code or its console output.

Example 10-6 defines a function called shellExecute that launches a program with the given arguments and returns its exit code and output as a tuple.

Example 10-6. Launching a new process

```
open System.Text
open System.Diagnostics

/// Spawns a new process. Returns (exit code, stdout)
let shellExecute program arguments =

    let startInfo = new ProcessStartInfo()
    startInfo.FileName  <- program
    startInfo.Arguments <- arguments

    startInfo.UseShellExecute        <- false
    startInfo.RedirectStandardOutput <- true

    let proc = new Process()
    proc.EnableRaisingEvents <- true

    // Add a handler to the 'OutputDataRecieved' event, so we can store
    // the STDOUT stream of the process.
    let driverOutput = new StringBuilder()
    proc.OutputDataReceived.AddHandler(
        DataReceivedEventHandler(
            (fun sender args -> driverOutput.AppendLine(args.Data) |> ignore)
        )
    )

    proc.StartInfo <- startInfo
    proc.Start() |> ignore
    proc.BeginOutputReadLine()

    proc.WaitForExit()
    (proc.ExitCode, driverOutput.ToString())
```

Automating Microsoft Office

Yet another possible application for F# scripts is automation, or programmatically performing otherwise mundane tasks. The following script illustrates how to automate simple tasks for Microsoft Office.

Example 10-7 automates Microsoft Word. It prints out all documents in the same folder as the script modifying the print options so that pages are printed with four pages per sheet.

The APIs for manipulating Microsoft Word are fairly straightforward, the only bit of trickiness in Example 10-7 is that the Word COM APIs expect to take byref<obj> objects as parameters, so the comarg function is introduced to convert a value into a mutable obj. (The byref<_> type is discussed in more detail in Appendix B.)

Example 10-7. Printing all documents in a folder

```
#r "stdole.dll"
#r "Microsoft.Office.Interop.Word"

open Microsoft.Office.Interop.Word

let private m_word : ApplicationClass option ref = ref None

let openWord()        = m_word := Some(new ApplicationClass())
let getWordInstance() = Option.get !m_word
let closeWord()       = (getWordInstance()).Quit()

// COM objects expect byref<obj>, ref cells will be
// converted to byref<obj> by the compiler.
let comarg x = ref (box x)

let openDocument filePath =
    printfn "Opening %s..." filePath
    getWordInstance().Documents.Open(comarg filePath)

let printDocument (doc : Document) =
    printfn "Printing %s..." doc.Name

    doc.PrintOut(
        Background  = comarg true,
        Range       = comarg WdPrintOutRange.wdPrintAllDocument,
        Copies      = comarg 1,
        PageType    = comarg WdPrintOutPages.wdPrintAllPages,
        PrintToFile = comarg false,
        Collate     = comarg true,
        ManualDuplexPrint = comarg false,
        PrintZoomColumn = comarg 2,  // Pages 'across'
        PrintZoomRow    = comarg 2)  // Pages 'up down'

let closeDocument (doc : Document) =
    printfn "Closing %s..." doc.Name
    doc.Close(SaveChanges = comarg false)

// ------------------------------------------------------------

open System
open System.IO

try
    openWord()

    printfn "Printing all files in [%s]..." __SOURCE_DIRECTORY__

    Directory.GetFiles(__SOURCE_DIRECTORY__, "*.docx")
    |> Array.iter
        (fun filePath ->
            let doc = openDocument filePath
```

```
            printDocument doc
            closeDocument doc)
finally
    closeWord()

printfn "Press any key..."
Console.ReadKey(true) |> ignore
```

Example 10-8 creates a new Microsoft Excel workbook and dumps the contents of the *My Pictures* folder to a spreadsheet. You could just as easily store the results of some computations.

The script starts up by loading up the Excel application, creating a new workbook, and allowing spreadsheet cells to be set using the setCellText function. The script then walks through each file in the *My Pictures* folder and prints the filename, size, and so on.

Example 10-8. Creating Excel worksheets

```
#r "Microsoft.Office.Interop.Excel"

open System
open System.IO
open System.Reflection
open Microsoft.Office.Interop.Excel

let app = ApplicationClass(Visible = true)

let sheet = app.Workbooks
                .Add()
                .Worksheets.[1] :?> _Worksheet

let setCellText (x : int) (y : int) (text : string) =
    let range = sprintf "%c%d" (char (x + int 'A')) (y+1)
    sheet.Range(range).Value(Missing.Value) <- text


let printCsvToExcel rowIdx (csvText : string) =
    csvText.Split([| ',' |])
    |> Array.iteri (fun partIdx partText -> setCellText partIdx rowIdx partText)


let rec filesUnderFolder basePath =
    seq {
        yield! Directory.GetFiles(basePath)
        for subFolder in Directory.GetDirectories(basePath) do
            yield! filesUnderFolder subFolder
    }

// Print header
printCsvToExcel 0 "Directory, Filename, Size, Creation Time"
```

```
// Print rows
filesUnderFolder (Environment.GetFolderPath(Environment.SpecialFolder.MyPictures))
|> Seq.map (fun filename -> new FileInfo(filename))
|> Seq.map (fun fileInfo -> sprintf "%s, %s, %d, %s"
                                    fileInfo.DirectoryName
                                    fileInfo.Name
                                    fileInfo.Length
                                    (fileInfo.CreationTime.ToShortDateString()))
|> Seq.iteri (fun idx str -> printCsvToExcel (idx + 1) str)
```

F# scripts allow you to use F# code outside of the normal "projects and solution" format of Visual Studio. F# scripts enable many new scenarios that would otherwise be prohibitively annoying to automate in a language like C#, or easy in a language like Python but requiring additional software to be installed and configured.

Using F# scripts you can automate tasks such as uploading files to a web server, analyzing and extracting data from log files, and so on. Using F# in a scripting context is just one more way you can apply the language toward helping you be more productive.

Data Processing

You have been exposed to just about every core feature of the F# programming language and seen how to program in the functional, imperative, and object-oriented styles. However, in order to develop a deep understanding of a language, you need to actually go out and *use* it. If you don't have an F# starter project in mind, well, this chapter should hopefully serve as the next-best thing.

This chapter focuses on the application of the F# programming language. However, there is not a canonical F# application. The language is well suited across multiple domains and industries. Yet in all cases, F# is best suited for the computational core of a program, or the numeric heavy lifting and data processing.

With that in mind, we will write a simple search engine using F#. Along the way, you will learn about MapReduce-style data processing and using Lex and Yacc for generating parsers. Although this F# search engine will not rival Google any time soon, it will serve as a large-enough code base to practice idiomatic F#.

Of course, a detailed look at the source code for a search engine and the technologies powering it could easily fill several books, so this chapter only covers the key concepts. For more detail, see the source code found on GitHub at: *https://github.com/aChris Smith/Programming-FS-Examples*

Before we begin, let's quickly cover the major components of the project, which, despite each one leading down a technically interesting rabbit hole, are not that difficult to grasp.

Indexing

>   Indexing is the process of transforming a corpus of data (in our case, the full text of books) and converting it into a more efficient format for retrieval. To perform this, we use MapReduce on so-called "cloud computing."

Querying

Querying is the intermediate step used to take a human-readable string such as "wherefore art thou Romeo" OR "to be, or not to be" and look for matching documents in our index. We parse user queries using industry-standard Lex and Yacc tools.

Serving

With the right querying and indexing infrastructure in place, all that is left is a way to provide a frontend for users and serve.

With a general notion of what the product looks like, it is now time to get started!

Indexing

The first component of our search engine is the *indexer*, which we will use to create a *reverse index*. A reverse index is an index data structure that maps items to their locations. In a search engine, a reverse index maps words to the documents and locations where they appear.

The Index Data Structure

To construct a reverse index, first each document gets assigned a unique document ID tracked by a DocumentID type (a type alias for int). The DocumentID is just a hash code of the original document name. Each document is then *tokenized*, or broken into individual words. Each token is represented by a TokenID, or a hash code of the original lexeme. In both cases, the integer ID is used as an optimization to conserve memory.

 The tokenizer presented here ignores the punctuation between words. However, a more sophisticated tokenizer would treat punctuation, HTML tags, and other non-word entities as special kinds of entities.

The following shows the tokenization of a poem by the syntax-loving poet E.E. Cummings:

```
> // Snippet from "Dying is Fine)but Death"
// By E.E. Cummings
let poem = @"
dying is fine)but Death

?o
baby
i

wouldn't like
```

```
Death if Death
were
good:for

when(instead of stopping to think)you

begin to feel of it,dying
's miraculous
why?be

cause dying is
...";;

val poem : string =
   "

dying is fine)but Death

?o
baby
i

wouldn't like

Death if "+[126 chars]

> // Break text into tokens, then tokenize each lexeme.
let rawTokens = breakText poem
let tokens = tokenizeText rawTokens;;

val rawTokens : Indexer.DataTypes.RawToken [] =
  [|"dying"; "is"; "fine"; "but"; "Death"; "o"; "baby"; "i"; "wouldn't";
    "like"; "Death"; "if"; "Death"; "were"; "good:for"; "when"; "instead";
    "of"; "stopping"; "to"; "think"; "you"; "begin"; "to"; "feel"; "of"; "it";
    "dying"; "'s"; "miraculous"; "why"; "be"; "cause"; "dying"; "is"|]
val tokens : Indexer. DataTypes.TokenID [] =
  [|80806596; -839403577; -1502834418; -1740700924; -2006800497; -842352703;
    1879991166; -842352697; -2126694611; -1099549881; -2006800497; -840648761;
    -2006800497; 1095172/3; 1246798081; -389758630; 1036624903; -840648767;
    -1985537974; -840190004; 48366728; 987527096; -1621728523; -840190004;
    -8273589; -840648767; -839469113; 80806596; -839403655; -544253080;
    -1693843354; -840583234; 1953640505; 80806596; -839403577|]
```

Token posting lists

A *token posting list* is the list of all document locations in which a specific token occurs.
For example, the token posting list for the word "is" would be rather long. The token
posting list for "legolas"—as in Legolas the elf from *The Lord of the Rings*—would only
list a handful of documents. Figure 11-1 illustrates several abbreviated token posting
lists.

Token posting lists, once constructed, provide an efficient way to map a search term to the list of documents and represent the heart of our search engine.

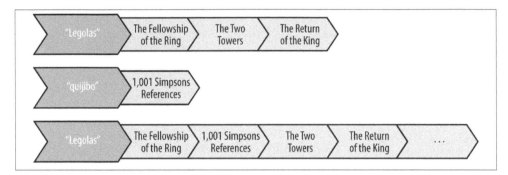

Figure 11-1. Token Posting Lists

In order for our search engine to do exact phrase matching (finding terms as they occur in a particular sequence), we also need to associate a position with each token. For example, to match the first sentence of *A Tale of Two Cities* ("It was the best of times, it was the worst of times ..."), we need to know that "it" occurs in positions 0 and 6, and "was" occurs in positions 1 and 7.

Surprising as it may seem, token posting lists with position information are all that is required to construct a basic search engine.

The final data structures and types required for constructing a reverse index are as follows:

```
/// Raw, unprocessed token. An individual word within a document. For example:
/// "Hello"; "World".
type RawToken = string

/// Unique ID to represent a token. (Case insensitive.)
type TokenID = int

/// Unique ID to represent a document.
type DocumentID = int

/// 0-indexed position within a document.
type DocumentPosition = int

/// TokenPositions are sorted by document ID first, and then document position.
type TokenPosition =
    { DocumentID : DocumentID; DocumentPosition : DocumentPosition }

/// Posting list for a given token. TokenOccurrences must be sorted.
type BasicTokenPostingList =
    { TokenID : TokenID; TokenOccurrences : seq<TokenPosition> }
```

F# type aliases can make code more declarative. The function converting a raw token into a token ID could have signature `string -> int`, but the signature `RawToken -> TokenID` is much more useful.

In the section titled "Querying" (page 302), we see how `BasicTokenPostingLists` can be used to efficiently retrieve documents based on a user query. But to complete the indexer, we need to find a way to construct a `BasicTokenPostingList` for each word in our corpus.

The naïve solution would:

- Tokenize each document to build a list of all unique tokens.
- For each unique token, rescan each document for its occurrences.

On a single machine, that approach might work for hundreds of tokens spread across hundreds of documents but probably not tens of thousands of tokens spread across tens of thousands of documents. Even using the asynchronous and parallel programming concepts covered in Chapter 9, any modestly sized corpus is just too much data for one machine.

To construct our index then, we need to distribute the computation from just one machine to dozens, if not hundreds more. Fortunately, distributed computing allows us to do just that.

MapReduce Processing

The terms "map" and "reduce" should be familiar to you, as you have seen then in the forms of `List.map`, `Seq.reduce`, and so on. However, the combined term "MapReduce" was not associated with large-scale distributed computation until 2004, when Google published *MapReduce: Simplified Data Processing on Large Clusters*. The paper describes how simple *map* and *reduce* functions—much like their F# analogs—can be combined to dramatically simplify large-scale computing problems.

In a MapReduce, the *map* operation takes an input data source and produces a list of key/value pairs. The *reduce* operation takes the key and list of values to produce a terminal list of values.

By expressing a computational task in terms of "map" and "reduce" operations, you can reap some interesting benefits. But first, let's look at a concrete example of a MapReduce task. Consider the following example for counting the number of occurrences of each word in a collection of documents.

First, the map operation takes its input document and emits tuples of the form (*word*, 1). So if the word "palabra" occurred twice, the output stream of the map operation would contain ...; ("palabra", 1); ...; ("palabra", 1); ... along with all the other words in that document.

The reduce operation will receive its input key and a list of values. In this case, the input key will be each word, such as "palabra" or "the". The list of values will be all map operation output tuples that had that word as the key. (Recall that the value for the map operation's output tuples was always 1.) For the reduce operation to generate the word count then, all it needs to do is count the total number of elements in the list of values passed to the reducer.

The word count MapReduce can be implemented using the following pseudo-code:

```
map(string inputKey, string inputValue):
  // inputKey: document name
  // inputValue: document contents
  for each word w in GetWords(inputValue):
    EmitOutput(w, "1");


reduce(String outputKey, Enumerator intermediateValues):
  // outputKey: a word
  // outputValues: a total count
  int result = 0;
  for each (word, value) in intermediateValues:
    result += ParseInt(value);
  EmitOutput(result);
```

 There are also two parts of a MapReduce that happen behind the scenes: first, there is a *shuffler*, which groups the mapper outputs by key before passing them to a reducer (e.g., group all (*word*, 1) tuples by word). Second, after the reduce phase, there is another process that aggregates the output results, and saves it off to disk.

The details of these steps, however, are usually taken care of by the underling MapReduce framework you are using.

Benefits

So what does constraining our computations into separate map and reduce operations buy us? In a word: scale.

Notice that both the map and reduce operations can each be performed in parallel. It makes no difference if there are 10 mapping processes computing the input space or 10,000. The only bound you have for mappers is the number of items in the input space (i.e., you should not have more than 10,000 mappers to index 10,000 documents).

Also, the mappers and reducers are idempotent. If any of the physical machines dies, crashes, or otherwise go caput, then the work can be restarted without corrupting the entire MapReduce job. (When performing computations across thousands of machines, hardware failures aren't a question of *if*, but rather is a question of when.)

 There are many other more subtle benefits to using MapReduce. For example, it makes file *sharding* very easy. Sharding is the process of breaking a large file or dataset into multiple pieces for redundancy and/ or ease of use.

Once you have mastered the MapReduce concept, you will probably want to use it for all of your large-scale data processing needs. But how do you actual *start* a MapReduce job? It is unlikely that you have a large-scale data center at your disposal. Fortunately, both you and I live in the future and can send our jobs to "the cloud."

Cloud hosts

There are several companies offering cloud computing for general computational tasks such as Google's App Engine, Google Compute Engine, Amazon's Web Services, and Microsoft's Windows Azure. By using one of these generic computing platforms, you can run your MapReduce job on their host hardware.

The original MapReduce framework that Google wrote about in their paper is proprietary. However, there are several open source libraries for performing MapReduce operations with the most popular being the open source Hadoop framework (*http:// hadoop.apache.org/*).

To construct the reverse index for our search engine, we will use Hadoop on Windows Azure. For more information on the boilerplate code to hook up F# projects to Windows Azure, see the source code for this project on GitHub.

Search Index Mapper

The mapper for our indexing MapReduce job will take an input document and emit `TokenID * TokenPosition` tuples. Note that the `DocumentID` for every `TokenPosi tion` will be the same.

Example 11-1 shows the basic mapper code we will use, stripped of any Hadoop-specific code.

Example 11-1. The search index mapper

```
type DocumentHitListMapper() =
    inherit Mapper<TokenID, TokenPosition>()

    default this.Map(fileName) =
```

```
    let docID = fileName.GetHashCode()

    tokenizeFile fileName
    |> Seq.mapi(fun i token -> token,
                               { DocumentID = docID;
                                 DocumentPosition = i })
    |> Seq.iter(fun (token, tokenPos) -> this.Output(token, tokenPos))
```

Once all the mappers have completed, the shuffler will group all `TokenID` * `TokenPo` `sition` tuples by the leading `TokenID`. In other words, it will identify all positions where each token occurs across all documents in our corpus.

Search Index Reducer

Merging these long lists of `TokenPositions` is done during the reduce phase.

Given a `TokenID` and all of its `TokenPositions` in the corpus, we just need to sort those occurrences in a standard ordering: `DocumentID` low to high, then `DocumentPosition` low to high. (We will see why this sort ordering is required when we begin to query documents.)

Once complete, the reducer emits a `BasicTokenPostingList`, and our reverse index is ready for searching!

Example 11-2 shows the reducer code to use—again, stripped of any Hadoop-specific code.

Example 11-2. The search index reducer

```
type TokenPostingListReducer() =
    inherit Reducer<TokenID, TokenPosition, BasicTokenPostingList>()

    default this.Reduce(key, values) =
        // Sort the values by the document ID and then by position.
        let sortedTokenOccurrences = new List<TokenPosition>()
        sortedTokenOccurrences.AddRange(values)
        sortedTokenOccurrences.Sort()
        this.Output({ TokenID = key; TokenOccurrences = sortedTokenOccurrences })
```

That's it. That is all the code we need to do to construct our search engine's index; and by using MapReduce, we can scale our system from 1 machine to 10 to 10,000.

Querying

With an efficient lookup mechanism for our search engine, we want to enable actual querying. There are three key features to support:

Basic keyword queries such as `"eggs" or "ham"`

A basic keyword query retrieves all documents that contain the given keyword. This requires returning all documents from the appropriate token posting list.

Exact phrase queries such as `"green eggs and ham"`

An exact phrase query searches for several keywords at the same time and in a specific sequence. This requires searching through multiple token hit lists at the same time and ensuring that tokens occur in the specific sequence.

Logical operators such as `"(planes OR trains) AND automobiles"`

Logical operators group queries together, returning all matching documents. Token position does not matter when using this type of query.

However, before we can implement returning queries, we first need to define how users will actually submit queries to the system. For example, what happens when the user enters "where's waldo" or "((a OR b) AND (c OR d))"?

To accept arbitrarily complex (but still valid) queries, we will create a proper lexer and parser for queries, which will handle the conversion of the raw text into a custom data structure.

Lex and Yacc

To complete this task, we will use `FSLex.exe` and `FSYacc.exe`, two F# implementations of classic tools for generating parsers. The tools do not ship with Visual Studio and are instead a part of the *F# PowerPack*, which is a library of tools and utilities for F#. It is available at: *http://fsharppowerpack.codeplex.com/*.

Converting a query string into a custom data type requires through a two-step process known as *lexing* and *parsing*.

Lexing converts input text into lexical tokens. (Similar to the way we tokenized documents during our indexing step.) Consider the F# code:

```
let x = 1 * f()
```

After lexing by the F# compiler, the text becomes a token sequence similar to:

```
LET; VAR("x"); EQUAL; Number(1); ASTERISK; VAR("f"); LPARAN; RPAREN
```

This step makes it much easier to describe acceptable inputs to parse, and frees us from needing to deal with string manipulation.

Parsing converts lexed token streams into higher-level abstractions, forming a parse tree. For example, the previous example would parse into something resembling:

```
Declaration(
    "x",
    Expression(
        Multiplication(
            Number(1),
```

```
        FunctionCall(
            "f",
            ArgumentList([]))
        )
    )
)
```

 For more information on lex and yacc—including how they are imple‐
mented—see the "Purple Dragon Book": *Compilers: Principles, Techni‐
ques, and Tools 2nd Edition* by Aho, Lam, Sethi, and Ullman (Prentice
Hall, 2006).

The `FSlex.exe` and `FSyacc.exe` tools generate F# source code for lexers and parsers.
`FSlex.exe` requires a set of regular expressions to identify each individual token and
emits the source code for the lexer. `FSyacc.exe` requires a set of grammar productions
(i.e., the "structure" of the language) and emits the source code for the parser. By com‐
bining the two, you have the ability to convert raw text into a parsed representation.

 Although there is no direct Visual Studio support for FSlex and FSyacc,
you can use custom MSBuild targets so that you can regenerate your lex
and yacc code output as part of your project's build. This is documented
in the SearchEngine project source code on GitHub.

The target output of our parser is shown in Example 11-3. The code generated by
`FSlex.exe` and `FSyacc.exe` will be able to convert any valid string input into a `Query`
object.

Example 11-3. The Query type

```
type Query =
    | Term of string
    | Phrase of string list
    | And  of Query * Query
    | Or   of Query * Query
    | SubQuery of Query
```

Parsing

The parser file specifies the language *grammar*, which defines a set of *productions* or
valid token sequences. All a parser does is essentially pattern match valid sequences of
tokens (from the grammar) against the input stream.

The following is a yacc grammar for parsing simple arithmetic expressions such as `"1
+ 2"` or `"(8 - 4) / 2"`. The grammar defines several *non-terminals*: `Equation`, `Expr`,

Term, and Factor. Each of these non-terminals is associated with several *productions*. A grammar production is a sequence of tokens or non-terminals that produces the non-terminal. In the example, terminal symbols (lexical tokens) are in all caps, whereas non-terminals are Pascal cased:

```
Equation:
    | Expr EOF                    { $1 }

Expr:
    | Expr PLUS Term              { Plus($1, $3)  }
    | Expr MINUS Term             { Minus($1, $3) }
    | Term                        { Term($1)      }

Term:
    | Term ASTER Factor           { Times($1, $3)  }
    | Term SLASH Factor           { Divide($1, $3) }
    | Factor                      { Factor($1)     }

Factor:
    | FLOAT                       { Float($1)   }
    | INT32                       { Integer($1) }
    | LPAREN Expr RPAREN          { ParenEx($2) }
```

With this grammar, the token sequence [INT32(1); PLUS; INT32(2)] would parse as a valid expression because of the Expr PLUS Term production. Both operands—INT32(1) and INT32(2)—produce Factor, which produces Term, which can also produce an Expr.

However, token sequence [INT32(8); PLUS; PLUS] cannot be matched to any known production sequence, and therefore would produce a parse error.

The text within the curly braces on the right of each grammar production corresponds to what F# code should be emitted when the parser encounters tokens in that order. $1, $2, and so on refer to any data associated with the tokens on the left.

So the resulting parse tree from the token sequence [INT32(1); PLUS; INT32(2)] would be Expr(Plus(Term(Integer(1)), Term(Integer(2)))).

Focusing back on the search engine, we can now encode our search query syntax into a parser grammar, as seen in Example 11-4.

Example 11-4. Search engine query parser

```
UserQuery:
    | UserQuery EOF        { $1 }
    | SingleQuery          { [ $1 ] }
    | UserQuery SingleQuery { $2 :: $1 }

SingleQuery:
    | TERM                                    { Term($1)   }
    | QUOTATION_MARK Phrase QUOTATION_MARK { Phrase($2) }
```

```
| SingleQuery AND SingleQuery         { And($1, $3)  }
| SingleQuery OR SingleQuery          { Or($1, $3)   }
| LEFT_PAREN SingleQuery RIGHT_PAREN  { SubQuery($2) }

Phrase:
| TERM         { [$1] }
| Phrase TERM  { $2 :: $1 }
```

Lexing

With the parser in place, we just need to define what constitutes each *terminal* symbol, or lexical element of our language. This is done by defining a regular expression for each valid symbol.

To go back to the simple four-function calculator example, consider the following lexer file. Operators such as PLUS and MINUS can be matched by basic regular expressions such as "+" and "-". However, more complex tokens such as INT32 require more effort:

```
let digit = ['0'-'9']
let whitespace = [' ' '\t' ]
let newline = ('\n' | '\r' '\n')

rule tokenize = parse
// Eat whitespace
| whitespace     { tokenize lexbuf }
| newline        { tokenize lexbuf }
// Operators
| "+"                 { PLUS }
| "-"                 { MINUS }
| "*"                 { ASTER }
| "/"                 { SLASH }
// Misc
| "("                 { LPAREN }
| ")"                 { RPAREN }
// Numeric constants
| ['-']?digit+
    { INT32 (Int32.Parse(lexeme lexbuf)) }
| ['-']?digit+('.'digit+)?
    { FLOAT (Double.Parse(lexeme lexbuf)) }
// EOF
| eof    { EOF }
```

Example 11-5 shows the lex file used for the query parser in its entirety.

Example 11-5. The lex file

```
// These are some regular expression definitions
let digit = ['0'-'9']
let whitespace = [' ' '\t' ]
let newline = ('\n' | '\r' '\n')

// Just grab a sequence of characters to form a token. We will turn that into
// a 'document token' later.
```

```
let wordcharacter = ['a'-'z''A'-'Z''\'']
let softcharacter = ['.' ',' '!' '?']
let term = (wordcharacter | softcharacter)+

rule tokenize = parse
// Eat whitespace
| whitespace    { tokenize lexbuf }
| newline       { tokenize lexbuf }
// Symbols
| "\""          { QUOTATION_MARK }
| "("           { LEFT_PAREN }
| ")"           { RIGHT_PAREN }
// Keywords
| "AND"
| "and"         { AND }
| "OR"
| "or"          { OR }
// Any other string is considered a term in a search query.
| term          { TERM(LexBuffer<_>.LexemeString(lexbuf)) }
// EOF
| eof   { EOF }
```

Once the parser and lexer source files have been built by FSLex.exe and FSYacc.exe, they can be used together to work and parse user queries.

Example 11-6 shows using the supporting code found in the F# PowerPack for parsing queries. It defines a function called parseQuery which takes a string, and prints the resulting token stream and parse tree.

Example 11-6. Using the parser and lexer

```
> // Load the F# PowerPack.
#r "FSharp.PowerPack.dll"

// Contains the definition of the final data type:
// type Query =
//     | Term of string
//     | Phrase of string list
//     | And of Query * Query
//     | Or of Query * Query
//     | SubQuery of Query
//     | NoOpQuery
#load "QueryTypes.fs"

// Parser generated from fsyacc
#load "QueryParser.fs"

// Lexer generated from fslex
#load "QueryLexer.fs";;

--> Referenced
    'C:\Program Files (x86)\FSharpPowerPack-2.0.0.0\bin\FSharp.PowerPack.dll'
```

```
[Loading QueryTypes.fs]

... snip ...

[Loading QueryParser.fs]

... snip ...

[Loading QueryLexer.fs]

... snip ...

> // Code against the generated lexer/parser.
open System
open Microsoft.FSharp.Text.Lexing

// Parse a query.
let parseQuery rawQuery =
    printfn "Lexing [%s]..." rawQuery

    let lexbuff = LexBuffer<char>.FromString(rawQuery)
    while not lexbuff.IsPastEndOfStream do
        let token = Query.Lexer.tokenize lexbuff
        printfn "\tToken %A" token

    // We need a new lex buffer since we advanced through it to print
    // each token.
    printfn "Parsing..."
    let lexbuff = LexBuffer<char>.FromString(rawQuery)
    let query =  Query.Parser.start Query.Lexer.tokenize lexbuff

    printfn "\r%A" query;;

val parseQuery : string -> unit

> // Simple two-term query.
parseQuery "Hello, World";;
Lexing [Hello, World]...
    Token TERM "Hello,"
    Token TERM "World"
    Token EOF
Parsing...

[Term "World"; Term "Hello,"]
val it : unit = ()
> // Use of phrase and conjunction.
parseQuery "\"Neither a borrower nor a lender be\" AND Hamlet";;
Lexing ["Neither a borrower nor a lender be" AND Hamlet]...
    Token QUOTATION_MARK
    Token TERM "Neither"
    Token TERM "a"
```

```
    Token TERM "borrower"
    Token TERM "nor"
    Token TERM "a"
    Token TERM "lender"
    Token TERM "be"
    Token QUOTATION_MARK
    Token AND
    Token TERM "Hamlet"
    Token EOF
Parsing...

[And
   (Phrase ["be"; "lender"; "a"; "nor"; "borrower"; "a"; "Neither"],
    Term "Hamlet")]
val it : unit = ()
> // Error: Invalid input
parseQuery "Foo AND Bar AND AND";;
Lexing [Foo AND Bar AND AND]...
    Token TERM "Foo"
    Token AND
    Token TERM "Bar"
    Token AND
    Token AND
    Token EOF
Parsing...
System.Exception: parse error
   at Microsoft.FSharp.Text.Parsing.Implementation.
popStackUntilErrorShifted@273[tok,a](Tables`1 tables, LexBuffer`1 lexbuf, Stack`1
                          stateStack, Stack`1 valueStack, AssocTable actionTable,
                          FSharpOption`1 tokenOpt)
   at Microsoft.FSharp.Text.Parsing.Implementation.
interpret[tok,a](Tables`1 tables, FSharpFunc`2 lexer, LexBuffer`1 lexbuf,
                          Int32 initialState)
   at FSI_0006.parseQuery(String rawQuery)
   at <StartupCode$FSI_0011>.$FSI_0011.main@()
Stopped due to error
```

Query Processing

Now that we can parse user input into Query objects, our last step is to look at how to
return queries. If you recall, the MapReduce processing we did produced a BasicToken
PostingList for every token (word) in our corpus:

```
type BasicTokenPostingList =
    { TokenID : TokenID; TokenOccurrences : seq<TokenPosition> }
```

Knowing every occurrence of the word "Mark" might not be useful if you are searching
for the phrase "Mark Twain." However, the trick is to compose multiple BasicToken
PostingList objects into new, higher-level enumerators (one that returns a TokenPo
sition object for every location that "Mark Twain" occurs in the corpus).

These super-charged `BasicTokenPostingLists` are given the unfortunately bland title of `TokenPostingList`. However, they will be powerful enough to handle OR, AND, term, and phrase queries.

Token posting lists

The `TokenPostingList` type can be thought of as an imperative wrapper over a `seq<To kenPosition>`. You can call `Current`, `MoveNext`, and `AtEnd` to list all positions the enumerator hits.

However, there are a couple of more advanced methods that take advantage of the fact that the `TokenPosition` sequence is ordered. (This is why we sorted the `TokenPosi tion` objects by `DocumentID` first and then by `DocumentPosition`.)

`MoveNextDocument` fast-forwards to the next document in the posting list. Once we know that a search query mentions a document, there is no need to continue reporting different locations *within* that document as matching the query (imagine a Google search for "news" where the first 100,000 links were all to *CNN.com*).

`AdvanceTo` fast-forwards the token posting list to the first token after a `TokenPosi tion`, or `DocumentID` and `DocumentPosition` tuple. You will see why we need this when we implement phrase queries.

Example 11-7 shows the implementation of the `TokenPostingList` type, which we will use as our core data structure for iterating through documents.

Example 11-7. The TokenPostingList type

```
type TokenPostingList(basePostingList : seq<TokenPosition>) =
    let underlyingEnumerator = basePostingList.GetEnumerator()
    // Move enumerator to initial position and initialize m_atEnd.
    // ... is how you would initialize a normal enumerator. A seq<_> from the F#
    // compiler however appears to not support Reset().
    // do underlyingEnumerator.Reset()
    let mutable m_atEnd = not <| underlyingEnumerator.MoveNext()

    /// If the enumerator as reached its final position. Reset by calling
    member this.AtEnd = m_atEnd

    member this.AdvanceTo(tokenPosition) =
        while (not this.AtEnd) && (this.Current < tokenPosition) do
            this.MoveNext()

    member this.Current =
        if not m_atEnd then
            underlyingEnumerator.Current
        else
            TokenPosition.InvalidTokenPosition

    member this.MoveNext() =
```

```
        m_atEnd <- not <| underlyingEnumerator.MoveNext()
        ()

    member this.MoveNextDocument() =
        let startingDoc = this.Current.DocumentID
        while not this.AtEnd && this.Current.DocumentID = startingDoc do
            this.MoveNext()
```

Keyword queries

Keyword queries are the easiest to construct. They simply return each `TokenPosition`
found in the term's `BasicTokenPostingList`.

Exact phrase queries

Exact phrase queries such as `"to be, or not to be"`, on the other hand, require looking
through multiple token posting lists at the same time. This is where the `AdvanceTo`
method comes in handy.

We will create a `TokenPostingList` for each term in the phrase, and loop through the
first word. For each occurrence of that word, we call `AdvanceTo` on the next word's
posting list. With any luck, that word occurred immediately after the first. If so, we repeat
the process all the way down the line.

Example 11-8 shows the implementation of handling exact phrase queries. Notice that
the cord simply creates a sequence expression that passes a `seq<TokenPosition>` to the
constructor for `TokenPostingList`.

Example 11-8. Exact phrase queries

```
/// Exact phrase enumerator. Returns all document positions where the given
/// tokens occur in a specific order.
///
/// This is done by finding all hits of the enumerators where the positions
/// differ by one.
///
/// Returns a new TokenPostingList enumerating all occurrences of the
/// phrase.
let createExactPhraseEnumerator(phraseParts : TokenPostingList[]) =
    new TokenPostingList(
        seq {
            if phraseParts.Length > 0 then
                while not <| phraseParts.[0].AtEnd do
                    let firstTokenPosition = phraseParts.[0].Current

                    // Advance all other enumerators to that point (if possible).
                    for i = 1 to phraseParts.Length - 1 do
                        phraseParts.[i].AdvanceTo(firstTokenPosition)

                    // Check if they all line up.
                    // Takes two tupled arguments.
```

```
                    let foldFunc (expectedDocID, expectedPos, lineUp)
                                (phraseEnum : TokenPostingList) =
                        let lineUp' =
                            lineUp &&
                            (phraseEnum.Current.DocumentID = expectedDocID) &&
                            (phraseEnum.Current.DocumentPosition = expectedPos)
                        (expectedDocID, expectedPos + 1, lineUp')

                    let initialState =
                        (firstTokenPosition.DocumentID,
                         firstTokenPosition.DocumentPosition,
                         true)

                    let allLineUp =
                        phraseParts
                        |> Array.fold foldFunc initialState
                        |> (fun (_, _, lineUp) -> lineUp)

                    if allLineUp then
                        yield firstTokenPosition

                    // Move to the next start of the phrase and continue.
                    phraseParts.[0].MoveNext()
        })
```

Logical operators

Local operators join pairs of queries together, returning documents that occur in either
query or only those that occur in both.

For *OR* operators, we simply retrieve the union of all unique documents returned by
both queries. This is another situation where the canonical ordering of `TokenPosi`
`tion` objects is required. Given two `TokenPostingList` objects, we return a hit for
whichever list has the lowest `DocumentID`.

Example 11-9 shows our implementation of *OR* queries.

Example 11-9. Using OR in queries

```
let disjunctiveEnumerator (iter1 : TokenPostingList) (iter2 : TokenPostingList) =
    new TokenPostingList(
        seq {
            while (not iter1.AtEnd) || (not iter2.AtEnd) do
                if iter1.AtEnd then
                    yield iter2.Current
                    iter2.MoveNextDocument()
                elif iter2.AtEnd then
                    yield iter1.Current
                    iter1.MoveNextDocument()
                else
                    let i1Current = iter1.Current
                    let i2Current = iter2.Current
```

```
        if i1Current.DocumentID = i2Current.DocumentID then
            // Take care not to yield the same document more than once.
            yield i1Current
            iter1.MoveNextDocument()
            iter2.MoveNextDocument()
        elif i1Current < i2Current then
            yield i1Current
            iter1.MoveNextDocument()
        else
            yield i2Current
            iter2.MoveNextDocument()
    })
```

AND works in a similar way, except that it advances whichever list has the lowest
DocumentID until the current document for both lists match.

Example 11-10 shows our implementation of *AND* queries.

Example 11-10. Using AND in queries

```
/// Combine two enumerators to return only documents found in both enumerators.
let conjunctiveEnumerator (iter1 : TokenPostingList) (iter2 : TokenPostingList) =
    new TokenPostingList(
        seq {
            while (not iter1.AtEnd) && (not iter2.AtEnd) do
                let i1Current = iter1.Current
                let i2Current = iter2.Current
                if i1Current.DocumentID = i2Current.DocumentID then
                    yield i1Current
                    iter1.MoveNextDocument()
                    iter2.MoveNextDocument()
                elif i1Current < i2Current then
                    iter1.MoveNextDocument()
                else
                    iter2.MoveNextDocument()
    })
```

Putting them together

With the basic enumerators in place, we can now compose them to handle arbitrarily
complex search queries. Query "(planes OR trains) AND automobiles" requires a
combination of five TokenPostingList objects: three term enumerators, and both a
conjunction and disjunction enumerator.

Fortunately, it isn't that difficult to construct a sophisticated TokenPostingList because
they can be easily nested. The following is the implementation of the getIterator
method that takes a Query object and returns a TokenPostingList:

```
/// Map a query object into a single document interator.
let rec getIterator (index : Index) query =
    match query with
    | Term(term) ->
```

```
    let tokenID = getTokenID term
    let tokenHitList = index.GetPostingList(tokenID).TokenOccurrences
    new TokenPostingList(tokenHitList)
| Phrase(phrase) ->
    let individualTokenIterators =
        phrase
        |> List.rev
        |> List.map getTokenID
        |> List.map(fun tokenID ->
                        index.GetPostingList(tokenID).TokenOccurrences)
        |> List.map(fun tokenHits -> new TokenPostingList(tokenHits))
        |> List.toArray
    createExactPhraseEnumerator individualTokenIterators
| And(x, y) ->
    conjunctiveEnumerator (getIterator index x) (getIterator index y)
| Or(x, y) ->
    disjunctiveEnumerator (getIterator index x) (getIterator index y)
| SubQuery(q) -> getIterator index q
```

With that, the bulk of our core structure of our engine is complete. The following shows a console dump of the search engine in action:

```
Query System
Loading index...
237 documents with 256243 tokens in index.
:"Much Ado About Nothing"
[Phrase ["Nothing"; "About"; "Ado"; "Much"]]
Results =

 Nov 1998 Much Ado About Nothing, by William Shakespeare    [2ws22xxx.xxx]
 Nov 1998 Much Ado About Nothing, by William Shakespeare    [3ws22xxx.xxx]
 Jun 1999 Much Ado About Nothing, by Shakespeare       [WL][1ws2211x.xxx]
 Oct 1999 Elinor Wyllys, by Susan Fenimore Cooper[Volume 2] [2wyllxxx.xxx]
 Oct 1999 Elinor Wyllys, by Susan Fenimore Cooper[Volume 1] [1wyllxxx.xxx]


:Ophelia
[Term "Ophelia"]
Results =

 Nov 1998 Hamlet, by William Shakespeare                    [2ws26xxx.xxx]
 Jul 2000 Hamlet, by William Shakespeare               [FF] [0ws26xxx.xxx]
 Dec 1997 Hamlet, Prince of Denmark, by Wm Shakespeare  [WL][1ws26xxx.xxx]
 Jun 1999 Hamlet, by Shakespeare                        [WL][1ws2611x.xxx]
 Jul 2000 The Complete Shakespeare's First Folio [35 Plays] [00ws1xxx.xxx]


:"Much Ado about Nothing" OR Ophelia
[Or (Phrase ["Nothing"; "about"; "Ado"; "Much"],Term "Ophelia")]
Results =

 Nov 1998 Hamlet, by William Shakespeare                    [2ws26xxx.xxx]
 Nov 1998 Much Ado About Nothing, by William Shakespeare    [2ws22xxx.xxx]
 Nov 1998 Much Ado About Nothing, by William Shakespeare    [3ws22xxx.xxx]
 Jul 2000 Hamlet, by William Shakespeare               [FF] [0ws26xxx.xxx]
```

```
Dec 1997 Hamlet, Prince of Denmark, by Wm Shakespeare  [WL][1ws26xxx.xxx]
Jun 1999 Hamlet, by Shakespeare                        [WL][1ws2611x.xxx]
Jun 1999 Much Ado About Nothing, by Shakespeare        [WL][1ws2211x.xxx]
Jul 2000 The Complete Shakespeare's First Folio [35 Plays] [00ws1xxx.xxx]
Oct 1999 Elinor Wyllys, by Susan Fenimore Cooper[Volume 2] [2wyllxxx.xxx]
Oct 1999 Elinor Wyllys, by Susan Fenimore Cooper[Volume 1] [1wyllxxx.xxx]
```

:Gandalf
```
[Term "Gandalf"]
No hits.
```

So is this all there is to making Google? No. In addition to scaling our corpus up to hundreds of billions of documents, our results do not consider *relevance*. Users can narrow down their search by adding more terms, but they still come in the order defined by the docId. Sorting the document matches by "what the user wanted to search for in the first place" is what makes Google magical.

Next steps

From here, there are many more things to do. For example, we could create an ASP.NET MVC website in F# to gather user search queries. That website could use Windows Communication Foundation to make remote procedure calls to a dedicated service sitting in front of the index. We could also write Windows Services in F# to monitor our website and serving instances to track memory usage and reliability...you get the idea.

Extending the F# Language

Reflection

We have covered almost all of the raw syntax of F#, and the programming paradigms it enables. In this chapter, you won't learn any new capabilities of the F# language *per se*; instead you will learn how to harness the *.NET Reflection APIs*.

Reflection allows you to access the runtime metadata information about executing code. Metadata can be raw type information, such as the methods a class has, or it can come in the form of *attributes*, which are programmer-supplied code annotations.

The most common usage of .NET reflection is for *metaprogramming*, which is writing programs that reason about themselves, or modify themselves, such as those that can load plug-ins to add new functionality at runtime. In other words, allowing other developers to extend your application without them needing to have access to the source code.

But before you can do full-on metaprogramming, you must first understand how to annotate code to provide metadata.

Attributes

Attributes are a form of metadata you can attach to assemblies, methods, parameters, and so on. These annotations can then be inspected at runtime using reflection, which we get to later in this chapter. The F# compiler will recognize attributes as well; in fact, you have been using attributes for a while now to provide hints for how to compile your code.

Recall from Chapter 5 that in order to mark a class as abstract, you need to provide the [<Abstract>] attribute to the type declaration. When the F# compiler sees that attribute, it will generate the code differently than if the attribute had not been present. The same is true for [<Struct>], [<ReferenceEquality>], and other attributes:

```
[<AbstractClass>]
type Animal =
    abstract Speak : unit -> unit
    abstract NumberOfLegs : int with get
```

In .NET programming, there are many common attributes that the F# compiler will recognize as well. For example, the System.ObsoleteAttribute is used to mark deprecated methods and classes. When using code entities marked with [<Obsolete>], the F# compiler will generate an error or warning based on usage.

Example 12-1 shows some F# code that has been refactored since originally written. An [<Obsolete>] attribute has been added to help guide consumers of the class to update their code.

As you have seen earlier, to place an attribute, simply insert the attribute's name surrounded by [< >] above the class or method you want the attribute to annotate. When applying an attribute, if the attribute's name is suffixed with *Attribute*, you can omit the word *Attribute*. For example, to apply an instance of System.ObsoleteAttribute, you just need to write [<Obsolete>] if the System namespace has been opened.

Example 12-1. The Obsolete attribute

```
open System

type SafetyLevel =
    | RecreationalUse
    | HaveMcCoyOnDuty
    | SetPhasersToKill

type HoloDeck(safetyLevel : SafetyLevel) =

    let mutable m_safetyLevel = safetyLevel

    member this.SafetyLevel with get () = m_safetyLevel

    [<Obsolete("Deprecated. Cannot update protocols once initialized.", true)>]
    member this.SafetyLevel with set x = m_safetyLevel <- x
```

Figure 12-1 shows the Visual Studio 2010 editor when trying to call a method or property marked with [<Obsolete>].

```
    let deck = new HoloDeck(RecreationalUse)
    deck.SafetyLevel <- SetPhasersToKill
```

100 %   ▾ ⏐ ◁

Error List

▼ ▾ ⊗ 1 Error   ⚠ 0 Warnings   ⊙ 0 Messages

Description

⊗ 1 This construct is deprecated. Deprecated. Cannot update protocols once initialized.

Figure 12-1. Warnings and errors in the Visual Studio Editor

Applying Attributes

Later in this chapter, we look at how to analyze type information to examine any attributes provided. But first, in order to have metadata to analyze, let's take a deeper look at adding attributes to your code.

Attribute targets

Most of the time, putting the attribute directly above the type or method you want to annotate will be sufficient. However, there are times when the attribute's target can be ambiguous. To have the attribute apply to a specific construct, you can use an *attribute target*, which is a keyword indicating what the attribute applies to.

For example, assembly-level attributes are global, in the sense that they do not belong to a particular class or method, but rather apply to the whole assembly. So an attribute target is required to make clear that the assembly-level attribute doesn't apply to the next type or value declared.

The most common assembly-level attributes are those for setting the assembly's version and copyright information. Note in the example that character trigraphs \169 and \174 are used to encode the © and ™ characters, respectively:

```
open System.Reflection

[<assembly:AssemblyDescription("RemoteCombobulator.exe")>]
[<assembly:AssemblyCompany("Initech Corporation")>]
[<assembly:AssemblyCopyright("\169 Initech Corporation. All rights reserved.")>]
[<assembly:AssemblyProduct("Initech \174 RemoteCombobulator")>]
do()
```

 Assembly-level attributes must be placed inside of a module on a do binding.

The list of common attribute targets are listed in Table 12-1.

Table 12-1. Attribute targets

Target Name	Description
Assembly	Applies to the assembly.
Field	Applies to a class field.
Param	Applies to a parameter of a method.
Return	Applies to the return value of a method or property.

Applying multiple attributes

When you apply multiple attributes, you have the choice to either place each attribute individually, or group all the attributes together in a semicolon-delimited list.

Example 12-2 shows the same assembly-level attributes from the previous code snippet, but in a slightly cleaned up form.

Example 12-2. Applying multiple attributes

```
open System.Reflection

[<
    assembly:AssemblyDescription("RemoteCombobulator.exe");
    assembly:AssemblyCompany("Initech Corporation");
    assembly:AssemblyCopyright("\169 Initech Corporation. All rights reserved.");
    assembly:AssemblyProduct("Initech \174 RemoteCombobulator")
>]
do()
```

Defining New Attributes

To define new attributes of your own, simply create a class that inherits from `System .Attribute`. Defining your own custom attributes is instrumental for creating custom type annotations.

Example 12-3 defines a couple of custom attributes for adding descriptions for classes and methods. XML-Doc comments are unavailable at runtime, whereas the custom `ClassDescription` and `MethodDescription` attributes are available.

Note that the custom attributes have the optional `AttributeUsage` attribute applied to them. This attribute for custom attributes determines where the attribute can be applied. (Meta-meta-programming indeed!) In Example 12-3, the `AttributeUsage` attribute indicates that the `MethodDescriptionAttribute` can only be applied to methods; otherwise, an error will be issued by the F# compiler. Similarly, the `ClassDescrip tionAttribute` can only be applied to classes.

Example 12-3. Defining custom attributes

```
open System

/// Provide a description for a given class
[<AttributeUsage(AttributeTargets.Class)>]
type ClassDescriptionAttribute(desc) =
    inherit Attribute()
    member this.Description = desc

/// Provide a description for a given method
[<AttributeUsage(AttributeTargets.Method)>]
type MethodDescriptionAttribute(desc) =
    inherit Attribute()
    member this.Description = desc

type Widget =
    | RedWidget
    | GreenWidget
    | BlueWidget

/// XML Doc comments like this one are great for describing a class,
/// but are only available at compile-time. Metadata encoded into
/// attributes is available at runtime.
[<ClassDescription("Represents a stack of Widgets.")>]
type WidgetStack() =

    let mutable m_widgets : Widget list = []

    [<MethodDescription("Pushes a new Widget onto the stack.")>]
    member this.Push(x) = m_widgets <- x :: m_widgets

    [<MethodDescription("Access the top of the Widget stack.")>]
    member this.Peek()  = List.head m_widgets

    [<MethodDescription("Pops the top Widget off the stack.")>]
    member this.Pop()   = let top = List.head m_widgets
                          m_widgets <- List.tail m_widgets
                          top
```

Type Reflection

So you have learned how to attribute code, but what if you want to inspect those at-tributes? The way you access attributes on code is through *type reflection*.

Recall that everything in .NET inherits from System.Object, and therefore every value in .NET has a GetType method, which returns an instance of System.Type. The Type class describes everything there is to know about a type—including its attributes.

Accessing Types

The following FSI session defines a custom type named Sprocket and then uses two different methods to access its type information. The first method used in the sample is the generic typeof<_> type function, which returns the type of the supplied type parameter. The second method used is to call the GetType method found on an instance of Sprocket, because it inherits from obj:

```
> // Simple sprocket type
type Sprocket() =
    member this.Gears = 16
    member this.SerialNumber = "WJM-0520";;

type Sprocket =
  class
    new : unit -> Sprocket
    member Gears : int
    member SerialNumber : string
  end

> // Get type information via typeof<_>
let type1 = typeof<Sprocket>;;

val type1 : System.Type = FSI_0002+Sprocket

> // Get type information via GetType
let aSprocket = new Sprocket()
let type2 = aSprocket.GetType();;

val aSprocket : Sprocket
val type2 : System.Type = FSI_0002+Sprocket

> type1 = type2;;
val it : bool = true
> type1.Name;;
val it : string = "Sprocket"
```

Accessing generic types

Although typeof<_> is helpful for getting type information, when used on generic types, it must fix any unknown generic type parameter to obj. If you want the returned type to be fully generic, use the typedefof<_> type function.

The following snippet shows getting type information from a sequence. Notice that the returned type information from using typedefof<_> is fully generic, whereas typeof<_> indicates that the sequence is of type obj, which is potentially incorrect:

```
> let fixedSeq = typeof< seq<float> >;;

val fixedSeq : Type = System.Collections.Generic.IEnumerable`1[System.Double]
```

```
> let genSeq = typeof< seq<'a> >;;

val genSeq : Type = System.Collections.Generic.IEnumerable`1[System.Object]

> let fullyGenSeq = typedefof< seq<'a> >;;

val fullyGenSeq : Type = System.Collections.Generic.IEnumerable`1[T]
```

Inspecting methods

Once you have an instance of Type, you can inspect the type's methods and properties by calling GetMethods and GetProperties, and so on.

Example 12-4 defines a function called describeType, which will print all methods, properties, and fields for a type to the console.

The BindingFlags enum is passed in to filter the results. For example, BindingFlags .DeclaredOnly is used so that the call to GetMethods doesn't return inherited methods, such as GetHashCode and ToString.

Example 12-4. Inspecting and analyzing types

```
open System
open System.Reflection

/// Prints the methods, properties, and fields of a type to the console
let describeType (ty : Type) =

    let bindingFlags =
        BindingFlags.Public    ||| BindingFlags.NonPublic |||
        BindingFlags.Instance ||| BindingFlags.Static    |||
        BindingFlags.DeclaredOnly

    let methods =
        ty.GetMethods(bindingFlags)
        |> Array.fold (fun desc meth -> desc + sprintf " %s" meth.Name) ""

    let props =
        ty.GetProperties(bindingFlags)
        |> Array.fold (fun desc prop -> desc + sprintf " %s" prop.Name) ""

    let fields =
        ty.GetFields(bindingFlags)
        |> Array.fold (fun desc field -> desc + sprintf " %s" field.Name) ""

    printfn "Name: %s" ty.Name
    printfn "Methods:    \n\t%s\n" methods
    printfn "Properties: \n\t%s\n" props
    printfn "Fields:     \n\t%s" fields
```

The following FSI session shows using describeType on string:

```
Name: String
Methods:
    Join get_FirstChar Join nativeCompareOrdinal nativeCompareOrdinalEx
nativeCompareOrdinalWC SmallCharToUpper EqualsHelper CompareOrdinalHelper
 Equals Equals Equals Equals Equals op_Equality op_Inequality get_Chars
CopyTo ToCharArray ToCharArray IsNullOrEmpty GetHashCode get_Length
get_ArrayLength get_Capacity Split Split Split Split Split Split
InternalSplitKeepEmptyEntries InternalSplitOmitEmptyEntries MakeSeparatorList
MakeSeparatorList Substring Substring InternalSubStringWithChecks
InternalSubString Trim TrimStart TrimEnd CreateString

    ...snip...

Properties:
    FirstChar Chars Length ArrayLength Capacity

Fields:
    m_arrayLength m_stringLength m_firstChar WhitespaceChars TrimHead snip
```

Now let's use `describeType` on a custom class. First, define a type called Cog. Note the private accessibility modifiers on the class's field and property:

```
/// Unit of measure for milliliter
[<Measure>]
type ml

type Cog =

    val mutable private m_oilLevel : float<ml>

    new() = { m_oilLevel = 100.0<ml> }

    member private this.Gears = 16
    member this.SerialNumber = "1138-THX"

    member this.Rotate() =
        // Rotating loses a bit of oil on each turn...
        this.m_oilLevel <- this.m_oilLevel - 0.01<ml>
```

Now, in an FSI session, call `describeType` on the type of Cog. Notice how all type information is printed out, including members marked with the private accessibility modifiers:

```
> describeType (typeof<Cog>);;
Name: Cog
Methods:
    get_Gears get_SerialNumber Rotate

Properties:
    SerialNumber Gears
```

```
Fields:
     m_oilLevel
val it : unit = ()
```

 Code accessibility is a language-level restriction to help programmers;
however, declaring something private or internal offers no security at
runtime. When using .NET reflection, you can access any fields and
members of objects. You should keep this in mind when persisting sensitive information in memory.

Inspecting attributes

Inspecting a type's attributes is done in much the same way as inspecting its methods
and properties. The only difference, however, is that attributes can be put in many more
places.

Example 12-5 shows inspecting a type for the ClassDescription and MethodDescrip
tion attributes from earlier in this chapter. Note how the full list of custom attributes
on a type needs to be pared down to just the ClassDescription or MethodDescrip
tion attributes.

Example 12-5. Inspecting type attributes

```
open System

/// Displays data attributed with the MethodDesc or ClassDesc attributes
let printDocumentation(ty : Type) =

    // Return if an object has a given type
    let objHasType ty obj = (obj.GetType() = ty)

    let classDescription : string option =
        ty.GetCustomAttributes(false)
        |> Seq.tryFind(objHasType typeof<ClassDescriptionAttribute>)
        |> Option.map(fun attr -> (attr :?> ClassDescriptionAttribute))
        |> Option.map(fun cda -> cda.Description)

    let methodDescriptions : seq<string * string option> =
        ty.GetMethods()
        |> Seq.map(fun mi -> mi, mi.GetCustomAttributes(false))
        |> Seq.map(fun (methodInfo, methodAttributes) ->
            let attributeDescription =
                methodAttributes
                |> Seq.tryFind(objHasType typeof<MethodDescriptionAttribute>)
                |> Option.map(fun atr -> (atr :?> MethodDescriptionAttribute))
                |> Option.map(fun mda -> mda.Description)
            methodInfo.Name, attributeDescription)

    let getDescription = function
```

```
                       | Some(desc) -> desc
                       | None       -> "(no description provided)"

    printfn "Info for class: %s" ty.Name
    printfn "Class Description:\n\t%s" (getDescription classDescription)
    printfn "Method Descriptions:"

    methodDescriptions
    |> Seq.iter(fun (methName, desc) -> printfn
                                    "\t%15s - %s"
                                    methName
                                    (getDescription desc))
```

When run on the `WidgetStack` type from Example 12-3, the `printDocumentation` function has the following output:

```
> printDocumentation (typeof<WidgetStack>);;
Info for class: WidgetStack
Class Description:
    Represents a stack of Widgets.
Method Descriptions:
              Push - Pushes a new Widget onto the stack.
              Peek - Access the top of the Widget stack.
               Pop - Pops the top Widget off the stack.
          ToString - (no description provided)
            Equals - (no description provided)
       GetHashCode - (no description provided)
           GetType - (no description provided)
val it : unit = ()
```

Reflecting on F# Types

Although the .NET reflection APIs are easy to use, they were written long before F# existed and as such don't have any concept of special F# types. As a result, when inspecting things like records or discriminated unions, you might get unexpected results.

Consider the following discriminated union to describe playing cards. Conceptually, the `PlayingCard` type is a very simple data structure:

```
type Suit =
    | Club
    | Diamond
    | Heart
    | Spade

type PlayingCard =
    | Ace   of Suit
    | King  of Suit
    | Queen of Suit
    | Jack  of Suit
    | ValueCard of int * Suit
    | Joker
```

However, when analyzed using reflection by our describeType function, you can see all the work the F# compiler does behind the scenes to map the discriminated union onto the object-oriented .NET runtime:

```
> describeType (typeof<PlayingCard>);;
Name: PlayingCard
Methods:
      get_Joker get_IsJoker NewValueCard get_IsValueCard NewJack
get_IsJack NewQueen get_IsQueen NewKing get_IsKing NewAce get_IsAce
get_Tag __DebugDisplay CompareTo CompareTo CompareTo GetHashCode
GetHashCode Equals Equals Equals

Properties:
      Tag Joker IsJoker IsValueCard IsJack IsQueen IsKing IsAce

Fields:
      _tag _unique_Joker
val it : unit = ()
```

Fortunately, the F# library contains a few additional APIs for reflecting over functional types in the Microsoft.FSharp.Reflection namespace.

Tuples

The underlying type used for tuples is System.Tuple<_>. To decompose a particular instance of a tuple and get the type of its elements, you can use the FSharpType.GetTupleElements method, which will return the types of the tuple's elements in order as an array:

```
> let xenon = ("Xe", 54);;

val xenon : string * int - ("Xe", 54)

> // Get the tuple's element's types
open Microsoft.FSharp.Reflection
let tupleElementTypes = FSharpType.GetTupleElements (xenon.GetType());;

val tupleElementTypes : Type [] = [|System.String; System.Int32|]
```

Discriminated unions

You can reflect over discriminated union data tags by using the FSharpType.GetUnionCases method. This will return an array of the UnionCaseInfo type, which will describe each data tag.

The following snippet reflects over the PlayingCard type and prints each data tag name to the console:

```
> // Reflect the PlayingCard discriminated union type
FSharpType.GetUnionCases typeof<PlayingCard>
|> Array.iter (fun unionCase -> printfn "%s" unionCase.Name);;
Ace
```

```
King
Queen
Jack
ValueCard
Joker
val it : unit = ()
```

Records

You can use the FSharpType.GetRecordFields method to get all of the properties on a record type:

```
> // Type definitions
[<Measure>]
type far // Degrees fahrenheit

type Outlook = Sunny | Cloudy | Rainy

type Weather = { Outlook : Outlook; High : float<far>; Low : float<far> };;

...snip...

> // Reflect over the Weather record type
FSharpType.GetRecordFields typeof<Weather>
|> Array.iter (fun propInfo -> printfn
                                "Name [%s], Type [%s]"
                                propInfo.Name propInfo.PropertyType.Name);;

Name [Outlook], Type [Outlook]
Name [High], Type [Double]
Name [Low], Type [Double]
val it : unit = ()
```

Dynamic Instantiation

In the previous section, you saw ways to examine types and reflect on their metadata. However, the real power of reflection lies in *dynamic instantiation*, which is a fancy way to say "creating values at runtime whose type you didn't know about at compile time." In other words, given an instance of System.Type, create a new instance of the type it describes.

Instantiating Types

Dynamically instantiating types can be done using the Activator class. Example 12-6 defines a type PoliteWriter, and creates a new instance dynamically using Activator.CreateInstance.

The parameters to PoliteWriter's constructor are passed in as an obj array. The result of CreateInstance is an obj, which will need to be cast as the type you want.

Example 12-6. Dynamic instantiation

```
> // Define a polite text writer
open System
open System.IO

type PoliteWriter(stream : TextWriter) =

    member this.WriteLine(msg : string) =
        sprintf "%s... please" msg
        |> stream.WriteLine;;

type PoliteWriter =
  class
    new : stream:IO.TextWriter -> PoliteWriter
    member WriteLine : msg:string -> unit
  end

> // Dynamically create an instance of that class
let politeConsole =
    Activator.CreateInstance(typeof<PoliteWriter>, [| box Console.Out |]);;

val politeConsole : obj

> (politeConsole :?> PoliteWriter).WriteLine("Hello, World!");;
Hello, World!... please
val it : unit = ()
```

Now you have the ability to not only load types, but also create new instances of them at runtime. This opens up powerful new capabilities for F# applications such as loading plug-ins.

Instantiating F# Types

Just like the custom F# reflection APIs for doing type inspection of functional code, there are special methods to do dynamic instantiation as well. Table 12-2 shows some common methods in the FSharpValue module for dynamically instantiating functional types like tuples and discriminated unions.

Table 12-2. Common methods in the FSharpValue module

Signature	Description
MakeTuple: obj[] * Type -> obj	Creates a new tuple value.
MakeRecord: Type * obj[] -> obj	Creates a new record value.
MakeUnion: UnionCaseInfo * obj[] -> obj	Creates a new instance of a discriminated union. You can get an instance of UnionCaseInfo by calling FSharpType.GetUnionCases.

Dynamic Invocation

If you can go about dynamically loading and instantiating types, why stop there? In .NET, you can do *dynamic invocation*, which is a fancy term for *late binding*, which is in turn a fancy way to say "calling methods at runtime which you didn't know about at compile time." Using reflection you can get an instance of a method or property and call it.

Example 12-7 defines a class Book and dynamically gets an instance of the type's Cur rentPage property. That property can then be updated dynamically without manipulating an instance of Book directly, but rather calling SetValue on the returned Proper tyInfo object.

Example 12-7. Dynamic invocation

```
> // Type for representing a book
type Book(title, author) =
    // Current page, if the book is opened
    let mutable m_currentPage : int option = None

    member this.Title  = title
    member this.Author = author
    member this.CurrentPage with get () = m_currentPage
                            and  set x  = m_currentPage <- x

    override this.ToString() =
        match m_currentPage with
        | Some(pg) -> sprintf "%s by %s, opened to page %d" title author pg
        | None     -> sprintf "%s by %s, not currently opened" title author;;

    ...snip...

> let afternoonReading = new Book("The Mythical Man Month", "Brooks");;

val afternoonReading : Book =
  The Mythical Man Month by Brooks, not currently opened

> let currentPagePropertyInfo = typeof<Book>.GetProperty("CurrentPage");;

val currentPagePropertyInfo : PropertyInfo =
  Microsoft.FSharp.Core.FSharpOption`1[System.Int32] CurrentPage

> currentPagePropertyInfo.SetValue(afternoonReading, Some(214), [| |]);;
val it : unit = ()
> afternoonReading.ToString();;
val it : string = "The Mythical Man Month by Brooks, opened to page 214"
```

Using late binding isn't that common because normally if you are given an obj, you know what types to expect, so you can use a dynamic cast (:?>) and then call the expected method. Late binding is typically used in dynamic languages, in which methods and properties can be added to objects at runtime. So you need to look up if the given method or property even exists before calling it!

The Question Mark Operators

As you saw in the previous example, dynamically getting a property and calling it can feel clunky in F#. For that reason, the question mark (?) and question mark setter (? <-) operators were introduced. Functions defined with that name are treated specially by the F# compiler, and make late binding much easier to perform.

If a symbolic operator named ? is defined, then when it is called, the first parameter will be the expression on the left hand side and the text on the right hand side will be passed in as a string parameter.

The following example defines a question mark operator that checks if a property exists on a type, printing the result to the screen. When using the . operator to access class members, whether or not the member exists is checked at compile time. With the question mark operator you get the text of the member name and can do the check at runtime:

```
> // Use the Question Mark operator to check if a type
// contains a given property.
let (?) (thingey : obj) (propName : string) =
    let ty = thingey.GetType()

    match ty.GetProperty(propName) with
    | null -> false
    | _    -> true;;

val ( ? ) : obj -> string -> bool

> // All strings have a Length property
"a string"?Length;;
val it : bool = true
> // Integers don't have an IsPrime property
42?IsPrime;;
val it : bool = false
> // Cast a string as an obj, works because check is dynamic
("a string" :> obj) ? Length;;
val it : bool = true
```

Using the question mark operator, we can clean up our code from Example 12-7. The following snippet defines both a question mark and question mark setter for dynamically accessing a class and updating a class property:

```
> // Get a property value. Notice that the return type is generic.
let (?) (thingey : obj) (propName: string) : 'a =
    let propInfo = thingey.GetType().GetProperty(propName)
```

```
        propInfo.GetValue(thingey, null) :?> 'a

// Set a property value.
let (?<-) (thingey : obj) (propName : string) (newValue : 'a) =
    let propInfo = thingey.GetType().GetProperty(propName)
    propInfo.SetValue(thingey, newValue, null);;

val ( ? ) : obj -> string -> 'a
val ( ?<- ) : obj -> string -> 'a -> unit

> let book = new Book("Foundation", "Asimov");;

val book : Book = Foundation by Asimov, not currently opened

> book?CurrentPage <- Some(14);;
val it : unit = ()
> let currentPage : int option = book?CurrentPage;;

val currentPage : int option = Some 14
```

In most applications, you will rarely encounter a type wherein you know of its available properties but not its actual type. So the question mark operators are of somewhat limited use. But consider situations where the property being checked contains additional information. For example: `book?CurrentPageTextInSpanish`. The question mark operators add extra flexibility when pushing the limits of what F# code can do.

Using Reflection

So now that you know all about reflection, what *do* you do with it? In other words, what is metaprogramming?

Next, we look at two specific applications of .NET reflection: declarative programming and writing plug-in systems.

Declarative Programming

Perhaps the simplest thing to do when using reflection is to create more declarative code. Rather than hardcoding data into properties and methods, you can encode data by using attributes. This leads to potentially cleaner and more readable code.

Consider Example 12-8, which defines a function `determineBoxToUse` to calculate the proper container to ship an item in. Each item that can be shipped inherits from the `ShippingItem` class and overrides the `Weight` and `Dimension` properties, which are used to determine the correct box size.

No reflection or declarative programming is used just yet; we'll see how we can improve upon this code next.

Example 12-8. Simple shipping software

```fsharp
/// Pounds
[<Measure>]
type lb

[<Measure>]
type inches

type Container =
    | Envelope
    | Box
    | Crate

type Dimensions =
    { Length : float<inches>; Width : float<inches>; Height : float<inches> }

[<AbstractClass>]
type ShippingItem() =
    abstract Weight : float<lb>
    abstract Dimension : Dimensions

// Piece of paper describing what is in the box
type ShippingManifest() =
    inherit ShippingItem()

    override this.Weight = 0.01<lb>
    override this.Dimension =
            {
                Length = 11.00<inches>
                Width  =  8.50<inches>
                Height =  0.01<inches>
            }

// Will it blend?
type Blender() =
    inherit ShippingItem()

    override this.Weight = 14.00<lb>
    override this.Dimension =
            {
                Length =  6.0<inches>;
                Width  =  5.0<inches>
                Height = 12.0<inches>
            }

/// Partial active pattern which matches only if the input is
/// greater than its parameter.
let (|GreaterThan|_|) (param : float<'a>) input =
    if param > input
    then Some()
    else None
```

```
let determineBoxToUse(item : ShippingItem) =

    match item.Weight, item.Dimension with
    // Heavy orders must always go into a crate
    | GreaterThan 10.0<lb>, _
        -> Crate

    // Large orders must always go into a crate
    | _, { Length = GreaterThan 24.0<inches>; Width = _; Height = _}
    | _, { Length = _; Width = GreaterThan 24.0<inches>; Height = _}
    | _, { Length = _; Width = _; Height = GreaterThan 24.0<inches>}
        -> Crate

    // Beefy orders must go into a box
    | GreaterThan 2.0<lb> _, _
        -> Box

    // Min dimensions for a box
    | _, { Length = GreaterThan 10.0<inches>; Width = _; Height = _}
    | _, { Length = _; Width = GreaterThan 10.0<inches>; Height = _}
    | _, { Length = _; Width = _; Height = GreaterThan 10.0<inches>}
        -> Box

    // Looks like an envelope will do
    | _ -> Envelope
```

Example 12-8 seems simple enough, but the code doesn't scale very well. Imagine you need to extend it so that you can add special handling instructions. For example, suppose you need to account for the fact that some shipping items are fragile or flammable.

Using the fully object-oriented approach, you might extend the ShippingItem base class and add new properties:

```
[<AbstractClass>]
type ShippingItem() =
    abstract Weight : float<lb>
    abstract Dimension : Dimensions
    abstract Fragile  : bool
    abstract Flammable : bool
```

But because you are adding a new property to the base class, you either need to give the Fragile property a default implementation, or you need to provide an implementation for every single class that inherits from ShippingItem. You then suffer this same problem every time you want to extend ShippingItem in some way—edit every single class or provide a default implementation.

Providing a default implementation may seem simple, but remember that it adds complexity to the type. If you are inheriting from ShippingItem and see 15+ abstract methods or properties, it may take some time to determine which ones are important and which ones are not.

For many items it would be far easier to have them declare any special handling needs themselves, rather than adding dozens of "one-off" properties to the ShippingItem base class. You can use attributes to annotate these types with their special needs.

Example 12-9 defines several attributes for annotating types to be shipped, so that later special shipping requirements can be determined. This frees the base type from needing to modify any special flags, and allows new shipping items to be written in a more declarative way. (In fact, the Weight and Dimension properties could also be replaced with attributes.)

Example 12-9. Using attributes for declarative programming

```
open System

type FragileAttribute() =
    inherit System.Attribute()

type FlammableAttribute() =
    inherit System.Attribute()

type LiveAnimalAttribute() =
    inherit System.Attribute()


/// A real, live wombat delivered right to your door!
[<LiveAnimal>]
type Wombat() =
    inherit ShippingItem()

    override this.Weight = 60.0<lb>
    override this.Dimension =
            {
                Length = 39.0<inches>
                Width  = 10.0<inches>
                Height = 13.0<inches>
            }

[<Fragile; Flammable>]
type Fireworks() =
    inherit ShippingItem()

    override this.Weight = 5.0<lb>
    override this.Dimension =
            {
                Length = 10.0<inches>
                Width  = 8.0<inches>
                Height = 5.0<inches>
            }
```

The following snippet defines a `getShippingRequirements` function that uses an inner function named `containsAttribute` to check if a given object is marked with a specific attribute. This is then used to check the items to be shipped and determine additional requirements:

```
open System.Collections.Generic

type ShippingRequirements =
    | NeedInsurance  of ShippingItem
    | NeedSignature  of ShippingItem
    | NeedBubbleWrap of ShippingItem

/// Get any additional requirements for shipping the package
let getShippingRequirements (contents : ShippingItem list) =

    let containsAttribute (targetAttrib : Type) x =
        x.GetType().GetCustomAttributes(false)
        |> Array.tryFind(fun attr -> attr.GetType() = targetAttrib)
        |> Option.isSome

    let itemsWithAttribute attr =
        contents |> List.filter (containsAttribute attr)

    let requirements = new HashSet<ShippingRequirements>()

    // Include fragile items
    itemsWithAttribute typeof<FragileAttribute>
    |> List.iter (fun item -> requirements.Add(NeedBubbleWrap(item)) |> ignore)

    // Include flammable items
    itemsWithAttribute typeof<FlammableAttribute>
    |> List.iter (fun item -> requirements.Add(NeedInsurance(item)) |> ignore)

    // Include live animals
    itemsWithAttribute typeof<LiveAnimalAttribute>
    |> List.iter (fun item -> requirements.Add(NeedSignature(item)) |> ignore)

    // Return the list of special shipping requirements
    Seq.toList requirements
```

Plug-in Architecture

Another use of reflection is to allow for a plug-in architecture, where other developers can extend your application by creating new .NET assemblies that conform to a specific contract. You can then use reflection to dynamically load those assemblies and call into the other programmer's code.

Typically this is done through a two-step process. First, you create an assembly to define the core infrastructure pieces, such as an interface and/or custom attributes to define new plug-ins. Then you have your application search other assemblies for types that look like plug-ins and instantiate them.

The following examples continue our delivery system implementation by allowing other developers to create new methods for delivering packages.

 If your application has more serious requirements around extensibility, consider using the *Managed Extensibility Framework*. It is a library built into the .NET Framework for writing and consuming plug-ins like the one described here.

Plug-in interfaces

Example 12-10 defines the code for `DeliverySystem.Core.dll`, which is a library future plug-ins will need to reference. It defines an interface `IDeliveryMethod`, which future plug-ins must implement.

Example 12-10. DeliverySystem.Core.dll

```
// DeliverySystem.Core.dll

namespace DeliverySystem.Core

/// Represents a package to be delivered
type Package =
    class
    (* ... *)
    end

/// Package destination
type Destination =
    {
        Address : string
        City    : string
        State   : string
        Zip     : int
        Country : string
    }

/// Interface for new delivery systems to be added
type IDeliveryMethod =
    interface
        abstract MethodName : string
        abstract DeliverPackage : Package * Destination -> unit
    end
```

Next, let's author a simple plug-in. Example 12-11 defines a new assembly, which references *DeliverySystem.Core.dll*, and implements a new, high-speed delivery system called CarrierPigeon.

Example 12-11. CarrierPigeonPlugin.dll

```
// CarrierPigeonPlugin.dll

// References DeliverySystem.Core.dll

open DeliverySystem.Core

type CarrierPigeon() =
    interface IDeliveryMethod with

        member this.MethodName = "Carrier Pigeon"

        member this.DeliverPackage (pkg, dest) =
            (* A lot of code using the System.Animals.Pigeon APIs *)
            ()
```

Loading assemblies

The final piece to our plug-in system is loading other assemblies and any desired types into the executing process.

You can dynamically load assemblies by using the Assembly.Load method, which will return an instance of System.Assembly. Once you have an Assembly object you can then examine its types and reflect over them—inspecting and/or instantiating the types.

Example 12-12 defines a method loadAsm that opens an assembly by name and later prints out the number of types in a set of common assemblies.

 The 1,614 types defined in FSharp.Core certainly may seem like a lot, but remember you don't need to know them all.

Example 12-12. Loading assemblies

```
> // Load the assembly
open System.Reflection
let loadAsm (name : string) = Assembly.Load(name)

// Prints assembly info to the console
let printAssemblyInfo name =
    let asm = loadAsm name
    printfn "Assembly %s has %d types" name (asm.GetTypes().Length);;

val loadAsm : string -> Assembly
```

```
val printAssemblyInfo : string -> unit

> // Some common assemblies
[ "System"; "System.Core"; "FSharp.Core"; "System.Windows.Forms" ]
|> List.iter printAssemblyInfo;;
Assembly System has 2272 types
Assembly System.Core has 929 types
Assembly FSharp.Core has 1614 types
Assembly System.Windows.Forms has 2271 types
val it : unit = ()
```

Loading plug-ins

Now that we can load assemblies, let's finish our plug-in demo. Example 12-13 defines a method loadPlugins that searches the current directory for .dll files, loads the assemblies, gets their types, and then filters them for those that implement IDelivery Method.

Finally, it uses the Activator class to instantiate external plug-ins.

Example 12-13. Loading plug-ins

```
// DeliverySystem.Application.dll

open System
open System.IO
open System.Reflection

open DeliverySystem.Core

let loadPlugins() =

    // Returns whether or not a type implements the given interface
    let typeImplementsInterface (interfaceTy : Type) (ty : Type) =
        printfn "Checking %s" ty.Name
        match ty.GetInterface(interfaceTy.Name) with
        | null -> false
        | _    -> true

    Directory.GetFiles(Environment.CurrentDirectory, "*.dll")
    // Load all of the assembly's types
    |> Array.map (fun file -> Assembly.LoadFile(file))
    |> Array.map(fun asm -> asm.GetTypes())
    |> Array.concat
    // Just get types that implement IDeliveryMethod
    |> Array.filter (typeImplementsInterface typeof<IDeliveryMethod>)
    // Instantiate each plugin
    |> Array.map (fun plugin -> Activator.CreateInstance(plugin))
    // Cast the obj to IDeliveryMethod
    |> Array.map (fun plugin -> plugin :?> IDeliveryMethod)

[<EntryPoint>]
```

```
let main(_) =

    let plugins = loadPlugins()

    plugins |> Array.iter (fun pi -> printfn "Loaded Plugin - %s" pi.MethodName)

    (* Ship some packages! *)

    0
```

It may seem like a lot of extra work to go loading external assemblies and instantiating their types, but remember that the final application has *no knowledge* of the types it will load ahead of type. So, by using reflection, you can extend and modify the behavior of an application without actually modifying its source.

Computation Expressions

In Chapters 2, 3, and 4, we covered list, sequence, and array comprehensions, which are ways to write integrated F# code that ultimately produces a collection of ordered elements in list, sequence, or array form. These comprehensions are not just syntactic sugar built into the language, but rather an advanced feature at work called *computation expressions* (less formally referred to as *workflows*).

In fact, this same technique that simplifies declaring sequences can also be applied to asynchronous programming or creating domain specific languages.

In short, computation expressions allow you to take F# code and determine *how* it gets executed. Having the workflow do some of the heavy lifting behind the scenes can dramatically reduce redundant code and in some ways extend the F# language itself.

Toward Computation Expressions

Let's review briefly what's possible with sequence expressions—they allow you to define a sequence by embedding some F# code into a `seq` computation expression. Example 13-1 shows a sequence expression for generating the days of the year.

Notice that you can write pretty much any F# code inside the `seq { }` block, and elements are produced from the sequence as items are returned with the `yield` keyword.

Example 13-1. Sequence expression for enumerating days of the year

```
> // Sequence for producing month, day tuples
let daysOfTheYear =
    seq {
        let months =
            [
                "Jan"; "Feb"; "Mar"; "Apr"; "May"; "Jun";
                "Jul"; "Aug"; "Sep"; "Oct"; "Nov"; "Dec"
            ]
```

```
    let daysInMonth month =
        match month with
        | "Feb"
            -> 28
        | "Apr" | "Jun" | "Sep" | "Nov"
            -> 30
        | _ -> 31

    for month in months do
        for day = 1 to daysInMonth month do
            yield (month, day)
    };;

val daysOfTheYear : seq<string * int>

> daysOfTheYear;;
val it : seq<string * int> =
  seq [("Jan", 1); ("Jan", 2); ("Jan", 3); ("Jan", 4); ...]
> Seq.length daysOfTheYear;;
val it : int = 365
```

It is clear that the code you can put inside of a sequence expression—and, by extension, any computation expressions—is sufficient for performing powerful computations. In fact, the only limitations to the F# code you can put inside of a computation expression are:

- No new types may be declared within a computation expression.
- Mutable values cannot be used inside computation expressions; you must use ref cells instead.

I've claimed that computation expressions can dramatically simplify code. To demonstrate this, let me provide a motivating example.

Example 13-2 tries to do some basic math, except rather than leaving division up to chance—and potentially throwing a DivideByZeroException—each division is wrapped into a custom type that will indicate success or failure.

The computation performed is a simple electrical calculation: the total resistance of three resistors in parallel, which requires four division operations. Because we want to check the result of division against Success or DivByZero, the code ends up looking excessively complex, because after each division we must check if we should continue the computation or stop with a DivByZero.

Example 13-2. Setting the state for custom workflows

```
type Result = Success of float | DivByZero

let divide x y =
```

```
    match y with
    | 0.0 -> DivByZero
    | _   -> Success(x / y)

// Total resistance of three resistors in parallel is given
// by: 1/R_e = 1/R_1 + 1/R_2 + 1/R_3
let totalResistance r1 r2 r3 =
    let r1Result = divide 1.0 r1
    match r1Result with
    | DivByZero
        -> DivByZero
    | Success(x)
        -> let r2Result = divide 1.0 r2
           match r2Result with
           | DivByZero
              -> DivByZero
           | Success(y)
              -> let r3Result = divide 1.0 r3
                 match r3Result with
                 | DivByZero
                    -> DivByZero
                 | Success(z)
                    -> let finalResult = divide 1.0 (x + y + z)
                       finalResult
```

Although this code works as expected, programming in this style is tedious and error prone. Ideally, you could define a new function called let_with_check that did the result checking for you. This function could check the result of a call to divide and if it was Success, then the next line of code would execute; otherwise, the function would return DivByZero. The following snippet shows what this might look like:

```
let totalResistance r1 r2 r3 =
    let_with_check x = divide 1.0 r1
    let_with_check y = divide 1.0 r2
    let_with_check z = divide 1.0 r3
    return_with_check 1.0 (x + y + z)
```

However, the special function let_with_check cannot be added to the F# language because it would have to abnormally break control flow. That is, in F#, there is no way to exit a function prematurely other than throwing an exception.

If only there was a way to chop this function up into different parts, and have the let_with_check take two parameters, the first being the result of divide, and the second being a function that represents the rest of the computation to be performed. (If you recall from Chapter 7, this is known as a *continuation*.)

Example 13-3 defines a function let_with_check that does just that. It takes two parameters, the result of a division operation, and a function representing the rest of the computation. If the result returns DivByZero, then the rest of the computation is not executed.

Example 13-3. Defining let_with_check

```
let let_with_check result restOfComputation =
    match result with
    | DivByZero  -> DivByZero
    | Success(x) -> restOfComputation x

let totalResistance r1 r2 r3 =
    let_with_check
        (divide 1.0 r1)
        (fun x ->
            let_with_check
                (divide 1.0 r2)
                (fun y ->
                    let_with_check
                        (divide 1.0 r3)
                        (fun z -> divide 1.0 (x + y + z))
                )
        )
```

With the nested indentation and additional lambda expressions spanning multiple lines, it looks even worse than it did before. Let's try to rewrite our `totalResistance` function once more, but this time putting the lambdas on the same line.

If we write it the following way, the code almost looks like we originally wanted; giving the appearance that the function will abruptly stop as soon as the first `DivByZero` is encountered (at the expense of obscuring the fact, we are passing nested lambdas as parameters):

```
let totalResistance r1 r2 r3 =
    let_with_check (divide 1.0 r1) (fun x ->
    let_with_check (divide 1.0 r2) (fun y ->
    let_with_check (divide 1.0 r3) (fun z ->
    divide 1.0 (x + y + z) ) ) )
```

Computation Expression Builders

Computation expressions in a nutshell are syntactic transforms for F# code, just like `let_with_check` in the previous example. Let's look at how you can simplify your code with computation expressions.

Example 13-4 shows how to create a custom workflow. We'll go over what's going on behind the scenes in a moment. For now, just look at the implementation of the `Bind` method, the `defined { }` block, and the use of the `let!` keyword.

Example 13-4. The success/failure computation expression

```
type Result = Success of float | DivByZero

let divide x y =
    match y with
```

```
    | 0.0 -> DivByZero
    | _   -> Success(x / y)

type DefinedBuilder() =

    member this.Bind ((x : Result), (rest : float -> Result)) =
        // If the result is Success(_) then execute the
        // rest of the function. Otherwise terminate it
        // prematurely.
        match x with
        | Success(x) -> rest x
        | DivByZero  -> DivByZero

    member this.Return (x : 'a) = x

// Create an instance of our computation expression builder
let defined = DefinedBuilder()

let totalResistance r1 r2 r3 =
    defined {
        let! x = divide 1.0 r1
        let! y = divide 1.0 r2
        let! z = divide 1.0 r3
        return divide 1.0 (x + y + z)
    }
```

You can test this in FSI and verify that the computation expression version gets the same results, and in one-third the lines of code!

```
> totalResistance 0.01 0.75 0.33;;
val it : Result = Success 0.009581881533
> totalResistance 0.00 0.55 0.75;;
val it : Result = DivByZero
```

All computation expressions do is break the expression into multiple function calls to the *computation expression builder*. In the previous example, it was of type Defined Builder. To use the computation expression builder, all you need to do is put an instance of it out in front of two curly braces, { }, surrounding the code you want to execute. In the previous example, it was an instance of DefinedBuilder via value defined.

Every let! is replaced with a call to the builder's Bind method, where the evaluation of the right hand side of the equals sign is the first parameter, and the second parameter is the function representing the rest of the computation to be performed. This is how the computation stops after the first DivByZero is reached. In the computation expression builder's implementation of Bind, the rest of the computation isn't executed if the result is DivByZero. If the result is Success, then the rest of the computation is performed.

Example 13-5 shows the expansion of this in a desugared form of the defined workflow, which is strikingly similar to the code you saw in Example 13-3.

Example 13-5. Desugared form of a computation expression

```
// De-sugared form
let totalResistance r1 r2 r3 =
    defined.Bind(
        (divide 1.0 r1),
        (fun x ->
            defined.Bind(
                (divide 1.0 r2),
                (fun y ->
                    defined.Bind(
                        (divide 1.0 r3),
                        (fun z ->
                            defined.Return(
                                divide 1.0 (x + y + z)
                            )
                        )
                    )
                )
            )
        )
    )
```

Inside of a custom workflow builder, you can write normal F# code, but in addition you have access to new keywords and abilities such as let!, return, and yield. By using these new primitives in the body of the computation expression, you can extend how F# processes the code. (For example, adding custom semantics for when the yield keyword is encountered.)

By defining a Bind method, you provided a way to determine how let! was computed. Similarly, defining a Return method will enable you to determine how the return keyword works. But a workflow builder can provide more methods to determine how F# code gets executed—a full list is in Table 13-1.

 Another way to think about computation expressions is that they enable you to insert code in-between the various steps of the computation, doing any necessary background processing without requiring you to explicitly write the code.

Table 13-1. Computation expression methods

Method Signature	Description
member For: seq<'a> * ('a -> Result<unit>) -> Result<unit>	Enables execution of for loops. The parameters are the values which the loop executes on and the body of the for loop.
member Zero: unit -> Result<unit>	Enables execution of unit expressions, such as the result of an if expression without a matching else if the predicate evaluates to false.

Method Signature	Description
`member Combine: Result<unit> * Result<'a> -> Result<'a>`	Used to link together computation expression parts (e.g., two for loops in sequence).
`member While: (unit -> bool) * Result<unit> -> Result<unit>`	Enables execution of `while` loops. The parameters are the function which determines whether or not the `while` loop should continue and the body of the loop.
`member Return: 'a -> Result<'a>`	Enables execution of the `return` keyword.
`member ReturnFrom: 'a -> Result<'a>`	Enables execution of the `return!` keyword.
`member Yield: 'a -> Result<'a>`	Enables execution of the `yield` keyword.
`member YieldFrom: seq<'a> -> Result<'a>`	Enables execution of the `yield!` keyword.
`member Delay: (unit -> Result<'a>) -> Result<'a>`	This operation is typically used in conjunction with `Combine` to make sure that operations get executed in the correct order (in case they have side effects).
`member Run: Result<'a> -> Result<'a>`	If provided, the method will be called at the very start of the computation expression.
`member Using: 'a * ('a -> Result<'b>) -> Result<'b> when 'a :> System.IDisposable`	Enables execution of `use` and `use!` keywords. The implementation of `Using` is responsible for calling `IDisposable.Dispose`.
`member Bind: Result<'a> * ('a -> Result<'b>) -> Result<'b>`	Enables execution of the `let!` and `do!` keywords (`do!` is a specialized form of `let!`, when binding against `Result<unit>`).
`member TryFinally: Result<'a> * (unit -> unit) -> Result<'a>`	Enables execution of `try`/`finally` expressions. The parameters are the result of the `try` block and the function representing the `finally` block.
`member TryWith: Result<'a> * (exn -> Result<'a>) -> Result<'a>`	Enables execution of `try`/`with` expressions. The parameters are the result of the `try` block and the function representing the `with` block.

If your computation expression builder contains an implementation for the given function, then you can use the associated construct inside the computation expression. In the previous example, if you didn't include the Return method, you would get an error because you use the return keyword on the last line:

```
        return divide 1.0 (x + y + z)
--------^^^^^^^^^^^^^^^^^^^^^^^^^^^^^^^^
```

```
stdin(259,9): error FS0708:This control construct may only be used if the
    computation expression builder defines a 'Return' method.
```

The pattern of looking for a computation expression method by its name alone has a couple of interesting ramifications. First, computation expression builder methods can be added via extension methods—enabling unexpected types to be the root of the computation expressions. Second, due to method overloading, you can have multiple implementations of a computation expression method such as Bind.

Custom Computation Expression Builders

Now you have the capability to customize how various language constructs get executed by defining extra work to be carried out. But when would this be useful? It is clear that F# workflows are helpful when trying to determine the success or failure of a computation, but you might be skeptical that the same technique can make asynchronous programming easier.

Asynchronous Workflows

Think about the most tedious aspects of parallel and asynchronous programming—dealing with threads. If you want your program to have two things going on at once, you need to spawn new threads, give them appropriate work, and then marshal their results back. It is just as painful to exploit I/O-level parallelism. The .NET Framework provides asynchronous I/O operations via `FileStream.BeginRead` and `FileStream`
`.BeginWrite`. However, using these constructs requires a messy combination of `IAsyn`
`cResult` interfaces, `AsyncCallback` delegates, and a lot of tedious code.

Even if you didn't mind handling all the thread hopping and the managing of incomplete tasks yourself, it is still a pain to deal with exceptions. To make matters worse, there is no good way to cancel the operation once it starts.

If only there were a way to abstract the code and wire in the thread hopping... Fortunately, this library does exist and it is built into F#. *F# asynchronous workflows* is a type of computation expression builder specifically designed for asynchronous tasks.

Example 13-6 shows how to use an asynchronous workflow for reading and writing file data asynchronously. Note the use of `let!` to perform asynchronous operations; all the thread hopping will be performed in the implementation of the `async` builder's `Bind` method. (You may recall the details for how the `async` computation expression builder and how `Async.Start` work are covered in Chapter 9.)

Example 13-6. F# asynchronous workflows

```
open System.IO

let asyncProcessFile (filePath : string) (processBytes : byte[] -> byte[]) =
    async {
```

```
    printfn "Processing file [%s]" (Path.GetFileName(filePath))

    let fileStream = new FileStream(filePath, FileMode.Open)
    let bytesToRead = int fileStream.Length

    let! data = fileStream.AsyncRead(bytesToRead)

    printfn
        "Opened [%s], read [%d] bytes"
        (Path.GetFileName(filePath))
        data.Length

    let data' = processBytes data

    let resultFile = new FileStream(filePath + ".results", FileMode.Create)
    do! resultFile.AsyncWrite(data', 0, data'.Length)

    printfn "Finished processing file [%s]" <| Path.GetFileName(filePath)
} |> Async.Start
```

Computation expressions weren't added to the F# language with ultra-useful asynchronous workflows in mind; rather, they just enable certain patterns of code that have the potential to be quite useful.

 If you want to get fancy, you could call computation expressions "monads" or *monoids in the category of endo-functors.*

The Rounding Workflow

When doing some types of mathematical calculation, it can be desirable to enforce a specific degree of precision—for example, to make sure calculations to compute real-world lengths are feasible (unless, of course, they start selling rulers that go down to the picometer).

Example 13-7 defines the RoundingWorkflow. Notice that the Bind method changes the value of what is passed to it. In addition, because Bind constraints its input to type float, you will get a compiler error if you use let! with any other type.

Example 13-7. Implementation of a rounding workflow

```
open System

// Computation expression builder which rounds bound computations
// to a fixed number of significant digits.
type RoundingWorkflow(sigDigs : int) =

    let round (x : float) = Math.Round(float x, sigDigs)
```

```
// Due to result being constrained to type float, you can only use
// let! against float values. (Otherwise will get a compiler error.)
member this.Bind(result : float, rest : float -> float) =
    let result' = round result
    rest result'

member this.Return (x : float) = round x
```

```
let withPrecision sigDigs = new RoundingWorkflow(sigDigs)
```

The following shows the rounding workflow in action:

```
> // Test the rounding workflow
let test =
    withPrecision 3 {
        let! x = 2.0 / 12.0
        let! y = 3.5
        return x / y
    };;

val test : float = 0.048
```

The State Workflow

To see a more real-world example of a useful computation expression, consider a work-flow to keep track of state. Imagine creating a library for web scripting. Each action such as clicking a link or button, changes the current state—current URL, HTML, session cookies, etc.—before passing it on to the next step of the computation.

Example 13-8 shows some hypothetical code to script a web session, which quickly becomes tedious, as the state information needs to be piped through to every single stage of the computation. (It may seem tempting to simply use the pipe forward operator, |>. The problem with using the pipe-forward operator in a situation like this is that it would require that every method in the sequence return the same state object, which wouldn't make sense for some functions.)

Example 13-8. Code passing around a state object

```
let reviewBook() =
    let state1 = openPage "www.fsharp.net"
    let state2 = clickLink "F# Books" state1
    let (table, state3) = getHtmlTableFromHeader "Programming F#" (state2)
    let state4 = clickButton table "Five Star Rating" state3
    ...
```

By using a computation expression, you can eliminate the need for passing a state object throughout the computation. The intuition here is that computation expressions are used to do "extra work" behind the scenes of normal F# code. So perhaps we can have that extra work persist state information:

```
let reviewBook() =
    state {
        do! OpenPage "www.fsharp.net"
        do! ClickLink "F# Books"
        let! table = GetHtmlTableWithHeader "Programming F#"
        do! ClickButton table "Five Star Rating"
    }
```

Building up the computation

We can achieve this illusion of persisting state information by using a single-case discriminated union type called StatefulFunc, which represents a function that takes an initial state and returns a tuple of the result and the updated state:

```
type StatefulFunc<'state, 'result> = StatefulFunc of ('state -> 'result * 'state)
```

Each call to Bind will take an existing StatefulFunc object and produce a new, larger StatefulFunc object by executing the function attached to the existing StatefulFunc object and then executing the rest of the computation (the continuation that is passed to Bind).

So, for example, we want to write a workflow to power the following code:

```
state {
    do! OpenWebpage "www.google.com"     // Sets the state
    do! EnterText "Funny Cat Pictures"   // Uses the state
    do! ClickButton "Search"             // Uses and Sets the state
}
```

When encoded into the StatefulFunc type, the steps would look something like the following:

```
// do! OpenWebpage "www.google.com"
let step1 =
    StatefulFunc(fun initialState ->
        let result, updatedState = OpenWebpage "www.google.com" initialState
        result, updatedState)

// do! EnterText
let step2 =
    StatefulFunc(fun initialState ->
        let result, updatedState = EnterText "Funny Cat Pictures" initialState
        result, updatedState)

// do! ClickButton "Search"
let step3 =
    StatefulFunc(fun initialState ->
        let result, updatedState = ClickButton "Search" initialState
        result, updatedState)
```

The result of a state workflow is a single StatefulFunc object that has a function that will perform the full computation associated with it. It will pass along a state object as well, built out of the calls to Bind within the workflow.

Once the StatefulFunc has been built up, the full computation would end up looking similar to the following:

```
StatefulFunc(fun initialState ->

    let result1, updatedState1 = OpenWebPage "www.google.com" initialState

    updatedState1 |> (fun initialState ->
        let result2, updatedState2 = EnterText "Funny Cat Pictures" initialState

        updatedState2 |> (fun initialState ->
            let result3, updatedState3 = ClickButton "Search" initialState

        result3, updatedState3
        )
    )
)
```

Implementation

Example 13-9 shows the implementation of the full state workflow. With additional methods like Combine and TryFinally, the full range of possible F# code is available within the workflow.

 Explicit type annotations have been provided to each method signature to make it clear what the signatures are, but in practice they can usually be omitted.

Example 13-9. Implementation of a state workflow in F#

```
open System

// Type to represent a stateful function. A function which takes an input state and
// returns a result combined with an updated state.
type StatefulFunc<'state, 'result> = StatefulFunc of ('state -> 'result * 'state)

// Run our stateful function
let Run (StatefulFunc f) initialState = f initialState

type StateBuilder() =

    member this.Bind(
                    result : StatefulFunc<'state, 'a>,
                    restOfComputation : 'a -> StatefulFunc<'state, 'b>
                ) =

        StatefulFunc(fun initialState ->
            let result, updatedState = Run result initialState
            Run (restOfComputation result) updatedState
        )
```

```
member this.Combine(
                partOne : StatefulFunc<'state, unit>,
                partTwo : StatefulFunc<'state, 'a>
              ) =

    StatefulFunc(fun initialState ->
        let (), updatedState = Run partOne initialState
        Run partTwo updatedState
    )

member this.Delay(
                restOfComputation : unit -> StatefulFunc<'state, 'a>
              ) =

    StatefulFunc (fun initialState ->
        Run ( restOfComputation() ) initialState
    )

member this.For(
            elements : seq<'a>,
            forBody : ('a -> StatefulFunc<'state, unit>)
            ) =

    StatefulFunc(fun initialState ->
        let state = ref initialState

        for e in elements do
            let (), updatedState = Run (forBody e) (!state)
            state := updatedState

        // Return unit * finalState
        (), !state
    )

member this.Return(x : 'a) =
    StatefulFunc(fun initialState -> x, initialState)

member this.Using<'a, 'state,
                'b when 'a :> IDisposable>
                (
                  x : 'a,
                  restOfComputation : 'a -> StatefulFunc<'state, 'b>
                ) =

    StatefulFunc(fun initialState ->
        try
            Run (restOfComputation x) initialState
        finally
            x.Dispose()
    )
```

```
    member this.TryFinally(
                        tryBlock : StatefulFunc<'state, 'a>,
                        finallyBlock : unit -> unit
                    ) =

    StatefulFunc(fun initialState ->
        try
            Run tryBlock initialState
        finally
            finallyBlock()
    )


    member this.TryWith(
                        tryBlock : StatefulFunc<'state, 'a>,
                        exnHandler : exn -> StatefulFunc<'state, 'a>
                    ) =

    StatefulFunc(fun initialState ->
        try
            Run tryBlock initialState
        with
        | e ->
            Run (exnHandler e) initialState
    )

    member this.While(
                        predicate : unit -> bool,
                        body : StatefulFunc<'state, unit>
                    ) =

    StatefulFunc(fun initialState ->

        let state = ref initialState
        while predicate() = true do
            let (), updatedState = Run body (!state)
            state := updatedState

        // Return unit * finalState
        (), !state
    )

    member this.Zero() =
        StatefulFunc(fun initialState -> (), initialState)

// Declare the state workflow builder
let state = StateBuilder()

// Primitive functions for getting and setting state
let GetState          = StatefulFunc (fun state -> state, state)
let SetState newState = StatefulFunc (fun prevState -> (), newState)
```

With the full workflow defined, Example 13-10 uses the `state` workflow to script a four-function calculator. (You can use the same `state` workflow for creating a web crawler, but the code to do that properly would easily dwarf the text in this chapter.)

The state is represented by the current total and the calculator's operational history. The functions Add, Subtract, Multiply, and Divide will take an input state, modify it, and return a new StatefulFunc object.

Example 13-10. Using the state workflow to create a calculator

```
let Add x =
    state {
        let! currentTotal, history = GetState
        do! SetState (currentTotal + x, (sprintf "Added %d" x) :: history)
    }

let Subtract x =
    state {
        let! currentTotal, history = GetState
        do! SetState (currentTotal - x, (sprintf "Subtracted %d" x) :: history)
    }

let Multiply x =
    state {
        let! currentTotal, history = GetState
        do! SetState (currentTotal * x, (sprintf "Multiplied by %d" x) :: history)
    }

let Divide x =
    state {
        let! currentTotal, history = GetState
        do! SetState (currentTotal / x, (sprintf "Divided by %d" x) :: history)
    }
```

Using functions like Add and Subtract within the state workflow will give the illusion that you are not passing the state around while in actuality a large StatefulFunc object is built up, which can be executed by passing it to the Run function:

```
> // Define the StatefulFunc we will use, no need to thread
// the state parameter through each function.
let calculatorActions =
    state {
        do! Add 2
        do! Multiply 10
        do! Divide 5
        do! Subtract 8

        return "Finished"
    }

// Now run our StatefulFunc passing in an intial state
let sfResult, finalState = Run calculatorActions (0, []);;
```

```
val calculatorActions : StatefulFunc<(int * string list),string> =
  StatefulFunc <fun:Delay@324>
val sfResult : string = "Finished"
val finalState : int * string list =
  (-4, ["Subtracted 8"; "Divided by 5"; "Multiplied by 10"; "Added 2"])
```

The creation of custom computation expressions is a rather advanced concept that can be difficult to grasp even by expert developers. But they can be used to simplify code by giving you the ability to execute code in-between computation steps. If you find yourself writing a lot of redundant, boilerplate code, consider looking into whether or not you can wrap that functionality inside of a computation expression.

Quotations

Earlier, we looked at .NET reflection as a way to do metaprogramming, analyzing static type information to reason about program code. Although metaprogramming using reflection can do things like load program plug-ins, if you want to reason about how that code *operates*, you are out of luck. The .NET reflection APIs allow you to get at the raw MSIL op codes, but you have to reverse engineer what that code does—a daunting task at best.

However, there are many applications where knowing not only the structure of program code but also how it operates can be beneficial. For example, taking a function written in F# and converting it into a form that can execute on a graphics card's GPU (presumably to be executed much, much faster).

F# provides a mechanism called *quotation expressions* by which you can access not only the static type information for a block of code, but also see the F# compiler's internal representation of the code (sometimes referred to as an *abstract syntax tree*, or *AST*).

Using F# quotations you can:

- Perform code analysis and inspection
- Defer computation to other platforms (SQL, GPU, etc.)
- Generate new code

We look at these capabilities shortly, but first let's look at how we can get started with this language feature. Be warned though, quotations are deep wizardry, and not for the faint of heart. This chapter only provides a crash course on the subject. To truly master quotations, refer to online resources at the F# developer center at *http://fsharp.net*.

Quotation Basics

Simply put, a *quotation* is an object representing the structure of some F# code. You can get a hold of a quotation by placing quotation markers, `<@ @>` or `<@@ @@>`, around an expression:

```
> // Simple addition
<@ 1 + 1 @>;;

val it : Quotations.FSharpExpr<int> =
  Call (None, op_Addition, [Value (1), Value (1)])
    {CustomAttributes = [NewTuple (Value ("DebugRange"),
          NewTuple (Value ("stdin"), Value (7), Value (3), Value (7), ...))];
     Raw = ...;
     Type = System.Int32;}

> // Lambda expression
<@@ fun x -> "Hello, " + x @@>;;

val it : Quotations.FSharpExpr =
  Lambda (x,
        Call (None, op_Addition,  [Value ("Hello, "), x]))
      {CustomAttributes = [NewTuple (Value ("DebugRange"),
            NewTuple (Value ("stdin"), Value (10), Value (4), Value (10),
                        Value (26)))];
       Type = Microsoft.FSharp.Core.FSharpFunc`2[System.String,System.String];}
```

F# exposes quotations using the `Expr<_>` type defined in the `Microsoft.FSharp.Quotations` namespace. The generic type parameter of `Expr<_>` is the result of the expression; for example, `<@ 1 + 1 @>` evaluates to `Expr<int>` because the expression `1 + 1` evaluates to an integer.

Using `<@@ @@>` will produce an untyped quotation, of type `Expr`, which doesn't contain the expression's return type. In most situations, it won't matter which way you quote code. Note that an `Expr<_>` can always be converted into an `Expr` by accessing its `Raw` property.

You can quote any arbitrary F# expression with the only restriction being that you cannot quote the use of an object expression (which if you recall is how F# introduces anonymous classes).

Decomposing Quotations

Once you have a quotation, deconstructing the AST is done using active patterns defined in the F# library. So although an `Expr<_>` represents a complicated tree-like data structure, you can use pattern matching to match against what the code represents with the additional benefit of being able to bind new values from the results of the pattern match.

Example 14-1 defines a function `describeCode`, which takes a quotation expression and prints a description of the code to the console. Notice that the pattern match does not use a dynamic type test to get the type of the expression, but rather is matching against what the computation represents. So you can not only check if the quoted code is a function call, but even bind that call's parameters.

Example 14-1. Basic quotations

```
open Microsoft.FSharp.Quotations
open Microsoft.FSharp.Quotations.Patterns
open Microsoft.FSharp.Quotations.DerivedPatterns

let rec describeCode (expr : Expr) =
    match expr with

    // Literal value
    | Int32(i)  -> printfn "Integer with value %d" i
    | Double(f) -> printfn "Floating-point with value %f" f
    | String(s) -> printfn "String with value %s" s

    // Calling a method
    | Call(calledOnObject, methInfo, args)
        ->  let calledOn = match calledOnObject with
                           | Some(x) -> sprintf "%A" x
                           | None    -> "(Called a static method)"

            printfn "Calling method '%s': \n\
                     On value:  %s \n\
                     With args: %A" methInfo.Name calledOn args

    // Lambda expressions
    | Lambda(var, lambdaBody) ->
        printfn
            "Lambda Expression - Introduced value %s with type %s"
            var.Name var.Type.Name
        printfn "Processing body of Lambda Expression..."
        describeCode lambdaBody

    | _ -> printfn "Unknown expression form:\n%A" expr
```

Using this, we can call our `describeCode` method in an FSI session, which will produce the following output:

```
> describeCode <@ 27 @>;;
Integer literal with value 27
val it : unit = ()

> describeCode <@ 1.0 + 2.0 @>;;
Calling method 'op_Addition':
On value:  (Called a static method)
With args : [Value (1.0); Value (2.0)]
val it : unit = ()
```

```
> let localVal = "a string";;

val localVal : string = "a string"

> describeCode <@ localVal.ToUpper() @>;;
Calling method 'ToUpper':
On value:  PropertyGet (None, System.String localVal, [])
With args : []
val it : unit = ()

> describeCode <@ fun x y -> (x, y) @>;;
Lambda Expression - Introduced value x with type Object
Processing body of Lambda Expression...
Lambda Expression - Introduced value y with type Object
Processing body of Lambda Expression...
Unknown expression form:
NewTuple (x, y)
val it : unit = ()
```

The F# library provides a full range of active patterns for discerning any form of quotation expression. All available active patterns can be found in the `Micro soft.FSharp.Quotations.Patterns` namespace.

Before continuing, let's take a closer look at the active patterns used in Example 14-1.

Literal values

There are active patterns available for every type of primitive value type in F#, from `int` to `float` to `string` and so on. Matching against these constant literals gives you an opportunity to bind their value:

```
// Literal value
| Int32(i)  -> printfn "Integer with value %d" i
| Double(f) -> printfn "Floating-point with value %f" f
| String(s) -> printfn "String with value %s" s
```

Function calls

Function calls can be matched against the `Call` active pattern. If it matches, the pattern introduces three values: the instance of the object on which the method is called (or `None` if the method is static), the `MethodInfo` containing reflection information for the method, and the list of arguments passed to the method:

```
// Calling a method
| Call(calledOnObject, methInfo, args)
    -> let calledOn = match calledOnObject with
                      | Some(x) -> sprintf "%A" x
                      | None    -> "(Called a static method)"

       printfn "Calling method '%s': \n\
                On value:  %s \n\
                With args: %A" methInfo.Name calledOn args
```

The **Call** active pattern can be cumbersome to use if you are looking for a specific function call. For this reason, the SpecificCall active pattern was created. Using it within a pattern match makes it possible for you to identify when a certain function is used and allows you to bind the function call's parameters. (It also binds the types of any generic function parameters required, although these can usually be safely ignored.) So rather than matching any function call, SpecificCall only matches the function you want.

Example 14-2 shows using the SpecificCall active pattern for describing an arithmetic operation. In the example, only the function's parameters are bound and the generic types instantiated are ignored.

Example 14-2. The SpecificCall active pattern

```
let describeArithmatic operation =
    match operation with
    | SpecificCall <@ (+) @> (_, _, [lhs; rhs]) ->
        printfn "Addition."

    | SpecificCall <@ (-) @> (_, _, [lhs; rhs]) ->
        printfn "Subtraction."

    | SpecificCall <@ (*) @> (_, _, [Int32(0); _])
    | SpecificCall <@ (*) @> (_, _, [_; Int32(0)]) ->
        printfn "Multiplication by zero."

    | SpecificCall <@ (*) @> (_, _, [lhs; rhs]) ->
        printfn "Multiplcation."

    | SpecificCall <@ (/) @> (_, _, [lhs; Int32(0)]) ->
        printfn "Division by zero."

    | SpecificCall <@ (/) @> (_, _, [lhs; rhs]) ->
        printfn "Division."

    | _ -> failwith "Unknown quotation form."
```

Function values

Function values are matched using the Lambda active pattern. The two values bound in the active pattern are of type Var and Expr:

```
    // Lambda expressions
    | Lambda(var, lambdaBody) ->
        printfn
            "Lambda Expression - Introduced value %s with type %s"
            var.Name var.Type.Name
        printfn "Processing body of Lambda Expression..."
        describeCode lambdaBody
```

The Expr is simply the body of the lambda expression. The Var represents the new value introduced by the lambda expression (its parameter).

When quoting code, any time you decompose an expression that introduces a new value, such as a let binding, the newly introduced value is represented as a Var.

Quoting Method Bodies

Although enclosing an expression in <@ @> marks returns the F# compiler's representation of that code, it is usually insufficient. This is because that code calls into functions, which then call into other functions and so on. To get the full abstract syntax tree of the expression, you need to drill into method bodies as well. By default, the F# compiler cannot return the quoted form of functions and class member bodies in a quotation.

To allow function bodies to be included inside of a quotation, you can provide the [<ReflectedDefinition>] attribute. Methods marked with this attribute can be further expanded upon by using the (|MethodWithReflectedDefinition|_|) active pattern.

Example 14-3 is the same describeCode function with a slight modification to add support for processing methods annotated with the [<ReflectedDefinition>] attribute. The function determines the MethodInfo object returned by the (|Call|_|) active pattern and checks if the body of the method is known. If so, then the body of the method being called is processed as well.

Example 14-3. Using the ReflectedDefinition attribute

```
open Microsoft.FSharp.Quotations
open Microsoft.FSharp.Quotations.Patterns
open Microsoft.FSharp.Quotations.DerivedPatterns

let rec describeCode2 (expr : Expr) =
    match expr with

    // Literal value
    | Int32(i)  -> printfn "Integer literal with value %d" i
    | Double(f) -> printfn "Floating point literal with value %f" f
    | String(s) -> printfn "String literal with value %s" s

    // Calling a method
    | Call(calledOnObject, methInfo, args)
        -> let calledOn = match calledOnObject with
                          | Some(x) -> sprintf "%A" x
                          | None    -> "(static method)"

           printfn "Calling method '%s': \n\
                    On intance: %s \n\
                    With args : %A" methInfo.Name calledOn args

           match methInfo with
           | MethodWithReflectedDefinition(methBody) ->
```

```
                printfn
                    "Expanding method body of '%s'..." methInfo.Name
                describeCode2 methBody
        | _ ->
                printfn
                    "Unable to expand body of '%s'. Quotation stops here."
                    methInfo.Name

    // Lambda expressions
    | Lambda(var, lambdaBody) ->
        printfn
            "Lambda Expression on value '%s' with type '%s'"
            var.Name var.Type.Name

        printfn "Processing body of Lambda Expression..."
        describeCode2 lambdaBody

    | _ -> printfn "Unknown expression form:\n%A" expr
```

The following FSI session shows the processing of two quotation expressions. de
scribeCode2 can process the body of the invertNumberReflected function because it
has been decorated with the [<ReflectedDefinition>] attribute:

```
> // Define functions with and without ReflectedDefinition
let invertNumber x = -x

[<ReflectedDefinition>]
let invertNumberReflected x = -1 * x;;

val invertNumber : int -> int
val invertNumberReflected : int -> int

> // Describe code without ReflectedDefinition
describeCode2 <@ invertNumber 10 @>;;

Calling method 'invertNumber':
On intance:  (static method)
With args : [Value (10)]
Unable to expand body of 'invertNumber'. Quotation stops here.
val it : unit = ()

> // Describe code with ReflectedDefinition
describeCode2 <@ invertNumberReflected 10 @>;;
Calling method 'invertNumberReflected':
On intance:  (static method)
With args : [Value (10)]
Expanding method body of 'invertNumberReflected'...
Lambda Expression on value 'x' with type 'Int32'
Processing body of Lambda Expression...
Calling method 'op_Multiply':
```

```
On intance:  (static method)
With args : [Value (-1); x]
Unable to expand body of 'op_Multiply'. Quotation stops here.
val it : unit = ()
```

Decomposing Arbitrary Code

Armed with just a few active patterns, we were able to decompose many code types in the describeCode method. However, whenever code wasn't matched, it fell through the pattern match and hit the generic wildcard case.

Most applications of active patterns decompose an arbitrary AST, intercepting only the nodes that the code cares about and ignoring the rest. However, it is important to traverse the entire AST. Abruptly stopping the traversal at a given node isn't a valid option, because it ignores a large amount of the tree and potentially some code constructs you cared about.

However, it also doesn't make sense to match against every possible active pattern available, from ForIntegerRangeLoop (for loops) to IfThenElse (if expressions) to LetRecursive (recursive let bindings) and so on.

Fortunately, there is a "catchall" active pattern that matches the most general forms of F# expressions. The catchall active pattern is in the ExprShape module and converts any F# quotation expression into a ShapeVar, ShapeLambda, or ShapeCombination. Example 14-4 introduces a new function, generalizedDescribeCode, for decomposing any quotation. The quotation matches against a ShapeVar if the expression is looking up a value and ShapeLambda is matched whenever a new function value is introduced. The majority of F# quotations fall into the third active pattern case, ShapeCombination. ShapeCombination is intentionally nondescript, only giving you an opaque handle to what was used to generate it and the subexpressions from the code construct (meaning that you cannot determine what the code represents—you are just given a list of its subexpressions).

Example 14-4. Generalized quotation traversal

```
open Microsoft.FSharp.Quotations
open Microsoft.FSharp.Quotations.ExprShape

let rec generalizedDescribeCode indentation expr =

    let indentedMore = indentation + "    "

    match expr with
    // A variable being used
    | ShapeVar(var) ->
        printfn "%s Looking up value '%s'" indentation var.Name

    // A new lambda expression
    | ShapeLambda(var, lambdaBody) ->
```

```
        printfn
            "%s Lambda expression, introducing var '%s'"
            indentation var.Name
        generalizedDecribeCode indentedMore lambdaBody

    // Other
    | ShapeCombination(_, exprs) ->
        printfn "%s ShapeCombination:" indentation
        exprs |> List.iter (generalizedDecribeCode indentedMore)
```

The following FSI session shows the `generalizedDescribeCode` method in action:

```
> generalizedDescribeCode "" <@ (fun x y z -> x + y + z) @>;;
  Lambda expression, introducing var 'x'
      Lambda expression, introducing var 'y'
          Lambda expression, introducing var 'z'
              ShapeCombination:
                  ShapeCombination:
                      Looking up value 'x'
                      Looking up value 'y'
                  Looking up value 'z'
val it : unit = () >
```

You are then free to add new pattern-match rules earlier in the match expression to "intercept" the things you care about, like in earlier versions of the `describeCode` method.

Application: Deferring Computation to Other Platforms

You have seen ways to decompose F# quotation expressions to analyze the compiler-generated form of the code, but what do you *do* with it? Perhaps the best usage of F# quotations is deferring computation to other platforms. By processing the F# quotation expressions, you can take F# code and transport it to another platform, such as a GPU or on an SQL database. By walking the AST, you can transform the F# code into a format that is amenable to another computing environment. This technique allows you to avoid the use of a second language, and use the existing F# toolset (IntelliSense, type checking, and so on).

For example, rather than writing assembly code for your graphics card encoded as a `string`, you can write F# code, and then convert that quotation of that code to the appropriate assembly language.

To provide a simple example of this, let's use quotations to convert F# mathematical expressions into *reverse polish notation*, or RPN.

RPN is a form of expressing mathematical equations without the need for parentheses. It works by using a hypothetical stack of numbers, where algebraic functions such as addition pop the top two items from the stack and push the result back on.

For example, the expression 2 * 3 + 4 would be represented by the operations listed in Table 14-1.

Table 14-1. Evaluation of 2*3 + 4 in RPN

Operation	Stack
Push 2	2
Push 3	3, 2
Call (*)	6
Push 4	4, 6
Call (+)	10

Encoding functions in RPN can be difficult and error-prone. Instead, you can use quotations to write F# code—letting the compiler build up the expression tree preserving the order of operations—and then transform the quotation of that code into RPN.

Example 14-5 defines a function called `fsharpToRpn`, which takes a quotation expression and decomposes the expression building up a list of operations to express the equation in RPN.

The example works by intercepting arithmetic operations and recursively generating the list of RPN operations to compute the left and right hand sides of the operator. Then, it simply adds those operators to the list of RPN operations in the correct order.

Example 14-5. Converting F# code to RPN

```
open Microsoft.FSharp.Quotations
open Microsoft.FSharp.Quotations.Patterns
open Microsoft.FSharp.Quotations.DerivedPatterns

let rec fsharpToRpn code stackOperations =
    match code with

    | Int32(n)  -> (sprintf "Push %d" n) :: stackOperations
    | Double(f) -> (sprintf "Push %f" f) :: stackOperations

    | SpecificCall <@ (+) @> (_, _, [lhs; rhs]) ->
        let lhs = fsharpToRpn lhs stackOperations
        let rhs = fsharpToRpn rhs stackOperations
        lhs @ rhs @ ["Call (+)"]

    | SpecificCall <@ (-) @> (_, _, [lhs; rhs]) ->
        let lhs = fsharpToRpn lhs stackOperations
        let rhs = fsharpToRpn rhs stackOperations
        lhs @ rhs @ ["Call (-)"]

    | SpecificCall <@ (*) @> (_, _, [lhs; rhs]) ->
        let lhs = fsharpToRpn lhs stackOperations
        let rhs = fsharpToRpn rhs stackOperations
```

```
        lhs @ rhs @ ["Call (*)"]

    | SpecificCall <@ (/) @> (_, _, [lhs; rhs]) ->
        let lhs = fsharpToRpn lhs stackOperations
        let rhs = fsharpToRpn rhs stackOperations
        lhs @ rhs @ ["Call (/)"]

    | expr -> failwithf "Unknown Expr:\n%A" expr
```

The following snippet shows the fsharpToRpn function in action:

```
> fsharpToRpn <@ 1 + 2 @> [];;
val it : string list = ["Push 1"; "Push 2"; "Call (+)"]
> fsharpToRpn <@ 2 * 3 + 4 @> [];;
val it : string list = ["Push 2"; "Push 3"; "Call (*)"; "Push 4"; "Call (+)"]
> // A little more complex
fsharpToRpn <@ (2 + 10) / (3 * (2 - 6 / 7 - 2)) @> []
|> List.iter (printfn "%s");;
Push 2
Push 10
Call (+)
Push 3
Push 2
Push 6
Push 7
Call (/)
Call (-)
Push 2
Call (-)
Call (*)
Call (/)
```

Generating Quotation Expressions

Decomposing quotation expressions gives you a way to inspect and transform ASTs, but you can build up quotation expressions dynamically at runtime as well.

Generating quotation expressions is especially useful when creating mini programming languages. Rather than writing F# code and processing the AST, you can parse another, perhaps simpler, language to generate the expression tree and then process that.

Any active pattern you see for decomposing quotation expressions has a complementary static method on the Expr class for producing an equivalent Expr<_> value.

The following snippet shows taking the quotation of a simple expression and the equivalent way to build up that same expression value:

```
let organicQuotation =
    <@
        let x = (1, 2, 3)
        (x, x)
    @>
```

```
let syntheticQuotation =
    Expr.Let(
        new Var("x", typeof<int * int * int>),
        Expr.NewTuple( [ Expr.Value(1); Expr.Value(2); Expr.Value(3) ] ),
        Expr.NewTuple( [ Expr.GlobalVar("x").Raw; Expr.GlobalVar("x").Raw ] )
    )
```

Expression Holes

Using methods on the `Expr` type isn't the only way to generate quotation expressions. Quotations may contain *expression holes*, which are locations for new instances of `Expr<_>` to be placed, allowing you to build up expression trees by simply patching holes in an existing expression.

To declare an expression hole, simply use a percent sign, `%`, in front of any expression within the quotation, and the result of that expression will be bound to the generated quotation expression tree. (Similar to `<@@ @@>`, using `%%` will leave a hole for an `Expr` type instead of `Expr<_>`.)

Example 14-6 defines a function called `addTwoQuotations` that takes two quoted values and builds a new expression, adding the two `Expr<_>`s together. So calling `addTwoQuotations` with the quoted form of two integer literals `<@ 1 @>` and `<@ 2 @>` is the same as quoting `<@ 1 + 2 @>`. Moreover, the generated quotation is identical to the static version of the quotation.

Example 14-6. Quotation holes

```
> let addTwoQuotations x y = <@ %x + %y @>;;

val addTwoQuotations : Expr<int> -> Expr<int> -> Expr<int>

> // Generate the quotation and describe it
addTwoQuotations <@ 1 @> <@ 2 @>
|> describeCode;;
Calling method 'op_Addition':
On value:  (Called a static method)
With args: [Value (1); Value (2)]
val it : unit = ()

> // Generate and describe a more complex quotation
addTwoQuotations <@ "a string".Length @> <@ (2 * 2) @>
|> describeCode;;
Calling method 'op_Addition':
On value:  (Called a static method)
With args: [PropGet (Some (Value ("a string")), Int32 Length, []);
 Call (None, op_Multiply, [Value (2), Value (2)])]
val it : unit = ()
```

Evaluating Quotations

You can not only analyze quotations—but *execute* them too. The F# PowerPack contains an experimental library for converting F# quotation expressions to LINQ expression trees. LINQ expression trees are a very similar feature to F# quotation expressions, both are ways to represent compiler ASTs. Although F# quotation expressions can express more forms of code than expression trees alone, the main advantage is that expression trees can be compiled and executed.

 The F# PowerPack does not come with Visual Studio 11 and is a separate download from the F# PowerPack's homepage on CodePlex, *http:// fsharppowerpack.codeplex.com/*.

To evaluate or compile F# quotations you will need to download and add a reference to `FSharp.PowerPack.dll` and `FSharp.PowerPack.Linq.dll` and open up the `Micro soft.FSharp.Linq.QuoationEvaluation` namespace. That will add extension methods to `Expr` and `Expr<_>` allowing you to evaluate and compile quotations via the `Eval` and `Compile` methods.

The following example shows simple evaluation and compilation of F# quotation expressions:

```
> // Reference required libraries
#r "System.Core.dll"
#r "FSharp.PowerPack.dll"
#r "FSharp.PowerPack.Linq.dll"

// Adds extension methods to Expr<_>
open Microsoft.FSharp.Linq.QuotationEvaluation;;

--> Referenced
    'C:\Windows\Microsoft.NET\Framework\v4.0.30319\System.Core.dll'


--> Referenced
    'C:\Program Files (x86)\FSharpPowerPack-2.0.0.0\bin\FSharp.PowerPack.dll'


--> Referenced
    'C:\Program Files (x86)\FSharpPowerPack-2.0.0.0\bin\FSharp.PowerPack.Linq.dll'

> // Evaluate a simple expression
let x = <@ 1 + 2 * 3 @>;;

val x : Quotations.Expr<int> =
  Call (None, op_Addition,
     [Value (1), Call (None, op_Multiply, [Value (2), Value (3)])])

> // Evaluate it. (Use PowerPack magic.)
```

```
x.Eval();;
val it : int = 7
> // Compile a function value expression
let toUpperQuotation = <@ (fun (x : string) -> x.ToUpper()) @>
let toUpperFunc = toUpperQuotation.Compile() ();;

val toUpperQuotation : Quotations.Expr<(string -> string)> =
  Lambda (x, Call (Some (x), ToUpper, []))
val toUpperFunc : (string -> string)

> toUpperFunc "don't panic";;
val it : string = "DON'T PANIC"
```

Application: Generating Derivatives

The ability to evaluate or compile F# quotation expressions adds a bold new capability to your F# applications—namely, the ability to generate new code. Example 13-7 analyzes the raw quotation and then generates a new Expr<_> representing the function's derivative.

The derivative of a function f(x) is the rate at which function f changes at point x. If f is increasing in value from f(x) to f(x+0.0001), then the derivative will be positive. Likewise, if f(x) is decreasing at point x, the derivative will be negative. Derivatives may seem like complicated business, but computing them is simple with a few easy rules.

Example 14-7 defines a function generateDerivative, which just like previous examples, matches basic arithmetic functions. When each arithmetic operation is encountered, the corresponding derivative rule is applied so that the resulting Expr represents the derivative of the operation. From there, you can use the F# PowerPack to compile and execute the generated function.

Example 14-7. Using quotations to create a derivative

```
#r "FSharp.PowerPack.dll"
#r "FSharp.PowerPack.Linq.dll"

// Adds extension methods to Expr<_>
open Microsoft.FSharp.Linq.QuotationEvaluation

open Microsoft.FSharp.Quotations
open Microsoft.FSharp.Quotations.Patterns
open Microsoft.FSharp.Quotations.DerivedPatterns

// Get the 'MethodInfo' object corresponding to basic arithmetic functions.
// These will be used to generate new Expr<_>.
type Operations =
    static member Add (x, y) : float = x + y
    static member Sub (x, y) : float = x - y
    static member Mul (x, y) : float = x * y
    static member Div (x, y) : float = x / y
```

```
let addMi = (typeof<Operations>).GetMethod("Add")
let subMi = (typeof<Operations>).GetMethod("Sub")
let mulMi = (typeof<Operations>).GetMethod("Mul")
let divMi = (typeof<Operations>).GetMethod("Div")

let rec generateDerivative (equation : Expr) =

    match equation with

    // Lamda - Begining of a function
    | Lambda(arg, body) ->
        Expr.Lambda(arg, generateDerivative body)

    // Method Call - Begining of a function
    | Call(None, MethodWithReflectedDefinition(methBody), [ arg ]) ->
        generateDerivative methBody

    // Property Getter - For module-bound properties
    | PropertyGet(None, PropertyGetterWithReflectedDefinition(body), []) ->
        generateDerivative body

    // Addition
    // [d/dx] f(x) + g(x) = f'(x) + g'(x)
    | SpecificCall <@ (+) @> (_, _, [f; g]) ->
        let f' = generateDerivative f
        let g' = generateDerivative g
        Expr.Call(addMi, [f'; g'])

    // Subtraction
    // [d/dx] f(x) - g(x) = f'(x) - g'(x)
    | SpecificCall <@ (-) @> (_, _, [f; g]) ->
        let f' = generateDerivative f
        let g' = generateDerivative g
        Expr.Call(subMi, [f'; g'])

    // Product Rule
    // [d/dx] f(x) * g(x) = (f'(x) * g(x)) + (f(x) * g'(x))
    | SpecificCall <@ ( * ) @> (_, _, [f; g]) ->
        let f' = generateDerivative f
        let g' = generateDerivative g
        Expr.Call(addMi,
            [ Expr.Call(mulMi, [f'; g]);
              Expr.Call(mulMi, [f; g']) ]
        )

    // Quotient Rule
    // [d/dx] f(x) / g(x) = ((f '(x) * g(x)) - (f(x) * g'(x))) / (g^2(x))
    | SpecificCall <@ ( / ) @> (_, _, [f; g]) ->
        let f' = generateDerivative f
        let g' = generateDerivative g
```

```
        let numerator =
            Expr.Call(subMi,
                [ Expr.Call(mulMi, [f'; g])
                    Expr.Call(mulMi, [f; g'])]
            )
        let denominator = Expr.Call(mulMi, [g; g])

        Expr.Call(divMi, [numerator; denominator])

    // Value
    // [d/dx] x = 1
    | Var(x) ->
        Expr.Value(1.0, typeof<double>)

    // Constant
    // [d/dx] C = 0.0
    | Double(_) ->
        Expr.Value(0.0, typeof<double>)

    | _ -> failwithf "Unrecognized Expr form: %A" equation

let f = (fun x -> 1.5*x*x*x + 3.0*x*x + -80.0*x + 5.0)

let f'  =
    let quote : Expr =
        generateDerivative <@ (fun x -> 1.5*x*x*x + 3.0*x*x + -80.0*x + 5.0) @>

    let typedQuote : Expr<float -> float> = Expr.Cast quote

    // Compile the Expr<_> into an actual method
    let compiledDerivative = typedQuote.Compile()
    compiledDerivative()
```

With function f and its derivative f', we can quickly plot their values on a graph, resulting in Figure 14-1:

```
    open System.IO

    let generatePlot() =
        use csvFile = new StreamWriter("Plot.csv")
        csvFile.WriteLine("x, f(x), f'(x)")

        [-10.0 .. 0.1 .. 10.0]
        |> List.iter (fun x -> csvFile.WriteLine(sprintf "%f, %f, %f" x (f x) (f' x)))

        csvFile.Close()
```

X	F(x)	F'(x)
-10.00	-4260.00	1245.00
-9.80	-4015.85	1196.68
-9.60	-3781.26	1149.32
-9.40	-3556.06	1102.92
-9.20	-3340.03	1057.48
-9.00	-3133.00	1013.00
-8.80	-2934.77	969.48
-8.60	-2745.14	926.92
-8.40	-2563.94	885.32
-8.20	-2390.95	844.68
-8.00	-2226.00	805.00
-7.80	-2068.89	766.28
-7.60	-1919.42	728.52
-7.40	-1777.42	691.72
-7.20	-1642.67	655.88
-7.00	-1515.00	621.00
-6.80	-1394.21	587.08
-6.60	-1280.10	554.12
-6.40	-1172.50	522.12
-6.20	-1071.19	491.08
-6.00	-976.00	461.00
-5.80	-886.73	431.88
-5.60	-803.18	403.72
-5.40	-725.18	376.52
-5.20	-652.51	350.28
-5.00	-585.00	325.00
-4.80	-522.45	300.68
-4.60	-464.66	277.32
-4.40	-411.46	254.92

Figure 14-1. Graph of a computed derivative

Quotations allow you to write applications that would otherwise require you to write your own parser, compiler, or both. Using the F# compiler's representation of code allows you to focus on transforming the AST instead of parsing another language and building up an internal representation yourself.

Type Providers

Connecting to an SQL database or retrieving data from a web service might seem like a mundane thing to do in a programming language, but the mechanism F# uses for connecting to data providers sets it apart from other languages by the use of a feature called *type providers*. But before we can look at the power and flexibility type providers bring to the F# language, let's look at why they are needed.

Typed Data Versus Typed Languages

F# is a statically typed programming language and goes well out of its way to encourage F# programmers to embrace types. For example, not many other languages have features like:

- Type abbreviations such as `type NodeList = List<Node>` allowing you to create ad hoc types.

- Units of measure such as `32.0f<Fahrenheit>` that allow you to further specialize primitive data types.

But F#'s type system has a crucial limitation. (Actually, this is true for most any programming language.) Types only describe the shape of data *within* programs. The outside world—and the data it contains—is also typed, but in a way that is completely divorced from the program code.

The API for opening XML documents just returns a generic `XElement` back, even if the underlying document contains data with a well-known structure or schema.

The API for reading a web request's response just returns a byte buffer, which could represent JSON, an XML SOAP message, or a custom binary format such as a Protocol Buffer.

If protobufs and JSON are familiar to you, then you should immediately see the problem: "typed" data from the outside world doesn't fit well into programming languages. Extra work must be done in order to correctly unify data from the outside and the type system of a programming language.

Wrapper Assemblies

The traditional solution has been to use custom tools to generate *wrapper libraries* that act as a shim on top of the data source. The output of these tools is either a separate .NET assembly or source code to be compiled in with you programs.

The custom tool knows how to read type information from the data source, and generates custom code to replicate the data source's types in the programming language. This is illustrated in Figure 15-1.

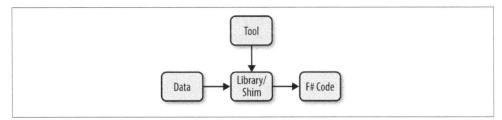

Figure 15-1. Wrapper assemblies

To go back to our XML example, there is an old tool to generate wrappers on top of XML documents called `xsd.exe`. `xsd.exe` will inspect an XML file (or schema) and generates source code for a typed object model. This way you can write code as if the XML document and its types were written in .NET.

The following XML document was retrieved from the National Oceanic and Atmospheric Administration's National Digital Forecast Database web service (*http://graphi cal.weather.gov/xml/*); also, the unfortunate realities of living in the Pacific Northwest have been highlighted in the forecast below:

```xml
<?xml version="1.0"?>
<dwml version="1.0" xmlns:xsd="http://www.w3.org/2001/XMLSchema">
  <head>
    <product srsName="WGS 1984" concise-name="dwmlByDay" ...
      <title>NOAA's Weather Service Forecast by 24 Hour Period</title>
      <field>meteorological</field>
      <category>forecast</category>
      <creation-date refresh-frequency="1H">2012-06-20T01:49:48Z</creation-date>
    </product>
    <source>
      <more-information>http://graphical.weather.gov/xml/</more-information>
      <credit>http://www.weather.gov/</credit>
    </source>
```

```
      </head>
      <data>
        <location>
          <location-key>point1</location-key>
          <point latitude="47.45" longitude="-122.30"/>
        </location>
        <time-layout time-coordinate="local" summarization="12hourly">
          <layout-key>k-p12h-n2-1</layout-key>
          <start-valid-time>2012-02-17T18:00:00-08:00</start-valid-time>
          <end-valid-time>2012-02-18T06:00:00-08:00</end-valid-time>
          <start-valid-time>2012-02-18T06:00:00-08:00</start-valid-time>
          <end-valid-time>2012-02-18T18:00:00-08:00</end-valid-time>
        </time-layout>
        <parameters applicable-location="point1">
          <probability-of-precipitation type="12 hour" units="percent">
            <name>12 Hourly Probability of Precipitation</name>
            <value>95</value>
          </probability-of-precipitation>
        </parameters>
      </data>
    </dwml>
```

Example 15-1 shows how to generate C# source code to wrap the types exposed from the previous XML document using xsd.exe (unfortunately, xsd.exe cannot emit F# code).

Example 15-1. Using xsd.exe

```
C:\TypeProviders>xsd.exe SampleXmlDoc.xml
Microsoft (R) Xml Schemas/DataTypes support utility
[Microsoft (R) .NET Framework, Version 4.0.30319.17020]
Copyright (C) Microsoft Corporation. All rights reserved.
Writing file 'C:\TypeProviders\SampleXmlDoc.xsd'.

C:\TypeProviders>xsd.exe SampleXmlDoc.xsd /language:CS /classes
Microsoft (R) Xml Schemas/DataTypes support utility
[Microsoft (R) .NET Framework, Version 4.0.30319.17020]
Copyright (C) Microsoft Corporation. All rights reserved.
Writing file 'C:\TypeProviders\SampleXmlDoc.cs'.
```

After compiling the emitted C# source code into a separate assembly, we can finally write F# code that interacts with the data and get all the safety guarantees of the type system to a certain extent. The generated library treats all XML attributes and element bodies as string. However, the structure and relationship between the elements and attributes is maintained:

```
> #r @"C:\TypeProviders\SampleXmlDocWrapperLibrary.dll"

open System.Xml.Serialization
open System.IO

// 'dwml' is a type from the generated wrapper library.
```

```
let deserializer = new XmlSerializer(typeof<dwml>)

// Pass the raw XML file to the XML deserializer.
let filePath = @"C:\TypeProviders\SampleXmlDoc.xml"
let fileStream = new FileStream(filePath, FileMode.Open)

let parsedXmlDoc = deserializer.Deserialize(fileStream) :?> dwml;;

--> Referenced 'C:\TypeProviders\SampleXmlDocWrapperLibrary.dll'


val deserializer : System.Xml.Serialization.XmlSerializer
val filePath : string = "C:\TypeProviders\SampleXmlDoc.xml"
val fileStream : System.IO.FileStream
val parsedXmlDoc : dwml

> let probabilityOfPercipitation =
    parsedXmlDoc
    .data.[0]
    .parameters.[0]
    .probabilityofprecipitation.[0]
    .value.[0].Value;;

val probabilityOfPercipitation : string = "95"
```

It works! Using a custom tool, we can integrate external, typed data sources into our programs. So life is good, right?

Well, think for a moment about what a pain this is. As soon as you want to bring in any data source you need to exit your code editor, break into a command line, generate source code, compile it into a separate assembly, reference it, and then finally get back to programming. Also, what if when you finish you realize that you referenced the wrong dataset and need to start the process all over again?

Wouldn't it be better if you didn't need to deal with the wrapper assembly at all? Ideally, you could just write code that used the data source without needing to futz with external tools.

The desire to remove this detour when using typed data is the motivation behind F#'s *type providers*. Type providers allow you to just focus on code, leaving all the type-wrapper-conversion-generation "stuff" to the F# compiler.

F# Type Providers

Example 15-2 shows an F# interactive session loading the same XML file, but this time going through an XML type provider. Notice that no reference to a separate assembly is required, yet the XML types are still available to program against (and provide IntelliSense in the Visual Studio editor!).

Example 15-2. Using an XML type provider

```
// The StructuredXml type provider is defined in the FSharpx library's
// FSharpx.TypeProviders.dll
open FSharpx

type NOAANDFDFile = StructuredXml<
    FileName="C:\weather.xml">

let reasonI'llStayInside : string =
    query {
        let document = NOAANDFDFile().Root
        for data in document.GetDatas() do
        for parameter in data.GetParameters() do
        where (parameter.ApplicableLocation = "point1")
        for percipitationProb in parameter.GetProbabilityOfPrecipitations() do
        let probabilityElement = Seq.head <| percipitationProb.GetValues()
        select (probabilityElement.Element.Value.ToString())
        head
    }
```

Of course, the F# compiler isn't entirely black magic—there still is a tool generating a wrapper assembly. Except that by using F# type providers the wrapper is generated *at design time*, while you are writing code in the IDE or FSI window.

At compile time, the type information from the type provider will be baked into your program. So there is no extra cost to using type information from type providers; whatever "shim" data types that would have been in a separate library are compiled directly into your F# program.

Advantage over shim libraries

With F# type providers, the way to get typed data into your programs now looks much simpler (see Figure 15-2).

Figure 15-2. Programming with type providers

When using type providers, you no longer need to generate or maintain wrapper code, nor do you have to distribute any shim libraries along with your application. If you have ever used the Add Service Reference dialog in Visual Studio while under source code control, you know just how much extra metadata can get added to your project as part of the shim generation.

Advantage over IDEs

On the surface, it looks like F# type providers don't actually eliminate any overhead because IDEs already do most of this heavy lifting. In fact, C# and VB.NET programmers have been using wizards, designers, and code generators to deal with typed data for years.

The key difference here is that the F# type provider approach scales much better than relying on the IDE to manage the code generation for you.

IDEs like Visual Studio, although as powerful as they might seem, only provide support along a specific path. As soon as you want to write code to interact with data sources outside of that path—for example, web services returning protocol buffers or working with OData—it is highly unlikely that your IDE will "just work." You will instead need to resort to the detour of going to the command line and working with custom tools directly.

F# type providers, on the other hand, provide a seamless way to bring typed data into your programs without relying on IDE support. All you need to do is fire up your favorite code editor and write F# code. The F# compiler and type provider assembly—not an IDE—will take care of all the work of type generation for you.

Also, and perhaps more importantly, if there isn't a type provider for your needs, the F# type provider system is easily extensible. It is much easier to write an F# type provider for a new data source than create a new add-in to your favorite IDE.

Type Providers

To create an instance of the type provider, construct the type provider by passing a string literal to the type provider type. Once created, you can use IntelliSense to navigate any exposed types freely. At no point in time do you need to leave the comfort of your editor:

```
[<Literal>]
let ConnectionString =
    "Data Source=MYSERVER\INSTANCE;\
    Initial Catalog=MyDatabase;\
    Integrated Security=SSPI;"

// Use the SqlDataConnection type provider.
type dbSchema = SqlDataConnection<ConnectionString>
```

There are several type providers that ship with F# in the FSharp.Data.TypeProviders.dll assembly. However, you can download more type providers for different data types from the Internet.

Be careful when using third-party type providers. F# type providers execute while you type, so only use type providers from sources you trust.

SQL Data Type Providers

Perhaps the most common use case for type providers is to read and write data from an SQL database. Databases store their contents in a very specific format. Type providers allow these typed data sources to be integrated directly into F# and act as the object-relational mapping, or ORM, without the need for additional tools and libraries.

However, SQL is a very broad technology and has many manifestations. F# provides four (!) different type providers to connect to SQL data, each with different tradeoffs. However, all of them can be used in the same way and work well with F#'s query expressions.

 The following examples use the prototypical Northwind database, an example database for Microsoft Access and SQL Server.

LINQ to SQL

The `SqlDataConnection` type provider uses a technology called LINQ to SQL and is the simplest of all the SQL-related type providers.

Example 15-3 shows using the `SqlDataConnection` type provider to lookup a customer by their ID in the database.

Example 15-3. Using the SqlDataConnection type provider

```
type dbSchema = SqlDataConnection<"Data Source=MYSERVER\INSTANCE;\
        Initial Catalog=MyDatabase;\
        Integrated Security=SSPI;">
let db = dbSchema.GetDataContext()

// Enable the logging of database activity to the console.
db.DataContext.Log <- System.Console.Out

let getCustomerByID id =
    query {
        for customer in db.Customers do
        where customer.CustomerID = id
        select c
        head
    }
```

The type alias dbSchema contains all of information about the data housed within the database specified by the connection string. Its GetDataContext method is used to construct the value db, which can be used to reference the live database tables.

The SqlDataConnection type provider also has parameters to customize how it generates types. For example, the Timeout parameter can be used to adjust the timeout, in milliseconds, to use when connecting to the database.

 Note that the connection string passed to the type provider—including any applicable passwords—is visible within your program's binary.

For accessing sensitive data, make sure to retrieve the database password from the user at runtime. There is an overload of the type provider's GetContext method to provide a connection string at runtime to do this.

DbmlFile

One drawback of the SqlDataConnection provider is that it requires a *live* connection to the database during development, so that the type provider can generate type information from the database's tables. Although a connection to the database is only created at runtime when the data is actually queried, this can cause friction in your development environment.

The DbmlFile provider allows you to generate the same type information as the Sql DataConnection type provider, except that it operates on a schema file describing the database's structure. (A .dbml file can be created by the Visual Studio Object Relational Designer from a data source.)

Example 15-4 shows using the DbmlFile provider to provide the same getCustomer ByID function of the previous example.

Example 15-4. Using the DbmlFile type provider

```
open Microsoft.FSharp.TypeProviders

[<Generate>]
type dbml = DbmlFile<"DataBaseSchema.dbml",
                     ContextTypeName = "DataContext">

// This connection string can be specified at run time.
let connectionString = "Data Source=MYSERVER\INSTANCE;Initial Catalog=MyDatabase;
    Integrated Security=SSPI;"

let db = new dbml.DataContext(connectionString)

let getCustomerByID id =
    query {
        for customer in db.Customers do
```

```
    where customer.CustomerID = id
    select c
    head
}
```

Entity Framework

The `SqlDataConnection` and `DbmlFile` type providers enable an elegant way to bring SQL data into your F# programs. However, for some users, the types generated are too primitive. The Microsoft Entity Framework is designed to address all the (supposed) limitations of LINQ to SQL. In Microsoft's own words (*http://msdn.microsoft.com/en-us/library/bb386876.aspx*):

> The ADO.NET Entity Framework supports data-centric applications and services, and provides a platform for programming against data that raises the level of abstraction from the logical relational level to the conceptual level. By enabling developers to work with data at a greater level of abstraction, the Entity Framework supports code that is independent of any particular data storage engine or relational schema.[1]

For programmers looking to work with data at a "greater level of abstraction" and "independent of any particular data storage engine or relational schema," the `SqlEntity Connection` and `EdmxFile` type providers are available.

Web Service Type Providers

Another major area where typed data can come from is the Internet. There are two built-in type providers for accessing data from web sources.

The WsdlService Provider

The classic notion of a web service is described using the *web service description language*, or WSDL. WSDL is an XML-based format for describing the interchange of information over a network.

The following is an example WSDL service definition for retrieving stock quotes from the W3C (the W3C is the standards body that codified the WSDL specification back in 2001):

```
<?xml version="1.0"?>
<definitions name="StockQuote"

targetNamespace="http://example.com/stockquote.wsdl"
        xmlns:tns="http://example.com/stockquote.wsdl"
        xmlns:xsd1="http://example.com/stockquote.xsd"
        xmlns:soap="http://schemas.xmlsoap.org/wsdl/soap/"
```

---

1. Retrieved September, 2012.

```
        xmlns="http://schemas.xmlsoap.org/wsdl/">

<types>
   <schema targetNamespace="http://example.com/stockquote.xsd"
         xmlns="http://www.w3.org/2000/10/XMLSchema">
      <element name="TradePriceRequest">
         <complexType>
            <all>
               <element name="tickerSymbol" type="string"/>
            </all>
         </complexType>
      </element>
      <element name="TradePrice">
         <complexType>
            <all>
               <element name="price" type="float"/>
            </all>
         </complexType>
      </element>
   </schema>
</types>

<message name="GetLastTradePriceInput">
   <part name="body" element="xsd1:TradePriceRequest"/>
</message>

<message name="GetLastTradePriceOutput">
   <part name="body" element="xsd1:TradePrice"/>
</message>

<portType name="StockQuotePortType">
   <operation name="GetLastTradePrice">
      <input message="tns:GetLastTradePriceInput"/>
      <output message="tns:GetLastTradePriceOutput"/>
   </operation>
</portType>

<binding name="StockQuoteSoapBinding" type="tns:StockQuotePortType">
   <soap:binding transport="http://schemas.xmlsoap.org/soap/http"/>
   <operation name="GetLastTradePrice">
      <soap:operation soapAction="http://example.com/GetLastTradePrice"/>
      <input>
         <soap:body use="literal"/>
      </input>
      <output>
         <soap:body use="literal"/>
      </output>
   </operation>
</binding>

<service name="StockQuoteService">
   <documentation>My first service</documentation>
```

```
        <port name="StockQuotePort" binding="tns:StockQuoteBinding">
           <soap:address location="http://example.com/stockquote"/>
        </port>
     </service>

  </definitions>
```

Although the specification is uncomfortably verbose, it contains all the necessary in‐
formation for describing what methods the service exposes (via the <**service**> element)
and the type of data messages passed across the network (via the <**types**> element).

The WsdlService type provider understands how to convert the WSDL description of
a service into types and methods for use in your programs.

Example 15-5 shows using the WsdlService type provider to connect to
w3school.com's temperature conversion service. Notice how the web service client is
obtained by calling the GetTempConvertSoap method on the type provider's provided
type.

Example 15-5. Using the WsdlService type provider

```
> // FSI session using the WsdlService type provider.
#r "FSharp.Data.TypeProviders.dll"
#r "System.ServiceModel.dll"

open Microsoft.FSharp.Data.TypeProviders

[<Literal>]
let WsdlAddress = "http://www.w3schools.com/webservices/tempconvert.asmx?WSDL"

type TemperatureConversionService = WsdlService<WsdlAddress>
let serviceClient = TemperatureConversionService.GetTempConvertSoap();;

--> Referenced
        'C:\Program Files (x86)\Reference Assemblies\Microsoft\FSharp\3.0\Runtime\
        v4.0\Type Providers\FSharp.Data.TypeProviders.dll'


--> Referenced
        'C:\Windows\Microsoft.NET\Framework\v4.0.30319\System.ServiceModel.dll'


val WsdlAddress : string =
  "http://www.w3schools.com/webservices/tempconvert.asmx?WSDL"
type TemperatureConversionService =
  class
    static member GetTempConvertSoap : unit ->
    SimpleDataContextTypes.TempConvertSoapClient
     + 1 overload
    static member GetTempConvertSoap12 : unit ->
    SimpleDataContextTypes.TempConvertSoapClient
     + 1 overload
```

```
    nested type ServiceTypes
  end
val serviceClient :
  TemperatureConversionService.ServiceTypes.SimpleDataContextTypes
  .TempConvertSoapClient

> let waterFreezesAt = serviceClient.CelsiusToFahrenheit("0.0");;

val waterFreezesAt : string = "32"
```

The ODataService Provider

Although WSDL is a useful standard, a more modern way to access data from the Internet is to use OData. OData is protocol for querying, updating a data store using common Internet Protocols such as HTTP and JSON. In other words, it is a way to get the basic functionality of an SQL-like database using nothing but a URL.

The Netflix service—a DVD-by-mail and movie streaming company—exposes their movie data to the Internet through OData. For example, the following URL/query can be used to find all movies titled "Avatar":

http://odata.netflix.com/Catalog/Titles?$filter=Name%20eq%20'Avatar'

When accessing that URL, the following data will be returned:

```
<?xml version="1.0" encoding="iso-8859-1" standalone="yes"?>
<feed xml:base="http://odata.netflix.com/Catalog/"
      xmlns:d="http://schemas.microsoft.com/ado/2007/08/dataservices"
      xmlns:m="http://schemas.microsoft.com/ado/2007/08/dataservices/metadata"
      xmlns="http://www.w3.org/2005/Atom">
  <title type="text">Titles</title>
  <id>http://odata.netflix.com/Catalog/Titles/</id>
  <updated>2012-02-04T16:51:42Z</updated>
  <link rel="self" title="Titles" href="Titles" />
  <entry>
    <id>http://odata.netflix.com/Catalog/Titles('BVlLw')</id>
    <title type="text">Avatar</title>
    <summary type="html">Disabled Marine Jake Sully (Sam Worthington) travels to
planet Pandora to become an avatar, ingratiate himself with the natives and help
Americans mine lucrative unobtainium. But he finds himself in an interstellar
conflict after falling for Na'vi warrior Neytiri (Zoe Saldana). James Cameron
writes and directs this Golden Globe-winning CGI odyssey that has broken box
office records. Sigourney Weaver and Stephen Lang co-star.</summary>
    <updated>2011-03-31T14:35:13Z</updated>
  ...
```

Similar to the WSDL specification of before, OData is self-describing to the point that a sophisticated client can parse the data for any application. For example, to retrieve the results from the previous using JSON, simply modify the URL with *&$format=json*:

http://odata.netflix.com/Catalog/Titles?$filter=Name%20eq%20'Avatar'&$format=json

JSON, or JavaScript Object Notation, is a format for describing objects that is compatible with a subset of the JavaScript programming language. Meaning that data formatted in the JSON format can be easily converted into full-fledged JavaScript objects (and, most importantly, not need to be parsed by an external library like XML).

The ODataService type provider allows you to connect to any OData web service. And, similar to the raw SQL data sources we saw before, you can query the data as well.

Example 15-6 shows using the ODataService type provider to connect to the Netflix OData web service from F#.

Example 15-6. Using the ODataService type provider.

```
> // FSI session using the WsdlService type provider.
#r "FSharp.Data.TypeProviders.dll"
#r "System.ServiceModel.dll"
#r "System.Data.Services.Client.dll"

open System
open Microsoft.FSharp.Data.TypeProviders

type NetFlixCatalog = ODataService<"http://odata.netflix.com/Catalog/">
let netflixDB = NetFlixCatalog.GetDataContext();;

--> Referenced
        'C:\Program Files (x86)\Reference Assemblies\Microsoft\FSharp\3.0\Runtime\
        v4.0\Type Providers\FSharp.Data.TypeProviders.dll'


--> Referenced
        'C:\Windows\Microsoft.NET\Framework\v4.0.30319\System.ServiceModel.dll'


--> Referenced
        'C:\Windows\Microsoft.NET\Framework\v4.0.30319\System.Data.Services.Client
        .dll'


type NetFlixCatalog =
  class
    static member GetDataContext : unit -> NetflixCatalog
    + 1 overload
    nested type ServiceTypes
  end
val netflixDB :
  NetFlixCatalog.ServiceTypes.SimpleDataContextTypes.NetflixCatalog

> // Check if the film is available for streaming over the Internet.
let isInstant filmName =
```

```
    query {
        for film in netflixDB.Titles do
        where  (film.Name = filmName)
        head
    }
    |> (fun movie -> movie.Instant.Available);;

val isInstant : string -> bool

> isInstant "Iron Man";;
val it : bool = false
> isInstant "The Terminator";;
val it : bool = true
```

 While OData services allow you to query data on the Internet, it comes with rather strict limitations on the nature of the queries possible. For example, you cannot perform joins against two tables.

Custom Type Providers

A big advantage to F#'s type provider system is that it is extensible, allowing you to author new type providers. Although the API for creating new type providers is not be covered in this book, the source code for many excellent type providers is available on GitHub in the *FSharpx* project, available at: *https://github.com/fsharp/fsharpx*.

FSharpx is an open source library built on top of Microsoft's FSharp.Core.dll in order to extend core F# capabilities. For example, the library contains extensions to asynchronous workflows, new computation expression builders, and other functionality. Of note are its type providers for common data sources like Microsoft Excel workbooks and XML files.

F# type providers represent a new way of writing software, and can dramatically reduce the friction for exploratory development. Using type providers you can test algorithms against live data sources in an FSI window, opposed to the build-compile-test cycle of other languages.

Appendixes

Overview of .NET Libraries

The .NET ecosystem has incredible breadth—by enabling you to run .NET code on various platforms, like on your phone, the X-Box gaming system, or even on the Internet via Silverlight. It also has incredible depth—by providing a wealth of powerful libraries from visualization, to communications, to databases, and so on.

This appendix provides a quick overview of some existing .NET libraries that can help you transition from the sample applications in this book to real-world problem solving. The APIs covered are divided into three main areas: visualization, data processing, and storing data.

Visualization

F# is a great tool for processing raw data, but visualizing that data doesn't need to be constrained to just the command line.

There are two main visualization APIs available for .NET: *Windows Forms* (WinForms) and *Windows Presentation Foundation* (WPF). WinForms is the older of the two and is an object-oriented wrapper on top of core Windows APIs. With WinForms, it is easy to create a functioning UI with buttons and common controls, but it can be difficult to create a rich and dynamic interface. WPF, on the other hand, is a much more design-centric library that allows for sophisticated interfaces at the cost of added complexity and a steeper learning curve.

 F# doesn't support code generation, so you cannot use the WYSIWYG editors of Visual Studio. The examples you see in this chapter build UIs programmatically; however, it is recommended that you write your presentation layer code in C# or VB.NET to take advantage of the rich tool support available.

Windows Forms

WinForms is conceptually very simple. Each window on the screen is an instance of a Form, which contains a collection of UI elements of type Control. As users interact with the Form's controls, they will raise events, which the programmer can listen to. For example, a Button control has a Click event, which will be fired whenever the button is clicked.

Note the assembly references to System.Windows.Forms.dll and System.Draw ing.dll; these are required for WinForms development:

```
#r "System.Drawing.dll"
#r "System.Windows.Forms.dll"

open System.Windows.Forms

// Create a form
let form = new Form()

// Create a button
let btn = new Button(Text = "Click Me")
btn.Click.AddHandler(fun _ _ ->
    MessageBox.Show("Hello, World")
    |> ignore)

// Add the button to the form
form.Controls.Add(btn)

// Display the form
form.ShowDialog()
```

Example A-1 creates a form that displays a progress bar while counting the number of words in the complete works of Shakespeare. The form contains two controls: a Pro gressBar and a Label (a control that displays text). As files are processed asynchronously, the two form controls will be updated to indicate progress.

Example A-1. Using Windows Forms

```
#r "System.Drawing.dll"
#r "System.Windows.Forms.dll"

open System.IO
open System.Windows.Forms

// Count the number of words in a given text file.
let countWords filePath =
    System.Threading.Thread.Sleep(2000)
    let lines = File.ReadAllText(filePath)
    let words = lines.Split([| ' ' |])
    words.Length

// The complete works of Shakespeare
```

```
let filesToProcess = Directory.GetFiles(@"D:\CompleteWorksOfShakespeare\")

// Setup the WinForm
let form = new Form(Text = "The Words of Shakespeare", TopMost=true, Height=130)

let wordCountText = new Label(Dock = DockStyle.Bottom)
let progress = new ProgressBar(Minimum = 0,
                               Maximum = filesToProcess.Length - 1,
                               Dock = DockStyle.Fill)

form.Controls.Add(progress)
form.Controls.Add(wordCountText)
form.Show()

// Begin processing files asynchronously. Once each file has been
// processed the status of the progress bar and label will be updated.
async {

    let totalWords = ref 0

    for i in 0 .. filesToProcess.Length - 1 do
        totalWords := !totalWords + (countWords filesToProcess.[i])

        // Update progress bar value and text
        progress.Value <- i
        wordCountText.Text <- sprintf "%d words counted so far..." (!totalWords)

} |> Async.Start
```

When the code from Example A-1 is executed, a form similar to Figure A-1 will be displayed.

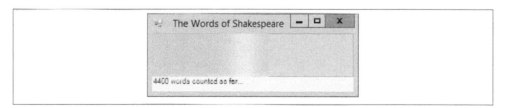

Figure A-1. Windows forms

Windows Presentation Foundation

WinForms provides a simple API for putting together a functioning user interface, but to build more advanced UIs with "sizzle" you will need to take a different approach. Windows Presentation Foundation (WPF) was added as part of .NET 3.0 with the aim of changing how people write and develop user interfaces.

WPF was designed around a couple of key tenets:

Enable rich media

Make it easy to embed rich media like video and animation into application. Whereas WinForms applications typically rely on bland operating system controls, the hallmarks of a WPF application are smooth corners, translucency, and clear text. In addition, WPF applications benefit from hardware acceleration where possible.

Declarative programming model

Another problem with WinForms applications is that the design of the UI and the code that powers it are inextricably linked. It is nearly impossible to change the interface of a WinForms application without needing to rewrite most of the program code. In WPF, the UI layout is separate from the code, and therefore much easier to refactor.

Getting a simple WPF app up and running doesn't take much more work than Win-Forms. Example A-2 does the prototypical "Hello, World"-style application using WPF.

Example A-2. Hello, World in WPF

```
#r "PresentationCore.dll"
#r "PresentationFramework.dll"
#r "WindowsBase.dll"

open System
open System.Windows
open System.Windows.Controls

let win = new Window(Height = 128.0, Width = 360.0)

let label = new Label()
label.FontSize <- 62.0
label.Content <- "Hello, World"

win.Content <- label

let app = new Application()
app.Run(win)
```

Figure A-2 shows our Hello, World application in action. Notice how smooth the text looks. This is because WPF is vector-based, meaning that displays created with WPF can be zoomed without pixellation, making the overall experience much cleaner and more visually appealing.

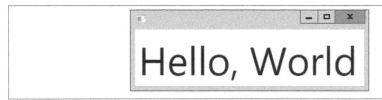

Figure A-2. Hello, World in WPF

XAML, the eXtensible Application Markup Language

Although you can create WPF user interfaces entirely in code, a key component of WPF development is *XAML* (pronounced "zam-el") or the eXtensible Application Markup Language. XAML is an XML-dialect that enables you to express application UI elements declaratively. This enables black-turtleneck-wearing designers to create application interfaces without impacting the coding done by caffeine-guzzling programmers. In addition to enabling designers to add "sizzle" to applications, XAML solves the problems we experienced with WinForms programming where the code and UI were too tightly coupled.

Example A-3 defines a simple WPF application that accepts user input, and when a button is pressed, displays "Hello, Name". The application interface is described in XAML, which is then parsed at runtime using the XamlReader class. (The specifics of the XAML itself are not be covered here.)

Example A-3. Hello, World in WPF

```
#r "PresentationCore.dll"
#r "PresentationFramework.dll"
#r "WindowsBase.dll"

open System
open System.Windows
open System.Windows.Controls
open System.Windows.Markup

/// Declare the UI in XAML
let windowXaml = "
<Window
    xmlns='http://schemas.microsoft.com/winfx/2006/xaml/presentation'
    xmlns:sys='clr-namespace:System;assembly=mscorlib'
    xmlns:x='http://schemas.microsoft.com/winfx2006/xaml' >

    <StackPanel>
        <TextBlock>Who do you want to say hello to?</TextBlock>
        <TextBox Name='NameTextBox'> [name goes here] </TextBox>
        <Button  Name='SayHelloButton'>Say Hello!</Button>
    </StackPanel>

</Window>
```

```
" // End string-based XAML

// Load our XAML markup
let getWindow() =
    let xamlObj = XamlReader.Parse(windowXaml)
    xamlObj :?> Window

let win = getWindow()

// Get instance of the XAML-based UI controls, and wire up event handlers
let textBox = win.FindName("NameTextBox")    :?> TextBox
let button  = win.FindName("SayHelloButton") :?> Button

button.Click.AddHandler(fun _ _ -> let msg = sprintf "Hello, %s" textBox.Text
                                   MessageBox.Show(msg) |> ignore)

let app = new Application()
app.Run(win)
```

The example enabled us to express the UI layout in XAML, but the program code and interface are still too tightly coupled. Because the program code gets a reference to the TextBox and Button controls by their Name property, the layout *has* to have a button and text box with specific names or else the application will stop working. Ideally, there would be a way to write code so that it didn't depend on the specific type of interface elements.

Binding

The designers of WPF wanted to make progress and enable a true separation of the UI and the code powering it. To achieve this, XAML supports *binding*, or linking live program objects with UI elements.

Let's rewrite our "Say Hello" application by first focusing on what we want the code to model. We can then worry about grafting an interface on top of it later.

To power our "Say Hello" application, we want a class that has an introductory message, a Name property the user can set, and a command to greet the user. Example A-4 defines this simple Greeter class as well as a GreetUserCommand, which displays a message box. This is all the code required to power our WPF application. Note the lack of any reference to UI elements.

Example A-4. Greeter for the SayHello application

```
// Greeter.fs

namespace GreetersNamespace

open System
open System.Windows
open System.Windows.Input
```

```
/// Greet command - when executed displays a message box
type GreetUserCommand() =

    let m_canExecuteChangedEvent = new Event<System.EventHandler, EventArgs>()

    interface ICommand with
        member this.CanExecute(param : obj) = true

        member this.Execute(param : obj) =
            MessageBox.Show(sprintf "Hello, %s" (string param))
            |> ignore

        [<CLIEvent>]
        member this.CanExecuteChanged with get() = m_canExecuteChangedEvent.Publish


/// Greeter class - Used to model greeting an end user
type Greeter() =

    let m_greetCommand = new GreetUserCommand()
    let mutable m_name = " [name goes here] "

    /// Introductory text
    member this.Introduction = "Hello, what is your name?"

    member this.Name with get () = m_name
                     and  set x  = m_name <- x

    member this.GreetCommand = m_greetCommand
```

Now that we have a model for how the code should execute, we want to define some XAML to use that model.

First, we need to let our XAML know about the namespace where our code lives. The following snippet defines a new XML namespace, g, to be an alias for the GreetersNa mespace in the current assembly (named WPFinFSharp):

```
<Window
    xmlns='http://schemas.microsoft.com/winfx/2006/xaml/presentation'
    xmlns:x='http://schemas.microsoft.com/winfx/2006/xaml'
    xmlns:g='clr-namespace:GreetersNamespace;assembly=WPFinFSharp'
    Title='Greeter' Height='220' Width='450'>
```

Next, we add a resource to the window of type Greeter called TheGreeter. With this resource in the XAML code, an instance of Greeter will be created behind the scenes and stored in a resource dictionary. This will enable future UI elements to bind to it:

```
<!-- Add an instance of 'Greeter' to the Window's resources -->
<Window.Resources>
    <g:Greeter x:Key='TheGreeter' />
</Window.Resources>
```

Now we can refer to that live object using WPF binding. The following XAML associates the live `Greeter` object with a `StackPanel`. It then adds a `TextBlock` that will display the `Introduction` property of resource TheGreeter:

```
<StackPanel DataContext='{Binding Source={StaticResource TheGreeter}}'>

    <TextBlock Margin='7.5' FontSize='36.0'
        Text='{Binding Introduction}' />
```

Likewise we can bind the `TextBox`'s value to `TheGreeter`'s `Name` property. So whenever the textbox is updated, the `Name` property is updated accordingly:

```
<TextBox Margin='7.5' FontSize='36.0'
    Text='{Binding Name}' />
```

Finally, we bind clicking the button to our `GreetCommand` property, which is an instance of `GreetUserCommand`. When activated, this will carry out greeting the user by calling the `Execute` method of the command:

```
<Button
    Margin='7.5' FontSize='36.0'
    Content='Say Hello' Command='{Binding GreetCommand}'
    CommandParameter='{Binding Name}' />
```

This introduction of another abstraction layer—the window resource—seems like additional complexity, but the code is no longer explicitly tied to the layout of the UI.

Example A-5 shows the updated XAML, which uses proper WPF binding, and the rest of the refactored "Say Hello" application. The XAML also adds a `LinearGradient Brush` element to add a vibrant splash of color to the UI.

 Note that the XAML references the `Greeters` namespace from the currently executing assembly, `WPFinFSharp`. You'll need to update that with the name of the application you build, which may be different—for example, *Application1*.

Example A-5. XAML for the SayHello application

```
// Program.fs

open System
open System.Windows
open System.Windows.Input
open System.Windows.Markup

module XamlCode =
    let xamlUI = "
        <Window
            xmlns='http://schemas.microsoft.com/winfx/2006/xaml/presentation'
            xmlns:x='http://schemas.microsoft.com/winfx/2006/xaml'
            xmlns:g='clr-namespace:GreetersNamespace;assembly=WPFinFSharp'
```

```
                Title='Greeter' Height='240' Width='450'>

                <!-- Add an instance of 'Greeter' to the Window's resources -->
                <Window.Resources>
                    <g:Greeter x:Key='TheGreeter' />
                </Window.Resources>

                <StackPanel DataContext='{Binding Source={StaticResource TheGreeter}}'>

                    <!-- Add a gratutious use of gradient brushes -->
                    <StackPanel.Background>
                        <LinearGradientBrush>
                            <GradientStop Color='Red'    Offset='0.00' />
                            <GradientStop Color='Orange' Offset='0.16' />
                            <GradientStop Color='Yellow' Offset='0.33' />
                            <GradientStop Color='Green'  Offset='0.50' />
                            <GradientStop Color='Blue'   Offset='0.66' />
                            <GradientStop Color='Indigo' Offset='0.83' />
                            <GradientStop Color='Violet' Offset='1.00' />
                        </LinearGradientBrush>
                    </StackPanel.Background>

                    <!-- Set the TextBlock's Text property equal to the Greeter's
                         Introduction property -->
                    <TextBlock Margin='7.5' FontSize='36.0'
                        Text='{Binding Introduction}' />

                    <!-- Bind the TextBox's data to the Greeter's Name property -->
                    <TextBox Margin='7.5' FontSize='36.0'
                        Text='{Binding Name}' />

                    <!-- When you click the button, execute the Greeter's GreetCommand,
                         passing in the Name property as its parameter -->
                    <Button
                        Margin='7.5' FontSize='36.0'
                        Content='Say Hello' Command='{Binding GreetCommand}'
                        CommandParameter='{Binding Name}' />
                </StackPanel>
            </Window>
        "

[<EntryPoint; STAThread>]
let main(args) =

    let getWindow() =
        let o = XamlReader.Parse(XamlCode.xamlUI)
        o :?> Window

    let win = getWindow()
```

```
let app2 = new Application()
let result = app2.Run(win)

result
```

When the "Say Hello" application is compiled and executed, the result looks like Figure A-3.

Figure A-3. Data-bound XAML

It is impossible to show the full extent of WPF data binding in a single example. But you now have a glimpse of how WPF's support for data binding allows you to cleanly separate presentation layer from code and write rich media applications.

 There is far more to learn about WPF. If you are interested in doing serious WPF development, I recommend *Windows Presentation Foundation Unleashed* by Adam Nathans (Sams, 2006).

Data Processing

Once you have a fancy user interface set up for your application, the next step is *doing* something. There are plenty of great data-processing libraries in .NET for whatever your application needs. (Also, see Chapter 11 for in-depth examples of data processing in F#.)

Regular Expressions

Manipulating text is one of the most common tasks you will encounter, and fortunately .NET has the full support for regular expressions to aid you.

Regular expressions are a formal language for searching text for particular words or sequences of characters. You can use regular expressions in .NET to simplify processing textual data to do things like:

- Validate input against a particular format
- Identify substrings that match a particular structure
- Create new strings that are modified versions of the input

To start with, consider the following code snippet. It defines a symbolic function =~= that takes a string and a regular expression—the format for which we cover shortly— and returns if the string matches the given regular expression. The regular expression provided, "\d+", checks if the string contains a number:

```
> // Simple regular expressions
open System.Text.RegularExpressions

let (=~=) str regex = Regex.IsMatch(str, regex);;

val ( =~= ) : string -> string -> bool

> "Does this contain a number?" =~= "\d+";;
val it : bool = false
> "Does this (42) contain a number?" =~= "\d+";;
val it : bool = true
```

Metacharacters

Regular expressions are built on their own language of metacharacters. The metacharacters and syntax for .NET regular expressions are defined in Table A-1.

Table A-1. Regular expression metacharacters

Character	Description
Most characters	Characters other than . $ { [(	)] } * + ? / ^ are matched verbatim.
.	Matches any character except for \n.
[aeiou0-9]	Matches any of a series of characters, including those in a range.
[^aeiou0-9]	Matches any character except those specified.
\w	Matches any word character [a-zA-Z_0-9].
\W	Matches any non-word character [^a-zA-Z_0-9].
\d	Matches any decimal digit [0-9].
\D	Matches any non-decimal digit [^0-9].
\s	Matches any whitespace or separator character.
\S	Matches any non-whitespace or non-separator character.
\	Used to escape metacharacters, such as matching . $ { [(	)] } * + ?
+	Match the previous character one or more times.

Character	Description
*	Match the previous character zero or more times.
?	Match the previous character zero or one times.

In the previous code snippet, the regular expression \d was used to match any digit character, and with the + suffix the regular expression matched any digit one or more times. So "1", "42", and "888" would match the regular expression, but not "foo" or "bar".

A great application for regular expressions is to validate input. Consider the following regular expression for validating if the input is a phone number:

```
"(\(\d\d\d\))?\s*\d\d\d\s*-\s*\d\d\d\d"
```

Even for regular expression pros, the syntax can seem cryptic. Let's look at this regex piece by piece.

First, a phone number can start with an optional three-digit area code. This is done by writing a regular expression to look for parentheses around three digits. Note that the parentheses need to be escaped:

```
\(\d\d\d\)
```

To indicate that the optional area code can only be matched zero or one times, it is enclosed in parentheses and suffixed with a question mark. The parentheses around \(\d\d\d\) treat the sequence of five characters as a single entity, for which the question mark will apply:

```
(\(\d\d\d\))?
```

Next, there can be zero or more whitespace characters \s* followed by three digits \d\d\d, then optional whitespace on either side of a dash separating the first three digits of a phone number from the rest \s*-\s*, and finally four sequential digits \d\d\d\d.

Example A-6 defines a function isValidPhoneNumber for validating input. The regular expression itself is processed using the static Regex.IsMatch method.

Example A-6. Validating input with regular expressions

```
> // Matching a phone number
open System.Text.RegularExpressions

let phoneNumberRegEx = "(\(\d\d\d\))?\s*\d\d\d\s*-\s*\d\d\d\d"
let isValidPhoneNumber text = Regex.IsMatch(text, phoneNumberRegEx);;

val phoneNumberRegEx : string = "(\(\d\d\d\))?\s*\d\d\d\s*-\s*\d\d\d\d"
val isValidPhoneNumber : string -> bool

> isValidPhoneNumber "(707) 827-7000";;
val it : bool = true
> isValidPhoneNumber "123-4567";;
```

```
val it : bool = true
> isValidPhoneNumber "123      -      4567";;
val it : bool = true
> isValidPhoneNumber "(this is not a phone number)";;
val it : bool = false
> isValidPhoneNumber "(123) 456-????";;
val it : bool = false
```

String manipulation

The Regex class offers methods to help build new strings based on existing ones. Split can be used to break a string into parts separated by a regex; Replace replaces all instances of a regex with a static string.

These two methods allows us to go a long way toward parsing semi-structured textual data.

The most widely used file format for storing Chess games is *Portable Game Notation*, or PGN. The format starts with data/value pairs enclosed in brackets—it can have comments enclosed in curly braces, and each move is prefixed with a number and one or three dots.

The following snippet shows an example PGN file describing a match between Bobby Fischer and Boris Spassky:

```
[Event "F/S Return Match"]
[Site "Belgrade, Serbia Yugoslavia|JUG"]
[Date "1992.11.04"]
[Round "29"]
[White "Fischer, Robert J."]
[Black "Spassky, Boris V."]
[Result "1/2-1/2"]

1. e4 e5 2. Nf3 Nc6 3. Bb5 {This opening is called the Ruy Lopez.} 3... a6
4. Ba4 Nf6 5. O-O Be7 6. Re1 b5 7. Bb3 d6 8. c3 O-O 9. h3 Nb8 10. d4 Nbd7
11. c4 c6 12. cxb5 axb5 13. Nc3 Bb7 14. Bg5 b4 15. Nb1 h6 16. Bh4 c5 17. dxe5
Nxe4 18. Bxe7 Qxe7 19. exd6 Qf6 20. Nbd2 Nxd6 21. Nc4 Nxc4 22. Bxc4 Nb6
23. Ne5 Rae8 24. Bxf7+ Rxf7 25. Nxf7 Rxe1+ 26. Qxe1 Kxf7 27. Qe3 Qg5 28. Qxg5
hxg5 29. b3 Ke6 30. a3 Kd6 31. axb4 cxb4 32. Ra5 Nd5 33. f3 Bc8 34. Kf2 Bf5
35. Ra7 g6 36. Ra6+ Kc5 37. Ke1 Nf4 38. g3 Nxh3 39. Kd2 Kb5 40. Rd6 Kc5 41. Ra6
Nf2 42. g4 Bd3 43. Re6 1/2-1/2
```

In order to access the game move data, all comments and metadata must first be removed. Using Regex.Replace, this task is very straightforward. In the game format, all comments and metadata are enclosed between [ ] or { }. So with two regular expressions, any text that matches any sequence of characters between [ ] or { } can be replaced with the empty string, effectively stripping out all comments and metadata:

```
// Remove comments and markup from the PGN file
let removeMarkup text =
    let tagPairs = new Regex(@"\[[^\]]+\]")
```

```
    let noTagPairs = tagPairs.Replace(text, "")

    let comments = new Regex(@"\{[^\}]+\}")
    let noComments = comments.Replace(noTagPairs, "")

    // Trim any leading whitespace and convert to a single-line
    noComments.Trim().Replace("\r", "").Replace("\n", " ")
```

Within the raw move-data blob, the next step is to separate the list of chess moves from the move markers. This can be done using `Regex.Split` on any sequences of digits followed by periods:

```
    // Get the list of moves, each prefixed with a number and one or three dots
    let getMoves text =
        let movePrefix = new Regex(@"\d+\.+")
        movePrefix.Split(text)
```

Using the `removeMarkup` and `getMoves` methods in conjunction will get you access to the meat of the PGN file. Although there certainly is need for more format-specific code to be written, Example A-7 shows how using regular expressions can quickly transform a chunk of textual data into a form that can be more easily processed.

Example A-7. PGN file parser

```
> // Starting to parse a PGN file
open System.Text.RegularExpressions

let pgnGameText = "
[Event \"F/S Return Match\"]
[Site \"Belgrade, Serbia Yugoslavia|JUG\"]
[Date \"1992.11.04\"]
[Round \"29\"]
[White \"Fischer, Robert J.\"]
[Black \"Spassky, Boris V.\"]
[Result \"1/2-1/2\"]

1. e4 e5 2. Nf3 Nc6 3. Bb5 {This opening is called the Ruy Lopez.} 3... a6
4. Ba4 Nf6 5. O-O Be7 6. Re1 b5 7. Bb3 d6 8. c3 O-O 9. h3 Nb8  10. d4 Nbd7
11. c4 c6 12. cxb5 axb5 13. Nc3 Bb7 14. Bg5 b4 15. Nb1 h6 16. Bh4 c5 17. dxe5
Nxe4 18. Bxe7 Qxe7 19. exd6 Qf6 20. Nbd2 Nxd6 21. Nc4 Nxc4 22. Bxc4 Nb6
23. Ne5 Rae8 24. Bxf7+ Rxf7 25. Nxf7 Rxe1+ 26. Qxe1 Kxf7 27. Qe3 Qg5 28. Qxg5
hxg5 29. b3 Ke6 30. a3 Kd6 31. axb4 cxb4 32. Ra5 Nd5 33. f3 Bc8 34. Kf2 Bf5
35. Ra7 g6 36. Ra6+ Kc5 37. Ke1 Nf4 38. g3 Nxh3 39. Kd2 Kb5 40. Rd6 Kc5 41. Ra6
Nf2 42. g4 Bd3 43. Re6 1/2-1/2
"

// Remove comments and markup from the PGN file
let removeMarkup text =
    let tagPairs = new Regex(@"\[.*\]")
    let noTagPairs = tagPairs.Replace(text, "")

    let comments = new Regex(@"\{.*\}")
    let noComments = comments.Replace(noTagPairs, "")
```

```
    // Trim any leading whitespace and convert to a single-line
    noComments.Trim().Replace("\r", "").Replace("\n", " ")

// Get the list of moves, each prefixed with a number and one or three dots
let getMoves text =
    let factRegex = new Regex(@"\d+\.+", RegexOptions.Multiline)
    factRegex.Split(text)

let normalizedText = removeMarkup pgnGameText

let listMoves() =
    getMoves normalizedText
    |> Array.map (fun move -> move.Trim())
    |> Array.iter (printfn "%s");;

val pgnGameText : string =
    "
[Event "F/S Return Match"]
[Site "Belgrade, Serbia Yugoslavi"+[684 chars]
val removeMarkup : string -> string
val getMoves : string -> string []
val normalizedText : string =
    "1. e4 e5 2. Nf3 Nc6 3. Bb5   3... a6 4. Ba4 Nf6 5. 0-0 Be7 6. "+[464 chars]
val listMoves : unit -> unit

> listMoves();;

e4 e5
Nf3 Nc6
Bb5
a6
Ba4 Nf6
0-0 Be7
Re1 b5
Bb3 d6
c3 0-0
h3 Nb8
d4 Nbd7
c4 c6
...
```

Capture groups

Regular expressions can be used for more than just validating input and manipulating text. You can also use regular expressions to extract textual data that matches a given format.

If you want to use a metacharacter like ?, +, or * to apply to a sequence of characters, you can group them in parentheses. For example, "(foo)+" matches the phrase "foo" one or more times. Without the parentheses, "foo+" the regular expression would match the letters f, o, and then another o one or more times.

Grouping can be more useful than adding expressiveness to regular expression syntax, if you use the Regex.Match method a Match object will be returned that you can use to refer back to the string captured in each captured group.

Example A-8 defines a regular expression to parse out word analogies found on standardized tests. Each part of the regular expression associated with a word is enclosed in parentheses, and therefore its own group.

The example takes the returned Match object and prints each captured group to the console. Notice that the full regular expression is considered the "first" group, which in the example is the full word analogy.

Example A-8. Capturing regular expression groups

```
> // Capturing regex groups
open System
open System.Text.RegularExpressions

let analogyRegex = "(\w+):(\w+)::(\w+):(\w+)"
let m = Regex.Match("dog:bark::cat:meow", analogyRegex);;

val analogyRegex : string = "(\w+):(\w+)::(\w+):(\w+)"
val m : Match = dog:bark::cat:meow

> // Print captures
printfn "Group captures..."
for i = 0 to  m.Groups.Count - 1 do
    printfn "[%d] %s" i (m.Groups.[i].Value);;
Group captures...
[0] dog:bark::cat:meow
[1] dog
[2] bark
[3] cat
[4] meow
```

We've already seen a great example of when to use regular expression group captures, and that is in conjunction with active patterns.

Example A-9 is from Chapter 7. Notice how the partial active pattern returns a tuple of three strings, which are the result of three captures in the given regular expression. List.tail is used to skip the first group's value—the fully matched string—and instead returns each individual group capture.

The example uses the (|RegexMatch3|_|) partial active pattern to match different ways to specify a date, while binding the year, month, and day to values in the pattern-match rule.

Example A-9. Regular expression captures via active patterns

```
let (|RegexMatch3|_|) (pattern : string) (input : string) =
    let result = Regex.Match(input, pattern)

    if result.Success then
        match (List.tail [ for g in result.Groups -> g.Value ]) with
        | fst :: snd :: trd :: []
            -> Some (fst, snd, trd)
        | [] -> failwith "Match succeeded, but no groups found.\n \
                          Use '(.*)' to capture groups"
        | _  -> failwith "Match succeeded, but did not find exactly three groups."
    else
        None

let parseTime input =
    match input with
    // Match input of the form "6/20/2008"
    | RegexMatch3 "(\d+)/(\d+)/(\d+)" (month, day, year)
    // Match input of the form "2000-3-6"
    | RegexMatch3 "(\d+)-(\d+)-(\d+)" (year, month, day)
        -> Some( new DateTime(int year, int month, int day) )
    | _ -> None
```

 If you are interested in learning more about regular expressions, consider reading *Mastering Regular Expressions* by Jeffrey E. F. Friedl (O'Reilly, 2006).

Working with XML

Working with XML allows you to easily create and store structured data without the fuss of writing your own parser. It means that you can leverage .NET APIs for manipulating XML documents as well.

There are two separate XML libraries for .NET, an early version in the System .Xml.dll assembly, which is somewhat painful to use, and a newer, friendlier library in System.Xml.Linq.dll, which is covered here.

Writing XML

Writing XML documents is as simple as constructing a hierarchy of XElement objects. Example A-10 defines a Book type that knows how to convert itself into an XML document, via the ToXml method.

Example A-10. Writing XML documents

```
#r "System.Xml.dll"
#r "System.Xml.Linq.dll"

open System.Xml.Linq

// Convert a string into an XName object
let xname thing = XName.Get(thing.ToString())

type Book =
    | ComicBook of string * int
    | Novel of string * string
    | TechBook of string * string
    member this.ToXml() =
        match this with
        | ComicBook(series, issue) ->
            new XElement(xname "ComicBook",
                new XElement(xname "Series", series),
                new XElement(xname "Issue",  issue))

        | Novel(author, title) ->
            new XElement(xname "Novel",
                new XElement(xname "Author", author),
                new XElement(xname "Title",  title))

        | TechBook(author, title) ->
            new XElement(xname "TechBook",
                new XElement(xname "Author", author),
                new XElement(xname "Title",  title))

/// Generates an XML document from a list of books
let bookshelfToXml (bookshelf : Book list) =
    let books = bookshelf
                |> List.map (fun book -> book.ToXml())
                |> Array.ofList
    new XElement(xname "Bookshelf", books)
```

You can see how easy it is to construct XML documents in the following FSI session. Saving XML documents is as simple as calling the `Save` method on an `XElement` object:

```
> // Convert a list of Book union cases to an XML document
[
    ComicBook("IronMan", 1)
    ComicBook("IronMan", 2)
    TechBook("Machine Learning", "Mitchell")
    TechBook("Effective C++", "Meyers")
    Novel("World War Z", "Max Brooks")
    ComicBook("IronMan", 3) ]
|> bookshelfToXml
|> (printfn "%A");;

<Bookshelf>
```

```
<ComicBook>
  <Series>IronMan</Series>
  <Issue>1</Issue>
</ComicBook>
<ComicBook>
  <Series>IronMan</Series>
  <Issue>2</Issue>
</ComicBook>
<TechBook>
  <Author>Machine Learning</Author>
  <Title>Mitchell</Title>
</TechBook>
<TechBook>
  <Author>Effective C++</Author>
  <Title>Meyers</Title>
</TechBook>
<Novel>
  <Author>World War Z</Author>
  <Title>Max Brooks</Title>
</Novel>
<ComicBook>
  <Series>IronMan</Series>
  <Issue>3</Issue>
</ComicBook>
</Bookshelf>
val it : unit = ()
```

Reading XML

To open XML documents, use the static methods XElement.Parse and XElement
.Load. The XElement.Parse method takes a string containing structured XML data and
return an instance of XElement; XElement.Load on the other hand takes a file path to a
valid XML file:

```
> // Load an existing XML document from disk
let shelf = XElement.Load("LordOfTheRings.xml")
printfn "Loaded Document:\n%A" shelf;;

Loaded Document:
<Bookshelf>
  <Novel>
    <Author>The Two Towers</Author>
    <Title>Tolkien</Title>
  </Novel>
  <Novel>
    <Author>Fellowship of the Ring</Author>
    <Title>Tolkien</Title>
  </Novel>
  <Novel>
    <Author>The Return of the King</Author>
    <Title>Tolkien</Title>
  </Novel>
```

```
</Bookshelf>
val it : unit = ()

> // Parse an XML document from a string
do
    let shelf = XElement.Parse("<Bookshelf>
                                    <TechBook>
                                        <Author>Steve McConnell</Author>
                                        <Title>CodeComplete</Title>
                                    </TechBook><TechBook>
                                        <Author>Charles Petzold</Author>
                                        <Title>Code</Title>
                                    </TechBook>
                                </Bookshelf>")
    printfn "Parsed Document:\n%A" shelf;;

Parsed Document:
<Bookshelf>
  <TechBook>
    <Author>Steve McConnell</Author>
    <Title>CodeComplete</Title>
  </TechBook>
  <TechBook>
    <Author>Charles Petzold</Author>
    <Title>Code</Title>
  </TechBook>
</Bookshelf>
val it : unit = ()
```

Storing Data

Once you've computed the values you need, you will probably want to save that data to disk or in a database. There are numerous ways of storing data in .NET, each with varying degrees of performance and ease of use.

File I/O

Most .NET I/O facilities are based around the abstract `System.IO.Stream` class, which defines a primitive interface between the stream and the backing store (backing store is just a fancy term for "where the data comes from"). Classes inherit from `Stream` and add specialized ways to read or write from a particular backing store. For example, `MemoryStream` is used to read or write data from memory, `NetworkStream` is used to read or write data from a network connection, `FileStream` is used to read or write data from a file, and so on.

The simplest way to read or write data from disk is to use the `File.ReadAllLines` and `File.WriteAllLines` methods. `WriteAllLines` takes a file path and a string array of textual data to be written to the file, whereas `ReadAllLines` takes a file path and returns the string array of the file's lines:

```
> // Solving the fizz buzz problem
open System.IO

let computeFileContents() =
    [| 1 .. 100 |]
    |> Array.map(function
                    | x when x % 3 = 0 && x % 5 = 0 -> "FizzBuzz"
                    | x when x % 3 = 0 -> "Fizz"
                    | x when x % 5 = 0 -> "Buzz"
                    | _ -> ".");;

val computeFileContents : unit -> string []

> File.WriteAllLines("FizzBuzzSln.txt", computeFileContents());;
val it : unit = ()

> let fileContents = File.ReadAllLines("FizzBuzzSln.txt");;

val fileContents : string [] =
  [|"."; "."; "Fizz"; "."; "Buzz"; "Fizz"; "."; "."; "Fizz"; "Buzz"; ".";
    "Fizz"; "."; "."; "FizzBuzz"; "."; "."; "Fizz"; "."; "Buzz"; "Fizz"; ".";
    "."; "Fizz"; "Buzz"; "."; "Fizz"; "."; "."; "FizzBuzz"; "."; "."; "Fizz";
    "."; "Buzz"; "Fizz"; "."; "."; "Fizz"; "Buzz"; "."; "Fizz"; "."; ".";
    "FizzBuzz"; "."; "."; "Fizz"; "."; "Buzz"; "Fizz"; "."; "."; "Fizz";
    "Buzz"; "."; "Fizz"; "."; "."; "FizzBuzz"; "."; "."; "Fizz"; "."; "Buzz";
    "Fizz"; "."; "."; "Fizz"; "Buzz"; "."; "Fizz"; "."; "."; "FizzBuzz"; ".";
    "."; "Fizz"; "."; "Buzz"; "Fizz"; "."; "."; "Fizz"; "Buzz"; "."; "Fizz";
    "."; "."; "FizzBuzz"; "."; "."; "Fizz"; "."; "Buzz"; "Fizz"; "."; ".";
    "Fizz"; "Buzz"|]
```

Data Serialization

Although the ability to read and write data to files is quite useful, you're still out of luck if you have no way to convert your classes to a form that can be easily written to disk. For that, you will need to use *serialization*. Serialization is the process of converting an object into a binary format, which can then be persisted on disk or transferred across a network.

You can write your own mechanisms for serialization, but built into the .NET framework is support to do this for you. To opt into the default serialization provided by .NET simply add the `[<Serializable>]` attribute to the type.

Just because a type has the [<Serializable>] attribute doesn't mean that it can be serialized in arbitrary ways, however. Different forms of serialization apply special constraints.

For example, the .NET XML serializer, which serializes objects into XML, requires that types have a parameterless constructor. This restriction disallows you from using F# types such as records and discriminated unions with XML serialization.

Consider the following types defining a baseball team from a discriminated union, record, and class; each marked with the [<Serializable>] attribute:

```
open System
open System.Collections.Generic

// Discriminated Union
[<Serializable>]
type Position =
    // Battery
    | Pitcher      | Catcher
    // Infield
    | ShortStop    | FirstBase    | SecondBase    | ThirdBase
    // Outfield
    | LeftField    | CenterField  | RightField

// Record
[<Serializable>]
type BaseballPlayer =
    {
        Name : string
        Position : Position
        BattingAvg : float
    }

// Class
[<Serializable>]
type BaseballTeam(name : string ) =

    let m_roster = new List<BaseballPlayer>()

    member this.TeamName = name

    member this.DraftPlayer(player) = m_roster.Add(player)
    member this.BenchPlayer(player) = m_roster.Remove(player)

    member this.Roster = m_roster |> Seq.toArray
```

Serializing an object to a byte[] is as simple as passing a stream to an instance of BinaryFormatter. Example A-11 shows an FSI session where the method serialize Thing serializes an arbitrary obj into a byte[] and a method saveTeam saves a Base ballTeam object to disk.

The serializeThing method works by creating a MemoryStream, which allows the BinaryFormatter to write the serialized version of the obj into memory. Then, the function returns the MemoryStream's data in the form of a byte[].

Example A-11. Serialization

```
> // Serializing an object
open System.IO
open System.Runtime.Serialization.Formatters.Binary

/// Serialize an object
let serializeThing(thing) =
    let bf = new BinaryFormatter()
    use mstream = new MemoryStream()
    bf.Serialize(mstream, thing)

    mstream.ToArray()

/// Saves a baseball team to disk
let saveTeam(team : BaseballTeam, filePath : string) =

    let byteArr = serializeThing team

    use fileStream = new FileStream(filePath, FileMode.CreateNew)
    fileStream.Write(byteArr, 0, byteArr.Length)
    fileStream.Close()

    ()
;;

val serializeThing : 'a -> byte []
val saveTeam : BaseballTeam * string -> unit

> // Creating a baseball team
let M's = new BaseballTeam("Mariners")
let ichiro =
    {
        Name = "Ichiro Suzuki"
        Position = RightField
        BattingAvg = 0.330
    }
let griffeyJr =
    { Name = "Ken Griffey, Jr."; Position = LeftField; BattingAvg = 0.287 }
M's.DraftPlayer(ichiro)
M's.DraftPlayer(griffeyJr);;

val M's : BaseballTeam
```

```
val ichiro : BaseballPlayer = {Name = "Ichiro Suzuki";
                               Position = RightField;
                               BattingAvg = 0.33;}
val griffeyJr : BaseballPlayer = {Name = "Ken Griffey, Jr.";
                                  Position = LeftField;
                                  BattingAvg = 0.287;}

> // Serialize poor Ichiro into a byte[]
serializeThing ichiro;;
val it : byte [] =
  [|0uy; 1uy; 0uy; 0uy; 0uy; 255uy; 255uy; 255uy; 255uy; 1uy; 0uy; 0uy; 0uy;
    0uy; 0uy; 0uy; 0uy; 12uy; 2uy; 0uy; 0uy; 0uy; 67uy; 70uy; 83uy; 73uy; 45uy;
    65uy; 83uy; 83uy; 69uy; 77uy; 66uy; 76uy; 89uy; 44uy; 32uy; 86uy; 101uy;
    114uy; 115uy; 105uy; 111uy; 110uy; 61uy; 48uy; 46uy; 48uy; 46uy; 48uy;
    46uy; 48uy; 44uy; 32uy; 67uy; 117uy; 108uy; 116uy; 117uy; 114uy; 101uy;
    61uy; 110uy; 101uy; 117uy; 116uy; 114uy; 97uy; 108uy; 44uy; 32uy; 80uy;
    117uy; 98uy; 108uy; 105uy; 99uy; 75uy; 101uy; 121uy; 84uy; 111uy; 107uy;
    101uy; 110uy; 61uy; 110uy; 117uy; 108uy; 108uy; 5uy; 1uy; 0uy; 0uy; 0uy;
    23uy; 70uy; 83uy; 73uy; 95uy; ...|]
> saveTeam(M's, @"D:\MarinersTeam.bbt");;
val it : unit = ()
```

Deserialization

Deserializing data is done in much the same way it is serialized, except the Deserial ize method is called on the BinaryFormatter. Deserialize returns an obj, which will need to be cast as another type.

Example A-12 provides the complement of saveTeam, called loadTeam. The method opens up a FileStream object, which the BinaryFormatter will read from and deserializes a BaseballTeam type.

Example A-12. Deserialization

```
> // Deserialization
let loadTeam(filePath) =

    use fileStream = new FileStream(filePath, FileMode.Open)

    let bf = new BinaryFormatter()
    let result = bf.Deserialize(fileStream)

    (result :?> BaseballTeam);;

val loadTeam : string -> BaseballTeam

> let loadedM's = loadTeam @"D:\MarinersTeam.bbt";;

val loadedM's : BaseballTeam

> // Print the loaded data
loadedM's.Roster
```

```
|> Array.iter (fun player -> printfn "%s - Batting %.3f"
                                      player.Name
                                      player.BattingAvg);;
Ichiro Suzuki - Batting 0.330
Ken Griffey, Jr. - Batting 0.287
val it : unit = ()
```

F# Interop

This book shows how F# can be a great language for helping you to be more productive, while seamlessly integrating with the existing .NET stack. Although it is true that F# is a great language, the word *seamlessly* may need to be qualified.

The dominant languages used in .NET today are C# and Visual Basic .NET (VB.NET), and although in F# you can write and call into object-oriented assemblies to interact with C# and VB.NET code, some concepts may get lost in translation.

This appendix is focused on how to ease interop with F#. By the end of this appendix, you'll be able to identify problem areas when doing multilanguage programming. In addition, you'll be able to have your F# interoperate with unmanaged (native) code as well by using Platform Invoke and COM.

 Although F# allows you to work with both C# and Visual Basic .NET, in this appendix, I'm just going to refer to C# for convenience. Whenever you see the term C#, you can replace it with the phrase *C# or Visual Basic .NET* depending on your preference.

.NET Interop

The key to interoperation between .NET languages is to make sure that the types and methods in the public surface area of a class library are available to all languages consuming the code. Intuitively, if a library exposes constructs that are not native to the consuming language, things can look a little strange. Or, even worse, the library exposes different idioms for the concepts in both languages.

Nullable Types

Nullable types are for unfortunate C# and VB.NET programmers who don't have pattern matching, discriminated unions, and the ability to use option types. In order for them to express that an object may or may not have a value, they must use the System.Nullable<T> type.

For example, the following expresses a nullable integer type, which has value zero, one, or null:

```
> // Nullable types
open System

let x = new Nullable<int>(1)
let y = new Nullable<int>();;

val x : Nullable<int> = 1
val y : Nullable<int> = null

> printfn "HasValue: x = %b, y = %b" x.HasValue y.HasValue;;
HasValue: x = true, y = false
val it : unit = ()
> x.Value;;
val it : int = 1
> y.Value;;
System.InvalidOperationException: Nullable object must have a value.
   at System.ThrowHelper.ThrowInvalidOperationException(ExceptionResource resource)
   at <StartupCode$FSI_0057>.$FSI_0057.main@()
Stopped due to error
```

 In pure F# code, stick to using option types wherever possible. However, if interoperating with other .NET code or reading from an SQL database, using nullable types might be unavoidable.

Linq.NullableOperators

Once you have a nullable value, you cannot use the standard set of operators on it (because (+) doesn't default to having semantics for adding two null values). Fortunately there is a plethora of operators for using nullable types.

As soon as you open the Microsoft.FSharp.Linq namespace, the NullableOperators module will auto-open and add a slew of custom operators.

The semantics for operating on nullable types is as follows: if both operands have a value, then the result is as you would normally expect. However, if either or both of the values is null, then the result will be null.

The general pattern is to add a question mark ,?, for each operand which is nullable. For example, use (?+) to add two values if the left side is nullable, (+?) if the right side is nullable, and (?+?) if both operands are nullable:

```
> // Nullable operators
open Microsoft.FSharp.Linq
(?+);;
val it : (Nullable<int> -> int -> Nullable<int>) = <fun:it@46-2>
> (+?);;
val it : (int -> Nullable<int> -> Nullable<int>) = <fun:it@47-3>
> (?+?);;
val it : (Nullable<int> -> Nullable<int> -> Nullable<int>) = <fun:it@48-4>
> let x = new Nullable<int>(12);;

val x : Nullable<int> = 12

> // ERROR: (+) doesn't work on nullable types.
x + 1;;

  x + 1;;
  ----^

stdin(49,5): error FS0001: The type 'int' does not match the type 'Nullable<int>'
> // Works
x ?+ 1;;
val it : Nullable<int> = 13
```

C# Interoperating with F#

When writing F# code, you should refrain from exposing functional types such as discriminated unions, records, and function values directly. Instead, use them for internal-types and values, and expose regular class types for public-facing methods. Otherwise, the C# consumers will have a difficult time working with your types.

Discriminated unions

Discriminated unions are types that define a series of possible data tags, and an instance of the discriminated union may only hold the value of one data tag at a time. To enforce this property, the F# compiler relies on inheritance and polymorphism behind the scenes.

Example B-1 shows a simple discriminated union in F# for describing the employees of a company.

Example B-1. Discriminated union exposed from F#

```
// HumanResources.fs - F# code declaring a discrimianted union

namespace Initech.HumanResources

type PersonalInfo = { Name : string; EmployeeID : int }
```

```
type Employee =
    | Manager of PersonalInfo * Employee list
    | Worker  of PersonalInfo
    | Intern
```

Discriminated unions seem simple in F# when you have pattern matching and syntax support; however, when consumed from C#, they are quite a pain to use.

Example B-2 shows the same F# code for the `Initech.HumanResources.Employee` discriminated union as it would look in C# (and therefore the API a C# developer would have to program against). In the example, interfaces and compiler-generated methods have been omitted.

You can see how treacherous navigating the type is in C#, but it should also give you an appreciation for how much legwork the F# compiler is doing to make pattern matching so elegant.

Example B-2. F# discriminated unions when viewed from C#

```csharp
using System;
using Microsoft.FSharp.Collections;

namespace Initech.HumanResources
{
    [Serializable, CompilationMapping(SourceConstructFlags.SumType)]
    public abstract class Employee
    {
        // Fields
        internal static readonly Employee _unique_Intern = new _Intern();

        // Methods
        internal Employee()
        {
        }

        [CompilationMapping(SourceConstructFlags.UnionCase, 0)]
        public static Employee NewManager(PersonalInfo item1,
                                          FSharpList<Employee> item2)
        {
            return new Manager(item1, item2);
        }

        [CompilationMapping(SourceConstructFlags.UnionCase, 1)]
        public static Employee NewWorker(PersonalInfo item)
        {
            return new Worker(item);
        }

        // Properties
        public static Employee Intern
        {
```

```
        [CompilationMapping(SourceConstructFlags.UnionCase, 2)]
        get
        {
            return _unique_Intern;
        }
    }

    public bool IsIntern
    {
        [CompilerGenerated, DebuggerNonUserCode]
        get
        {
            return (this is _Intern);
        }
    }

    public bool IsManager
    {
        [CompilerGenerated, DebuggerNonUserCode]
        get
        {
            return (this is Manager);
        }
    }

    public bool IsWorker
    {
        [CompilerGenerated, DebuggerNonUserCode]
        get
        {
            return (this is Worker);
        }
    }

    public int Tag
    {
        get
        {
            Employee employee - this,
            return (!(employee is _Intern) ? (!(employee is Worker) ? 0 : 1) :
                                            2);
        }
    }

    // Nested Types
    [Serializable]
    internal class _Intern : Employee
    {
        // Methods
        internal _Intern()
        {
        }
```

```
}

[Serializable]
public class Manager : Employee
{
    // Fields
    internal readonly PersonalInfo item1;
    internal readonly FSharpList<Employee> item2;

    // Methods
    internal Manager(PersonalInfo item1, FSharpList<Employee> item2)
    {
        this.item1 = item1;
        this.item2 = item2;
    }

    // Properties
    [CompilationMapping(SourceConstructFlags.Field, 0, 0)]
    public PersonalInfo Item1
    {
        get
        {
            return this.item1;
        }
    }

    [CompilationMapping(SourceConstructFlags.Field, 0, 1)]
    public FSharpList<Employee> Item2
    {
        get
        {
            return this.item2;
        }
    }
}

public static class Tags
{
    // Fields
    public const int Intern = 2;
    public const int Manager = 0;
    public const int Worker = 1;
}

[Serializable]
public class Worker : Employee
{
    // Fields
    internal readonly PersonalInfo item;

    // Methods
    internal Worker(PersonalInfo item)
```

```
        {
            this.item = item;
        }

        // Properties
        [CompilationMapping(SourceConstructFlags.Field, 1, 0)]
        public PersonalInfo Item
        {
            get
            {
                return this.item;
            }
        }
    }
}
}
```

Function values

Function values represent a similar problem when consuming F# code from C#. Although C# supports lambda expressions just like F#, the way the C# compiler handles them is much different.

In C#, the method for representing function values is to use delegates. C# 3.0 introduced two generic delegate types to help aid C# developers when doing functional programming: System.Action<_> and System.Func<_,_>.

The Action<_> type represents a function that does not return a value. The Func<_,_> type, on the other hand, does return a value. In both cases, the generic type parameters are the types of the function's parameters (with the last being the return type in the case of Func).

The following snippet shows F# code for creating Action<_> and Func<_,_> function values:

```
> // Using the System.Action type
#r "System.Core.dll"

open System

let fsAction = new Action<string>(fun arg -> printfn "Hello, %s" arg);;

--> Referenced 'C:\Windows\Microsoft.NET\Framework\v4.0.20620\System.Core.dll'


val fsAction : Action<string>

> fsAction.Invoke("World");;
Hello, World
val it : unit = ()
> // Using the System.Func type
```

```
let fsFunc = new Func<string, int>(fun s -> Int32.Parse(s) * Int32.Parse(s));;

val fsFunc : Func<string,int>

> fsFunc.Invoke("4");;

val it : int = 16
```

Function values created in F# are not of type `Action<_>` or `Func<_,_>`, but instead of type `FSharpFunc<_,_>`. Another difference in F# is that function values may be partially applied, so passing in the first parameter of a function returns a new function with one fewer parameter.

Example B-3 shows the type `MathUtilities`, which has a method named `GetAdder` that returns an F# function value taking three string parameters.

Example B-3. Function values in F#

```
namespace Initech.Math

open System

type MathUtilities =
    static member GetAdder() =
        (fun x y z -> Int32.Parse(x) + Int32.Parse(y) + Int32.Parse(z))
```

The type returned by `GetAdder` is an `FSharpFunc<_,_>` object, which in F# can be expressed by:

```
string -> string -> string -> int
```

However, to declare that same function type in C# you must write:

```
FSharpFunc <string, FSharpFunc <string, FSharpFunc <string, int>>>
```

Just imagine what the function signature would look like if it took more parameters! Curried function values are an elegant way to simplify code in functional languages, but be wary of exposing them to languages that don't support currying natively.

F# Interoperating with C#

Consuming C# code from F# is typically no problem because F# contains most all of the language features found in C# and VB.NET. However, there are a few things you can do in C# that you cannot do easily in F#; so if you have control over the C# libraries you will consume from F#, keep the following points in mind.

Byref and out parameters

In C#, you can declare out and ref parameters, which enable a function to return more than one value by modifying its parameters. ref indicates that a parameter's value may be changed during the execution of a function call, and out indicates that the parameter's value will be set as a result of the function call.

F# supports both ref and out parameters natively, and can make use of C# code that exposes them.

Consider the following C# code, which defines two functions taking either out or ref parameters:

```
public class CSharpFeatures
{
    public static bool ByrefParams(ref int x, ref int y)
    {
        x = x * x;
        y = y * y;
        return true;
    }

    public static bool OutParams(out int x, out int y)
    {
        x = 10;
        y = 32;
        return true;
    }
}
```

In F#, to pass a parameter to a function accepting ref arguments, you have two options. You can either pass in a ref<'a> value or use the F# address-of operator & on a mutable value.

The following FSI session shows calling into the CSharpFeatures.ByrefParams method using both a ref value and the address-of operator. Notice that after the function executes, both parameters have been modified:

```
> // Declare ref / out parameter values
let x = ref 3
let mutable y = 4;;

val x : int ref = {contents = 3;}
val mutable y : int = 4

> CSharpFeatures.ByrefParams(x, &y);;
val it : bool = true
> x;;
val it : int ref = {contents = 9;}
> y;;
val it : int = 16
```

In F#, out parameters have the special property that they are not required to be passed to the function, and if they are omitted, the out parameters are returned with the function's result as a tuple. To pass in an out parameter in F#, the same rules for ref arguments apply. It must be of type ref<'a> or mutable value called with the address-of operator.

The following FSI session shows calling into the CSharpFeatures.OutParams method three times. Notice how the return type of the function changes based on whether or not the out parameters were passed in:

```
> // Declare ref / out parameter values
let x = ref 0
let mutable y = 0;;

val x : int ref = {contents = 0;}
val mutable y : int = 0

> // Pass in both out parameters, return value is bool
CSharpFeatures.OutParams(x, &y);;
val it : bool = true
> // Pass in just one out parameter, return value is bool * int
CSharpFeatures.OutParams(x);;
val it : bool * int = (true, 32)
> // Pass in no out parameters, return value is bool * int * int
CSharpFeatures.OutParams();;
val it : bool * int * int = (true, 10, 32)
```

To expose a method parameter from F# as a ref parameter, simply give the parameter type byref<'a>. You can then treat that parameter as a local, mutable variable. To expose an out parameter, give the parameter type byref<'a> as well but also attribute it with System.Runtime.InteropServices.OutAttribute. The following snippet defines an F# function that takes a ref and an out parameter respectively:

```
open System.Runtime.InteropServices

let fsharpFunc (x : byref<int>, [<Out>] y : byref<int>) =
    x <- x + 1
    y <- y + 1
```

Dealing with null

Another F#-C# interop area is dealing with null. Types created in F# cannot be null, but any reference type in C# can have null as a proper value. This can lead to sticky situations when round-tripping types defined in F# through C# libraries (because the C# library could return null when the F# library doesn't expect it).

To enable types defined in an F# assembly to permit null as a possible value, you can add the AllowNullLiteral attribute. This attribute is only available on class and interface types; so records, structs, and discriminated unions still may not be null.

The following FSI session shows the `AllowNullLiteral` attribute in action. Notice that when trying to create an instance of `Widget` with a value of null, a compiler error is given. However, you can have a value of type `Sprocket` equal to null because it was decorated with the `AllowNullLiteral` attribute:

```
> // Define two classes, one with [<AllowNullLiteral>] and one without
type Widget() =
    override this.ToString() = "A Widget"

[<AllowNullLiteral>]
type Sprocket() =
    override this.ToString() = "A Sprocket";;

type Widget =
  class
    new : unit -> Widget
    override ToString : unit -> string
  end
type Sprocket =
  class
    new : unit -> Sprocket
    override ToString : unit -> string
  end

> // ERROR: Widget cannot be null
let x : Widget = null;;

  let x : Widget = null;;
  ----------------^^^^

stdin(12,18): error FS0043: The type 'Widget' does not have 'null'
as a proper value
> // Works
let x : Sprocket = null;;

val x : Sprocket = null
```

Unmanaged Interop

Although the .NET platform offers a wealth of functionality and is a great platform for writing new applications, there are many times when you will want to interoperate with legacy code; for example, calling into frameworks written in C or C++.

F# supports all of the same mechanisms as C# for interoperating with unmanaged code.

Platform Invoke

Platform invoke, also referred to as P/Invoke, is how managed applications can call into unmanaged libraries, such as Win32 API functions. When you have a non-.NET library that you wish to call into, P/Invoke is how you do it.

P/Invoke isn't limited to just Windows. Any CLI implementation, such as Mono, may use P/Invoke in order to access libraries outside of the CLI runtime environment.

In F#, to make a P/Invoke call, you must first declare the function signature. This means defining the function signature so that the .NET framework knows how to call into it correctly (the library where the function exists, the number and types of parameters, etc.).

Example B-4 shows calling into the Win32 function `CopyFile`, defined in the library `kernel32.dll`. The `DllImport` attribute shows which library and the name of the method the F# function is bound to. After that, the function is declared using the `extern` keyword followed by the function signature as it would be declared in a C-like language (types coming before parameter names).

Once the P/Invoke signature is declared, the actual function can be called like any normal F# function value. The F# compiler will take care of passing data to the unmanaged library. The process of transferring data between managed and unmanaged code is known as *marshaling*.

Example B-4. Using platform invoke in F#

```
open System.Runtime.InteropServices

/// PInvoke signature for CopyFile
[<DllImport("kernel32.dll", EntryPoint="CopyFile")>]
extern bool copyfile(char[] lpExistingFile, char[] lpNewFile, bool bFailIfExists);

let file1 = @"D:\File.dat"
let file2 = @"D:\Backups\File.dat"

// Calls the CopyFile method defined in kernel32.dll
copyfile(file1.ToCharArray(), file2.ToCharArray(), false)
```

For more advanced interop scenarios, you can customize how data gets marshalled by providing hints to the F# compiler.

Example B-5 declares two structs, `SequentialPoint` and `ExplicitRect`, for use with the Win32 API function `PtInRect`. The function `PtInRect` returns whether or not a given point exists inside of a rectangle. However, because the Win32 function has no knowledge of the .NET type system, it simply expects structs with a specific layout to be passed on the stack.

The `StructLayout` attribute determines how the struct's data gets laid out in memory, to ensure that it lines up with the way data is expected to be received on the unmanaged half of the P/Invoke call.

For example, the `PtInRect` function expects the rectangle to be made up of four, four-byte integers in left, top, right, and bottom order. In the example, the `ExplicitRect` doesn't declare its fields in that order. Instead, it uses the `FieldOffset` attributes so that when the F# compiler generates code for the `ExplicitRect` type, its fields are laid out in the expected order.

Example B-5. Customizing marshalling

```
open System.Runtime.InteropServices

/// Define a Point using the sequential layout
[<Struct; StructLayout(LayoutKind.Sequential)>]
type SequentialPoint =

    new (x, y) = { X = x; Y = y }

    val X : int
    val Y : int

/// Define a rectangle struct explicitly
[<Struct; StructLayout(LayoutKind.Explicit)>]
type ExplicitRect =

    new (l, r, t, b) = { left = l; top = t; right = r; bottom = b }

    [<FieldOffset(12)>]
    val mutable bottom : int
    [<FieldOffset(0)>]
    val mutable left : int
    [<FieldOffset(8)>]
    val mutable right : int
    [<FieldOffset(4)>]
    val mutable top : int

/// P/Invoke signature for PtInRect
[<DllImport("User32.dll", EntryPoint="PtInRect")>]
extern bool PointInRect(ExplicitRect& rect, SequentialPoint pt);
```

 There are many other ways to customize the marshaling of data between managed and unmanaged code. For more information, refer to MSDN documentation of the `System.Runtime.InteropServices` namespace.

COM Interop

The .NET world where multiple languages use the same runtime to interoperate seamlessly isn't a terribly new idea; in fact, many of .NET's core architectural principles are rooted in another technology called *Component Object Model* or COM. COM is a 1990s-era technology to support binary interoperability between different programs. So a C++ application written by one developer could interact with a Visual Basic application written by another.

Most large, unmanaged applications expose COM interfaces as their way of loading add-ins, enabling programmatic access, and so on. For example, rather than writing your own web browser you could just host the Internet Explorer COM control inside of your application.

Although COM components don't execute on top of the .NET runtime, just like unmanaged libraries you can call into COM objects from .NET applications.

The easiest and most common way to call into COM objects is through a *runtime callable wrapper* (RCW). An RCW is a .NET assembly that provides wrapper classes on top of COM interfaces. So to the developer, it looks as though you are programming against any other .NET assembly, when in fact every function call and class instantiated is actually using the COM-interop machinery of the .NET runtime.

To generate an RCW you use the `tlbimp.exe` tool, which comes with Visual Studio as part of the .NET framework SDK. The following snippet shows using `tlbimp.exe` to create an RCW for the Apple iTunes COM interfaces (declared in `iTunes.exe`). The iTunes COM interfaces allow programmatic control of the iTunes software, such as playing music or manipulating the music library:

```
C:\Program Files\iTunes>tlbimp iTunes.exe /out:NETiTunesLibrary.dll
Microsoft (R) .NET Framework Type Library to Assembly Converter 3.5.21022.8
Copyright (C) Microsoft Corporation. All rights reserved.

Type library imported to C:\Program Files\iTunes\NETiTunesLibrary.dll
```

With the RCW in place, you can reference the library like any other .NET library and write applications that interact with iTunes. Example B-6 shows an FSI session where the RCW for calling into the iTunes APIs is used to print out a list of top-rated albums for the current music library.

This is done by creating an instance of the `iTunesAppClass`, and accessing the `LibrarySource` property. These all correspond to COM interfaces defined in the iTunes API, but with the generated RCW it looks just like any other .NET assembly. Moreover, if you add a reference to an RCW within Visual Studio you will get full IntelliSense support.

Example B-6. COM interop

```
> // Reference required libraries
#r "System.Core.dll"
#r @"C:\Program Files\iTunes\NETiTunesLibrary.dll";;

--> Referenced 'C:\Program Files\Reference
Assemblies\Microsoft\Framework\v3.5\System.Core.dll'
```

```
--> Referenced 'C:\Program Files\iTunes\NETiTunesLibrary.dll'

> // Bind to the iTunes app
open System.Linq
open NETiTunesLibrary

// Load up the main iTunes library
let iTunes = new iTunesAppClass()
let iTunesLibrary = iTunes.LibrarySource.Playlists.[1];;
Binding session to 'C:\Program Files\iTunes\NetiTunesLibrary.dll'...

val iTunes : NetiTunesLibrary.iTunesAppClass
val iTunesLibrary : NetiTunesLibrary.IITPlaylist

> // Search my iTunes music library to sort albums by average song rating
// Return type is seq< albumName * avgRating * tracksInAlbum>
let albumsByAverageRating : seq<string * float * seq<IITTrack>> =
    iTunesLibrary.Tracks.OfType<IITTrack>()
    |> Seq.groupBy(fun track -> track.Album)
    |> Seq.map(fun (albumName, tracks) ->
        // Get average track rating
        let trackRatings = tracks |> Seq.map (fun track -> float track.Rating)
        albumName, (Seq.average trackRatings), tracks);;

val albumsByAverageRating : seq<string * float * seq<IITTrack>>

> // Return whether or not the majority of tracks in the album have been rated
let mostTracksRated tracks =
    let rated, notRated =
        Seq.fold
            (fun (rated, notRated) (track : IITTrack) ->
                if track.Rating <> 0 then
                    (rated + 1, notRated)
                else
                    (rated, notRated + 1))
            (0, 0)
            tracks
    if rated > notRated then
        true
    else
        false

// Print top albums, filtering out those with few ratings
let printTopAlbums() =
    albumsByAverageRating
    |> Seq.filter(fun (_,_,tracks) -> mostTracksRated tracks)
    |> Seq.sortBy(fun (_, avgRating, _) -> -avgRating)
    |> Seq.iter(fun (albumName, avgRating, _) ->
        printfn
            "Album [%-18s] given an average rating of %.2f"
```

```
        albumName avgRating);;

val mostTracksRated : seq<IITTrack> -> bool
val printTopAlbums : unit -> unit

> printTopAlbums();;
Album [Aloha From Hawaii ] given an average rating of 100.00
Album [Sample This - EP  ] given an average rating of 95.00
Album [Dark Passion Play ] given an average rating of 83.08
Album [When I Pretend to Fall] given an average rating of 80.00
Album [Weezer (Red Album)] given an average rating of 78.30
Album [The Best Of The Alan Parsons Project] given an average rating of 76.36
Album [Karmacode        ] given an average rating of 64.00
val it : unit = ()
```

The subject of .NET and COM interop is a very complex one where attention must be paid to details like security models, threading, and garbage collection. Fortunately, F# doesn't have any special requirements over C# when it comes to COM interop.

 If you are interested in learning more about COM interop, I recommend *.NET and COM: The Complete Interoperability Guide* by Adam Nathan (Sams, 2002).

Index

We'd like to hear your suggestions for improving our indexes. Send email to index@oreilly.com.

A

abs function, 18
[<Abstract>] attribute, 319
abstract classes, 160, 160
abstract keyword, 159
abstract syntax tree (AST)
    about, 359
    decomposing arbitrary code, 366
    deconstructing, 360
[<AbstractClass>] attribute, 160
abstracting data access, 222
accessibility modifiers, 154–156
accessor methods, 147
accumulator pattern, 211–212
Activator class (System)
    CreateInstance method, 330
    instantiating plug-ins, 341
active patterns
    about, 185–186
    combining, 192
    function calls and, 362
    function values and, 363
    literal values and, 362
    multicase, 190
    nesting, 193–195
    parameterized, 189
    partial, 187–189
    quotation expressions and, 362
    single-case, 187
    usage considerations, 192–195
addition (+) operator, 17, 26, 228
aggregate operators
    about, 39
    Array module, 117
    List module, 39–42
    Seq module, 89
AggregateException exception, 276
aliasing reference types, 101
all operator, 94
[<AllowNullLiteral>] attribute, 236
Alt-Down keyboard combination, 12
Alt-Enter keyboard combination, 11
Alt-Up keyboard combination, 12
and (&&&) bitwise operator, 20, 179
and (&&) Boolean operator, 23
And (&) pattern, 73, 193
and keyword, 60, 77, 235
angle brackets (<>), 144
anonymous functions, 55, 75

anonymous modules, 46
APM (asynchronous programming model),
    259–262
apostrophe ('), 144
append (@) operator, 35, 203
application development (see writing applica-
    tions)
arithmetic operators, 17, 199
array comprehensions, 111
Array module (F# Library)
    aggregate operators, 117
    fold function, 116, 117, 224
    foldBack function, 117
    init function, 114, 116
    iter function, 116, 117
    iteri function, 117
    map function, 116, 117
    partition function, 116
    tryFind function, 116
    tryFindIndex function, 116
    zeroCreate function, 114, 116
array slices, 113
Array.Parallel module, 272
Array2D module, 118
Array3D module, 118
arrays
    about, 110
    array slices, 113
    creating, 114
    enumerable for loops and, 125
    equality in, 115
    indexing, 111–113
    jagged, 119
    multidimensional, 117–119
    pattern matching, 115
    rectangular, 118
arrow (->), 25, 55, 68
assemblies
    about, 165
    attributes for, 321
    loading, 340
    wrapper, 378–380
Assembly attribute target, 321
Assembly.Load method, 340
AST (abstract syntax tree)
    about, 359
    decomposing arbitrary code, 366
    deconstructing, 360

Microsoft.FSharp.Collections namespace, 38, 38, 54
    (see also specific modules)
Microsoft.FSharp.Core namespace, 69, 69, 199
    (see also specific modules)
Microsoft.FSharp.Linq namespace, 201, 420
Microsoft.FSharp.Linq.QuoationEvaluation namespace, 371
Microsoft.FSharp.Quotations namespace, 360
Microsoft.FSharp.Quotations.Patterns namespace, 362
Microsoft.FSharp.Reflection namespace
    FSharpType class, 329
    FSharpValue class, 331
module keyword, 46
module scope, 27
modules
    accessibility modifiers in, 155
    anonymous, 46
    controlling usage, 200–201
    converting to classes, 195–198
    creating, 46
    extending, 175
    nesting, 46
    shadowing values, 198
modulus (%) operator, 18
MSIL (Microsoft Intermediate Language), 165
multicase active patterns, 190
multidimensional arrays, 117–119
multiplication (*) operator, 17
mutable keyword, 102
mutable values
    about, 53
    in closures, 102
    functional patterns, 220
    records and, 104
    storing on heap, 103
mutually recursive discriminated unions, 77
mutually recursive functions, 59

N

named patterns, 70
names, binding to values, 6, 16
namespaces, 47
    (see also specific namespaces)
    about, 47, 195
    extending modules and, 175
naming conventions, 151
negate function, 54

nesting
    active patterns, 193–195
    functions, 28
    if expressions, 30
    modules, 46
.NET platform
    about, 165
    CLI support, xii, 165
    enumerations and, 176–179
    extending modules, 175
    extension methods and, 174
    F# interoperating with, 8
    garbage collection, 166–167
    interfaces and, 168–171
    interoperation, 419–421
    naming conventions, 151
    object expressions, 171–174
    Parallel Extensions, 239
    structs and, 179–182
    Unicode support, 20
.NET Reflection APIs (see reflection)
.NET thread pool, 254
Netflix service, 388
new keyword, 172
New Project dialog box, 4
[<NoEquality>] attribute, 236
not Boolean operator, 23
not equal to (<>) comparison operator, 24
null constraints, 236
nullable types, 420–421
NullableOperators module, 201, 420
NullReferenceException exception, 101
numeric primitives
    about, 16
    arithmetic operators and, 17
    bitwise operators and, 20
    conversion routines for, 19
    large integers, 19
    mathematical functions supported, 18
    specifying values for, 17

O

Object class (System)
    about, 134
    common methods, 135
    dynamic casts and, 163
    Equals method, 24, 136, 138
    GetHashCode method, 136
    GetType method, 137, 323

sharing data, 255–259
spawning, 253–254
tilde (~), 228
token posting lists, 297, 310
tokenization, 296
TPL (Task Parallel Library)
    about, 273
    concurrent data structures and, 278–281
    primitives and, 274–277
trademark character, 321
tree structures, discriminated unions and, 78
truth tables, 23
try-catch expressions, 127
try-finally expressions, 129
Tuple class, 329
Tuple class (System), 32
tuple type (F#)
    about, 31, 32–34
    equality and, 139
    pattern matching and, 73
    type reflection and, 329
type annotations, 26, 234
Type class (System), 137
    about, 99, 323
    GetMethods method, 325
    GetProperties method, 325
type constraints, 236
type functions, 99
type inference
    about, 25
    compilation order and, 11
    processing order in, 62
    records and, 83
    units of measure and, 109
type keyword, 76, 175
type providers
    about, 377
    creating instances, 382
    custom, 390
    Entity Framework, 385
    F#, 380–382
    SQL data, 383–384
    web service, 385–389
type reflection, 323–330
typedefof function, 324
typeof function, 99, 324
types
    about, 15
    accessing, 324–328

core, 31–46
F# limitations, 377–382
instantiating, 330
nullable, 420–421
operator overloading and, 227
primitive, 15–23
proactive, 237–238
reflecting on, 328–330

U

uint16 numeric type
    about, 16
    conversion routine for, 19
uint32 numeric type
    about, 16
    conversion routine for, 19
uint64 numeric type
    about, 16
    conversion routine for, 19
unary operator, 228, 229
Unchecked.defaultof function, 99
underscore (_) as wildcard, 69
Unicode standard, 20
union cases, 76
unit type (F#)
    about, 31, 32
    control flow example, 31
units of measure
    about, 105–106
    atomic mass units, 121
    Common Language Runtime and, 110
    converting between, 108
    defining, 107–108
    generic type and, 109
    type inference and, 109
unmanaged code
    about, 165
    garbage collection and, 167
    interoperation and, 429–434
unmanaged constraints, 236
use keyword, 167
UTF-16 standard, 20

V

val keyword, 141
value equality, 24, 137
value type constraints, 235

About the Author

Chris Smith works at Google on developer tools. Before that he was at Microsoft on the F# team. Chris has a masters degree in computer science from the University of Washington. You can read his blog, Chris Smith's Completely Unique View, at *http:// blog.achrissmith.com/*.

Colophon

The animal on the cover of *Programming F# 3.0* is a bullfinch (*Pyrrhula pyrrhula*). Members of the *Fringillidae* family, bullfinches are small passerine birds that can be found throughout central and northern Europe, from the Atlantic coast of western Europe and Morocco to the Pacific coasts of Russia and Japan. They primarily inhabit woodland areas, orchards, and farmlands, and are somewhat notorious for the damage they do by eating the buds of fruit trees and flowering shrubs in spring.

Bullfinches are skittish, wary birds and are rarely seen on the ground. The common bullfinch grows to about six inches long. It has a thick neck and a short, stubby bill. Both sexes are primarily black and white, though males have rose-colored undersides while females have duller, brownish breasts.

The females make nests from small twigs, moss, and roots, and lay four or five eggs twice a year. Both parents share feeding responsibilities once the young have hatched. Between 1968 and 1991, there was a significant decline in the bullfinch population. While the specific cause is not known, one theory is that the trend of deforestation and overtrimming hedges on agricultural land compromised many nesting sites and removed the birds' primary food sources. Increased use of herbicides is also a probable culprit, as well as the fact that trapping and killing bullfinches was not regulated until relatively recently. However, bullfinch numbers are now abundant over most of their range and, with the exception of some local populations and subspecies, the birds are not considered threatened.

The cover image is from Cassell's *Natural History*. The cover font is Adobe ITC Garamond. The text font is Minion Pro; the heading font is Adobe Myriad Condensed; and the code font is Ubuntu Mono.

Have it your way.

Get even more for your money.

Join the O'Reilly Community, and register the O'Reilly books you own. It's free, and you'll get:

- $4.99 ebook upgrade offer
- 40% upgrade offer on O'Reilly print books
- Membership discounts on books and events
- Free lifetime updates to ebooks and videos
- Multiple ebook formats, DRM FREE
- Participation in the O'Reilly community
- Newsletters
- Account management
- 100% Satisfaction Guarantee

Signing up is easy:

1. **Go to: oreilly.com/go/register**
2. **Create an O'Reilly login.**
3. **Provide your address.**
4. **Register your books.**

Note: English-language books only

To order books online:
oreilly.com/store

For questions about products or an order:
orders@oreilly.com

To sign up to get topic-specific email announcements and/or news about upcoming books, conferences, special offers, and new technologies:
elists@oreilly.com

For technical questions about book content:
booktech@oreilly.com

To submit new book proposals to our editors:
proposals@oreilly.com

O'Reilly books are available in multiple DRM-free ebook formats. For more information:
oreilly.com/ebooks

Spreading the knowledge of innovators   oreilly.com

Lightning Source UK Ltd.
Milton Keynes UK
UKHW030629060921
389928UK00007B/46